Being Colonized

The Kuba Experience in Rural Congo, 1880–1960

Jan Vansina

The University of Wisconsin Press

The University of Wisconsin Press
1930 Monroe Street, 3rd Floor
Madison, Wisconsin 53711-2059
uwpress.wisc.edu

3 Henrietta Street
London WC2E 8LU, England
www.eurospanbookstore.com

1   3   5   4   2

Printed in the United States of America

Library of Congress Cataloging-in-Publication Data
Vansina, Jan.
Being colonized: the Kuba experience in rural Congo, 1880–1960 /
Jan Vansina.
p.   cm.—(Africa and the diaspora: history, politics, culture)
Includes bibliographical references and index.
ISBN 978-0-299-23644-1 (pbk.: alk. paper)
ISBN 978-0-299-23643-4 (e-book)
1. Kuba (African people)—Congo (Democratic Republic)—Social conditions—History.
2. Congo (Democratic Republic)—Colonization.
3. Congo (Democratic Republic)—History—To 1908.
4. Congo (Democratic Republic)—History—1908–1960.
I. Title.   II. Series: Africa and the diaspora.
DT655.V37   2010
305.896′397—dc22
2009040640

Being Colonized

AFRICA AND THE DIASPORA
History, Politics, Culture

SERIES EDITORS

Thomas Spear
David Henige
Michael Schatzberg

Contents

ILLUSTRATIONS

Maps

Figures

Acknowledgments

As this manuscript goes to press, I am very well aware of what it owes to the great number of people who contributed to it, for without knowing that I would ever write this history I started gathering background evidence for it well over fifty years ago. Hence the full list of acknowledgments encompasses a great many people, research or teaching institutions and grant-giving agencies such as my teachers and friends, academic and otherwise, in Europe and among the Bushong, as well as my colleagues and my own students, museums, universities, and libraries. Even though it is not practical to thank all of them by name, I am grateful for their input.

Still, as a practical matter, expressions of gratitude must be limited here to those who assisted me during the actual writing and publishing of this work. Professor Bogumil Jewsiewicki, Dr. Jos Van den Nieuwenhuizen, and Dr. Beatrix Heintze all helped me find and procure a rare book about the painter Djilatendo. When I contacted Father Willibrord Geysels, C.J., a former missionary of the Josephite order, for some help, he reacted with great enthusiasm and provided me not only with a large number of photographs and an indispensable ecclesiastical history of the Catholic missions in Mweka but also with a copy of the autobiography of Georges Kwete Mwana, a central personality among the Kuba.

I owe Professor Nancy R. Hunt, Dr. M. Wagner, and Dr. D. Henige a special debt of gratitude. They all spent a good deal of time reading the first rough draft, urged me to continue with it, and provided me with very useful suggestions and corrections. Although the input of the official readers for the University of Wisconsin Press was less crucial, some of their observations, I believe, also improved the final product.

As is so often the case, thankful mention must also be made of the Memorial Library of the University of Wisconsin and especially David

Henige, its bibliographer for Africa, for help with library materials. I also want to thank Mme Lutgart Doutrelepont of the Royal Museum of Central Africa Tervuren for her help with the procurement of some of the illustrations. Last but not least come the specialists at the University of Wisconsin Press, especially acquisitions editor Dr. Gwen Walker, who went well beyond the call of duty by contributing a great amount of time and effort to get this manuscript in shape.

MADISON, JANUARY 2009

A Note on Spelling and Pronunciation

Spelling

Bushong words are cited in simplified spelling without tones, without any distinctions between vowels of the second and third degree. Long vowels are indicated only when absolutely necessary; they are omitted whenever vowel length can be inferred from the context of the consonant clusters in the word: hence, for instance, *Bushong* and not *Bushoong*, *Ibanc* and not *Ibaanc*.

Outside the Kuba kingdom (the Territory of Mweka) place-names are spelled by their official colonial names. Within the kingdom most place-names are spelled according to the usage in my book *The Children of Woot* (Madison 1978). Hence we write *Nsheng* rather than *Mushenge* for the Kuba capital, and *Ibanc* instead of *Ibanshe* for the well-known town. But we keep the official spelling *Domiongo* rather than *Ndoomiyoong* for the town on the rail line inhabited by many non-Bushong.

Several spoken variants of the most common Bushong and Kete personal names occur. In such cases we have chosen to write the most commonly used form of the name: thus *Mbop* (class 1), rather than *Bop* (class 1a), *Mbo* (a common abbreviation), or *Mbopey* (an error). In another very common name, *Kwet*, the vowel varies according to dialect. We also render it as *Kwet* rather than *Kot*.

In this work all Bushong or Tshiluba texts are cited in translation, and all translations are the author's unless otherwise specified. Even then the author has checked all translations against the originals.

Pronunciation

In Bushong the consonants are pronounced as in English except for *c* and *p*.

C stands for *ch* as in *church:* hence read *cak* as *chak*.

P is a consonant unknown in European languages. It is the sound produced when blowing out a candle, not quite like either *f* or *h:* hence read *Mbop* as *Mbof* or *Mboh*.

In Bushong spelling long vowels are distinguished from short vowels by doubling the vowel letter. In this book vowel length is only marked in cases where confusion could otherwise arise. Length does not change the vowel sound in any way other than the time during which the sound is held. Whether long or short, vowels are pronounced as follows:

A always as *a* in *hat:* thus *ngady* is pronounced *ngady* and *baat* is *baat*.

E stands for two different sounds: sometimes for *ai* as in *pain*, sometimes for *e* as in *bread* or *mesh*. Thus *ngesh* is pronounced as *ngaish* and *ncyeem* as *nchaim;* but *Kwet* is read as *Kwet* and *Mbweky* as *Mbweky*.

I is always pronounced as *i* as in *pin:* thus *nyim* is read as *nyim* and *kiin* as *keen*.

O stands for two different sounds: sometimes for *oa* as in *boat*, sometimes for *o* as in *top*. Thus *iyol* is pronounced as *iyoal* and *Woot* as *Woat*, but *Lakosh* is pronounced as *Lakosh* and *ngwoom* as *ngwom* (never *ngwoum*).

U is always pronounced like *oo* or *ou* in *boot* or *would:* thus *kum* is pronounced as *koom/koum* and *ntuum* as *ntoom/ntoum*.

Changing Place-names

Place-names outside of the Kuba realm are written in the spelling that appears on official administrative maps of Belgian Congo. Places inside the Kuba region are named and spelled in the language spoken by their inhabitants. Hence it is the Bushong name *Nsheng* (not the Tshiluba *Mushenge*) or the Kete *BwaaNzeebwa* (not the Tshiluba *Bakwa Nzebwa* nor the Bushong *Baancep* nor *Baancap*). In the cases of the following mixed settlements the official names and spellings are preserved: *Domiongo, Kakenge, Mweka, Port Francqui*.

Congolese acquired new names after independence. The most relevant ones for this book are the following:

Former	Current
Elisabethville	Lubumbashi
Jadotville	Likasi
Léopoldville (Lipopo)	Kinshasa
Luluabourg	Kananga
Port Francqui	Ilebo (also called Ilebo before 1923)
Stanleyville	Kisangani

Bantu Prefixes

In Bushong as in many Bantu languages high pitch on any syllable in the stem of a word helps to determine its meaning. Despite this, pitch is not marked in this book.

All nouns in most Bantu languages, including Bushong, begin with prefixes, most of which change from singular to plural and can trigger other changes (e.g., *mwaan,* singular: "child"; *baan,* plural: "children").

Following a general convention, in this work all prefixes of simple nouns designating ethnic names or names of languages are dropped. Hence *Kete* and not *Mukete* "a Kete person"; *Bakete* "several Kete persons"; or *Tshikete* "the language of the Kete." One exception: *Tshiluba* for the language of the Luba of Kasai and not Luba to differentiate it from the different language spoken by the Luba of Katanga.

In compound ethnic nouns such as *Bashi + Bushong* "Bushong people," the initial element of the compound is usually dropped: hence *Bushong.* In a few cases such as *Bwaa + Nzeebwa* "the inhabitants of the village cluster Nzeebwa," the existing literature has chosen to maintain the initial element.

Nouns that are not ethnic names and hence keep their prefixes are always cited with the prefix for the singular even when they refer to plurals. For example, *mwaanyim* both for "royal child" and "royal children" although the latter should be *baanyim.*

Currency

Congo's monetary unit was the Congolese franc, which was equivalent to the Belgian franc. The "gold franc" remained stable until 1914, after which its buying power began to erode (but there was deflation in the early 1930s). The currency was devalued in 1927, 1935, and 1946. Its rate of exchange to the dollar usually fluctuated between forty and fifty francs per dollar. In addition the dollar also suffered its own bouts of inflation and deflation. Hence it becomes quite difficult to translate historic francs into today's dollars or euros. For the purposes of this book it makes better sense to establish the value of francs in comparison to wages, prices, or taxes current at the time, rather than to try to calculate its equivalent in dollars.

Being Colonized

The old man on the hill (photo by author)

Introduction

The old man stood there in his compound on top of the hill, silent now, lost in dreams and gazing over the landscape. He had just retold us how the colonial soldiers came to capture the town and his freedom. He stood there for a long while, recalling perhaps all that happened to him and those he had known since then until this day in the waning years of the era these men had ushered in. If so, his vision of colonial history had certainly very little in common with the standard accounts one finds in textbooks about the period.

Most of the latter begin with the creation of colonies by European powers through treaties with the other powers accompanied by occupation on the ground. These accounts then continue by writing about the initiatives the colonizing powers took and the structures they implanted in order to exploit these territories and to "civilize them"—that is, in so far as possible, turn them into approximations of modern metropolitan societies. Or they tell the same tale refracted through the prisms of multiple abstract concepts. Such a top-down focus may well be admirably suited to explain the links between colonies and their metropolises and to detail the large place taken by the plans and activities of colonial intruders in the fields of economics, administration, justice, education, religion, and health, but these accounts have no room for histories retold by people such as the old man in his compound on the hill. For in such textbooks the colonized Africans were merely the potter's clay out of which splendid colonies were made.

3

For all their merits, such historical surveys provide then obviously only fragments of a much richer history. They are crippled for lack of the perspectives of those like the old man on the hill who lived through it all and went on into independence after that. For African subjects were just as much agents in this story as were their masters. Did they not have their own achievements, aspirations, joys, and suffering? Were they not shaped in part by their shared experience of colonialism? Were they not the mass of the people in the colonies at the time and the ancestors of today's citizens, whose countries inherited what they wrought? Yet, I do not know of any introductions to colonial history that emphasize the African experiences and place them at the heart of the tale, where they obviously belong. That is the reason why I wrote this work.

This book introduces its readers to the colonial period from the side of the colonized, as far as feasible, by keeping its focus on their concrete experiences, by underlining their active rather than their passive agency where appropriate in the overall narrative, and by letting them tell their own story as much as possible—and that does include some reminiscences of that old man on the hill. Such an endeavor cannot fully succeed, mainly because "the colonized" is a collective noun that includes myriad points of views, experiences, voices, and agents, yet it is one that to my mind presents a history that is more concrete, more realistic, richer, and more meaningful than any top-down alternative.

Given this goal, it becomes immediately evident that one cannot encompass all of tropical Africa in such a book, nor even all the peoples of a single colony without losing the immediacy of those voices into overgeneralization. In consequence this essay focuses only on one country, the Democratic Republic of Congo, also known as Congo-Kinshasa, and only on one group in that country, a group I call Middle Kuba. As it happens this country occupies the heart of Central Africa, and the group we study live at its center. By itself, however, that does not mean that either the colony or the Middle Kuba are representative for all of tropical Africa—and yet to a certain degree they are. As a colony Congo is exceptional in that it was the only one that had been founded as the domain of a single despotic ruler, that it later became the only Belgian colony in the world, and that its colonial rule ended in the most spectacular chaos. Yet that exceptionalism is often exaggerated: nearly all of its patterns of governance, economic exploitation, conversion to Christianity, and social modernization have on the whole been quite similar to those of other colonies.

The choice of the inhabitants of the central core of the Kuba kingdom in Congo as the subject of this study, however, had nothing to do at first with their representativeness. The choice simply flows from my own experience of the colonial period. I arrived among the Middle Kuba during the waning years of the period in early January 1953 as a young social anthropologist and stayed among them almost continuously for twenty-one months. In 1956 I returned again for several months. And later I remained in contact with some Kuba for many years afterward. As a researcher I diligently set out to obtain evidence about the functioning of daily life among the Kuba and the structures relating to this. At that time the orthodox methodology among British-trained social anthropologists was to rely only on direct observation. Explanations by locals should be distrusted because they had to be expressions of false consciousness, since local people lacked the necessary objectivity to be scientific. Still, luckily enough, most fieldworkers did not abide by those strictures—and anyway, how did anthropologists know exactly what to observe and where?

Because I had been trained as a historian, this methodology stuck in my craw. For me, local people were witnesses, and hence I felt that whatever they might tell about their personal experience in as unsolicited a way as possible had to be highly relevant. Since funding was available for quantitative social surveys I was able to employ about half a dozen literate young men whom I taught to write in their own language, Bushong, before encouraging them to write down all sorts of local news, gossip, and even dreams, to record information about customs they considered to be noteworthy, and to conduct interviews with local elders (especially their older relatives) about the latter's reminiscences of notable events and social practices in earlier days. The old man on the hill was one of these elders.

Recently these accounts convinced me that they could be used, along with more conventional ones, to write a book about the successive experiences of this concrete group of rural Congolese during the colonial period. These are the reasons for my choice of the Middle Kuba, rather than any supposedly exceptional representativeness of colonial experience for the whole rural Congo they might have had. Indeed, the choice of the Kuba to represent all the rural areas of the colony seems strange at first because among the 120 or so administrative territories in the Belgian Congo their kingdom was one of fewer than half a dozen that were placed under indirect rule. Nevertheless, as it happens, the substance of colonial rule and the experience of the Middle Kuba villagers turn out to be quite comparable to the experience of all rural Congolese—a group that encompassed nearly all of Congo's inhabitants at the outset of the period and still included two-thirds of them when it ended. All of them, the Middle Kuba included, shared the same colonial impulses from above, the same laws and regulations, the same market economy often embodied in the same companies and otherwise in companies with similar policies, and similar missionary practices whatever the differences in denomination.

However, the experiences of those people who lived in the industrial belt of Katanga, in the larger cities (especially after 1945), or in other small pockets of the country (including plantations especially in Kivu) where the landscape was completely reshaped by colonials were quite different from those of the Middle Kuba.

The Middle Kuba are located right in the middle of the colony, in the realm generally known as the Kuba kingdom, a realm lodged between the Lulua, Kasai, and Sankuru rivers on the southern edge of the great equatorial forests. It encompassed an area the size of New Jersey or, more significantly, over two-thirds the size of its colonial master, Belgium. From their power base in the central chiefdom inhabited by the Bushong, the kings and their courts ruled over more than a dozen acknowledged ethnic groups who shared most political and social institutions although they did not all share the same languages. Thus while the Ngende and Pyang tongues were but dialects of the Bushong language and the Kel and Ngongo spoke closely related tongues, several of the groups along the Sankuru, including the Shoowa, spoke idioms that were much closer to those spoken in the equatorial rainforests of the Central Congo than to any of their neighbors in the kingdom. Kete and Coofa speech was far closer to Tshiluba, the language of the Lulua and Luba people who lived south of the kingdom in central Kasai province, than they were to Bushong, while the language of the Cwa foragers in the east differed considerably from all other tongues.

Within this kingdom I focus on a block of people that formed and still form its central core. That block includes the whole of the Bushong chiefdom in the middle of the kingdom including the royal capital as well as the Kete villages on its southern and eastern fringes. For our purposes in this book that block is labeled Middle Kuba. During most of the colonial period the number of these Middle Kuba was estimated to be in the thirty thousands, but the number was significantly higher in the 1890s.

The precise goal of this work is to tell the story of colonialism in Congo from its earliest timid manifestations, along the twists and turns of its changes over time, to its tumultuous and precipitous unraveling as reflected in the experiences of the Middle Kuba people and, as far as

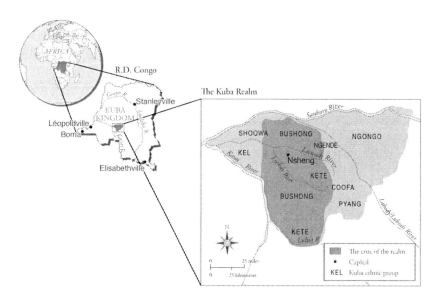

The Kuba realm: General orientation

possible, though their own eyes. The tale of what happened to these people necessarily leads us to encounter the local and concrete manifestations of a whole series of issues and processes that have been the subject of elaborate generalizations and theoretical discussions, and to throw unexpected new light on many of these. Thus we will meet such new realities and processes as racism, pacification, ethnogenesis, indirect rule, development, conversion, modernization, civilization, class formation, and changing gender relations, to mention but some of the most obvious themes. This implies that this tale allows our readers to test, verify, improve, and sometimes challenge many theories and generalizations along the way. Whatever their fascination, however, such matters are outside the scope of this book, which only aims to provide an introduction to colonial history.

Once the goal is clear, the first question that arises is, Are there enough appropriate data to document the experiences of the Middle Kuba? There are, and this work rests on a mass of concrete evidence. Indeed it may be rather unusual in its genre for its heavy reliance on primary sources—that is, on evidence directly gathered from written and other testimonies—rather than on evidence cited by other authors. The sources include masses of official (administrative and judicial) and unofficial written documents, as well as an exceptionally rich photographic

and even cinematographic record, all of it produced by resident colonials (administrators, missionaries, traders) and foreign visitors (commissions of enquiry, tourists, journalists, ethnographers).

Because these sources were all created by and mostly for foreigners,
they need to be complemented by more direct and reliable evidence
about Kuba perspectives on their experiences of colonial rule—that is,
sources emanating from or addressed to Kuba. These exist. The bulk of
them are found in the surviving papers of the Kuba king Mbop Mabinc
maKyeen, in the files and notebooks generated during my stay in the
field, and in the autobiography of Georges Kwete Mwana.[1] Besides information given to me by people of both genders and all ages from child-
hood onward, my papers also include a large number of texts written by
the young Bushong men I have mentioned before. Their notes cover not
just all sorts of topics contemporary for the 1950s but also the reminiscences of their elders about past episodes or situations ever since the conquest of the country in 1899–1900.

However, the dense mass of exceptionally diverse, rich, and well-
informed primary sources on which this study rests remains nearly invisible. That is because this book is not annotated as if it were addressed to
professional colleagues who are expected to follow up such annotations
but rather to undergraduate students and a general public who are not.
Nevertheless, readers interested in learning more will find at least a
short list of further readings at the end of each chapter. These readings
include some references that allow the reader to compare the Middle
Kuba to other "cases" so as to evaluate their representativity on points
discussed in the chapter. While these references are often not the best
ones, their main virtue is accessibility: with the exception of Ndaywel è
Nziem all are written in English and are available in many college libraries. In addition I have quoted some primary sources in whole or in
part, wherever it seemed most relevant to do so, in order to allow readers to at least taste a diversity of flavors from the primary evidence.

The tale of colonial rule of Congo is one of two different regimes that
succeeded one another. The first was a surrealistic oddity: a colony without a metropolis ruled dictatorially by Leopold II, king of the Belgians, in

1. My files (cited in the footnotes as Vansina Files) and Mbop Mabinc maKyeen's
papers can be found at the Memorial Library of the University of Wisconsin–Madison.
My notebooks (cited in the footnotes as Vansina Notebooks) and Kwete Mwana's autobiography are in my possession until a permanent repository can be found.

his imagined capacity as head of a federation of Congolese chiefs. It was as such that he was recognized by the European powers assembled at Berlin in February 1885, and the new colony was given the even more surrealistic name of the Independent Congo State, also known as the Congo Free State. His regime ended with the forced transfer of the colony to Belgium on November 15, 1908. It then remained under Belgian rule until it achieved independence on June 30, 1960.

This book opens with the story of the advent of colonialism in the region of Kasai, the Kuba kingdom included, and its incorporation into the Congo Free State rather than into the Portuguese colony of Angola. The second chapter is mainly devoted to those crucial first contacts that shaped their continuing mutual representations of each other between the Middle Kuba and colonials during the initial years of the colonial presence. The two following chapters relate first the conquest of the kingdom and then its subsequent rule by the concessionary Compagnie du Kasai, the latter of which concludes with the reforms that followed this episode. This account of the Congo Free State and its immediate aftermath closes with an examination of the supposed decline of the Kuba population.

The Belgian colonial period starts with a chronological overview of the main developments during the whole period in general, an overview that provides the necessary background for the five following thematic chapters, which are specifically devoted to the Kuba. These deal respectively with a history of colonial administrative rule, an account of the economic and social impact of the times on Middle Kuba villages, an exposition of the initiatives they took to redress the calamities that beset them, and finally the slow conversion of the region's inhabitants to modernity by means of missions and schools culminating in the emergence of a tiny new elite on the eve of their dramatic passage to independence.

FURTHER READINGS

Ndaywel è Nziem, Isidore. *Histoire générale du Congo*. Paris, 1997. Today this account of the colonial period is the standard reference for the history of Congo in the country itself. For the colonial period, see 309–560.

Nzongola-Ntalaja, Georges. *The Congo from Leopold to Kabila: A People's History*. London, 2002.

Vellut, Jean-Luc, ed. *The Memory of the Congo: The Colonial Time*. Tervuren, 2005.

Congo

Becoming a Colony

Kongo was the name given to an old African kingdom, most of which lies in Angola today. Later this realm, which straddled the lower reaches of the mighty dragon-shaped river coiled in the heart of Africa, bestowed its name, Congo, on that river. And when in the late nineteenth century a completely new political entity, Leopold's colony, emerged in the basin of that river, it was also called Congo after the river. Thus there is no link between the old kingdom along the coast and the new colony in the very heart of the continent. It is also true that the state now called the Democratic Republic of Congo, like most other states in Africa, did not exist before it was created as a colony.

Colonies emerged all over Africa at the end of a long process that began with the arrival of European ships and European traders as early as the late fifteenth century. The early traders made contact among others with existing kingdoms along the coast such as Kongo and founded commercial stations along the shores of the oceans. By the middle of the sixteenth century such posts existed all around the Atlantic, and within that framework of European economic expansion a slave trade soon sprang up between Africa and America. This was fertile ground for the development of some colonies. Thus in 1575 one of its wealthier noblemen convinced Portugal to formally proclaim a colony in Angola, just to the south of Kongo, and to outsource it to him. He launched an expedition, founded Luanda, and started a hundred-year war to occupy the hinterland.

Soon the transatlantic slave trade brought more and more wealth to Angola's Portuguese traders as well as to its government so that the colony flourished. Transatlantic slave traders shipped commodities from Europe to Luanda and other Angolan ports, where they used these goods to buy slaves to be shipped to the Americas. As part of this same endeavor, local caravans loaded with commodities began gradually to go further and further inland to buy slaves that they would then sell at the coast. Already around 1750 some caravans had reached the Upper Kasai River. Although the whole of Angola's economy and its institutions of governance were based on the slave trade for more than two centuries, eventually the transatlantic slave trade was formally abolished and forcibly brought to an end during the 1840s. Nearly every member of the establishment in the colony, whether born in Portugal or in Angola, whether Portuguese or Luso-African (that is, part Portuguese and part African in way of life, whatever their physical makeup), fought this development tooth and nail but to no avail. By 1850 the transatlantic slave trade was a thing of the past, and a frantic search was underway to find a new commodity of high intrinsic value for export overseas to avoid a complete collapse of the colony.

In Search of Ivory

The commodity that saved Angola from ruin was ivory from elephant tusks. Around 1850 Angolan caravans in the interior still continued their old trade in slaves but now for sale in the hinterland of the Portuguese colony. They had, however, discovered by then that they needed ivory to pay for the European commodities demanded by their trading partners in the interior. They also discovered that they could obtain large quantities of the ivory they craved from the inhabitants of the sparsely populated regions in eastern Angola and especially from one people among them, a hunting and farming people known as the Cokwe, who sold elephant tusks in return for textiles, guns, metal ware, and beads.

At first most ivory came from eastern Angola, but the harassed herds of elephants there began to flee northward by seeking refuge from the carnage in the even less inhabited forests along the tributaries of the Upper Kasai River, but to no avail. Parties of Cokwe hunters continued to pursue them there and forced the elephants to retreat further and further northward across the savannas of central Kasai toward the safe

haven of the equatorial forests in Kuba country. One result of this process was a great expansion of Cokwe territory accompanied by a large
increase in their population, fueled in part by their acquisition of
women as slave spouses.

From the start of their expansion Cokwe hunters were followed
by large commercial caravans from Angola organized by Portuguese
or Luso-African traders assisted and guided by people known as
Ambaquistas—that is, Africans who spoke and were literate to some
extent in Portuguese, who tended to be Catholic, who had partially
adopted a colonial Portuguese style of living, and among whom many
had mastered a "European" craft such as carpentry, tailoring, or making

Kasai

The Kasai River is the main affluent of the Congo River. It rises in
eastern Angola and soon turns northward. That stretch of river,
often designated as Upper Kasai, is not navigable and forms the
present boundary between Angola and Congo's modern province
of Katanga. In the following partially navigable stretch the Kasai
River takes a course in the shape of an inverted S. This stretch is
called the Middle Kasai. Finally the river, now fully navigable, takes
a sharp turn to the west-northwest and forms a long stretch
known as Lower Kasai before it joins the Congo River upstream of
Kinshasa.

Kasai is also the name given to a large region of the Congo
along the Middle Kasai stretch and the lands to its east. At first the
colonial state adopted it as an administrative label for a large district. Then in 1933 it also became the name for a province whose
inhabitants soon acquired an identity that distinguishes them from
other Congolese. After independence the province split into west
Kasai and east Kasai, but both together are still known as the
greater Kasai. Moreover, to designate two specific geographic regions in the savannas within the colonial province one distinguishes south Kasai, between Angola and Katanga, from central
Kasai, around Kananga (formerly Luluabourg), between the Lubilash and Kasai rivers, and south of the Kuba kingdom to its north.

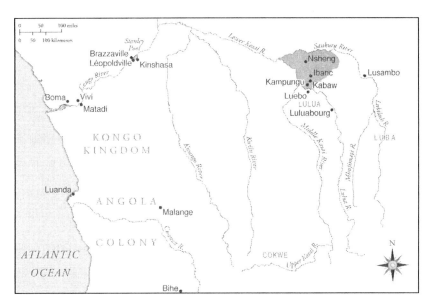

The Kuba in West Central Africa, ca. 1890

shoes. The Ambaquistas disseminated strong Angolan cultural influences wherever they went. In this fashion Cokwe advance parties reached the lands of central Kasai around 1865, a country then inhabited by a people now known as Lulua because most of them live in the basin of the Lulua River.

When the first Cokwe arrived in central Kasai they found a vibrant regional trade there that included the Kuba kingdom. Kete and Bushong had been trading with their Tshiluba-speaking neighbors from central Kasai for at least a century before the arrival of the Cokwe. Since unknown but remote times the Bushong and Kete had been so eager to import salt cakes from central and southern Kasai that the Bushong derived their word for "price" (*mbaan*) from the Tshiluba term for a "commercial salt cake" (*mbanda*). These cakes were so valued for their taste that Kuba parties went far south to obtain them, despite the existence of plantations of vegetal potassium salt near some of their own villages. Besides the salt sought by every household, Kuba traders were interested also in luxury items such as copper crosses from Katanga and glass beads or conus shells of transatlantic provenance mostly bought in return for their own raffia cloth.

This commercial landscape changed dramatically around 1865–70 when the first Cokwe hunters and Angolan caravans burst on the scene

Kuba raffia velvet cloth (Sheppard, *Presbyterian Pioneers in the Congo*, 1917)

in central Kasai. The first Cokwe chief to arrive there struck an alliance with one of the leaders of the Tshiluba-speaking people who lived in the valley of the Lulua in central Kasai. With some Cokwe help and with the invention of a cult of friendship that consisted of smoking pot together, this leader and his successor, Mukenge Kalamba, managed to unite most of the people in central Kasai. Indeed, beginning around 1870 the first Kalamba was strong enough to momentarily prevent Angolan caravans from traveling and trading beyond his residence near the Lulua River, even though the greatest stocks of ivory were then to be found further north in the Kuba kingdom.

By 1875 Mukenge Kalamba could no longer prevent the large caravans from proceeding further northward where they now reached Kampungu, the southernmost regional market within the Kuba kingdom. Almost immediately the Ambaquistas brought news about the open road, the Kuba realm, and the potential bonanza in ivory to be had there back to their bases in Angola. There the Luso-African Joannes Bezerra Caxavala, who was familiar with central Kasai since 1874, learned all about it and informed the German traveler Schütt in late December 1878. Schütt's book brought the first word about the existence of a

Kuba kingdom to Europe and right with it a first stereotype of Kuba as cannibals:

> Only Luquengo [Luba title for the Kuba king] who rules over the Luba on the Cassai and Lualaba [rivers] and governs an hereditary empire, similar to that of Muata-Jamvo [the ruler of the Lunda Commonwealth] can hold him in check. These Luba are naturally still cannibals just like the Meno [inhabitants along the lower Sankuru River].[1]

When the Angolan caravans reached the Kete market, Kampungu, the southernmost regional market of the Kuba kingdom, they faced a much more impressive polity than that of Kalamba. As soon as they appeared, the Kuba king Mbop Mabiinc maMbul barred them from proceeding further, although the limit was moved a few miles further to the north to Kabaw (Kabao) a few years later. Both settlements lay in Kete country north of the Lulua River and were ideally suited as marketplaces because the Kete language was fairly close to Tshiluba, the language of trade in central Kasai, but Kete culture was close to that of Bushong, and both markets stood under direct royal control. In this way the Middle Kuba safeguarded their position as middle-men between the caravans to their south, the interior of their own kingdom where elephants teemed, and the lands north and east of the Sankuru River that were even richer in ivory than their own realm.

The first European-born person to reach both markets was the celebrated Portuguese trader António Ferreira da Silva Porto at the head of his own Angolan caravan from Bihe. He reached Kampungu on August 13, 1880, and stayed only a few days to buy ivory, for which he paid with a mixture of goods including fine cloth worth three slaves. A little later he mentioned that the Kuba produced high-quality raffia textiles themselves, but that they were allowed to wear only wrappers of raffia cloth; only their king, his wives, and a few privileged persons could wear trade cloth. Therefore the Kuba usually refused to accept any imported cloth and sold their ivory for cowries or for slaves. This was bad news for the Angolan caravans that relied almost entirely on imported cloth to pay for the ivory they wanted to buy.

---

1. P. Lindenberg, *Reisen im Südwestlichen Becken des Congo von Otto Schütt* (Berlin, 1881), 146. By the end of January 1879 (page 157 and the end map) he learned that Luquengo's lands lay at the confluence of the Lulua and Kasai rivers and calculated its position surprisingly accurately as to latitude but half a degree too far east.

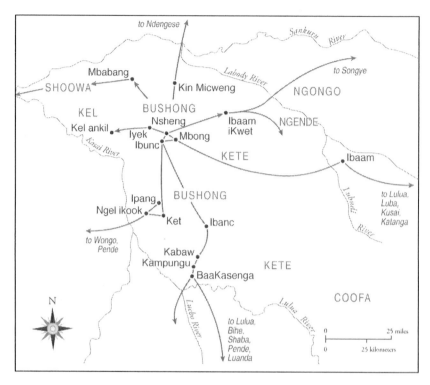

Main Kuba markets in the late nineteenth century

The consequences of this situation were considerable. The Kuba had a stranglehold on the trade in ivory: On the one hand, their kingdom was powerful enough to force the Angolan caravans to trade only at Kampungu and Kabaw and to prevent any hunting by outsiders inside its realm. On the other, most of the ivory still available in Kasai after 1875 stemmed from their country and was only available in or around these markets. Hence, their refusal to buy imported cloth resulted in the almost immediate reorganization of commercial activities in all of Kasai as far east as the lands beyond the Lubilash River. By 1880 or even earlier, the caravans from Angola began to travel first to those eastern lands in order to buy slaves there before turning westward toward Kampungu and Kabaw in order to sell them to the Kuba. This pattern of trade was to persist for nearly twenty years.

A year after Silva Porto's voyage, an expedition sponsored by the German society for the exploration of Africa arrived in Kasai. It consisted of a caravan of Ambaquistas under the direction of Paul Pogge and Hermann Wissmann. The travelers met a Kuba trading party on the road to central Kasai, which prompted Wissmann on August 12, 1881, to jot down the gist of the encounter in the following short note. Short it was, but nevertheless it managed to introduce the standard motif of savagery:

> On the twelfth [August 1881] we encountered a few Bakuba in Muketeba's village who were there to trade in salt. They live north of the Lulua and belong to the realm of the powerful Luquengo. Of exceptionally muscled savage appearance, they opined that they already knew Pogge: they took him for the Portuguese trader

---

Silva Porto Buys Tusks

Then we bought a tusk of ivory weighing 66 pounds paid for in the commodities that are cited in the following list . . .
    1,000 cowries, one *arroba* [30 pounds]
    500 mottled coral [beads], half a bundle
    30 fathoms of beads, 6 bundles as dash
    40 fine trade cloths, [value] two slaves
    1 tin cup
    1 knife
    1 copper crank [heavy ring?]
    ½ *arroba* [15 pounds] of salt
    1 mirror
    1 dish
    1 ax
    1 bell
    1 [metal] rattle
trinkets that we did not carry: we handed over 20 fine trade cloths instead [to the value of] one slave in order to remedy this lack.[2]

Note that the amount of imported cloth corresponded to a precise value in slaves. The seller likely intended to resell this for slaves elsewhere outside of the Kuba realm.

---

2. António Ferreira da Silva Porto, "Novas jornadas," *Boletim da Sociedade de Geografia de Lisboa* 6a (Lisbon, 1885–86), 450–51.

Silva Porto, the only White person who had penetrated that far with his people from Bihé.[3]

While Wissmann went on from central Kasai to cross the continent to the East Coast, Pogge returned to found a scientific station called Luluabourg on July 21, 1882. His Angolan companions created a town nearby that they called Malanje after the town from which the caravan had come in Angola. When his supplies were exhausted in November 1883, Pogge abandoned the station to return to Angola. Most of his Angolan companions, however, stayed and became ever more influential in the region as role models of modernity. On his way home Pogge met Wissmann again at Malanje, where he was fitting out a caravan for Luluabourg with a few of their compatriots, including a Dr. Wolf. This expedition in 1884, however, was financed by King Leopold II of Belgium. Once in central Kasai Wissmann first helped the Lulua potentate Kalamba to expand his authority there, while sending smaller German parties to explore the whole region. Meanwhile, however, the Ambaquistas of the new Malanje continued to exert great cultural influence on the inhabitants of the region all around their town who admired their skills and achievements, while a few Portuguese traders had also just arrived to settle in the region. Thus were it not for the Leopold-backed expedition in 1884, it looked as if Kasai was fast becoming part of the hinterland of the colony of Angola and might soon become part of it.

The Creation of the Congo Independent State

Officially the Congo Independent State came into being on February 23, 1885, when envoys of all the major powers, gathered in Berlin since November 1884 to discuss the scramble for African colonies, collectively recognized the existence of a new state with this name. On the same day the Belgian government also approved of its creation. Although Belgium was the smallest state present at the conference, its agreement was crucial because its monarch, Leopold II of the Belgians, was to become the absolute ruler of this new state that was to grow some eighty times larger than its metropolis. To understand how this was even possible one must realize that even though Belgium is about the size of Rhode Island, in those days it also was the second biggest industrial

3. Hermann Wissmann, *Unter Deutsche Flagge von West nach Ost* (Berlin, 1889), 75.

power in Europe, a power equal to that of the United States. Moreover, Belgium was truly neutral with regard to the dissensions between the great powers. Moreover, King Leopold had to accept that the Congo Basin was to be an international zone of free and unfettered access to any individual or company—commercial or religious—that wished to visit the region or settle there.

The recognition of the Congo Independent State in Berlin was a triumph for the personal diplomacy of King Leopold II, a diplomacy that had begun more than a decade earlier. The king had always been convinced that industrial Belgium needed a colony to thrive. After tentative probings, including some in Africa, he organized a large geographical conference at Brussels in 1876 and invited some of the most celebrated European travelers in Africa to attend. The conference created an International African Association with the mandate to explore the continent and to end the slave trade there. Chapters of the association were then created in several western European countries.

Barely a year later the sensational news broke that the journalist Henry Morton Stanley had descended the Congo River all the way from Maniema in eastern Congo to its mouth, thereby solving the main remaining mystery in European knowledge about Central Africa. Upon Stanley's arrival in Europe, Leopold II immediately invited him to become his agent. Given the lack of interest shown in Great Britain, Stanley agreed. By 1879 he was back in lower Congo with the mandate to create a colony. Over the next six years Stanley did just that. He set up an embryonic central government first at Vivi, then at Boma, both in lower Congo; he signed treaties with a plethora of chiefs there; he built a road between the lower Congo River below the last falls near Vivi and Léopoldville, a newly baptized town on the shores of Malebo Pool (formerly known as Stanley Pool).

He then oversaw the hauling of the myriad parts of small steam riverboats along the new road, their assembly at Malebo Pool, and their launch on the Congo River. With these paddlewheel steamers he and others then traveled up the Congo River and some of its tributaries as far upstream as today's Kisangani, and they set up a few posts all along the river. All of this was paid for from the king's private purse. Hence, Stanley could attend the conference of Berlin as the representative of a great political endeavor in Congo.

In addition to this whole venture, Leopold II still had found it advisable to attract Hermann Wissmann after his first crossing of Africa. He financed his second expedition from Malanje in Angola to Kasai, which, as we saw, arrived at Luluabourg in 1884. The story of the colonial experiences of the Kuba opens with the entry into their kingdom of Dr. Ludwig Wolf, second in command and physician to that expedition.

Just ten days before the day the Congo was officially born, Wolf arrived at the great marketplace of Ibanc within the Bushong heartland. At the head of a modest party, he had deviously attempted in vain to sneak into the country by back roads. Nevertheless, as soon as he reached the border he was stopped until word came from the capital that he should be brought to the market of Ibanc in order to meet "Mbotte kumambwa" (Mbot Ikumaam), the deputy ruler for the old, blind, and incapacitated ruler king Mbop Mabiinc maMbul. That suited Wolf, whose mission was to obtain the assent of the Kuba ruler to Wissmann's plan to descend the Kasai River along the realm's western border.

Wolf obtained the assurance that the Kuba would not oppose Wissmann's plans. And so two months after his visit the whole German expedition, accompanied by Kalamba of the Lulua and his men, embarked in canoes, descended the Lulua River, and then the hitherto unknown course (except by Kuba) of the Lower Kasai River. To their great surprise they found that the river joins the Congo River not very far upstream from Kinshasa. Thus the region of Kasai was physically linked to the Congo state.

In November 1885 Wolf returned from Kinshasa with most of Kalamba's party and a government official, the Englishman Bateman, on board the brand-new thirty-foot-long *Stanley*, the largest ship then afloat on the Congo River system and its first sternwheeler. The ship ascended the Lulua River as far as possible. There Wolf and Bateman founded Luebo at the first waterfalls that barred further navigation on the Lulua River. The site lay next to a Kete village and just within the outermost border of the Kuba kingdom. Bateman promptly declared that he was taking possession of the whole region for the new Congo State, although no one ever informed the Kuba of this. Thereupon Kalamba and his men returned home to central Kasai, Wolf left to explore the Sankuru, and Bateman remained at Luebo to build a station with a handful of Swahili-speaking workers and six or seven Zanzibari soldiers.

Five months later, in April 1886, Wissmann passed through Luebo on his way to the East Coast of Africa. He was accompanied by what can be described as an international sample of colonial society in the Congo State, namely two Belgian state agents, a famous English missionary, a prominent Dutch businessman, and a noble Swedish tourist, none of whom tarried at Luebo.

The *Stanley* (HP.1952.62.219, collection RMCA Tervuren; anonymous photo, © RMCA Tervuren)

Bateman left in December 1886. By then the Congo State could no longer afford to keep Luebo staffed, so it outsourced the post to an American commercial company, the Sanford Exploring Expedition. Luebo was thus demoted to a mere trading post on the road to the government station at Luluabourg. It was not to become a government station again until 1904. Sanford ran the post for a mere two years before it was obliged to cede it to a new and better financed Belgian rival, the Société Anonyme Belge. From then onward one lone commercial agent at the factory was relayed by another lone agent year after year, and they continued to trade in ivory and rubber as Bateman had. The only other settler at Luebo at this time was a Portuguese businessman who had come from Angola in between Wissmann's two expeditions. Every single one of these traders sought to establish profitable trade relations with the masters of most of the ivory, the successive Kuba kings, but to no avail.

Although Luebo was built on Kete land at the very limit of their kingdom, the Kuba kings merely reacted to its foundation by ignoring the foreigners there just as they did with foreigners at Luluabourg. Until 1892 they rebuffed all overtures of traders and government officials alike, returned all gifts, refused all communication, and continued to forbid access to the country just as in earlier days. Caravans could still not travel beyond Kabaw. The main reason for this policy of isolation seems to have been the precarious political state of the country. When Wolf entered the realm it had been on the very eve of a sequence of contested successions to the throne that pitted the partisans of the incumbents against those of the claimants. Although the situation deteriorated to the point that one formal battle was actually fought between two sides during those years and not far from Ibanc, a general civil war was narrowly avoided, thanks to the authority of the formal councils at the capital.

Two elderly kings succeeded each other within four or five years after Wolf's passage in 1885, the second one being Kwet aMbweky, a septuagenarian. He assumed power in 1890, ruled over most of the country, and stabilized the situation somewhat, even though his accession was disputed by the claimant next in line, who continued to occupy part of the country. Kwet aMbweky upheld the policy of barring access to his capital and the inland regions of the realm by forbidding anyone, on pain of death, to show any foreigner any road to the capital. He was probably unaware that by these orders and by remaining an unseen and mysterious king he was actually enhancing his reputation and that of his armed might in the imagination of the foreigners in Kasai.

In many ways Luebo at the time was rather typical for the whole Congo State in its infancy. The invaders from overseas did not stem predominantly from one country but from a host of nations. During its first three years of existence the place counted traders from Portugal, Germany, Great Britain, France, and Belgium. Like elsewhere in Congo the personnel of the administration, missions, and businesses alike were recruited from nearly every European country, including even Bulgaria and the Ottoman Empire, as well as from the United States. That reminds one that while the Congo Independent State belonged to the king of the Belgians, it was still an "international zone" and not a Belgian colony.

Luebo's almost immediate financial trouble was typical for the whole Congo as well. The state simply lacked sufficient income because the Conference of Berlin had outlawed any levy of custom duties. It operated nearly everywhere on a shoestring with a severe shortage of European personnel and at first only a token military presence consisting of a few Zanzibari or West African soldiers. Thus the lease of Luebo and the subsequent absence of any governmental presence there was typical of the situation elsewhere. Outsourcing to private enterprise was now resorted to whenever possible.

At Luebo this initial state of affairs lasted only until 1890–91 when the town suddenly took on a new lease of life with the foundation of a permanent mission station by two missionaries of the American Presbyterian Christian Mission and by the proliferation of new trading posts prompted by the arrival of new companies that were competing with each other to acquire rubber. From 1891 onward these companies flocked to Luebo rather than elsewhere for two reasons: first because this region, unlike most of the rest of Congo, was to remain an area of free trade until 1902, and second because it was there that the best rubber in Africa could be had. Seen in isolation, the history of the small post of Luebo, especially in its initial years, might well seem to be completely unimportant for the history of colonial Congo. But isolation distorts. The true place of Luebo in colonial history appears only when what happened there is firmly placed within its full regional context, a context to which we now turn.

An Influx of Slaves and Refugees

Wolf's report about his visit to the Kuba kingdom in 1885 includes the following: "Such a picture of an Inner African life, unadulterated and uninfluenced by European culture, remains permanently etched in the traveler's mind both because of its fascinating genuineness and of its rarity."[4]

Wolf's colonial successors fully accepted his claim of an unadulterated ancient civilization in the heart of Central Africa, yet it is entirely humbug. By the time of Wolf's visit, and contrary to his romantic picture, Kuba society had in fact been changing rapidly as the result of a significant influx of Luba slaves that had started more than five years before Wolf arrived and was to continue for almost another twenty years.

We have already seen that the Kuba trade policy was most inconvenient for Angolan caravans whose basic stock of trade was cloth because they now had to buy slaves with their cloth elsewhere first and then sell the slaves for ivory at Kampungu or Kabaw. Unfortunately they soon learned that at that time Luba people beyond the Lubilash River in eastern Kasai could be bought at rates as cheap as five slaves for a gun

---

4. Ludwig Wolf, "Wolf's Bericht über seine Reise in das Land der Bakuba," in Hermann von Wissmann, *Im Innern Afrikas* (Leipzig, 1891), 256.

or a single slave for four yards of calico. Slaves were so cheap because a number of local rulers in this region had been raiding people in the area for many years for sale to Arab or Swahili traders from the East Coast based on the Lualaba River. These rulers were just as willing to trade with caravans from Angola as with Arabs or Swahili, and already in Silva Porto's day large caravans, for the most part from Bihe like his own, were traveling eastward to buy slaves for the Kuba market in ivory. As a byproduct of the ivory trade, slaves in ever rising numbers came pouring into Kuba country from about 1878 onward to the point that in 1888 a Portuguese trader encountered no less than three caravans simultaneously at Chief Zappo Zap's town by the Lubilash River about to leave for Kabaw with eight hundred slaves at once. Indeed by then the largest Angolan caravans were no longer just buying slaves in Luba country: they were raiding there for slaves themselves. At the same time, however, the ever increasing number of slaves for sale was causing a steady fall in their value and hence an equivalent rise in the price of ivory bought with them. Whereas in 1886 a slightly middle-size damaged tusk was bought for 2 young girls, 5 copper crosses, 5,000 cowries, and 200 packets of *amandrilha* beads, a year later a 4-pound tusk cost 1 slave, a 10-pound tusk cost 2 slaves, a 20-pound tusk cost 6 slaves, a 30-pound tusk cost 10 slaves, a 50- to 60-pound tusk cost 20 slaves, and a large 92-pound tusk was sold for 54 slaves.

The earliest agents of the Congo at Luebo or Luluabourg were wholly unable to even attempt to break up this infamous trade. In 1887 there was not a single soldier left at their main base in Luluabourg, while Luebo's handful of Zanzibari soldiers were obviously unable to challenge any well-armed caravan. In that year foreign slave raiders and their local allies were causing such havoc in eastern Kasai that Chief Zappo Zap could no longer compete with his peers and sought asylum at Luluabourg with eight hundred followers. While this move provided the state with a well-armed ally around this post, the ravages further east only worsened. They culminated in 1890 with the first of several large-scale raids organized by Ngongo Leteta, the most notorious of all slavers and at that time an Arab ally. Two years later his plundering in eastern Kasai became so destructive that a large portion of the Luba population there was uprooted and, like Zappo Zap a few years earlier, fled to the vicinity of Luluabourg.

At the same time the large-scale conflict known as "Arab war" broke out in eastern Congo, and between 1892 and 1894 no government

Zappo Zap: A Person, a Title, an Ethnic Group

At first Zappo Zap was the name given in March 1883 by Wissmann, the first European traveler in this region, to a certain Nsapu
(a.k.a. Nsapu Nsapu, to distinguish him from Nsapu Kumwaba),
the man who had adopted him as a brother. Zappo Zap was then
ruling over Mpengie, a large settlement of at least one thousand
people, including hundreds of slave warriors. This town was located
in eastern Kasai southeast of Lusambo and well to the east of the
upper Sankuru River and north of Kabinda town. This Nsapu and
his people were Songye speakers, and their town was part of the
Ben'Eki kingdom. At the time Wissmann heard about them they
were slave raiders and traders involved both with caravans from
Bihe in Angola and from the towns on the Lualaba River then inhabited by Arab and Swahili merchants.

By 1883 trade had made Zappo Zap, who had begun his career
as a nobody, powerful and wealthy enough to challenge the king of
the Ben'Eki. This triggered a civil war that soon embroiled all the
major slave traders of the region After a first reverse in 1886,
Zappo Zap was obliged to move to the vicinity of Lusambo, where
he built a splendid establishment. But he lost a second battle
nearby on the right bank of the Sankuru River in 1887 during
which his older brother Nsapu Kumwaba died. That forced him
and his ally Mulumba Nkusu to cross the river with all their followers, estimated at about three thousand people. From then on,
Zappo Zap as well as these folk lost their former ethnic designations as Ben'Eki.

Near Lusambo Zappo Zap, the chief, met Lieutenant Paul Le
Marinel, the Congo Independent State commander for Kasai, and
Chief Mukenge Kalamba of the Lulua, who were retreating westward from the Lualaba in 1887. Zappo Zap died the following year.
He was succeeded by one of his sons, who from then on was also
known as Zappo Zap. Then in 1889 the new Zappo Zap moved
with all his people to settle near the post of Luluabourg. Some
later written documents claim that Le Marinel granted the original

Zappo Zap protection, supposedly because he foresaw how crucial their support could be for his feeble forces, but oral traditions claim that the original Zappo Zap allied himself with Kalamba and left his own senior wife as hostage in the household of Kalamba's sister. Contemporary documents confirm the hostage situation, but the move only occurred under the second Zappo Zap. He ruled only for a few years, died in 1894, and was succeeded by his brother, who also was referred to as Zappo Zap. Thus from 1888 onward the name of the original chief became the generic title given to the leader of the Zappo Zap people.

From the outset the settlement of the Zappo Zap people near Luluabourg flourished. Within the space of less than three years they proved to be the irreplaceable main allies of the Congo State in Kasai. They sided with the state against Kalamba in 1890 and drove him away from the vicinity of Luluabourg. A year later they helped defeat two large Angolan caravans south of the town. Later they defeated Kalamba again when he threatened Luluabourg in April 1895. When the garrison there rebelled in July 1895, they sided with the state and defied the rebels who were afraid of them. Weeks later they saved the Catholic mission from destruction by Kalamba's Lulua. Such sterling allies could do no wrong. Later they continued to gain considerable influence in colonial Kasai by informal means until well after 1900 by supplying most Europeans other than missionaries with mistresses.

Meanwhile these indispensable allies had also become important producers of foodstuffs and became the foremost traders in central Kasai. They developed sizeable commercial plantations, almost certainly worked by slave labor, as they continued to buy slaves for themselves as well as to trade in small numbers with local people all over Kasai. Although this was well known to all, the colonial establishment turned a blind eye on this activity, perhaps because it was not their main commercial activity. That was their participation in the ivory and rubber trade. They brought these commodities to the trading houses of Lusambo, Luebo, and Bena Makima, and they even settled in hamlets of their own in these commercial centers so as to expedite their commercial activities.

Hence, when Dufour, the commander of the Luluabourg post, planned to extract rubber as taxes from the Kuba in 1899, he

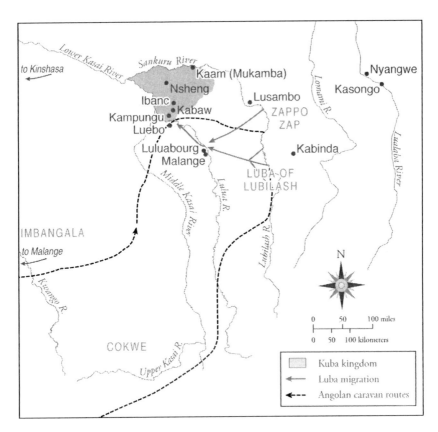

Kuba and Kasai, 1875–99

"naturally" turned to "his" Zappo Zap to provide the military muscle to do so. Zappo Zap then turned this task over to his subordinate ally, Mulumba Nkusu, whose men then caused such a massacre that it disgraced not only Dufour but the Congo State as well. After that experience the state agents no longer seem to have made any overt military use of their Zappo Zap allies. The latter gradually lost their privileged position and became just one tribe among others, a trend that accelerated when the colonial army was able to station more soldiers in central Kasai after 1897 and even more after Belgium took over the Congo in 1908.

troops at all were available to interfere with slave raiding in Kasai. As a result more and more people were uprooted among the Luba from the Lubilash valley in eastern Kasai, and by 1895 the initial trickle of refugees from there to Luluabourg had turned into a full-scale migration. By then the Arab wars had ended, yet the Congo Independent State was still unable to intervene, for this time a major military mutiny had broken out at Luluabourg and reduced the state to near impotence during the following few years. Over the next decade Luba people in the tens of thousands continued to flee their homeland to seek refuge near Luluabourg and Luebo. In central Kasai they soon began to outnumber the original inhabitants, who from now on were called Lulua to distinguish them from the Luba immigrants.

The effects of this migration were huge and long lasting. The immigrant Luba became faithful followers and willing workers for the colonial rulers, missions, and commercial agencies all over Kasai. They converted massively to Christianity and sent their children to mission schools in such numbers that by independence they were the most educated of all Congolese peoples. Meanwhile the occupation of so much Lulua land by so many Luba fueled an ever increasing friction between the two new ethnic groups over the next decades that finally erupted into civil war in 1959–60 on the very eve of independence.

Despite the initial military weakness of the Congo State in the region, however, Kasai did not become part of Angola. It was lost to Angola as soon as it was found that the Lower Kasai River route directly linked Kinshasa to Luebo. Under the rules set out during the Conference of Berlin, only the formal occupation of posts was a valid basis for any territorial claim, and by early 1886 there were Congo state agents both in Luebo and Luluabourg and no official Portuguese agents anywhere in Kasai. Hence, Leopold's claim to all land in Kasai north of the sixth parallel south was recognized by then. Thereafter and despite bitter protests in Lisbon and despite continued Angolan commercial activity in the region, the international boundary inexorably began to shift southward until the present boundary was finally reached around 1891 and agreed on in 1910.

The river route also decisively altered the existing commercial patterns in favor of the Congo State. Almost from the day Luebo was founded, caravans could no longer compete with the river route. A single ship carried more merchandise than several of even the largest caravans and brought them to Luebo at a significantly lower cost than any Angolan caravans could afford. The market in Kasai was soon flooded with goods from lower Congo so that the prices paid for ivory and rubber in commodities other than slaves soon rose to such an extent that the caravans from Angola with their much higher costs of transportation could no longer compete.

Prices had already sharply risen in early 1885 as a result of the large quantity of merchandise carried by Wissmann's caravan from Angola. Late in 1885, prices rose again by a further 50 percent as soon as the first shipload of merchandise from Kinshasa hit the market at Luebo. By December 1887 one of the Portuguese traders on the Mwanzangoma River complained that rubber, which had been very cheap before 1885, now cost three times as much and had become scarce while ivory had become a rarity and was too expensive to buy for any legal market in Angola. Indeed, the following year an experienced Belgian trader also remarked that ivory at Luebo was traded at steep prices. Yet tusks were still not scarce nor too expensive for slave traders from Angola.

Nevertheless, despite a decline in the number of tusks for sale on the market, business in Luebo turned from undistinguished into a boom by 1893, mainly thanks to increased and lucrative rubber sales while the market in ivory did not wholly decline. In later years and despite the continued presence of some Angolan slave traders, European merchants still managed to buy ivory in deals with Kuba individuals or villages outside of the market places. By then also, Angolan slave caravans had begun to avoid Luebo, Kampungu, and Kabaw altogether, leaving more ivory for sale to the legitimate Luebo merchants either directly or through their Zappo Zap allies who still continued to import small numbers of slaves into the Kuba realm.

After the middle 1890s the number of Angolan caravans around Luebo dwindled. A growing scarcity of ivory played a minor role in this decline, but most of this decrease resulted from the suppression of their trade in slaves, especially after state agents finally acquired enough military means in the early 1900s to attack even the largest slave-trading caravans. By then, however, the Angolans had learned to operate wholly out of sight of all Europeans posts. They moved their trading routes west of the Kasai River bend and secretly traded with the Kuba, including agents of their king, at places west of the Kasai River, just across from the kingdom, and they continued to do so until 1910. Nevertheless, concomitant with the decline in the official number of Angolan caravans, the use of Portuguese as the trade language and the Angolan style of living also began to fade away in Kasai, even though the Angolan connection never completely disappeared.

Luba Slaves in the Kuba Heartland

One result of the conjunction of events we have discussed was that the Kuba actually acquired most of their slaves only during the early colonial period, not earlier. Yes, the first slaves were sold on their markets a year or two before Silva Porto's arrival at Kampungu. After this visit slave imports steadily grew but only reached their peak between 1885 (when Luebo was founded) and the middle 1890s. Later their numbers began to decline, although some slaves were still being bought until about 1910. Hence, the slave trade here must be considered an integral part of the early colonial period and not just the tail end of earlier developments, and this despite the fact that the state was committed to suppressing the slave trade.

Kuba from all parts of the kingdom, not just Kete and Bushong in the south, began to buy Luba slaves perhaps seven years or so before Wolf's visit and continued to do so in ever increasing numbers afterward. Ordinary people were allowed to trade only in ivory they had bought beyond the kingdom's borders, usually north of the Sankuru. Most of the ivory on offer, however, belonged to the king by virtue of the rule that the tusks of all elephants killed in the country were his, a rule that was strictly enforced. As late as the 1950s, for instance, old people still remembered that a thief had sold some of the king's ivory to Silva Porto at Kabaw in August 1880. But the thief was recognized, caught by official Bushong traders, and carried off to the capital. As the foremost trader in ivory in the country, the king had his men buy most of the slaves available on the market. In addition he occasionally acquired more such persons as tribute from small Lulua chiefs east of Kabaw and Kampungu. One such "gift" of some forty slaves had still not been forgotten in the 1950s.

Royal slaves were used mostly as agricultural labor, as porters, and as construction workers around the capital, although either King Mbop Mabiinc maMbul or his successor also settled some of the slaves in distant villages just as they had done with prisoners of war in earlier times. That was, for instance, how four to five hundred Luba slaves happened to occupy a village at Mukamba (Kaam) on the banks of the Sankuru River in 1888. Kuba commoners bought slaves to raise their standard of living. They served as servants to perform routine chores around the home and as additional farm labor alongside the women of the household.

They also preferred young women because these slaves could be wed to their masters and thus raise additional children for his own lineage, unlike the offspring of free women, who were members of their mother's lineage. The Kuba were a matrilineal society, a society in which descent was reckoned in the female line, and the lineage was therefore defined as a group that united men and women who were related through their mothers and female ancestors. But slave concubines were foreigners. They had no lineage of their own, and hence their children were incorporated into their father's lineage. These concubines thus boosted the growth of such a lineage compared to others, which then threatened to upset the local balance of power that existed between competing local lineages in favor of the enlarged one. It was this effect that encouraged all competing leading men to acquire as many concubines as they could obtain. As a result the demand for slaves never abated.

Even as late as the 1950s over 6 percent of the Kuba population as a whole and a higher percentage in the south was still of partly slave descent. Such a proportion of slave immigrants was sufficiently high to exert significant demographic and social effects, especially among the southern Kuba. While the influx of so much Luba slave labor generated an air of ever increasing prosperity in the region, these massive imports of unhappy Luba slaves were also beginning to undermine the stability of the Bushong and Kete villages. Thus in 1885, barely a week after Wolf arrived at Ibanc, a dispute broke out between the villagers and his party because one of his Luba porters had absconded with a local Luba slave woman. The couple had been caught and brought back to stand trial. First the village court and then the king's son's court in appeal set an amount required for ransom. This was paid, and the man was returned to Wolf.

Over time such cases became more and more common, provoked more unrest, and sometimes led to outright lawlessness. The story of Wembo, a Kete man whose wife, Mulanga, was kidnapped in Luebo and sold into the interior in 1897, was a common one. What followed, however, was less typical. Wembo traced Mulanga to "sixty miles" away in Kuba country. He hid along a trail that led to the spring of the town where she was held, and then he drew her attention when she passed by with a group of women by whistling a favorite old tune of theirs. On her way back from the spring she managed to be the last one in the file of women and to contact him briefly. That night they escaped together back home.

As the years went by, both kidnapping and attempts to rescue slaves raised tensions more and more frequently between villagers and nearby trading or mission stations. After 1893, trading stations began to multiply and to hire more and more workers recruited for the most part among Luba refugees or former slaves near Luebo. And, of course, these workers were often ready to help their fellow Luba escape from bondage.

Why did the Kuba buy so many slaves? That question puzzled Wissmann as early as 1885 and was raised over and over again—usually in a context of praise for the benefits of colonial intervention—by nearly all early overseas foreigners who followed him as late as 1904. Little did these colonials realize that slaves were mostly in demand by the Kuba as domestic labor and as a way to increase the size of their lineages. Nor did such writers readily acknowledge that they and their ilk also relied heavily on "liberated" slaves. They routinely bought slaves who were then tied to them by contract for a number of years before they were emancipated. Not only traders but also missionaries indulged in this practice. Thus most of the "abandoned and orphaned girls" in the care of the Presbyterian missionaries had actually been bought from slavers. Only after 1895 would the flood of refugees from eastern Kasai make such contracts unnecessary. Technically such redeemed refugees might be free labor, but in the eyes of the local Africans these workers were still held in bondage just like pawns for debt or slaves.

Ever since the days of Wissmann the standard answer given by all Africans to the question of why slaves were in such demand was that the Kuba needed large numbers of slaves to sacrifice them at funerals of kings, chiefs, and other important men. Bateman was told that "two thousand slaves" had been sacrificed in 1885–86 at the funeral of Mbop Mabiinc maMbul, a figure copied so often in later years that it became a standard figure of speech. According to the Presbyterian missionary Sheppard, King Kwet aMbweky told him a few years later that: "The burying of the living with the dead was far beyond the Bakete, who only bury goats with their dead, and that is why we bury slaves; they serve us here and then go with us on the journey to wait on us there."[5]

Yes, the Kuba (Kete included) sacrificed slaves at the funerals of important people. Nevertheless, the answer given in colonial accounts was but a half truth in that all of them with only one exception omit mentioning the role of slaves as domestic labor or as concubines. To raise this question was also a typically colonialist ploy because the answer invariably justified colonialism by the benefits of civilization. The accusation

5. William Sheppard, *Presbyterian Pioneers in Congo* (Richmond, Va., 1917), 137; more accessible in a new edition as *Four Presbyterian Pioneers in Congo* (Richmond, Va., 1965), 131.

of human sacrifice would remain a handy threat for a great many years to come. Although the last human sacrifices for a royal funeral seem to have occurred in the year 1900, eight years later Sheppard's fellow Presbyterian missionaries still routinely accused the Kuba kings of sacrificing large numbers of slaves at major funerals. They were wont to do this so regularly that by 1909 King Kwet aPe requested the presence of a European state official at the funeral of one of his close relatives simply to prove that human sacrifices were no longer carried out on such occasions.

Conclusion

In this chapter we have followed the long and complex process by which Congo became a colony, a process that required the crossing of two different developments: the expansion of an intercontinental trade in commodities within Central Africa and the ambition of a single monarch to acquire a colony. We have also seen that the territorial extent of the colony was by no means foreordained but gradually took shape as the result of various factors. In the case of Kasai the geographic location of Luebo at the end of a waterway to Kinshasa meant that the region became part of Congo and not Angola. Yet at the same time the government of the colonial Congo Independent State remained extraordinarily weak during the first fifteen years of its implantation here. During this substantial number of years the state remained unable to occupy the region effectively or to suppress the slave trade. In the Kuba kingdom north of Luebo the colonial footprint was so unimportant before 1899 that it would be ludicrous to speak about a Kuba experience of colonialism prior to that year. Yet, from 1885 onward the southern Kuba and some Bushong were in continual contact with the overseas foreigners and began to develop basic images of these colonizers in their minds, while the latter also developed their imagery about the Kuba. Already then these mutual representations began to shape the relationships between colonialist and colonized that were to characterize the whole colonial period. So important is this matter that the next chapter is devoted to this issue.

FURTHER READINGS

Bateman, Latrobe C. S. *The First Ascent of the Kasai.* London, 1887.
Carvalho, Henrique Augusto Dias de. *Lubuku: A Few Remarks on Mr. Latrobe Bateman's Book Entitled "The First Ascent of the Kasaï."* Lisbon, 1889.

Fabian, Johannes. *Out of Our Minds: Reason and Madness in the Exploration of Central Africa.* Berkeley, 2000.

Gann, L., and P. Duignan. *Rulers of Belgian Africa, 1884–1914.* Princeton, 1979.

Martens, Daisy S. "A History of European Penetration and African Reaction in the Kasai Region of Zaire, 1880–1908." Ph.D. dissertation, Simon Fraser University, Vancouver, 1980.

Slade, Ruth. *King Leopold's Congo.* London, 1962.

Stengers, Jean, and Jan Vansina. "King Leopold's Congo, 1886–1908." In *Cambridge History of Africa,* ed. John D. Fage and Roland Oliver, 6:315–58.

2

The Colonial Relationship

An absolutely essential foundation for the development of any colony was the creation of a special unequal relationship between people belonging to two different worlds: namely, all the foreigners from overseas, not just state personnel, with their own different and exotic culture, as masters and all the local African populations, with the variety of their cultures, as subjects. Without such a relationship the colonial state could not have endured. This relationship was backed by force, but ultimately it did not rest on force. In the eyes of the foreigners it was justified by the conviction of their absolute superiority, while their subjects mainly accepted it because of the foreigners' wealth and their superior magic-like technology that included their lethal weaponry.

The local populations accorded a special treatment to overseas foreigners and their agents from their very first appearance. Such a treatment was crucial even if it did not yet constitute a colonial relationship. This kind of behavior first appeared in Kasai as people witnessed the deference with which the Angolan caravans treated their Portuguese or German leaders, a behavior that was based in part on the centuries-old practice of colonialism in Angola. But caravans are temporary phenomena: when they arrived in the vicinity local people could either contact them—for instance, to trade—or ignore them.

They were compelled to become more involved when foreigners came to stay, founded stations, and began to interact daily first with willing local people and later by gradually forcing everyone into this new relationship of absolute inequality between locals and foreigners. It was a relationship expressed daily in conventional signs of superiority or submission, such as standard gestures to give or to receive, to claim precedence, or to yield it, a relationship vocalized by a tortured colonial jargon in which true verbs were always in the imperative mood and all other verbs became nouns, a jargon that bristled with a special lexicon referring to the benefits of superior civilization and the savagery of inferior culture. It was a relationship in which all terms of address invariably referred or alluded to the utter inequality of the relationship, and its jargon dripped with the condescension of the master toward the subject.

In addition and almost from the beginning the colonial relationship developed further on the basis of the preconceptions and the impressions each party built into its vision of the other during their initial encounters. However, this general vision then petrified almost immediately into a stereotype that was to last the whole colonial period, despite the accretions over time of further curlicues induced by later observations and by the very practice of colonial rule.

In the Kuba instance the crucial initial encounter was not the one involving Silva Porto but the one involving Wolf because he was supposedly the experienced white pioneer whose opinions were gospel for all his colonial followers. The followers of these followers then adopted the views of their predecessors as a matter of fact. Thus, even well before 1900 the essential colonial stereotypes had been formed about both the Bushong and the Kete. They would remain valid during the whole colonial period, just as the quintessential image of the foreigner did in the Kuba imagination. The impression their kingdom made on the imagination of the colonialists turned out to be crucial because it also conditioned the whole Kuba experience of colonial rule. Hence, this chapter deals first with the impressions left on both parties by their initial encounter, follows this up with a sketch of the organization of the Kuba kingdom and its villages, and only then turns to the colonial relationship proper.

Becoming Acquainted

Ludwig Wolf's unexpected irruption in the Kuba border settlements from an unusual direction created a stupendous surprise. In the first Bushong settlement where he arrived, the village of Ndong, the inhabitants completely lost their heads, as if they had seen something impossible, something out of a nightmare:

They first stood stock still as if spell-bound and yet it seemed as if they dearly wished to flee. Some silently held their hand in front of their mouth as a sign of surprise and others were aimlessly running around with their spears. All the while a woman kept staring at me with an expression of the greatest surprise and kept pinching the folds of her stomach with such force that her face mirrored the pain she was thus inflicting on herself.[1]

What precisely caused such a tremendous surprise, such an obvious challenge to the worldview of the villagers? Not just the sight of a white man, for five years earlier (in August 1880) Silva Porto had visited the nearby Kete market of Kampungu, and one or two other white Angolan traders may well have led or accompanied the caravans from Angola that had been frequenting these markets between Silva Porto's visit and that of Wolf. What every villager in Ndong saw was an impossibility or rather an awesome, fearful, yet also fascinating magical stunt: a person riding a buffalo, one of the most feared animals in Kuba country. For that is what Wolf perched on his tame bullock looked like to the spectators. Somewhat later that sight was sensational enough to attract thousands of sightseers to Ibanc on a market day. Even though later traders from Angola and even foreigners in Luebo also rode bullocks, the feat was still so impressive that "man riding an antelope" became thereafter a novel subject for some Kuba carvings.

A connection between white-skinned persons and a new kind of magic that produced wondrous new things, such as guns or compasses, had already impressed people in Silva Porto's time. Hence they nicknamed him Cingom, "the gun." Yet even in the 1950s people remembered that the magic of his gun had not prevented people from deriding his long beard. But riding a buffalo was altogether different and far more fearsome. To do this one had to be a powerful magician, somebody like Tooml Lakwey of yore, a magician of war and a hero so famous among the Bushong that a whole cycle of stories narrates his exploits. After Wolf's visit many Kuba believed for many years that some, if not all, Westerners were magicians of this ilk. Thus as late as 1892 King Kwet aMbweky accused the missionary Sheppard of provoking a heavy thunderstorm at the capital merely by stirring up soapsuds in the nearby brook.

Wolf is remembered as Mbol Woot, "The trace of/from Woot," an

---

1. Ludwig Wolf, "Wolf's Bericht über seine Reise in das Land der Bakuba," in Hermann Von Wissmann, *Im Innern Afrikas* (Leipzig, 1891), 227.

ominous but prestigious name that fitted his powerful magic. Woot was the common ancestor to all Kuba and the most powerful spirit known. Wolf was called by this name because he suddenly appeared from the direction in which Woot had vanished, namely upstream to the east. This was also the direction from which Woot had sent a number of calamities to the Bushong after his departure. Moreover, Wolf requested passage to go home downstream from where he later returned with a steamship and other Europeans. In the Kuba genesis stories (first recorded in 1905–8 but obviously much older) the absolute "downstream" or the ocean was the temporary abode of the dead. Once reborn they ascended the rivers to return to the kingdom, just as Wolf and his successors had done.

Indeed, Wolf's movements seemed to confirm the rumors that had been spread by the trading caravans from Angola for at least a decade or so. They held that Europeans actually lived in the sea and that was why their eyes were colored like those of fish and why their skin was bleached. So if anyone had told the Bushong or Kete in November 1885 that they had just become part of a new Congo state ruled by a bearded king somewhere underwater or overseas it would have sounded to them like a fairy tale. It probably was King Leopold's portrait, however, that inspired the account told to a trader for the Dutch rubber company at Ibanc in 1900 by his Lulua mistress. The trader's father was said to live on an island built up from rubber balls in a great water. He had a long beard, the end of which hung in the sea and attracted sardines there. From time to time he lifted his beard and harvested the fish—and that is why Europeans always have sardines to eat. As to the trader's mother, her portrait in full color could be found on the paper flyleaf inserted inside every box of his Dutch cigars.

Eventually someone did tell people about this new state to which they supposedly belonged and that was then already called Bula Matari, "the breaking of rocks" after Stanley, the man who had used a magic powder (dynamite) to blast a road from the lower river to Kinshasa in order to have ships launched on the Pool, ships like the sternwheeler *Stanley*, which had been the first ship to reach Luebo and remained its most frequent caller for many years thereafter.

In time Kuba views about Westerners slowly changed as they drew lessons from their relentless observations of everything every single European or American did or told them about the lands overseas, and they also made room for Europeans in their worldview and tales of Genesis. They soon became familiar with the routines of traders and missionaries, and somewhat later with those of government officials.

Yet some questions about all Europeans remained a mystery for decades, not least the one about why they came to Congo at all. On beholding the skyline of Antwerp for the first time in 1899, Kassongo, a servant of the missionary Verner, asked, "Master, why does the white man leave all this to go to our country?"[2] A year or so later the highest-ranked title-holder in a large Bushong village near the Dutch trading station of Ibanc asked the trader there why he had abandoned his family in Europe although there was no famine and although he loved his parents and his siblings. Moreover, his stock of trade showed that he was obviously extremely wealthy. So why then did he come to Ibanc to work so much? Would he never amass enough rubber and ivory to satisfy his father? Would there never come an end to all this toil? Already many Kuba, like many other Congolese, suspected that most Europeans came to Congo because they were poor, of low status, or unwanted at home, a suspicion that was to flourish all during the whole colonial period.

While the almost hypnotized Kuba could scarcely believe their eyes when they first met him, they in turn astonished Wolf, even though he was a seasoned traveler in Central Africa by the time he met them. His

---

A Fable and a Moral

A certain man left his village, saying that he wanted to travel in the forest, to cross the spring and to arrive in the middle of another savanna, the largest and the longest [known] where he had heard people talk and dance, a dance called "the perfect dance." He listened to it and said that he had to go there to see those people. Then when he arrived nearby he found himself in a big village. There was a lot to eat, he was attracted to the village, and the view from there was beautiful also. He returned quickly to his native village to take all his things and to settle in the village that he had found in the middle of the forest.

Moral of the story: This is like the Europeans who have landed here in Congo thanks to us: Otherwise they could almost never live here in Congo.[3]

---

2. Samuel P. Verner, *Pioneering in Central Africa* (Richmond, Va., 1903), 434.
3. Vansina Notebooks, 61: 1/2, April 25, 1956; Kwet Stéphane, *Fable.*

A raffia palm in the yard (photo by author)

writings do not betray this because he donned the mask of the detached
scientific observer like the good physician he was. Yet he too saw and did
not understand what he saw. For instance, he describes Mwanika—a
large Kete village, the first he saw in the kingdom—as a long rectangle
with a straight six-meter-wide main street and two one-and-a-half-
meter-wide parallel side streets along which were aligned some 350 to
400 small but elegantly shaped houses built with materials from the raffia palm. Palm trees and other huge shade trees stood in the middle of
the village. He was astonished because hitherto he had never seen any
settlement in Africa that seemed to have been built according to a defi-
nite plan.

    Wolf described Mwanika, but he did not really see it. He did not no-
tice its orientation, east to west, parallel to the nearest large river, the

A village street (photo by author)

Lulua, nor did he observe its internal divisions into clusters of houses inhabited by members of the same clan section. Hence the blatant objectivity of his report was quite misleading, not just because he missed so much but because that objectivity leaves the impression that he had described everything there was to see.

Just how much he missed is evident from his account of the next village he visited, the Bushong settlement of Ndong. This had a three-meter-wide main street along which lay forty small but elegantly built houses in materials from the palm tree. Again Wolf failed to notice the overall east-west orientation, nor did he distinguish the prestigious downstream part, inhabited by the founding lineages, from the upstream region inhabited by their lower-status followers, nor did he realize that the main street divided the village in right and left halves, each of which had its own leaders. He was unaware of the clustering of the houses along that street by clan section according to matrilineal family ties, and he simply could not see the extent, the use, and the meaning of the lands that constituted its domain.

Wolf vividly sketches the utterly hypnotized woman he saw there, but he was not aware of her as a social person since he knew only her gender but nothing else about her. Yet she had a name, a matrilineage, an age grade, probably a husband (unless she was a widow), a social rank, and a known history. She belonged to a social class and was perhaps famous for some special know-how such as making ceramics or being a priestess. Wolf knew nothing about this, yet neither does he seem to have been aware that he did not know. Actually it is especially striking that while Wolf was deeply impressed by the Kuba display of political might and rank, as well as by their manufactures and art objects, he still had no inkling that Kuba society was probably the most stratified and intricate then flourishing in Congo.

Moreover, the true significance of his concrete observations often escaped him for lack of experience, even when in hindsight it is quite evident to us. Thus he mentions that manioc was scarce at Ndong, but he did not realize that this was so because the village did not straddle any major caravan road. He ignored that local women bitterly resented its cultivation because processing manioc easily doubled their daily work as compared to processing maize or sorghum. Nor did he realize that the cultivation of this crop was recent in this region and had been induced by the demand of the caravan carriers from Angola. Indeed, the Bushong word for root of manioc stems directly from the Cokwe language and indirectly from Kimbundu, the language of Luanda, the capital of Angola.

In particular, Wolf could not know whether what he saw was routine or exceptional, although he tended to assume that everything he witnessed was routine. For instance, at the end of February he observed people busy cutting trees to prepare fields in the forest just north of Ibanc. We know that this is highly unusual because February falls during the main rainy season, a time when no one usually prepares fields. What caused people to do this in the year 1885? He did not ask, and hence we do not know. Similarly the account of his official encounter with the king's son at Ibanc presents that situation as absolutely normal whereas it was, in fact, a highly exceptional and ominous occurrence. It was part of the events that were bringing the kingdom just then to the brink of civil war. Indeed, the royal son's visit ended with the truly exceptional plunder of the market by his armed escort, an event for which the market women blamed Wolf.

Despite his detached stance Wolf was obviously profoundly impressed by the settlement planning of the Kuba, their intricate political display, their superior technological skills, and their artistic achievements, which his followers from Angola and even from central Kasai also seemed to admire without reservation. So impressed was he that he needed to explain the origins of such a "superior civilization." The profound astonishment that his appearance had created led him to believe that the Kuba had never seen any European before him and had not yet been influenced by things Western, despite their trade with Angolan caravans. He felt therefore that he had found that elusive entity eagerly sought by all explorers: a truly pristine African culture. He concluded that Kuba "culture" was superior to that of all the other Africans he had met, and suggested that this original, untainted, indigenous Central African culture was very likely related to ancient Egyptian civilization and the product of Semitic migrations.

The first colonials who succeeded him at Luebo accepted Wolf's sketch of Bushong and Kete society and culture without any reservations. In due time they added a few of their own observations as curlicues to it so that barely a decade later that sketch had become gospel truth. For example, to cite but a single instance, in 1896 the official description of the Kuba includes the following summary sentence: "The Kuba are excellent paddlers, very committed to trade, peaceful, not much given to farming, but very proficient in the handicrafts; they form a handsome population [French: *race*]; their women however are too tall." This sentence was still copied as late as 1908 by Morrissens and Goffart in a general geography book that then adds for good measure: "Considering themselves, rightly so, superior to the neighboring races the Bakuba carefully avoid to mix with them by custom and by tradition and remain scrupulously faithful to the ancient traditions."[4]

Moreover, usually they contrasted these Bushong perfections with the deficiencies of the miserable Kete around Luebo as in the following statement: "The Bakete are generally lazy and quite wild: they wear no European cloth," or succinctly, they are "lazy," "wild," and even "degenerate."[5] These descriptions are particularly striking in missionary Verner's work: "The surrounding natives generally look down upon the Bakete and they are extremely dirty and disorderly in their towns" as opposed to "These Bakuba [Bushong] were the most powerful, the most

4. C. Liebrechts, *L'état indépendant du Congo à l'exposition de Bruxelles-Tervueren* (Brussels, 1897), 190; G. Morrissens and F. Goffart, *Le Congo* (Brussels, 1908, 2d ed.), 154 (and 144–48). See also A. de Boeck, ed., *Notre colonie: Le Congo Belge* (Brussels, 1909), 78.

5. Morrissens and Goffart, *Le Congo*, 154. See also David A. Binkley and Patricia Darish, "'Enlightened but in Darkness': Interpretations of Kuba Art and Culture at the Turn of the Twentieth Century," in *The Scramble for Art in Central Africa*, ed. Enid Schildkrout and Curtis A. Keim (Cambridge, 1998), 42–44.

conservative, the least changed, the most tenacious of their own superstitions and customs of all the surrounding tribes. They are also probably the most capable and intelligent."[6]

Thus Bushong/Kete formed a pair of striking contrasts, but it was a
wholly spurious and imaginary one, considering that Kete daily life was
in general quite similar to that of the Bushong. Nevertheless, this negative opinion about the Kete as a counterfoil to the Bushong would last
until nearly the end of the colonial period. And even though the Kete
too were Kuba, colonialists excluded them when they spoke of the
"Kuba" as a "superior and ancient civilization," a sophisticated "feudal"
kingdom, very conservative, opposed to all innovation, a peaceful but
haughty people, great traders, indifferent farmers, and "the greatest artists and architects of central Africa." This superb reputation helps to explain why that kingdom and its rulers also enjoyed exceptionally favorable treatment by the administration during the whole colonial period.

The Kingdom

Wolf found an old, complex, multilingual, and flourishing kingdom—
even though just then in 1885 it was teetering on the brink of a major
civil war about the royal succession. He himself did not learn much
about the realm and its inhabitants. Today we known a good deal more
thanks to the records left by traders, missionaries, and anthropologists
who followed not long after Wolf. However incomplete and even misleading such records can sometimes be, they are still valuable because
they can be checked against the many local oral reminiscences, most of
which were recorded in the 1950s. These include items linked to every
succeeding generation from the 1880s until the 1950s. While this is not
the place to provide a detailed overview of the economic, social, political, and cultural situation of the Kuba in the late nineteenth century,
the reader still needs to know enough about the situation around 1885 so
as to evaluate the magnitude of the changes colonialism wrought.
Hence the summary information that follows.

The core of the kingdom in 1885 consisted of the single large central chiefdom called Bushong, whose inhabitants were known as Bashi

---

6. Verner, *Pioneering in Central Africa*, 116, 226, 282, 313. See also Liebrechts, *L'état
indépendant*, 190; Morrissens and Goffart, *Le Congo*, 144–48, 154.

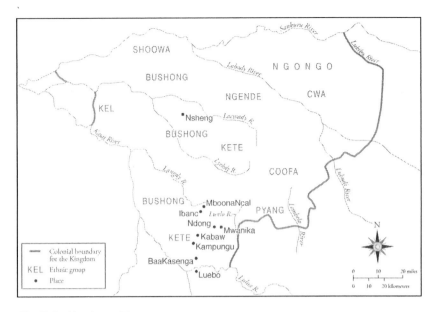

The Kuba kingdom, 1885

Bushong. An adjacent region composed of large autonomous but subject villages to its south and east was inhabited by Kete who spoke one or two languages different from Bushong. This core was surrounded by an outer band of smaller regions inhabited by various other peoples closely related to the Bushong in language and culture. The largest among these and the most significant in colonial times were the Ngende (Ngyeen) to the east of the central chiefdom, the Ngongo beyond the Labody (Lubudi) River east of the Ngende, the Pyang to the southeast of the Bushong chiefdom, and the Kel to the southwest of the Bushong chiefdom. To these should be added several groups living along the Sankuru River, where the languages and customs diverged further from Bushong practice than those of the previous set. These included the Shoowa northwest of the core chiefdom and a set of small ethnicities further upstream.

Each of these small ethnic regions was further subdivided into chiefdoms whose rulers wore eagle feathers in their cap as a sign of rank. Every chief of this rank was supervised by an official from the royal court and had to give a spouse to the king. These royal wives lived in the women's quarters of the royal court and were the permanent representatives of their chiefdoms at the capital.

In addition, from the 1850s onward the king also claimed overlord-ship over a group of freshly immigrant Lulua speakers who were fleeing from famine-stricken country further southeast and who formed an en-clave within the realm. They soon emerged as a new ethnic group known as the Coofa. Beyond the formal border of the kingdom in that direc-tion lay a number of other small satellite Lulua polities that sometimes made gifts to their powerful neighbor. Last but not least one must also mention a number of semi-nomadic foragers, known as Cwa. They were dispersed all over the kingdom, spoke yet another different language, and were reputed to be its earliest inhabitants.

The Bushong chiefdom and hence the whole kingdom was ruled from its capital, Nsheng (Mushenge, as the Europeans called it). This was a planned urban settlement, oriented on an axis from downstream to upstream in relation to the two nearest sizeable rivers that flow from east to west. The enclosed royal palace area occupied the most pres-tigious downstream portion of the town. In addition to the king's own dwellings this area contained sections for the successors and their fami-lies, for the royal slaves, for some royal notables, for the royal wives, for the royal storehouses, as well as guardhouses for its main gate. Each of these sections was separated from all the others by squares and a laby-rinth of walled passages. The town proper occupied the upstream por-tion of the capital. This was divided into a left and a right side by a succession of squares and a broad long road running from east to west along the daily path followed by the sun. An orthogonal grid of streets further divided each side into named and enclosed wards. In 1892, when the missionary Sheppard first saw this city, there seemed to be nothing even remotely comparable elsewhere in the whole Congo.

— The Bushong chiefdom was governed by the king acting in con-cert with a set of councils. These were staffed by ranked titleholders who formed part of an administration that comprised more than a hun-dred officials. Among them a small number of aristocratic titleholders of the highest rank, sometimes referred to as "ministers" by the sources, formed the council for routine affairs, a council that met almost daily. The degree to which the whole Bushong population was represented in this central government was perhaps its most remarkable feature. All the titleholders were elected by their peers in council without any royal input, so that the whole council truly represented the population of the capital and the free Bushong villages. It also greatly limited the influence of the king on the council for routine affairs. The same concern of rep-resentativeness dictated the composition of the tribunals. The number of judges on the bench and their particular competence varied for each case according to its particularities as to the offense involved (e.g., adultery, theft, debt), the social situations of the parties (especially by territorial origin, rank, class, and gender), and also the technical knowledge involved (e.g., metallurgy, hunting).

Royal supervision and administration of the villages within the Bushong chiefdom was close and detailed. As part of a canton, itself part of a province, itself part of the chiefdom, each village was indirectly linked to the center. It was also directly connected to the court through a royal spouse because each village was obliged to always have at least one of its women married to the king. According to its location, size, and economic profile, each village regularly paid tribute in food or the products of local crafts such as raffia cloth, iron, or palm oil and provided labor from time to time for porterage or for projects at the capital. The amounts of goods and services required varied further according to the status of each village involved because villages could be free or unfree.

Less onerous but far more crucial was the royal tribute in game. Whenever one of the so-called noble animals was killed in its territory, the village involved had to send to the king the part that made the animal noble—for example, the skin of the leopard, the horn of the buffalo, the tusks of the elephant, or the eagle's feathers. To send such a part was a declaration of renewed homage, while to eschew this was an open declaration of rebellion.

Why did the Bushong and especially the more exploited villagers accept this political regime? The first of two major reasons why nearly every one of them supported the central government was that people, even in the humblest of villages, felt that they had a stake in the government and that they participated in it. So widespread was the titleholding system at various territorial levels from the royal court down to that of the village that nearly every mature man and many women could hope to gain the recognition of their peers by being granted one or another title. Everyone was fascinated and overawed by the spectacle of government and power in action when royal dances were performed during which the special dance steps, the musical rhythms, the costumes, the jewels and emblems of the participants, all directly displayed the hierarchies and relationships of power while the spectators particularly noted the emblems of rank on display by titleholders in performance that they themselves could hope to achieve one day. At the same time, such spectacles legitimized the authority of the center. For instance, I suspect that when Wolf arrived at Ibanc, the royal son who received him arranged for such a dance on market day first and foremost to demonstrate his own power as a disputed regent of the kingdom to the thousands of people who had assemble there to see Wolf, and only incidentally to impress Wolf himself.

But the second and main reason why people accepted both kingship and the regime was a social contract between the king and his people. The king protected his people from major calamities and provided peace and with it fertility for plants, animals, and people to multiply and prosper. Once the king's protection was withdrawn from a village, it would soon be struck by a medical or natural catastrophe. More prosaically villagers also feared reprisals by the royal soldiers. Yet despite such a perspective and such fears, a large village like Mwek in 1907 might openly rebel against the king once the villagers had gained the conviction that he had failed in his duties and no longer protected them.

In sharp contrast to the care with which the ruling Bushong were represented in the personnel and the institutions of government, the other peoples of the kingdom had few representatives at its capital. Only the royal wives whom their leaders had to send to Nsheng acted as their agents at court; the particular titleholders and emissaries from the court who were responsible for transmitting orders to the subordinate chiefdoms or villages—and who gathered tribute there—were appointed by the king and the Bushong councils. The subordinate polities seem to have accepted their inferior status out of fear of the king's believed innate capacity to spread death and destruction but also in part because they feared his warriors. Still, the further away from the center the local groups were, the weaker such fears and the more rebellious they tended to be. Thus, in spite of royal claims to the contrary, a royal woman slave told Wolf at Ibanc that the kingdom did not extend beyond the Labody River to the east. Her assertion could be considered to be merely a spiteful exaggeration, yet the known events during the next decades make it clear that the royal will was indeed rarely heeded east of the Labody River or for that matter in the lands of the Coofa.

Villages and Villagers

For all its glamour the political structure of the kingdom rested ultimately on the humble village organization that underpinned it, a truth that seems to have eluded most outside observers, including its earliest anthropologists, perhaps because villages seemed to be so ephemeral to them. Indeed, most settlements moved from one site to another on average once every five years or so, and in addition there was a considerable turnover in their populations from one decade to another.

Yet villages were not so ephemeral after all: many of the settlements Wolf mentions still existed in the 1950s, and the ones that had disappeared had fused with other villages still in the same general location. How could there be this situation of stability despite mobility? Each village was endowed with a landed domain that belonged to the matrilineage of its founders and movements from site to site always occurred within the same domain. The term *matrilineage* refers to the lineage that is constituted by all the descendants of a single common ancestress through the female line only. Nearly every domain seems to have had its own nature spirit or *ngesh* whose priest, often a woman, resided in the village whose land it was. Moreover, village domains were the basic units whose aggregation formed all the higher-level territorial units within the kingdom.

The Kuba countryside was occupied by clusters of settlements, each of which contained one or two larger villages comprising several hundred inhabitants each, surrounded by a number of smaller villages counting less than one hundred and fifty inhabitants each. Because their internal structure facilitated the acceptance of new immigrant families more than that of the Bushong, most Kete villages were larger than their Bushong counterparts. In addition, the royal court directly limited the largest size that Bushong villages could reach. Most settlement clusters occupied a distinctive and usually named landscape. Often their largest village was a market town and, among the Bushong, also tended to be the administrative seat of a district or canton.

As to its social composition, each village contained a number of local wards. Each ward consisted of a group of houses whose inhabitants belonged to a single matriclan section—that is, a portion of a single matriclan together with their spouses and children. *Matriclan* is the designation for a large group of people who *believe* that they are all related by descent from a single ancestress through the female line only and who all share a common motto and a common avoidance of a particular food as a result. Kuba clans were dispersed in lineages between wards all over the country. At any time the number of such wards varied from one per village to well over a dozen and often more among the Kete, while every village waxed and waned over time as some of its resident families first increased in numbers and then split up, and as new clan sections were attracted to it or old ones left for elsewhere. Apart from matrilineal descent the inhabitants of every village were further structured by age, gender, and know-how. Every few years there were separate initiations for boys and girls so that every man and woman belonged to an age grade. Such peer groups did play a prominent social role.

Marriage required bridewealth, which is a set of payments handed over by the groom and his relatives to the relatives of the bride by which the marriage alliance was sealed. In the event of divorce these payments were returned. Marriage was forbidden between relatives of any degree and was monogamous with the exception of the king, his immediate successors, and eagle feather chiefs elsewhere. But divorce was frequent, and any man could also marry pawn women (*ngady*) as concubines in addition to his wife but for a much higher bridewealth. Since women went to live in the village of their husbands, since men moreover usually married outside their village of residence, and since men could reside in any of the four villages of their grandparents, one effect of those frequent divorces was a high rate of residential mobility within any given village and especially for women.

To make matters even more complex one must consider class and rank as well. In most wards there were free persons, pawns (half-free persons), and slaves, while at the village level there were "owners" (that is, members of the matrilineage who had founded the village—usually in a distant past), groups whose head was a child or a grandchild of a male "owner," and groups whose head was a friend or a spouse of one of the above. Moreover, some Bushong villages were serfs of the kingdom while others were free. Last but not least, every village was divided into two halves lying left and right (usually north and south) of the main street and led by their own titleholder. Each half was further divided into two less marked portions, a prestigious downstream and a more common upstream, an arrangement that reflected a further hierarchy of resident clan sections.

The government of a Bushong village included a village head, a male and a female leader each for the right and left halves, a head warrior (*iyol*) responsible for safety in the village, lesser female and male titleholders, and a council of elders that consisted of the heads of every clan section. That council met whenever common village affairs needed to be resolved. Every village further contained an enclosure in the central square for the shrine of the village charm (*kiin*). That charm supposedly protected the village against all evil from the outside, such as epidemics, disease, prolonged drought, lightning, or especially bad storms. In some cases the headman of the village seems to have been the guardian of the *kiin*, but sometimes it seems to have been tended by the priestess or priest of the village *ngesh*, or even by a resident diviner, when there was one. Such persons were also included in the village government along with the leaders of right and left and the *iyol*.

Collectively these notables dealt with all outside affairs such as the raising of tribute or labor for the kingdom, organizing communal commercial affairs, or inviting specialists in the supernatural to cope with particular calamities when required. They also kept peace inside the community by convening a local court and acting as judges whenever any conflict between villagers needed to be resolved. A separate court consisting of female titleholders settled only disputes between women. Such village courts enjoyed real authority:

> When after solemn treatment of the matter at hand to which the whole village has listened in silence, the village headman announces his decision; there is nothing more to argue and even the strongest man will accept it, or at least will not show his resentment openly, because that might well hurt him and do so in a terrible way.[7]

That "terrible way" is an allusion to the poison ordeal, *ipwemy*, whereby anyone accused of witchcraft could be subjected to the consumption of poison that was ordered by the village authorities and usually administered by a medicine man. The accused drank the poisoned potion and either vomited it soon, which was as a sign of innocence, or was affected by it, a sign of guilt. If the latter happened, the public lynched the accused and burned her or his bones.

The village was also the place where all economic production from agriculture to manufacturing and even mining was organized. In general, work was allotted according to a well-defined and efficient division of labor by gender and by age for nearly every kind of economic activity, from the preparation of fields to the provision of food and drink. Thus the fabrication of the celebrated embroidered Kuba raffia cloths, used primarily during funeral rites or in dancing costumes, required the following collaboration, as the Presbyterian missionary Lapsley discovered on his arrival at Baa Kasenga, a Kete town near Luebo:

> I saw the manufacture in all its stages—boys stripping off the outside of the leaf blade and leaving the delicate pale green ribbons [of raffia] within and tying them in hanks like yarn. Men were separating it; threading the loom with the warp; and then came the clack

---

7. Alfons Vermeulen, *De pioniersdagen van Chicongo* (Amsterdam, ca. 1933), 260.

of the simple but complete weaving machine, the simple, silent passage of the long polished stick which does duty as a shuttle, and thus the usual everyday waist or loin cloth is finished. But the women pound a few choice pieces in a mortar with flour of maize or manioc till it is soft and satiny to the feel. These are dyed [by women] and worn on swell occasions.[8]

Apparently he did not observe on his walk that day how women patiently embroidered many woven and softened pieces of cloth with different threads dyed in different colors (also by women) to produce the famous "Kasai velvets."

But the most distinctive feature of Kuba villages, as opposed to those of all their neighbors, was undoubtedly the extent of their specialization by know-how as attested by the great diversity and the quality of their celebrated artworks and other manufactures. While all men should be able to weave cloth, to plait mats and baskets, or even to carve simple tools, only a few were able smelters, smiths, jewelers, wood carvers, and tailors, just as only a small number of women were potters. Moreover, some persons were so much more talented than others that they also achieved a reputation as specialists. Thus we find among others specialized fishermen and women dyers, embroiderers, or sculptors in redwood paste. As the following quotes show, their contemporaries were struck by all this manufacturing activity and ability:

> In the middle of the small village a shed of the same [raffia] materials is the meeting place where the men gather to talk. Next to this shed, the village smith (*fundji*) has set up his primitive smithy and his bellows fixed in the ground are serviced with great diligence by a pair of alert, handy, naked boys. The *fundji* of a village is a very important personage, the craft is often inherited from father to son, each piece of work is inspected from all sides and is discussed in the shed adjacent to his atelier. . . .
>
> Under the shed a few men are plaiting some fishing baskets, mats, or baskets; they make nets and ropes, beat the bark from trees in solid rough patches of brown stuff, which they then dye with tukula—finely rasped redwood, or they are weaving pieces of raffia cloth, or they are just gossiping and philosophizing with each other.[9]

Such a pronounced specialization in manufacturing was complemented by a network of flourishing internal and external markets of

---

8. Samuel Lapsley, *Life and Letters of Samuel Norvell Lapsley* (Richmond, Va., 1893), 167.
9. Vermeulen, *De pioniersdagen van Chicongo*, 259.

which the great market at Ibanc was but one node. Besides goods produced by various groups of Kuba and Luba, imported sea salt, cowries, bush knives, and copper rings were in great demand from foreign parts, as were quantities of white cotton textiles and blue drill by 1900, although they were probably only destined for resale elsewhere outside of the kingdom.

At this point the reader may well feel overwhelmed by the incredible intricacy of the communal organization to be found within any seemingly anodyne village: every person in his or her place arranged in hierarchical order within several different overlapping social webs in such a way that no two individuals ever occupied the same social spot. A detailed description of the economic life within a village with its complex system and know-how of food production and its array of specialized knowledge in manufacturing would bring the reader to the same point of astonished wonder. Yet most foreigners at the time and most of the subsequent writers about the Kuba have remained wholly unaware of these intricacies of village life and culture. Hence they have been unable to truly grasp how much colonial change did transform the world of the rural Kuba.

This thumbnail sketch of the institutional structures of the kingdom and its constituent parts down to the village may well seem to be somewhat romanticized or idealized to some readers, and to a certain extent that cannot be avoided. Like nearly all similar short introductions to the makeup of a whole social structure, this sketch can only describe norms and not an ever-changing reality. Thus even while the institutions and arrangements sketched were real enough, the sketch actually describes a set of rules for the political and social game that were commonly agreed on in the minds of people rather than what they always did. Still, without the guidance provided by such a sketch, the significance of any concrete data cannot be assessed, while with it readers can easily discern when the reality of concrete circumstances differed from the expected and prescribed behaviors.

The Colonial Relationship

Internationally the colonial period began in 1885 with the recognition of the Independent Congo State. However, one may also consider that in the Kuba area this period began in 1900 when the kingdom was conquered or even as late as 1910 when the first state post was finally founded in its capital. Yet it is more realistic to argue that the colonial period started as soon as Luebo was founded in 1885 because the fundamental

colonial relationship between unequals was established in the region at
that moment. It was then a brand-new relationship, different from the
one that obtained between transient foreign travelers such as Europeans
or Luso-African caravan leaders, including Wolf on the one hand and
the personnel of their caravans and the local populations on the other.

The colonial relationship involved a different pattern of behavior,
and Luebo was its local incubator. Because it was a profoundly unequal
relationship, it was regulated by the requirements, orders, and moods of
the dominant partner. It had taken root in Luebo from the start even
though most of the available evidence on this point starts only in 1891.
To begin with, any resident European or North American, including
African American missionaries, was deemed to always be superior to
anybody else, more knowledgeable than anybody else, and endowed
with the authority to intervene in local affairs, such as to set themselves
up as judges in court cases or to hand out what they considered to be
summary justice.

Thus we see a trader and a missionary from Luebo suddenly set out to
attack and plunder a Luso-African caravan at the Kampungu market . . .
to liberate slaves or to loot ivory from the competition? In any case they
"took three pieces of ivory, seventeen slaves, and . . . we returned."[10]
Whereas their subordinates quickly learned to recognize the routine requirements of traders or missionaries, there always remained some surprising demands that seemed absolutely arbitrary to the colonized since
most dominant partners did not condescend to explain why they required something.

The moods of the colonizers mattered because they were the most
powerful. That is no doubt the reason why the special colonial whip
known as the *chicotte*, a whip with which one could inflict severe injuries
or even cause death, eventually became the symbol of the whole colonial relationship in Congo. The practice of whipping came to Luebo by
ship from the Lower Kasai, as a report about two incidents in early 1891
clearly shows. These incidents were linked to the "towering rage" of the
captain, who had "lost all control of his temper," a very common situation and a dangerous one, especially in the early colonial period when
there was often no check at all on such violent behavior.[11]

However, it is wrong to imagine a colonial relationship that was only
based on coercion with the *chicotte* never far away. Most foreigners were

10. Lapsley, *Life and Letters of Samuel Norvell Lapsley*, 195.
11. Lapsley, *Life and Letters of Samuel Norvell Lapsley*, 156–57.

Friends Chicongo and Mbop

Not all relationships between local men and colonials were hostile or coercive. Some became genuine comrades or friends even though such sentiments were frowned upon in the colonial world and are almost never mentioned in writing. Still they existed. Thus in 1900 Chicongo, the young and freshly arrived Dutch trader at Ibanc, became friends with Mbop, the young sculptor of the nearby Bushong village of Mboon aNcal (Bonzadi), and frequently refers to him.[12] In his book Vermeulen describes such friendships as follows:

> In Ibanc Chicongo had a few friends among the Kuba. He was himself only just over twenty years old and he needed to conclude a kind of comradeship with a few young men of that tribe from the village of Mboon aNcal, which was closest to his establishment. And, because he was generous and made these young men sometimes happy with small gifts they were keen about his friendship. One among them was Mbop whom we have already described. (277)

Vermeulen had described Mbop earlier in his account:

> He was a handsome Kuba youth. The greatest artist in the whole area as far as wood carving, the plaiting of baskets with naturalistic and geometric figures, extremely handy in forging flawless, symmetrical arrowheads and spear points with rows of hair-thin barbs that run around the arrowhead as a screw. And the manufacture of hafts for knives or swords, inlaid with bits of white iron from cans which he received from the White man and with little copper plates. Mbop was moreover Chicongo's hound when he went hunting in his free time. (200)

> Mbop is a youth of about seventeen or eighteen years old. A black person is then already an adult. He had just undergone his examination for "manhood" [boy's initiation] and had succeeded splendidly. Therefore he already wears the short plaited dancer's skirt which reached to the knees, with a pocket of leopardskin in front, the sign

---

12. Vermeulen, *De pioniersdagen van Chicongo*, 198, 200–201, 204–5, 212, 218, 223, 232–33, 276–78.

of virility for the Kuba. A single string with leopard and dog teeth around the neck completes this summary but virile toilet of our bronze Apollo. (201)

Other passages mentioning Mbop in the book make it clear that their friendship could only be a strongly unequal one, but a friendship nevertheless—even though Chicongo calls his friend a hound! In these passages Mbop appears when they are hunting, when he forges a needle for Chicongo, when he recruits a troop of small boys to trade salt from the shop in return for cowries, or when he tailors some trousers for the trader. On the other hand Chicongo spontaneously provides three thousand cowries "for his good services of all sorts and his many manifestations of friendship" (204). Those cowries are Mbop's bridewealth and allow him to marry. Elsewhere Chicongo further confides to his mistress that he wishes to be reborn a black person, just as handsome and talented as his friends Mbop and Kabea. But it all came to a tragic end around 1902:

> Among them was a Mbop whom we have already described. He was a particularly intelligent and Black person refined by nature. Suddenly one day Mbop stayed away and did no longer come to the establishment of his young friend. This went on for a few days, and soon for a few weeks. Then Chicongo began to look for information as to where Mbop could be, but he heard all sorts of excuses, and no one in Mboon aNcal wanted to inform him and to say where Mbop was. (277)

Six months later Chicongo learned that Mbop had been forced to undergo the poison ordeal and had died.

> His art and his friendship for the White man as well as his already considerable wealth in the eyes of these people had awakened the envy of some elders in the village. They had then spoken to the medicine man and they had concluded that this young man who was so expert in all sorts of things, who had won over such a difficult White man, who was so talented, had to be an unnatural being. There was witchcraft there, devilish arts. Mbop was forced to drink the poison ordeal and they had given him enough to put an end at once to the life of this young magnificent person. (277–78)

> And his most beautiful dancing sword hangs today in the national Dutch Museum of Ethnography in Leiden. (204)

young bachelors in their twenties in need of friendship and affection. Some, especially in isolated posts, struck up unequal friendships with local lads of their own age while nearly all of them kept a concubine or "housekeeper." Often such a couple became devoted to each other. The situation of the trader Ernest Stache and Chala, his mistress, is such a case. In 1891 even a Presbyterian missionary could not be wholly negative about it. "I would add, poor girl; but she is happy, and don't know that she wasn't married just as her husband would have married a wife in Belgium. When he was sick she would expose herself to a similar attack saying, as if it were a matter of course, 'If you die, I will die too.'"[13]

In his reminiscences Vermeulen, the Dutch rubber trader, illustrates how strong and long lasting such an affection could be. Much of his memoir is devoted to remembering his mistress Mulekedi and defending that devotion, more than twenty-five years after her death in childbirth. Nevertheless liaisons of even devoted couples usually ended with the return of the man to Europe or America. Social and racial taboos were so strong in that age that even devoted fathers abandoned their concubine and their children. Thus on his departure for Belgium, where he died soon thereafter, Stache had to leave both Chala, his wife, and Emma, his daughter, in the care of Sheppard and the mission station.

The foundations of the colonial dispensation had thus been laid well before the formal conquest of the kingdom, which we discuss in the next chapter. Colonial traders and missionaries had taken root all around the kingdom and even at a few places inside its borders, while by the mid-1890s the Kuba along the Sankuru River were beginning to experience destructive behavior caused by the people known as Bula Matadi, the agents of the colonial government. As we shall soon see, the years of conquest and subjugation were to be much more than merely a formal recognition that the colonial era had begun.

Further Readings

Josefsson, Claes. *The Politics of Chaos: Essays on Kuba Myth, Development and Death*. Gothenburg, 1994.
Vansina, Jan. *The Children of Woot*. Madison, 1978.

---

13. Lapsley, *Life and Letters of Samuel Norvell Lapsley*, 181.

3

Incidental Conquest

Recently the history of the Congo Independent State returned to the attention of a wider public when a sensational, century-old controversy flared up again. The original controversy had started in the 1890s when indignant missionaries began to report and denounce the atrocities they had witnessed. The scope and the tenor of such accusations grew until the British government ordered its consul Roger Casement to investigate in 1903. His report then led E. D. Morel to launch the Congo Reform Association in Great Britain and to orchestrate one of the first successful mass media campaigns there and elsewhere. The international success of the campaign led to the demise of the Independent Congo State when King Leopold was forced to hand over the colony to Belgium in 1908.

This issue flared up again in the early 1980s and has reached a large international audience since 1998 as a result of Adam Hochschild's *King Leopold's Ghost*, a Pulitzer Prize–winning book. He argues that the atrocities were all too true, that they included murder on a very large scale, that they caused demographic losses that he estimates at around ten million people or half of the total population over some thirty years, and finally that Leopold II and his government were well aware of the situation and hence were fully responsible for the huge loss of lives.

The main rebuttal of this position involves two points: first, atrocities are far from the whole story of colonial Congo, so focusing exclusively on them wholly distorts what is in reality quite a complex history, and second, the mortality figures quoted are unreliable and highly inflated, to say the least. No credible population counts had been conducted during the period, and hence all the figures we have are more or less well-informed guesses. In any case, such population losses as occurred did not result for the most part directly from the atrocities themselves.

As it happens, the regional experience of the Kuba kingdom allows us to evaluate these claims and counterclaims in a concrete manner, which we do in this and the following two chapters. According to some of the best-known accounts of the Congo Reform Association as well as those contained in Hochschild's book, the Kuba are alleged to have suffered two rounds of atrocities, one in 1899 and the other between 1905 and 1908. Both were linked to the gathering of rubber, and both are alleged to have triggered huge demographic losses. By using the Kuba experience, the reader can gain more familiarity with the kind of evidence that backs the allegations made in the early 1900s and a better sense of the historical context in which that evidence should be evaluated.

A New Dispensation for Congo

In the same year that business suddenly began to pick up at Luebo, King Leopold decreed a completely new dispensation on the colony. For several years it had become painfully clear to him and his closest advisers that Congo was headed for bankruptcy in the near future because significant revenues to cover the costs of the colony could not be raised. That resulted from one of the conditions that the main powers in 1885 had attached to their recognition of the state—trade in Congo was to be totally free, and hence no customs duties would ever be levied there.

But by 1890 the king found a brilliant solution to this predicament, a solution known as the *régime domanial*, and he imposed it immediately. The new dispensation started with the definition of the state's self-proclaimed ownership over all "vacant" land, defined as land that was not physically occupied by houses and standing crops. By definition this domain encompassed almost the whole country. Moreover, ownership of vacant land included everything it contained, such as elephants or rubber vines. Hence the solution for Congo's financial problem was for the state to become a business enterprise. From then on the main task of the agents of the state would be to gather ivory, rubber, and whatever other products were valuable in return for a commission. The state then sold these products on the European market.

However, the king realized that the country was too vast, the number of his agents too small, and the impression his business empire would create in the chanceries of Europe too unsavory to keep the whole exploitation for himself. So he set aside a royal slice of the country for direct exploitation as a "domain for the crown" and carved up the rest into a few huge chunks and "outsourced" them by awarding the monopoly of exploitation in each of these chunks to different concessionary companies, expressly created for this purpose, and in return for some of their shares as well as for hefty taxes.

Still, the new dispensation raised howls of protest from the two largest trading companies, the Dutch NAHV (Nieuwe Afrikaansche Handelsvereeniging) and the Belgian SAB (Société Anonyme Belge), which had already been established in the country for many years with King Leopold's blessing and which now were faced with the sudden loss of all of their business. So strong was their resistance that they forced the king into a compromise. In 1892 the regions of Lower Congo and central Kasai were formally set outside the *régime domanial*. They remained open to free trade as before, although in Kasai at least commercial freedom was limited only to the next decade.

In general, King Leopold's plan worked all too well. His new dispensation came just in time to profit from a long rubber boom. Hence it succeeded in eliminating Congo's deficits within the next five years, after which it began to generate huge profits. However, it also gave rise to the widespread abuses that became so notorious that they ended with the forced cession of Congo to Belgium.

Central Kasai and Kuba land escaped the effects of the new dispensation for a whole decade, in part as the result of Leopold's compromise, but also because in that same year of 1892 a large-scale war broke out between the Congo state and the Arab or Swahili merchant princes trading in ivory and slaves who dominated the whole of eastern Congo. Hostilities started when the district commissioner of Kasai at Lusambo on the Sankuru River attacked one of the major merchant princes on the Lualaba without any direct provocation. The war was extremely brutal, inflicted huge numbers of fatalities, and lasted for two years. During those years every Congolese soldier in Kasai who could be spared was sent to the front, and there was no question for the local post officer at Luluabourg to coerce anybody into producing anything for the state.

Within a year after the war's end the garrison stationed at Luluabourg mutinied and killed their commander. Once again every available loyal soldier was needed to cope with this emergency. As a result it was only in 1898 that some soldiers finally became available for the foundation of posts and the collection of "taxes" in the hinterland of Lusambo and also south and west of Luebo. Until that came about, though, the lands around Luebo as well as the Kuba kingdom remained an unexpected quiet corner where trade flourished all through the 1890s despite the raging turmoil all around them.

Hence the Kuba experience during those years was rather unusual compared to that of most Congolese elsewhere. But unfortunately it became as typical as that of almost any other corner in Congo during the decade that followed 1898: conquest followed by the brutal imposition of a concessionary company accompanied by significant loss of life and the outrage this provoked, which then resulted in takeover and major reform.

Red Rubber First Brings a Decade of Prosperity to Kasai

Meanwhile a commercial miracle woke up sleepy Luebo. From 1890 onward the price of rubber began to skyrocket as the result of technological development in Europe and North America—just as the price of coltan (columbite-tantalite) would about a century later. In the 1890s, however, the demand for rubber was not about cell phones but about electrification and transport. Rubber was needed to insulate wires and to make tires for bicycles and for the nascent automobile industry. Actually, rubber had been traded at the southern Kuba markets along with ivory for at least a decade before Luebo was even founded, but only as a subsidiary product. As we have seen, the first traders from overseas at Luebo who were competing with Angolan caravans soon discovered that most ivory was out of their reach, mainly because tusks had to be paid for in slaves. Hence, already by the late 1880s, traders were buying rubber mostly from the surrounding Kete and Bushong villages.

The rubber gathered in Kasai was technically known as "Kasai red rubber." In 1890 it suddenly acquired the reputation of being the best rubber in Africa and attracted the highest prices on the European markets. By March 1890 there was already talk of a "stupendous amount of business."[1] This "red rubber" was a product of the forests in the Kuba

---

1. Oscar Michaux, *Carnet de campagne* (Brussels, 1907), 88.

The NAHV rubber factory, 1897 (HP.1941.0.1099, collection RMCA Tervuren; anonymous photo, © RMCA Tervuren)

kingdom. There men would tap rubber by incising the *landolphia* vines and gathering their dripping sap. Then they let it coagulate into small balls. All of this was men's work because this tapping was analogous to the tapping of palm trees for wine, which was considered men's work because it involved climbing trees. The end product was the best and the most expensive variety of rubber in the whole Congo.

And so the export of rubber from Congo in general and Kasai in particular rose from year to year although it remained constrained by the need for huge numbers of porters to carry both products from Kinshasa, where they arrived by boat, to Matadi in the lower Congo. But this limitation was removed in 1898 when the railroad from Matadi to Léopoldville was completed. From then on both imports and exports grew by leaps and bounds. Indeed, so important was this railway that concessionary companies also began to flourish in the neighboring French colony of Congo Brazzaville.

The boom came just in time to save Luebo. In 1890 the capital of Kasai had been shifted from Luluabourg to Lusambo on the Sankuru River, a town that by then had become the strategic gate for access to both Katanga and eastern Congo. As a result the Sankuru River suddenly turned into the main highway into the interior at the expense of the Middle Kasai and Lulua rivers while Luebo, for the state at least, became a mere backwater. Actually this official neglect and the regime of commercial competition that continued to flourish in this part of Congo were the salvation of Luebo and its hinterland, including the Kuba kingdom. Business continued at Luebo much as usual after 1890 except that it grew to be more and more profitable and competitive as the prices for its high-quality rubber kept rising on the world market.

The rubber boom brought the quiet years of a commercial backwater to an abrupt end. Within less than a decade both the quality of its rubber and its trading regime attracted half a dozen rival new businesses to Luebo. In an effort to gain the advantage over their competitors, each of these companies began to found new trading posts around Luebo and along the banks of the Kasai and Sankuru rivers from 1892 onward. Soon every village within the whole Kuba kingdom became accessible to the rubber trade. As a result of the enhanced competition, the prices paid for rubber in the commodities demanded by its local suppliers rose from year to year and brought modest prosperity to villagers all over the Kuba kingdom. Yet at the same time the new trading posts summarily occupied large plots of land without any compensation to or any permission from the Kuba village on whose domain they were founded. In addition the new businesses also introduced sometimes large numbers of Luba or Lulua laborers around their posts. Needless to say, such practices caused considerable social strain between immigrants and older inhabitants.

The intense commercial rivalry not only ensured good prices for the Kuba but also led to fairly good relations between the local Europeans and the Kuba, simply because the African customers chose where to go and to whom to sell their rubber. In later testimony a magistrate claimed that peace and prosperity reigned in and around Luebo until 1902 when the brand-new Compagnie du Kasai gained a monopoly over all the wild rubber in the region. The memoirs of young Vermeulen, the trader for the NAHV company at its post in Ibanc between February 1900 and early July 1904, bear this out. His business was close to the Presbyterian mission station, but none of its missionaries objected to his business practices. His portrayal of the local rubber traders in 1900–1901, at the heyday when genuine competition was the rule and commercial rivalry was acute, eloquently shows how much the initiative was theirs (see "Pemba [Pyeem] Sells Rubber at Ibanc").

Pemba [Pyeem] Sells Rubber at Ibanc

Among the Kuba [Bushoong] the traders are often women. Every village has a few elder knowledgeable matrons endowed by nature with a strong dose of "commercial spirit" and a stupendous memory. They are born bargainers, not at all bashful, and they will do errands with the white trader for anybody. To do that they walk for days, indeed for a week, while John, Peter, and Nicholas from their own village and from the villages that they cross on their way to the factory give them balls of rubber. Thus they have their steady customers and thus they arrive sometimes at the factory with a huge basket of some forty kilogram [eighty pounds] balanced on their head with a value in those days of some 200 to 300 Dutch guilders.

Once near the factory our sturdy black woman trader greets us already from far away with a jolly "Good day, white person, here I am again." With a *dawé good lord*—and an artificial sigh of effort she puts the heavy basket on the ground followed by whatever else she carries such as half a dozen chickens, a few big packets of groundnuts and other merchandise, wipes the sweat from her brow with her hand and then sits down to recuperate a little on the mats of the veranda. And the white trader who knows her answers "Good day, mother Pemba." "Yes white man here I am again, am I not your girl?" says she. "But this time you are going to pay me well and you better give me a big, a very big present, or I won't ever come back to you." And she roars with laughter and slaps her heavy thighs.

Now she unpacks and she needs space for that. For she has up to fifty packets of different owners and out comes her ledger . . . that is, a bundle of sticks bearing all sorts of notches. She picks up one of these, rummages in her heap of packets, gets one of them out, thinks a little about it and says, "White man for this package I must have a bushknife."

The white man takes the package, unpacks the contents from their bundle of banana leaves, weighs the balls of rubber on his scale and says, "Mother, that is not doable but because you are my girl, I'll give you a bushknife for this once."

The bushknife is accepted, carefully examined to see if it does not have any flaw and put in the basket tied to the little stick.

Now comes little stock number two and its package: "*Mukalenge* [sir] for this one I want six *lopoto* beads"—that is, six big cut bunches (rosettas) of beads which were a very expensive sort of beads.

"You can imagine that," says the white man. "I'll give you three *lopoto*."

That provokes much praise and bargaining and finally one agrees for four *lopoto* and two spoons of salt.

The beads are put on a string of raffia together with tally stick number two. In this way the accounts are kept in order, and the whole goes neatly in the basket next to the bushknife. As for the salt, that goes into a tiny raffia basket.

And so one trades until all the packages are done, but it does not go just like that, it also needs a whole lot of talking.

Finally "Mother Pemba" is ready with the packing of her shopping and now she coaxes: "White man, didn't I bring you a whole lot of *dundu* [rubber], am I your girl? Give me a nice gift now, so then I will return soon to you, because you are my white man."

Mother Pemba now receives a few cups of salt, some beads, a copper bracelet and a few trinkets as a gift, as the white man assures her that he is crazy about her.

Whereupon she leaves happily and waddles out of the factory [the shop]. Now she will bring all her treasures to her customers who live days walking apart from each other, and if necessary she will defend her merchandise with her life. But then no one even thinks of robbing anything from these women. To the contrary, they are welcome everywhere, get to eat something in each house, and there too a place is found where she can sleep overnight on a mat . . . Happy mortals.

In this way her customers are served one after the other.

After the trade the white man makes a list of items sold, records the total weight of the rubber bought and writes it all down in his memorandum.[2]

But the commercial situation did not stand still. The volume of business at Ibanc increased fivefold in just two years so that Vermeulen also hired gangs of casual laborers as rubber gatherers. These people were Lulua or Luba just as all porters were and had always been, since the Bushong or Kete refused to be hired as labor because they considered this status to be akin to slavery. The introduction of so many aliens in the region raised tensions and eventually contributed to an uprising in 1904.

2. Alfons Vermeulen, *De pioniersdagen van Chicongo* (Amsterdam, ca. 1933), 166, 168, 223.

Ominous Portends: Missionaries and State Agents

The boom at Luebo was barely underway when two members of the southern American Presbyterian Christian Mission (APCM) unexpectedly landed there in April 1891 to found a mission station. This would not be a remarkable event at a time when many such stations were founded, including a Catholic mission at Luluabourg, were it not that this pair of missionaries consisted of an African American, William Sheppard, and a Euro-American, Samuel Lapsley. However, Lapsley died unexpectedly in early 1892, and Sheppard was left on his own. Unlike any other foreigner in the region, the flamboyant Sheppard was really enthused by everything Kuba and felt it to be his mission to convert this wonderful people. Hence he began to learn the "difficult" Bushong language, and even though he never spoke it very well, he still impressed the local people. Obviously he was not to be equated with other colonials at Luebo.

The next year he attempted to reach the capital by surreptitiously following local merchants from one market to the next, but this strategy was in vain. He was stopped along the way by royal warriors. When they reported to King Kwet aMbweky that this stranger spoke Bushong and was black, everyone there concluded that Sheppard had to be the reincarnation of some deceased Bushong. So the king had him brought to Nsheng, where the king declared that Sheppard was a reincarnation of one of his relatives. Sheppard stayed four months during which he made the acquaintance of many major titleholders, including Mishaamilyeng, a son of the king, who became a close friend. Finally the missionary was allowed to leave on condition that he would return to build a mission station at the capital.

But these plans suffered various delays and were finally cut short by the death of this king during the summer of 1896. However, Sheppard's visit had opened the road to the capital for others, so that henceforth either a trader or a missionary managed to visit the capital at least once every year until the conquest in 1900.

Yet there were already clouds on the horizon. Even King Kwet aMbweky was well aware of the reputation of state agents for violent behavior, and already in 1894 he flatly told a visiting missionary that he absolutely refused access to any Bula Matadi. So when the political situation turned to violence along the Sankuru River at the end of the year, he was certainly not surprised. The first district commissioners of Lusambo were very much Leopold's men on the spot, and they were acutely aware from the outset that they should use their men to exploit ivory, rubber, or whatever else would gain income for the state. At first this income consisted of rich stocks of ivory looted from the Arab Swahili traders during the war, but when the conflict ended in 1894 new resources had to be tapped.

So in December 1894 the district commissioner sent a young lieutenant with a few state soldiers who had been recruited on the Gold Coast to the village of Iyenga on the south bank of the Sankuru at the very edge of the Kuba kingdom. His instructions were to found a post there to gather "taxes"—that is, as much ivory or rubber as could be extracted. Since this officer, like any other agent of the state, stood to earn a handsome commission from the revenue he raised, he was eager to comply. On arrival he threatened the villagers with violence if they did not immediately bring rubber, ivory, and foodstuffs. They did not react at all, and hence on January 9, 1895, he captured the first canoe passing his camp. But the following night he was attacked, wounded by a poisoned arrow, and died, whereupon the district commissioner swore revenge and sent another lieutenant to carry it out. That man burned several villages along the river but had to be recalled soon to eastern Kasai. Three weeks later he was killed during a battle with mutineers from the garrison of the colonial army in Luluabourg. As to King Kwet aMbweky, he did not react to these events at all.

Kwet aMbweky's demise radically altered the situation. As soon as his successor, Mishaape, assumed power in the summer of 1896, he immediately consolidated it by having seven prominent sons of his predecessor killed. But Kwet aMbweky's favorite son Mishaamilyeng escaped, and his other main associates fled into hiding. At the same time the new king returned to the earlier policy of isolation despite strong opposition from a number of ivory and slave traders. Sheppard and his companion, the newly arrived Euro-American William Morrison, were also prevented from proceeding to the capital in July 1897. They were dismayed, yet they might have expected this. After all, in the eyes of the Bushong, Sheppard had been an obvious associate of the previous king and was still an ally of Mishaamilyeng. The king let the missionaries know that the question of a mission station at Nsheng would be discussed only after he had been formally installed as king. That in turn could happen only at the conclusion of a time-consuming sequence of rituals that would begin only after the building of a new capital, and only after all the Kuba chiefs had paid homage to him. The two thwarted missionaries waited at Ibanc. Then in August Mishaape's mother died. Because the queen mother was the king's equal, mourning for her was obviously going to delay the whole process of the king's coronation even further. Hence, on receipt of that news, the missionaries, tired of waiting, decided to found a temporary mission station at Ibanc until they could move to Nsheng. In this instance, temporary turned into permanent.

It was to Ibanc that Sheppard's friend Mishaamilyeng finally fled. This so infuriated the king that he first ordered Sheppard killed by a poisoned arrow. But he soon relented and called him instead to the capital to explain the rules of succession. As Sheppard understood it, he was told: "Do you not know, said he, that it is the custom when the crown passes from one family to another to murder all the sons of the old king?"[3] Obviously Sheppard had not understood the very principle of matrilineal succession that was being explained to him. He still continued to think that this particular succession was extraordinary in that the crown had passed from one "family" to another, whereas it was in fact a routine succession from uncle to sister's son within the same lineage. This incomprehension was to have lasting consequences because he continued to protect Mishaamilyeng and apparently to support him as a legitimate contender for the throne as well. That earned him and the whole mission the bitter enmity of several kings in succession.

Meanwhile time passed, and Mishaape had still not formally assumed kingship. By December 7, 1897, his mother had still not been buried, and the preparations for his accession to the kingship could be resumed only after her funeral. Despite a growing sense of urgency his installation was then further delayed all through 1898. Meanwhile the state began to assert itself along the Sankuru River in late 1897 with the establishment of an official post at Isaka on the north bank of that river just across from the kingdom and also with more and more frequent government interventions in and around Luebo. Perhaps most ominous among several incidents there was the arrival in March 1898 of a military detachment west of Luebo charged with the collection of taxes in ivory and rubber. Their claims and their unruly behavior aroused the whole country. The tension grew further all year long, first when it was rumored during the following summer that the state intended to send an expedition against the Kuba capital, later when the state agent in charge of Luluabourg set out to fight Lulua villagers in the valley of the

---

3. William Phipps, *William Sheppard: Congo's African American Livingstone* (Louisville, 1991), 112, 117.

Mwanzangoma River not very far from Luebo and on the southeastern borders of the Kuba kingdom, and finally when news about the mutiny of the main Congolese army far in the northeast of the colony reached the area. No wonder that "the country [around Luebo] was considerably disturbed everywhere around us, and the natives were restless and ill at ease."[4] It was perhaps then or a little later that Sheppard or Morrison sent word to Mishaape "that the state was coming, if he did not put in the feather (his crown) and open the roads for all to come and go."[5] In other words, the state would take action unless the missionaries could visit the capital as they pleased. Mishaape did not react to this veiled threat. When disaster finally struck, he was not ready to cope with it.

Conquest

In the historiography of colonial vintage there never was a real conquest, and the occupation of Congo had been a *conquête pacifique,* "a peaceful conquest," with the single exception of the oh so honorable campaign against Arab and East African slave traders during which all of eastern Congo was liberated—rather than conquered. Even the revisionists later on did not pay much attention to the processes of various local conquests, but they noted the loss of life involved. But then one must remember that in spite of appearances and notwithstanding all the clamor and indignation, this revisionism itself usually remains a colonial historiography in which Africans appear only as victims. Actually the conquest of Congo was a bloody and lengthy process. Still it is also true that in the grand colonial scheme of things the conquest of the Kuba kingdom was wholly unremarkable, whereas in the Kuba scheme of things their own subjugation was such a chaotic catastrophe that even as late as the waning days of colonial rule vivid recollections about its various episodes still occupied a prominent place in local memories.

The Kuba kingdom was conquered as the result of three successive attacks in 1899–1900: a raid on Nsheng from Isaka between April 4 and 25, 1899, an assault by Zappo Zap on the Pyang in the southeast in September 1899, and the sack and destruction of the capital in late July

---

4. Samuel P. Verner, *Pioneering in Central Africa* (Richmond, Va., 1903), 394.

5. Robert Benedetto, *Presbyterian Reformers in Central Africa: A Documentary Account of the American Presbyterian Congo Mission and the Human Rights Struggle in Congo, 1890–1918* (Leiden, 1996), 116–17 n4.

1900 by government forces within a week or two of Mishaape's sudden death. Some Bushong recollections summarized the whole process of conquest as the consequence of Mishaape's "noble" refusal to answer a summons to come to Isaka. But the underlying cause of everything, at least as indicated in a 1954 text about the conquest, was sheer racism (see "The European War").

The first raid on the capital was conducted by Edouard Schaerlaeken, the commander of the post at Isaka, and included twenty-seven soldiers of his garrison. He acted on his own initiative since the raid had not been ordered or approved by his district commissioner at Lusambo, and Schaerlaeken's report about it is a blatant attempt to obtain this agreement after the fact. The report first justifies the raid by the need to gather rubber. Schaerlaeken claimed that he had gone to a certain village because it was in arrears with its expected payment of one ton of rubber a month. Once there, he discovered that royal warriors were attacking the town "every day" for reasons unknown to him and had killed ten persons. He then continued his journey to subdue a local chief called Kampuku, from whom he learned that the Kuba king had no guns. So he decided to attack the king. After four days of marching hampered by skirmishing and by a last concerted attack by Mishaape's warriors, who were repulsed with heavy losses, the king submitted. Kuba casualties up that point were estimated at four hundred.

The report paints the king as a barbarian tyrant and mentions sanctimoniously that Schaerlaeken ordered him not to kill people, nor to loot, nor to burn border villages anymore. Thereupon the officer immediately left (no doubt, laden with booty) and returned safely to Isaka, in spite of further attacks by several villages along the road (he probably looted several villages). Schaerlaeken ordered the king to come to Isaka a month later to pay "tax" under penalty of renewed hostilities and urgently requested thirty soldiers from the district commissioner in the event that the king would not come. His report concludes apparently innocently by mentioning the great wealth of the kingdom in domestic animals, foodstuffs, rubber, and ivory, wealth that was no doubt the real reason for his invasion.

The raid was a bolt out of the blue because hitherto the Bushong court never had had any dealings with Isaka nor had any foreigner ever entered the country from the general direction of the Sankuru River or from across the Labody (Lubudi) River. The invaders must have been guided either by runaway Kuba slaves or by Kampuku's men. Regardless, the surprise factor helps to explain the success of what was after all—and despite its guns—just a small raiding party. At the time the sack of Nsheng must have been an event of huge significance to the Kuba because no one in living memory had ever taken the capital before. Yet the even more disastrous attack of 1900 would soon displace this incident in their recollections.

For the colonial foreigners the event was barely worthy of note at the time. The ancient kingdom fell victim to one greedy raid for rubber among countless others in Congo, led by someone who had barely

---

The European War

King Mishaape—They came to tell him that the people of white race have come: they want you to go and visit them. The king nobly refused to see them. He sent his son in *expensive* dress to deceive them [into thinking] that he really is the king but the Europeans were not caught by the deception; they immediately ordered people to bring the king to them.

King Mishaape said: "I will not go there; these people who have chased us away from downstream [the Bushong Eden] by insulting us that we have a bad skin, they are now provoking us into war— the SKIN WAS MOCKED/black white." The [Bushong] traders of that time who were trading in slaves and ivory gave the king good advice to wit: "leave these travelers alone for they might harm our area." The king refused these wise words saying: "As you have refused my orders, in tomorrow's world you will deal in their market [this became a well-known proverb]."

A few days after the king warned them that war was about to break out after the mistake he had just made, he died. Not long after the king's death and even before his body had been buried the Europeans entered his capital, killed men and women and took others prisoner.[6]

---

6. Vansina Files, *nyim—before 1920*; Vansina Files, Kwete Albert, *European War* (1954). The commentary inserted into the text including the capital letters is by Kwete. Other oral accounts made the same points. For example, see the same account in Conway T. Wharton, *The Leopard Hunts Alone* (New York, 1927), 79.

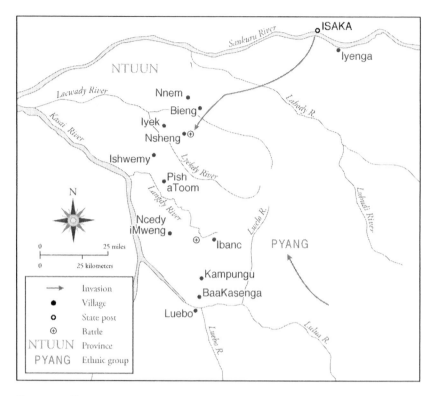

Conquest, 1899–1900

completed grade school in Belgium, which was not so unusual either.
His report is a typical specimen of such documents: justification for a
raid and the substantial number of casualties it caused by both moral
obligations and happy results. Namely the need to defend a village vic-
timized by a bloodthirsty monster, the subjection of that tyrannical adversary, and as a reward for virtue the promise of rich "tax" revenues to
come. This sort of all-too-routine abuse is precisely what the Congo Reform Association, helped by Morrison's later reports, would denounce
in later years.

Yet on April 13, 1899, a few days after the raid, all that Morrison and
Sheppard had to say about it according to the former's diary was to tell
Mishaape, who had urgently called them to the capital, that they had
warned him that Bula Matadi was coming, that Bula Matadi knew the
road and would more than likely return, to which the missionaries
added that they might wish at some time to found a mission station at
the capital. Unstated but obviously implied is that this mission would

then protect the capital. The Presbyterian headquarters in the United States were not very indignant either when they summarized the situation in a request to King Leopold II to obtain further concessions of land for new mission stations: "The people at Lukengu have suffered much from the effect of their superstitions and from the disturbances that have come to them from the outside."[7]

However, a few years later in a statement to the British government, Morrison had changed his tune:

> Upon arrival there [at Nsheng] we found the whole community in greatest excitement. We were told that the state men had fired upon them as they went out with their bows and arrows to defend their village. They reported fourteen men killed. Without leaving them any word as to the reason of his visit the officer departed almost immediately; at any rate he was not there when Mr Sheppard and I reached the place. The officer was from the state post Isaka on the Sankuru river.[8]

One effect of Schaerlaeken's raid was to throw the whole country open for travel by foreigners, and the first to benefit were the two APCM missionaries. After meeting the king they continued their trip through the kingdom for nearly three weeks all along the southern bank of the Sankuru River in search of a good place to found a mission station.

A few months after this raid it was the turn of Edmond Dufour, commander of Luluabourg, to try to raise revenue from Kuba country. We do not know whether he first attempted to do so by sending word to the capital that he expected delivery of tribute. But he, like Schaerlaeken, seems to have acted on his own because he never seems to have received any orders from the district commissioner in Lusambo, and he did not commit any regular troops at all. In July he ordered his Zappo Zap allies to go to the nearest region of the kingdom, the country of the Pyang and their neighbors, to gather "tax": in plain language to raise as much as they could in rubber, any foodstuffs, ivory perhaps, and—according to local memory a good thirty years later—slaves; that is, either recruits for the Congolese army or unauthorized slaves for private sale given that the Zappo Zap were still slave traders in Kasai at the time. Zappo Zap in turn sent his main lieutenant with about five hundred warriors, all armed with guns. They began by building a stockade

7. Benedetto, *Presbyterian Reformers*, 131.
8. Benedetto, *Presbyterian Reformers*, 153.

inside Pyang country. Then they called all the Pyang chiefs and headmen to a meeting and demanded sixty slaves, herds of goats, baskets of
food, and 2,500 balls of rubber. This, especially the slaves, was a tribute
of such proportions that the Pyang could not or would not pay, whereupon the Zappo Zap leader had the entrance gate to this camp locked.
The eighty or ninety titleholders who had come to the meeting found
themselves trapped and were massacred. After this bloodbath the Zappo
Zap swarmed out to kill, loot, and burn villages all around.

At this point, early in September 1899, Sheppard received an urgent
and desperate call out of the blue at Ibanc. The messengers told him of
great and ongoing massacres committed by the Zappo Zap warriors
nearby in the country inhabited by the Pyang and asked him to intervene posthaste. Despite the despair of the messengers, and although he
greatly cared for Kuba, Sheppard declined to go, probably sensing that
it would be to no avail. A few days later, however, a runner from Luebo
brought him a peremptory order from the Euro-American missionary
Morrison to proceed to Pyang country, stop the massacre, and document it with Kodak pictures. Although Morrison had no authority to
order Sheppard around, the latter still obeyed. He set out on September
13 and found first wholly deserted villages and then a wounded man
who told him the story of the trap. Traveling deeper into Pyang country
the next day, the missionary party found villages strewn with corpses,
some of which showed indications of cannibalism. Then they encountered a squad of warriors who were tracking possible survivors to shoot
them. They were led by a man who happened to be an acquaintance of
Sheppard from Luebo, and who recognized him. Hence Sheppard was
not attacked himself but was brought to the main stockade. There
Sheppard interviewed the Zappo Zap leader, recorded his observations
in his diary, and photographed scenes of outrageous carnage including
many mutilated bodies, a stack of eighty-one grilled right hands probably as justification for the use of ammunition, and some sixty terror-
ized women penned in a corral, no doubt as booty intended to be sold
into slavery as was Zappo Zap custom.

At first Morrison could not believe Sheppard's report and sent Lach-
lan Vass, a Euro-American colleague he particularly trusted, to double-
check the facts. Vass corroborated everything and provided more detail.
Then Morrison complained to the state authorities, who put an end to
the raid. A few months later the magistrate in charge came from Lusambo to Luebo to hear the case. Even while his own escort was looting
Kampungu and the other market towns between Ibanc and Luebo, the

magistrate found no one guilty except for the lieutenant of Zappo Zap. His whole attitude so infuriated Morrison that he wrote a letter to King Leopold and sent a copy of his report to a friend in London who passed it on to the Aborigines Protection Society. Brussels did not react, and the report caused only a ripple of sensation in London, after which the matter rested until Morrison's own visit to Europe.

The scale of terror and carnage visited by the Zappo Zap on the Pyang seems to have been unique in the region, and even Europeans did not quickly forget the outrage committed there. Six months later a young trading agent fresh from Europe heard about it in Luebo, and more than two years later he encountered nothing but deserted villages when he visited Pyang country to trade with them. Everyone had fled into the forests, and the only sign of human life was the sound of their signal drums. Nevertheless several months after that a few Pyang began to trickle one by one into his shop at Ibanc. The next visitor to Pyang country was Leo Frobenius. It was now 1905, and he knew nothing about the Zappo Zap affair. He was enchanted by the few days he had spent in Pyang country and declared that they were the highlight of his whole trip to Africa. He could not give enough praise to the artistic sense of the reconstructed Pyang villages, and he was enthralled by what he romantically interpreted as the Pyang's haughty, aristocratic, and reserved demeanor, a demeanor that was actually still one of extreme distrust. Indeed a generation later the Pyang still remembered the massacre and told a local administrator that it had been triggered by the Zappo Zap's demand for slaves, or recruits for the Congolese army, for even in the 1933 many Kuba still equated the one status with the other.

Yet in the 1950s one episode from that period was far better remembered in the whole region than the Pyang massacre: the final assault on the capital. This shows how significant that event had been to them when it happened. It was perhaps best remembered not only because it signaled an end to Kuba independence but also because as many or more people lost their lives on this occasion than had perished in the Pyang massacre. This second and final assault on Nsheng occurred in July 1900. It involved troops from Isaka led this time by Lieutenant Georges Henrion, also ominously known as Ndoom, "the bullet." Whether the attack was triggered by the death of King Mishaape (believed to be from smallpox) is disputed. Apart from short written and oral mentions, there exist only three accounts of these events: the report of Henrion, a short text by Morrison, who relied on hearsay from fugitives to Ibanc, and the recollections of a Bushong participant. I begin with the report.

On August 6, 1900, Henrion reported that while he was (once more) at chief Kampuku's place, a few Luba fugitives (almost certainly slaves) from the capital arrived there and told him that the king had died and that at least two hundred of their comrades had been sacrificed. He could not let such a blatant spectacle of human sacrifices proceed unchallenged. Therefore he assembled a force of thirty-three soldiers and fifty allies—from another tribe, wrote Ms. Sheppard—and left for Nsheng, where he arrived on the seventh day. He took the town after a battle lasting two hours and found ten to fifteen corpses in the houses surrounding the king's own dwelling. He then sent most of his force in pursuit. During the four following days these men scored many new "victories" every day as they continued their so-called pursuit of the enemy into the surrounding villages. Henrion then returned to Isaka with about a hundred prisoners, half Bushong and half Luba, of whom seventy to eighty remained the day he wrote his report. Had the others died or run away? He also carried about ten tusks and sixty goats. The reason that he could not stay in Nsheng any longer than he did was "because the soldiers and the people who accompanied me were heavily loaded with cloth, beads, cowries and so on [loot!]."[9] Despite his rapid departure he believed that the Kuba would now pay "taxes," particularly because he took some thirty wives of the late king as hostages. He closed with the remark that the Luba prisoners he took at Nsheng told him that they had arrived at Nsheng as slaves sold by the Zappo Zap.

It is telling that Henrion's final conquest of the Kuba kingdom was judged to be so unimportant for colonial history that it is not even worth a mention in the notice devoted to him in the Belgian colonial bibliography. When the raid was mentioned by King Leopold's secretary responsible for the Congo government several years later, it was presented as a wholly humanitarian action to save victims of human sacrifice, and the conquest was not even alluded to.

Sheppard and his wife at Ibanc were well aware at the time that something momentous had happened. Yet they did not raise any alarm about it, in part because King Mishaape had been their bitter enemy. In a letter from Ibanc dated August 7, a day after Henrion penned his report, Sheppard's wife wrote to a friend, Ms. Hawkins, that "just now this, the Bakuba, are experiencing some trouble. Very recently their king died, and while the people were in a state of mourning another

---

9. Jules Marchal, *L'état libre du Congo: Le paradis perdu* (Borgloon, 1996), vol. 1, 380.

tribe (we believe to have been sent by the State) invaded the capital, killed all of the royal family, and only one heir to the throne made his escape." She then goes on to suggest that the king who had just died was so bad because he did not allow any missionaries or state agents to settle in the region, nor did he permit any foreigners or people working for them to pass near his place. If only a mission had been started this would not have happened. But "while many have been killed, there are thousands remaining. They feel helpless, lost, because their leader, their earthly king is gone."[10]

On September 6 the mission committee at Luebo even said in passing: "The recent disturbances, caused by the death of the king and nearly all of the royal family, have scattered the Bakuba and it is quite likely that many of them will settle around Ibenj, and thus increase the opportunities a hundred fold."[11]

A year later in February 1901 Sheppard himself only wrote the following in a report about the mission at Ibanc: "Not long since the State was fighting with king Lukenga, and there were troops at four other points in our territory. Though hundreds were killed and captured, the natives did us no harm. On the contrary, they brought their ivory and other valuables and asked us to hide them away till all was quiet again."[12]

As for Morrison, he waited nearly two years before these events became a matter for indignation and protest. He then commented as follows: "About a year later another officer (or perhaps the same one) again paid a visit to this village [Nsheng had four or five thousand inhabitants], killed its chief [the king] and from native reports, which we have every reason to believe to be true, also killed a great number of men, women, and children, carrying away a large quantity of booty."[13]

And he continued by claiming that no missionary could possibly have gone to see what had happened. Yet a trader had done just that, and the Sheppards were well aware of what was going on. Morrison went on to write that this large and prosperous "village," dismissed by him as nearly in ruins in 1899, had been entirely broken up, and he incorrectly stated that only "within the past few months"—that is, nearly

10. Lucy Sheppard, "Letter," *Missionary*, December 1900, 55.
11. Mission Committee, *Missionary*, December 1900, 545–46.
12. William Sheppard, *Missionary*, May 1901, 212–13.
13. Benedetto, *Presbyterian Reformers*, 153.

two years after the event—were people beginning to return to the old site. He further added that he met Henrion on his way downriver to go home (probably in October 1901) and was then told "how the people, as they were being fired upon, ran about crying 'Shepite, Shepite!' They were calling their old friend, William Sheppard, to come to their assistance. He also said that he had obtained a splendid lot of ivory and many curios."[14]

Fifty-six years later Nyimilong a Mbobulaam's reminiscences about his experiences during the conquest were recorded by a young relative as best he could.[15] The text is too long to quote in full, but its first sentence highlights the most striking difference between this and the colonial reports: "Lengool, the slave of Mbokashaang a Kweetul, arrived at the ward Shoongl of the king's capital. He said: 'When we were sleeping at [the village] Bieng, we heard the signal drum speaking from [the village] Nnem.'" This remembrance abounds with the names of people and places that immediately give a sense of participated experience, in sharp contrast to the bloodless aloofness of the reports by colonialists to whom unnamed Africans are but generic abstractions. By its very detail, moreover, Nyimilong's testimony underlines how traumatizing the conquest was and how important it was to the history of the kingdom.

A summary of his account continues as follows. Lengool's message to King Mishaape was that someone at the village Nnem had found that the garrison from Isaka was on the march in the kingdom. The king immediately ordered both to bring the new queen mother to safety and to prepare the defense of the capital, by supernatural means. Meanwhile, Lengool was seen returning to his village. "Kir—too! They [the enemy] made their guns speak and he died. Then they began to march uphill [from Bieng] towards the capital. King Mishaape died. They did not carry him away any further than the quarter of the crown princes and very quietly."

At this point Nyimilong and a named friend of his were jointly ordered by those in charge to take the crown princes, including three later kings, away to safety. Immediately afterward the authorities killed a man called Lamboom as the first sacrificial victim for the funeral of Mishaape, whereupon all the other potential victims ran away to hide in the forests.

14. Benedetto, *Presbyterian Reformers*, 153–54; Phipps, *William Sheppard*, 115 and notes.
15. Vansina Files, notebook 61 (1956): 53–58.

When Nyimilong had finally found a safe place in the woods for the crown princes, well away from the lines of march of Henrion's column, he was sent back to the capital: "They went for instructions and near the place where the Catholic mission now stands Nyimilong saw a man laying on the ground. He said: 'who is this?' They answered 'Mbakam.' They found him as they found 400 other corpses that had died from their wounds. They also found that 150 prominent people such as 1/ NgoomNgady, 2/ PeshaMiang, 3/ Mbanc Ngokady had been taken prisoner and carried to the banks of the Sankuru."

Then follows a vignette of how a well-known princess hid herself away in a distant village but was later recognized by an acquaintance from the top of a palm tree where he was tapping wine. The recollections continue with Henrion's command to send him every month (in addition to rubber) forty goats, pots of oil, and copper crosses, of the kind used as currency by the state.

In a flashback Nyimilong ends his account with a description of the confusion that reigned at court before the war broke out. While some among Mishaape's advisers were wondering why Henrion would want to wage war, others claimed that it all was a false alarm: "Yet they themselves proclaimed the impending disaster, from mouth to mouth that war was about to erupt. And this is truly how the war at the capital began."

A comparison of Nyimilong's reminiscences with Henrion's report suggests that the latter is not completely truthful because Nyimilong makes it clear that the soldiers were well inside the kingdom, in the lands of the village of Nnem, *before* Mishaape died, not later. So much then for the agent's desire to save the intended victims from human sacrifice. Obviously, like his predecessor, he too was merely after booty.

The Immediate Aftermath

As its aftermath shows, the conquest was a decisive turning point for the Bushong. During the assault the inhabitants of the capital and the surrounding villages fled and did not return until long after the soldiers had left the town. The destruction of its capital immediately plunged the country into a political vacuum, for no state post was set up there nor anywhere else in the country, nor were any state agents left there. But almost as soon as it appeared, the vacuum was filled by the settlement of trading posts from different companies. Indeed, only days or a few weeks after the disaster a trader in search of rubber was already setting up shop at Nsheng.

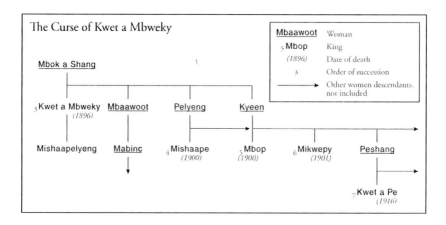

The Curse of Kwet a Mbweky

Mbok a Shang

₃ Kwet a Mbweky   Mbaawoot   Pelyeng   Kyeen
      (1896)

  Mishaapelyeng   Mabinc   ₄ Mishaape   ₅ Mbop   ₆ Mikwepy   Peshang
                                   (1900)   *(1900)*   *(1901)*

                                                                        ₇ Kwet a Pe
                                                                           (1916)

Mbaawoot   Woman
₅ Mbop   King
(1896)   Date of death
   3   Order of succession
──────►   Other women descendants,
            not included

As for the kingdom, it was unclear at this point whether it had survived or not. The court had fled downstream to the marshes near the
village of Yeek. There Mishaape's immediate successor died a few
months later during ceremonies for his installation, and that king's successor also passed away less than a year later in early 1902. In addition
several other members of the royal house who had lived in the ward
of the successors in the capital also died in rapid succession, probably
all struck down by the same epidemic that felled Mishaape. Indeed, it
seemed by 1902 that the royal dynasty was coming to an end. But the
next king, Kwet aPe, installed in July 1902, survived and thereby saved
the realm in Kuba eyes.

To the Bushong at the time, the sudden collapse of the kingdom and
the decimation of its dynasty was such a momentous change that it
seemed to be inconceivable in ordinary terms. Yes, the foreigners' superior magic had helped them to overcome the capital's supernatural
defenses, but in the final analysis the defeat had to be the result of a
curse, a supernatural attack, and it was not difficult to find who was to
blame: King Kwet aMbweky. Hence, still in 1902 the rumor circulated
that Kwet aMbweky had hated his own potential successors who had
been his adversaries in the civil war to such an extent that when he felt
himself dying, he crafted a supremely powerful noxious charm called
Nceemy ("God") to ensure that none of the men in the royal house would
have a long reign and that no royal woman would ever bear a child
again. His son Mishaamilyeng helped craft the charm and secretly
placed it in his father's coffin. From that moment onward the kings

Kwet aPe's countercharm, 1908 (Torday and Joyce, *Notes ethnographiques sur les peuples communément appelés Bakuba . . .*, 1911)

died soon after their accession, and no new children were born to the royal house. Was not the present sorry state of affairs in 1902 proof of this? Thus Kwet aPe was keen from the outset to capture or eliminate Mishaamilyeng, and it explains why at one juncture in 1903 he ordered the execution of Sheppard's friend and protector. Once again, though, the mission managed to save Mishaamilyeng, but this time at the price of the king's lasting distrust of the American mission.

In order to undo the curse, Kwet aPe called on a Zappo Zap sorcerer to fashion a countercharm for him that would destroy Kwet aMbweky's evil charm. Were not the Zappo Zap the fiercest and most feared warriors in Kasai, and did they not have the best sorcerers as well? The sorcerer made three enchanted statues that seemed to work: the king did not die, the royal women bore children, and the realm seemed to be saved. Kwet aPe and his successors prominently displayed these statues at the entrance of the royal palace, where the anthropologist Emil Torday and his party saw and photographed them in the fall of 1908.

The conquest also had an aftermath in Europe. We saw how the Pyang massacre and the stonewalling surrounding it so infuriated Morrison that he denounced it in letters to King Leopold and to a friend in England. Yet when Morrison went on leave early in 1903 this incident had practically been forgotten. He first visited Brussels, where he attempted to obtain more sites for mission posts from the government. (Was this in return for his silence? We don't know.) When this failed, he

---

Charm and Countercharm

The Story of King Kwet aMbweky

All the kings had a charm from birth. It is the *Nceemy*. When King Kwet aMbweky was about to die, he told his children Mancu ma-Shang and Mishaa miLyeng: "The day that I die you will bury the charm *nceemy* on me. I will take it with me to the underworld." They did put the charm in his coffin.

That charm is in a box in which the umbilical cords of all the kings were put. When a princess gave birth they put the cord in that *nceemy*.

The princes who survived, it was their business; they had buried the corpse of Kwet aMbweky. The Bashi Matoon [the royal dynasty] was done for.

They [the Bashi Matoon] went to consult a diviner among the people north of the Sankuru River. The diviner told them: "go disinter King Kwet aMbweky. But the Bashi Matoon did not bear children, King Kwet aPe made some charms of Mutwom, named Iyong [and then] the Bashi Matoon have born children until today."

A Battle of Charms

Kwet aMbweky had a son Mishaamilyeng: together they made a charm with an eagle's feather against their juniors to kill those who could succeed. His son put the feather in the coffin, and after one to two months all the potential successors of Kwet aMbweky and the seniors of Kwe aPe died after a month or two.

Kwet aPe took his precautions. He went to visit Labaam, a Luba, at Pish aToom. The latter called Nkishi Kasongo, the main medicine man of the Zappo Zap. The king sent him thirty slaves. He found the king at the village Ishwemy (between Domiongo and Kabwe).

proceeded to London and delivered a report about the Kuba conquest to the secretary of foreign affairs while the Aborigines Protection Society arranged for him to give a talk to a very distinguished audience. The talk was a resounding success, and as a result H. R. Fox Bourne denounced the Pyang massacre in his *Civilization in Congoland*, published in the same year. This book was one of the first telling shots in the media campaign against Leopold's government in Congo. It was the source of

---

He planted a palm tree there called *nceemy*. In the capital he then made two statues Mutoom and Mwem ("the thief"): Mutoom protected the king while Mwem disinterred Kwet aMbweky and took the feather. The king and the medicine man took Kwet aMbweky's skull and put it in the basket *nceemy* in front of the king. The food prohibitions linked to this charm were elephant meat and the *sheem* fish for anyone in the landed domain of the capital.

The Charm Mutoom

King Kwet aPe made the charm of Mutoom with a man, a man from Zappo Zap called Iyong. Mutoom was inside a wooden statue. They put a leaf of the *lanyung* plant and on the head a leaf of the *lapell* plant. It wore a kilt ornamented with cowries and brass rings on its arms and legs (only the king can wear them while the successors and the king can both wear cowries). They attracted the spirit of King Mbop Kyeen. They put it in the statue. They put in it hair from a person killed by lightning; they put the finger of a drowned person; they put a finger of a great evildoer; they put a finger of a madman; they put a piece of a snake that had bitten someone; they put a piece of a scorpion that had bitten someone. The women from the royal line have given birth until our own day. And the power of the Mutoom charm comes from sorcery.[16]

---

16. Vansina Files. The first two texts are from the file *nyim—before 1920* (1953, 1954). Text 1 is in Bushong and French translation; text 2 is as told by Shaam aNce Evariste to Vansina in 1953. The third text by Nyimilong a Mbobulaam, a contemporary of Kwet aPe, is as told to Shaam aKoong. According to written evidence, Kwet aPe complained about the killing charm and acquired the countercharm in 1903. The statues are well known since 1908, when they were photographed. They are in the Songye Zappo Zap style.

Mark Twain's scathing *King Leopold's Soliloquy*. Morrison's "big talk" was
also noted to some effect in British political circles because it happened
at a time when the House of Commons was debating whether the
government should become involved with the cause of Congo reform.
On his return home Morrison then launched a campaign of denunciation both in American political circles and in the press. He even managed to discuss the issue personally with President Theodore Roosevelt.

While the Pyang events told by Morrison were all too true, they were
not the only massacres that occurred. As we have seen, indignation
about massacres among the APCM missionaries was apparently selec-
tive and forcefully reminds one that the whistleblowers in Congo were
also colonialists themselves. In this instance neither Sheppard nor Morrison seem to have deplored the two attacks on Nsheng very much. On
the one hand they disliked Mishaape's policies, while on the other hand
the conquest removed an obstacle to their evangelization. Still, whatever their motives, one must remember that by itself the selectivity of
this indignation does not affect the credibility of their accounts about
the Pyang massacre, a truth well worth remembering when evaluating
other reports about atrocities in Congo at the time.

Conclusion

In this chapter we have seen how Kasai rubber suddenly surpassed
ivory as the main revenue earner for both the colony and the private
companies that operated there, at the very time in 1891 that Leopold II
laid claim to nearly all its lands and then outsourced large portions of it,
and how he was obliged to stay his hand for a whole decade in central
Kasai, including the Kuba kingdom, until the last days of 1901. As a result a competitive and peaceful trade in rubber flourished at and around
Luebo for most of the decade after 1891. But the state constantly needed
additional revenues, and its agents craved the commissions they earned,
in particular from exactions in high-value ivory rather than low-value
rubber. That explains the sudden and illegal attacks on the Kuba kingdom in 1899 and 1900, despite the fact that the kingdom lay in the free
trading zone. That in turn explains in part why the state did not establish any station there.

In the next chapter we will find out how at the end of the grace
period the handing over of a commercial monopoly to a company,
ruthless in its pursuit of profit, almost immediately visited the kind of
violence and misery on the kingdom that had accompanied similar

takeovers elsewhere in the colony. Hence it was not the trading of rubber by itself that somehow brought destruction with it, but the combination of a commercial monopoly allied to a complete abdication of any oversight by the state.

FURTHER READINGS

Benedetto, Robert, ed. *Presbyterian Reformers in Central Africa: A Documentary Account of the American Presbyterian Congo Mission and the Human Rights Struggle in Congo, 1890–1918.* Leiden, 1996.

Hinde, S. L. *The Fall of the Congo Arabs.* London, 1897.

Hochschild, Adam. *King Leopold's Ghost.* Boston, 1998.

Kennedy, Pagan. *Black Livingstone.* New York, 2002.

Shaloff, Stanley. *Reform in King Leopold's Congo.* Richmond, 1970.

Síocháin, Séamas O., and Michael Sullivan, eds. *The Eyes of Another Race: Roger Casement's Congo Report and 1903 Diary.* Dublin, 2003.

4

Company Rule and
Its Consequences

> One day rumors suddenly appeared with the effect of an explod-
> ing bomb. The whole Kasai area with all its business posts, har-
> bors, plantations etc. was to pass in the hands of the state; the
> private businesses were to be liquidated, their employees would
> be sent back to Europe, and they were to be replaced by state
> agents.[1]

This was how traders at Luebo learned in 1901 that Leopold II
was pressuring the fourteen companies that operated in Kasai to merge
into a single new concessionary company in a fifty/fifty partnership
with the state. The king succeeded, and the Compagnie du Kasai was
established by royal decree on the eve of Christmas 1901 with a monopoly over the trade in rubber, ivory, and other raw materials. With this action Kasai fell in line with the situation elsewhere in the colony. Indeed,
the effects of the merger were almost immediate, even though much
time was spent in 1902 disposing of the assets of the merged companies,
setting up a single uniform business, and integrating those agents whom
the company was willing to take over from its predecessors into a single
corps. As part of that operation Belgian agents were now favored to the
extent that fairly soon only a few nationals from other countries were

---

1. Paul Landbeck, *Malu malu: Erlebnisse aus der Sturm und Drang periode des Kongo-staates*
(Berlin, 1930), 41.

left, a general trend in Congo although before Belgium took over it was less evident in the hiring of state agents.

In 1901 rubber was paid a rate of 2.70 Belgian francs maximum per kilogram, but by 1904 the price had plunged to only 0.24 francs maximum. Moreover, in order to achieve this result, the high-quality goods sold by the company, such as the Dutch cloths known as *wax*, were replaced by the cheapest and shoddiest merchandise available. That provoked an immediate boycott by buyers such as mother Pyeem. Hence exports from Kasai dropped dramatically from 1,650 tons of rubber in 1901 to only 365 tons in 1902. Nevertheless as the new trading system came into full operation, by 1903 exports from Kasai rose again to 721 tons but then fell to 716 and 674 tons in 1904 and 1905, respectively. They then picked up to reach 824 tons in 1906. After that, overall production declined again in 1907 and 1908, albeit quite slowly.[2]

Profits hit a peak of 5.99 francs per kilogram in 1906 before falling by 40 percent early in 1907. From 1908 onward they gradually rose again for a few years, although the price paid to the African producers continued to worsen during that period as well. As a result the directors of the company were able to pay over 5 million francs as dividends in 1905 and even managed to double this amount the following year. Such results could only derive in large part from the ruthless cost cutting for which the company was famous. Cost cutting indeed: most of these profits resulted from the threat or actual instances of violence.

The Compagnie du Kasai had divided its territory into some fifteen "sectors." The chief of each sector left the running of individual trading posts (factories) to European managers he appointed, and some of the latter had one or more European agents. All these people were responsible for monthly accounts and stock in their realm, and they were often inspected. The anthropologist Leo Frobenius observed in 1905, however, that there were shortfalls in most of the local accounts. Some of these were due to pilfering by local Africans, while some, such as part of a sack of salt, were due to spoilage during storage. Each manager or agent was held responsible and had to pay for such losses.

But the most serious deficits apparently resulted from the unavoidable practice of allowing managers or agents to take small quantities of

---

2. Daisy S. Martens, "A History of European Penetration and African Reaction in the Kasai Region of Zaire, 1880–1908" (Ph.D. diss., Simon Fraser University, 1980), 285, table 2.

merchandise from stock to pay for their living expenses, their personal servants, and sometimes even a palm wine tapper, the expenses of their mistresses, and gifts to local leaders, although theoretically only sector chiefs were allowed to hand out such gratuities. Of course, the company expected all such withdrawals to be reported on the accounts, but most employees failed to do so. Rather, they tried to recover their deficit by buying rubber under the already very low floor price set by the company, or by cheating on measures and weight. They were wont, for instance, to dent the spoon with which they measured salt and beads. But—"dent in the spoon, dirt in the rubber"—once their customers were aware of such practices, they reacted by cheating in turn on the weight of the rubber they brought. Thus every transaction threatened to turn into a confrontation and spill over into violence. Such encounters were now very far from the amicable bargaining in the days of mother Pyeem at Ibanc only a few years earlier.

Ever since they first arrived from Angola, traders in Kasai practiced the ancient custom there of giving goods in advance to African entrepreneurs, called *capitas* (Portuguese: *capitaõ*), who then set out at the head of well-armed small parties to buy ivory and rubber in remote villages on behalf of their trader. These practices continued in large parts of Kasai under the new regime, although they often caused outbreaks of violence when capitas had used up their stock in whole or in part to liquidate personal debts such as bridewealth or fines, whereupon the store manager had to make up the losses.

Moreover, the pressure exerted by the new company on its own agents to produce all they could at the lowest possible cost was such that another form of advance payment emerged in some parts of Kasai, including Kuba country. A manager ordered his armed capitas and their crews to forcibly foist an "advance" of shoddy goods on villagers whether the latter wanted them or not. Often enough these people simply dumped the advance at the entrance to a village. A few weeks later they then returned to claim an arbitrary amount of rubber as their "due." If this was not forthcoming, they camped out in the village and brutalized the people until it was delivered.

From there it was but a step to set up armed capitas permanently in most larger villages and have them raise specified amounts of rubber every month as "taxes." That had long since been a standard procedure for the concessionary companies in the equatorial regions of Congo where it was precisely this practice of using armed sentries that had been the main cause for all manner of violence and appalling atrocities.

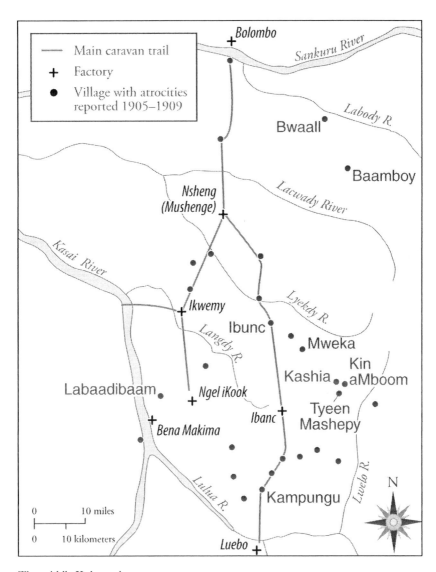

The middle Kuba realm, 1904-10

The state authorities in Lusambo had also invented yet another completely illegal gimmick to exploit the Africans even more. Already by 1899 state agents there began to levy an unspecified "tax" per month to be paid in a currency consisting of copper crosses imported from Katanga. Once the Compagnie du Kasai began to operate, it bought these crosses from the state at a low price. In 1903 the going rate was 3.5 francs

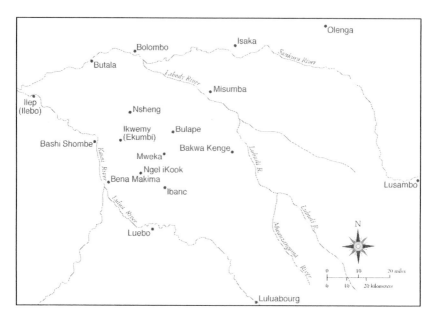

Kasai, 1900–1910

per cross. The company then paid villagers in this currency of crosses in return for rubber at an unknown rate, and finally the state obtained the crosses back from the villagers as "tax," but at a value that in 1903 was only a little less than half the rate the company had paid. In 1904 that declined even further to only a third. Hence the state made a handsome profit at the expense of the villagers. So did the company, for it required from five to seven kilograms of rubber per cross for a value of .24 francs per kilogram or less in 1904, and it further managed to force villagers to buy crosses by refusing to sell them anything else.

Most of the Kuba kingdom, including the post at Nsheng, belonged to the Compagnie du Kasai sector ten with headquarters at Luebo, but the northern and eastern parts lay in sector eleven with headquarters at Bolombo on the Sankuru. There were eight posts belonging to one or the other of these sectors in the kingdom, plus Luebo and Bolombo just across the boundary, and these stations were well placed to reach every Kuba village by means of capitas. The eight posts appear to have been placed in those large villages like Ibanc that had earlier been market towns within the kingdom. All the hired labor and nearly all the capitas working in or for these posts came from outside the kingdom. Most among them were Lulua, and while their managers seem to have considered this status as a good reason to give them more control over their labor force, the Kuba both despised and feared these people as slaves or relatives of their own slaves, while conversely the workers also bore the Kuba a deeply held grudge for the same reasons.

On one of its ten existing posts the company started a plantation for rubber trees and vines at Bena Makima on October 20, 1904. It had staffed this post with four Catholic missionaries of the Scheut order as agents in charge of both planting rubber and gathering wild rubber for the company. This deal was unique in Congo. The place counted as a company post but was in fact a Catholic mission station as well. In addition, the company also undertook to transport all the goods belonging to the missionaries of Scheut in Kasai free of charge on company boats from Kinshasa to Luebo. In return the company gained not only a few managers for free but more importantly also all the labor needed to run a plantation because the Catholic missionaries disposed of large numbers of bonded Luba laborers from central Kasai whom they had liberated from slavery during the Luba migration to the region of Luluabourg.

Neither the company nor the mission gave any thought to the disruption the plantation and its labor force settled in a large new village nearby caused to the regional network of landed village domains, a network that had already been disrupted twelve years earlier by the establishment of another rubber plantation accompanied by a large village inhabited by foreigners nearby at Ngel iKook, in addition to yet another sizable alienation of land that had accompanied the growth of a large foreign agglomeration around the Presbyterian mission and the trading post at Ibanc not so far away.

By 1903 a combination of the new business practices of the company, the introduction of the tax in copper crosses by a state in cahoots with the company, the state's attempts to recruit soldiers for its army, the Force Publique in the Kete villages around Luebo, the arrival of so many Luba or Lulua foreigners, and the loss of land all combined to cause severe social tensions. Signs of stress are evident in the region around Ibanc for which we have information. On the one hand there are the happy reports by Sheppard and his colleagues that the local Bushong and Kete suddenly began to flock to the mission, and on the other comes the sad news that a sudden spate of witchcraft accusations and the ensuing poison ordeals had erupted in the villages.

The obvious reason for the rush to join the mission was the need for protection, and protection was what Morrison in Luebo was always trying to obtain. Thus already in August 1902 he had asked the governor general of the colony to grant exemption from taxes and recruitment for the colonial army except for the delivery of foodstuffs to anyone in a radius of three kilometers around his mission post. The people living there provided workers for the mission and the traders and food for passing agents of the state, and they were very active as rubber-buying capitas in the interior. Most of them were Lulua and Luba. Moreover, Morrison also wanted a total exemption from recruitment or taxation, including the then brand-new tax in copper crosses, for the inhabitants of the Kete village nearest to the mission. "We only ask for their protection," he wrote.[3]

The outburst of witchcraft accusations and poison ordeals is even more revealing of trouble. "In those days this gruesome ordeal was an insatiable Moloch [a deity] who devoured a steady stream of victims, while nobody had enough influence to escape from it," wrote a trader from Ibanc who backed it up by citing several cases.[4] A wave of such accusations tended to occur only at times of severe stress. To the Kuba, witches are antisocial persons who killed family members or neighbors out of sheer envy, thanks to a deadly power innate within them. A wave of accusations therefore implies the recognition of an equal wave of envy between members of one's community. In 1903 this wave specifically betrayed the high level of tension within villages that pitted age groups, lineages, and families against each other as they tried to cope with the relentless increase in outside demands, mostly impositions for ever more rubber, accompanied by ever more frequent incidents of brutal aggression by capitas or traders. And remember all of this followed hard on the heels of the relative affluence two years earlier, an affluence that had suddenly evaporated as the Compagnie du Kasai imposed its rule.

According to magistrate Paul Bossolo, the Kasai region had hitherto enjoyed a well-deserved reputation for peace and quiet but became unsettled and the scene of multiple military interventions during 1902 after the constitution of the Compagnie du Kasai and because of its monopoly status. He even provided a list of military interventions between 1902 and 1904 to prove it. Indeed, by then the number of incidents related to intensive economic exploitation began to increase all around

3. Jules Marchal, *L'état libre du Congo: Paradis perdu: L'histoire du Congo, 1876–1900* (Borgloon, 1996), 1: 78–79.

4. Alfons Vermeulen, *De pioniersdagen van Chicongo* (Amsterdam, ca. 1933), 279.

the kingdom, and it would be naïve to think that the Kuba were not aware of them. Thus during the fall of 1903 in the south of the kingdom the company managers at Ngel iKook, Luebo, and Bena Makima all banded together to destroy two large Lele villages across the Kasai River as reprisals after the locals there, provoked by repeated ill treatment, had destroyed a post of the company in their neighborhood. The same insurgents and their friends also attacked company officials traveling along the Kasai River. At that point a military detachment sent from Lusambo intervened. But only two months later the military escort of a magistrate who was enquiring into the earlier events became involved in renewed hostilities.

Rebellion!

Given the climate of mounting unrest, an imminent general rebellion in Kuba country was a distinct possibility. Yet late in 1903 and again early in 1904 King Kwet aPe seems to have decided to become more conciliatory toward the various colonial agencies in his country. He started to cooperate with the American Presbyterian Christian Mission, the Compagnie du Kasai, and even the government agent who occupied a newly created government post at Luebo. Thus he let some Presbyterian evangelists build a chapel in Nsheng, he agreed with the company's request to approve the foundation of a Catholic mission at Bena Makima, he sent copper crosses as taxes to Luebo, and in April 1904 he even went to Luebo to settle a matter of supposed arrears in taxes when summoned by Captain Jacques-Paul-Felix De Cock (a.k.a. Ibulbul), who was the commanding officer in Kasai. But on that occasion De Cock's greed triggered a crisis. He unexpectedly jailed the king until a hundred thousand cowries were paid as a fine for the king's late arrival at Luebo. The royal detention lasted only a few days because the Presbyterian mission advanced the needed cowries, but the damage was done. The king, the court, and most villagers in the kingdom were outraged by this unprecedented insult.

A month or so before this was happening at Luebo, far to the northeast, the villagers of a locality called Olenga rebelled. The place lay halfway between the Sankuru and the Lukenye rivers and hence north of and well outside the kingdom. Moreover, it lay just on the border between the territory reserved for exploitation by the Compagnie du Kasai and the domain of the Crown reserved for direct exploitation by the government. Consequently the village had suffered much from the

The garrison of Luebo, 1905 (Frobenius, *Im Schatten des Kongostaates*, 1907)

depredations of state agents. As reported by a government inquiry in 1905, the villagers found a way out of their misery by deciding to be inducted into the cult for a new collective charm called Tongatonga (a.k.a. Inkunia), which the medicine man Ekpili kpili had just invented. But according to another government report in 1917, a villager testified that Inkunia originated quite far to the north of this region and had already been adopted in the region between the Sankuru and Lokenye rivers as early as 1900 to 1902.

Whatever its origin, by 1904 Tongatonga was spreading. The charm was to shield the inhabitants from any further exactions from the state or the company, because all the bullets fired at them would miss their targets. However, Tongatonga could only be effective if people avoided eating European salt, wearing European textiles, or eating certain species of antelopes.

The good news that Olenga had adopted this marvel of a charm spread like wildfire, and very soon nearby villages followed suit. In each settlement people raised funds to pay a competent medicine man to initiate them into this cult. And so Tongatonga diffused far and wide, including into the villages south of the Sankuru into the northeastern part of the Kuba realm. Rubber stopped flowing to the shops, state or company agents reacted with threats of force, and from June 1904 onward some of their posts were attacked and destroyed. And even though in each case the military eventually counterattacked, still by late July even the local manager of the Compagnie du Kasai in Ngongo country within the Kuba kingdom had to flee.

During the dry season news about Tongatonga also reached Nsheng as the cult was sweeping downstream along the Sankuru River. By August the northernmost Kuba settlements, including Bushong villages, had all adopted it. The rebels then blockaded Bolombo and killed some of the capitas there, whereupon all the others fled. By September the senior company trader of Ibanc was chased out of Baambooy, the northernmost Kete village in the same general area. By then the cult had also reached the confluence of the Sankuru and Kasai rivers and had been adopted upstream along the banks of the Kasai as far as the troublesome company factories at Ekumbi and Bashi Shombe. Yet at the same time Kwet aPe was in the north of his country to prevent the cult from spreading into the center of the kingdom. The local people, however, did not obey him without an argument because they stubbornly refused to believe that the charm was worthless, and they would not abandon the cult. He even had to fine a village for refusing to pay him the homage to which he was entitled.

Then suddenly in late September a fresh incident brought Kwet aPe in opposition with a state official and changed his mind. Paul Hubin (a.k.a. Bungyen), the new state agent for Luebo, had come to Ibanc with a detachment of soldiers to show the flag and to prevent disturbances from breaking out there. On that occasion the king had sent him some "tax" in copper crosses. But Hubin refused this and sent a message that he expected the king to come to Ibanc with some fifty Bushong recruits to serve a seven-year stint in the army. As every African in Kasai considered such a recruitment to be enslavement by another name, this demand was just too much. Kwet aPe did not go to Ibanc. By mid-October he warned the company agent responsible for Nsheng that henceforth he refused to pay any taxes to the state or to allow the recruitment of any of his subjects. He even added that he had lost his authority because he was still trading with Europeans, and he ordered all Europeans out of his realm. Under strong pressure from his own prime minister (*kikaam*), Kwete Mwana, and the councils at court who encouraged the rebellion in the north, he was now turning necessity into virtue. He may or may not have called for the cult to be brought to Nsheng, but he certainly paid for its introduction there and ordered that it be spread throughout his realm. As one remembrance goes: "There was a man named Mbop Mingambol [or Mbop Nyingambol]. When he arrived he told king Kwet aPe that he had a charm with which we can wage war against the Europeans. If you want this charm to be effective do like this: none of your men should eat with any women, nor should you eat the dwarf antelope. Then when we fight the whites the guns will almost not shoot."[5]

War was now unavoidable, and a well-organized general revolt broke out in the south on November 1–5. The Bushong and Kete attacked all the stations from Bashi Shombe on the Lele side of the Kasai River to Ibanc and overran all of them except for Bena Makima and Ngel iKook, where the resident Europeans were able to drive them off. Another force also planned to attack Luebo, but some of the Kete villages closest to the post refused to join it, so that a half-hearted assault was easily repulsed. As soon as possible the two state agents in Kasai, Captain De Cock and Hubin, rushed to the rescue with the soldiers at their disposal. Meanwhile the Presbyterians at Luebo armed a group of their own Luba and Lulua followers and counterattacked. By the ninth of November De Cock was at Bena Makima. From that day onward every available ship on the Kasai-Sankuru river system seems to have headed for the region loaded with agents and their small armed retinues until fresh troops dispatched from Lusambo landed at Bena Makima on the fourteenth of December.

Meanwhile, still in November, another army unit commanded by the assistant district commissioner Alexandre Knitelius subdued the rebellion in the villages around Bolombo, including those on the Kuba side of the Sankuru River. The colonial reaction to the Tongatonga insurrection thus dramatically demonstrated to any Kuba who might have doubted this that ultimately all foreigners from overseas were colonialists and stuck together, whatever their labels as traders, missionaries, state agents, or military officers might be.

5. Vansina Notebooks, *The Story of the Tongatong War*, 61: 33, 67, recorded by Kwet Stéphane.

Since the Kuba had no guns, the Congolese military easily defeated their enemies wherever they clashed with them as they tramped from village to village to reopen the roads and occupy the country. Nevertheless, some Bushong villages were tenacious and returned several times to the attack. One of the more notable clashes occurred at the passage of the Lyekdy River on the road to Nsheng, but resistance was of no more avail here than elsewhere. De Cock occupied the capital abandoned by its inhabitants and then went further toward the Sankuru River in pursuit of Kwet aPe. When he was halfway there, however, he returned to Nsheng on January 27, 1905, and informed the king in hiding through Bushong intermediaries that he would not be killed nor arrested because he had been drawn into the revolt against his will. This version of events was apparently suggested to the officer by local agents from the Compagnie du Kasai who hoped to turn the situation to their advantage. The king then left his hiding place and surrendered on February 7, 1905.

But the Bushong remembered the sequence somewhat differently. They did not say that the king sent for the charm Tongatonga, they underline that their attack was directed against Luba people as much as, if not more than, against Europeans, they stressed their own casualties but glossed over those they inflicted on the Luba, and they explained how contact between Captain De Cock and the king was established to negotiate a surrender. This is how a participant, MboMaloom, remembered it half a century later:

Story of the war of king Kwet aPe with Ibulbul [Captain De Cock]

All was quiet when Mbop Nyingambol [a medicine man] came to give the charm to the king. Once he had given it to the king, the latter called all the Bushong people and began to hand out the charm. And so the people from the Mitoom district began the war with the Luba. The Luba fled to Luebo with the Europeans and the people from Mitoom did nothing further. Then the people from the district "Valley of the Langdy" fought with Langang [a European]. Langang was not afraid. The Europeans wrote to Ibulbul that the Bushong had rebelled. Ibulbul went as far as Luebo. The [local] Kete said that they would not fight and they fled. Then he went to fight in the region called Malong and he killed many people there. From there he went to kill people from the Imbedim region and then went to stop at Iyop. From there he went towards Nsheng. When Ibulbul arrived at the river Lyekdy, the people from

the capital went to the Lyekdy [as well]. They broke all the bridges
and shot quiverfuls of arrows at Ibulbul. But Ibulbul discharged his
guns and they all fled to Nsheng. When Ibulbul arrived at Nsheng
he did not find anyone, so he proceeded directly on to Ntun province [in the north] killing people along the way. From there he went
to the village of Shabolitak where one of the king's sisters sought to
meet him. She saw Ibulbul, apologized to him, asked him to end
the war, and [if he did so] they would show where the king was
staying. Ibulbul returned to Nsheng and they did not find the king
there. After this the king sent Kec aKecy to see if Ibulbul was there.
Kec aKecy did not sleep but returned [immediately] to the king to
tell him that we should go to Nsheng. The king refused and stayed
where he was. Thereupon [after a delay] he did return. Ibulbul
then said, "Stay and take care of your town, I am leaving." And he
went away.[6]

The return of the king was not the end. According to contemporary
written documents Kwet aPe sent three medicine men to Ibanc in April
1905 with orders to murder Mishaamilyeng, whom he still viewed as
his rival to the throne. They arrived when Hubin and his escort also
happened to be there. Hubin arrested the emissaries and immediately
rushed to Nsheng, where Kwet aPe let himself be arrested rather than
provoking another massacre. This prevented a second uprising, but the
king was put in chains and brought first to Luebo and then by boat to
jail in Lusambo.

But on June 22, 1905, Governor General Théophile Wahis peremptorily ordered Kwet aPe's release and the complete restoration of his authority. Meanwhile, however, an estimated twenty thousand Kuba had
marched on Luebo to demand his freedom. Even if this number is probably a gross overestimate, it was a huge demonstration and the first, the
largest, and perhaps the only one organized in all of Kasai before the
last year of colonial rule. Perhaps Wahis knew about it and was influenced by it before he gave his orders. Be that as it may, the upshot was
that Kwet aPe was released from confinement in Lusambo and returned
via Luebo to his capital, where he arrived in August with a military
guard of honor. It was rumored at the time that he paid a ransom of five
hundred slaves to the state for his release. The rumor was certainly false,

6. Vansina Notebooks, MboMaloom, *The Story of the War of King Kwet aPe with Ibulbul*, 59: 5–7, 10–12. Recorded and translated by Mbanc Augustin.

but it does remind us how the state recruited both its labor and its soldiers at the time.

A Bushong remembrance recalls the episode in only slightly different terms and turns it into an example of the wisdom of the king:

> A story about king Kwet aPe. They took him in 1911 [*sic*, should be 1905] at Mingyenc [his capital] because he had killed the children of Mishaamilyeng; it was Mishaamilyeng himself who denounced him to Bungyen [Hubin], the state agent, and after that they came to arrest him and he [Hubin] asked "why are you killing people?" They brought him to Lashaam [Lusambo] and jailed him for five months. After that they let him go telling him to take care of his town [the capital].
>
> But the day they put the vine around his neck right in the middle of the capital his younger cousin [and crown prince] Mbop Mabinc maMbeky took his bow and arrows declaring that he was going to war. But then king Kwet aPe said "The snake on the calabash: if you kill the snake the calabash is broken; if you leave the calabash alone, the snake will leave." So his cousin remained quiet. But when he was released from jail back among his Bushong, he shook his head and said "All the parts of the body can be repaired, but when the head is broken it cannot be repaired." That is [the meaning of the saying] "The movement of the head."[7]

Although the uprising in the center and south of the kingdom lasted only a little over three months, it nevertheless was significant as measured by the number of soldiers and allied forces involved and the extent of the area disrupted by it. The events were followed almost immediately by speculation about who was to blame. The American missionaries surprisingly expressly acquitted the Compagnie du Kasai of any responsibility and joined the company in incriminating Hubin and De Cock for their repeatedly insensitive treatment of the Kuba king and for their delay in coming to the rescue. The director of the company and the Catholic mission blamed the Kuba: the reactionary notables had thwarted the king's desire to throw open the country to free trade and foisted a radical xenophobic policy on him. The two state agents apparently blamed the Presbyterian mission for its support of Mishaamilyeng as well as a company manager for his frequent whippings. A few colonials further away down on the Congo River and some magistrates

7. Vansina Files, *nyim*.

pointed the finger at company agents because of the bad treatments
they had inflicted on the Kuba, while for others the uprising was a reaction against the growing influence of the Catholic mission.

No one involved in this debate, however, remarked that the Tongatonga rebellion had started outside of the kingdom, was affecting an
area wider than the realm, and was not over. In the middle Lukenye
basin the rebellion continued well into 1906, and even then the cult was
not completely eradicated there. Hence, this had not been just a "Kuba
rebellion" but an uprising of the whole of north Kasai of which the coordinated Kuba action was only the most spectacular portion. Tongatonga's stated goal was to stop European exploitation, which makes its
cause clear. In the last resort the rebellion was caused by the unrelenting
pressure on villagers to produce rubber, often accompanied by outrages
that sometimes included rape and even murder. In Kuba country it was
the villagers and not the king who brought the movement into the country, and it was the villagers, backed by the notables, who finally forced
the king to join them. That too is ample evidence that exploitation was
the main cause of the rebellion.

Indeed, colonials at the time apparently did not realize the concrete
situations of particular villages such as that of Labaadibaam near Bena
Makima, which had lost most of its lands to two new Luba and Lulua
agglomerations that accompanied the foundation of the posts of Bena
Makima and Ngel iKook, respectively, and who feared that they were
about to lose the rest. No wonder that once Tongatonga was available
they revolted, chased the intruding villages away, and tenaciously continued both to attack and to resist until the ninth of November when De
Cock's troops killed thirty-three of them. In the context of such pressures for sheer survival, Hubin's demand for Bushong recruits was the
last straw that finally convinced the king to throw in his lot with the insurrection and to organize the assault against the colonial bastions in
the south.

In late colonial times some Bushong reminiscences such as Mbo-
Maloom's description of the uprising interpreted it as primarily a war to
chase away the despised Luba and Lulua who were swamping the country and provoking much unrest by assisting slaves, especially women, in
running away. Perhaps this point was stressed in the 1950s because by
then a quarter of the population in the kingdom was Luba and Lulua
and because it was convenient at the time to understate the role of colonial exactions. Nevertheless, as the example of Labaadibaam shows, this
interpretation was certainly well founded. Large numbers of foreign

workers, many of whom were still immigrating from eastern and central Kasai, had settled especially in the south of the kingdom before 1904. It is also due to them, in part at least, that the posts at Ngel iKook, Bena Makima, and even Luebo where not overrun. Moreover, some of the recently acquired Luba slaves all over the realm seem to have offered guidance and advice to the avenging government forces. Thus the influx of Luba speakers certainly was a contributory cause to the rebellion. It probably explains the destruction of the Protestant mission at Ibanc. In the last analysis, however, the presence in the whole region of Luba speakers was inseparable from that of colonial posts because all Luba in the region were still displaced persons, and it would be artificial to attribute the uprising wholly to their presence.

Ultimately Tongatonga was typical for nearly all uprisings in Congo triggered by the rush for rubber. While its specific character as a cult movement includes a number of features contingent to the area of its emergence and spread, its general claim to neutralize the effect of firearms was both an essential and a necessary feature of such movements elsewhere in Africa, including the best known one, Majimaji, which shook German East Africa in 1906. After independence many historians have interpreted such movements as nationalistic and labeled them "primary resistance." They were not nationalistic, and the Kuba case is especially convincing here. Not only were fellow Congolese targeted as enemies, but this was not a case where the governing elite organized an uprising from the top down to recover its lost independence. Rather, it was an uprising from the grassroots up against the stranglehold of colonial impositions. Still it is a case of "primary resistance" because it was the first local experience of resistance against colonialists and one that showed conclusively that violent uprisings could not succeed. Hence from now on other means of self-defense would have to be adopted.

Systematic Terror and Sporadic Resistance

The immediate toll of the rebellion on the African population was much heavier than might appear at first sight. The southern part of the kingdom especially was left in a sorry state. First the inhabitants of the Luba and Lulua villages abandoned most of their belongings and even some victims of the Bushong attacks to take refuge in Luebo. Then sizeable numbers of people, such as thirty-three of the Labaadibaam, were killed or wounded in many Bushong and Kete villages, while every inhabitant of the Bushong villages in the Bena Makima area at least, and many elsewhere, fled into the forests in spite of the frequent and heavy rains of the season. There they survived for weeks mostly on wild roots, with the result that an unknown number of particularly vulnerable people died among the wounded, the aged, the already ill, and the heavily pregnant. In the end the villagers did return to find their villages looted and usually burned. Meanwhile, they had missed a major planting season so that when the dry season began in late May, there was no harvest, there was fear of famine, and people soon went hungry. Indeed the company had to import manioc to feed its laborers in several places including Bena Makima.

In addition De Cock had imposed heavy fines on every village in his path, and while people were struggling to pay, the company agents were once again pressuring most of them to produce rubber as "taxes." On top of it all, many villages were also ordered to provide materials or laborers for the reconstruction of the trading posts and missions, even though they could hardly find the time to rebuild their own settlements. By July 1905, for instance, Frobenius saw the fierce Father Polet at Bena Makima bring in a number of village headmen in chains to his mission and jail them there until the arrival of the workmen whom he had requisitioned to finish rebuilding the mission. The excuse that they were probably absent because they were rebuilding their own houses was no doubt irrelevant. Even by year's end the mission station at Ibanc was still not fully rebuilt, and the Compagnie du Kasai post at Nsheng was still raising more men to send to Ibanc for reconstruction.

No wonder that by the dry season of 1905 some rural communities seem to have been unable to cope with the stress. Thus when Frobenius visited Labaadibaam in July, people (of different clan sections?) there were stealing objects from each other to sell to the anthropologist. Actually, as its own history tells us, that village never fully recovered. When villages move to a new site they give a name to commemorate the site they leave, and that name then becomes part of village history. Labaadibaam's landscape tells us first of a place they left because of lack of food and palm trees (most likely an effect of the European settlements nearby) to go to "The burning of the houses," no doubt as a result of the war. The place they moved to from there was called "The sadness of the corpses," and that was probably the site Frobenius visited.

Labaadibaam survived, yet, as a result of increased Luba and Lulua immigration, it was eventually forced to fuse with the five other Bushong villages in the vicinity of Bena Makima and Ngel iKook in order to retain sufficient landholdings for making a living. As to the inhabitants of the two main Luba and Lulua settlements near Ngel iKook and Bena Makima, they returned from Luebo slowly and fearfully at first, but then quickly and in numbers so large that by 1906 state officials were desperately trying to maintain some control over them and over a similar agglomeration around Ibanc. In order to do so they formally detached both areas from the Kuba kingdom and set up two independent and separate chiefdoms there where the immigrants would be ruled by one of their own. The seriousness and urgency of the situation are underscored by the fact that the main colonial law concerning chiefdoms had only barely been promulgated at the time.

After the war the company resumed operations as if nothing had happened that would cast doubt on its way of doing business. Nor did the state administration reconsider its position in Kasai. Although its military had put down the uprising, the state continued to abdicate its most essential responsibilities. It did not create any post within the kingdom itself, although earlier in 1904 it had established one at Luebo, staffed by a territorial officer and a small military detachment. As to the rest, the administration still continued to rely exclusively on the company, on the sole condition that the company should support the king. That had been the main lesson the governor general had learned from this and other uprisings.

This stance implied that the king could not be blamed in any way for the war. That was an official view conveniently shared by the company and the Catholic mission as well. In return they all expected the king to deliver a pliable workforce. One of the fathers put it rather ominously: "Lukengo moves and shakes the secular laziness of his subjects, and Lukengo should be supported rather than a few old blacks [his councils!] who believe that it is easier to wallow in vermin than to work."[8]

Given such expectations, the Compagnie du Kasai left the governance of the kingdom, including the administration of justice and the maintenance of public order, in the hands of the king. It focused fully on its business: the extraction of the maximum amount of rubber possible through its own network of armed capitas placed in all larger villages, the use of forced advances, and the delivery of copper crosses for rubber as payment for state "taxes." The king was not directly involved in the collection of rubber but could be called upon when a village

---

8. Léon Van der Molen, "Encore une réponse," *Mouvement des missions* (1906): 148. This passage occurs in a text defending the Compagnie duKasai.

openly rebelled against its capita. What did it matter to the company that nearly all its capitas were Lulua or Luba with a long list of grievances against the Kuba, including the losses they had suffered during the last rebellion? What did it matter that the country had not yet fully recovered from that war? Only rubber mattered.

So in addition to its former way of doing business the company now also began to pay a set of monthly gifts such as cloth or salt to Kwet aPe to secure his cooperation. Meanwhile the king also continued to extract "customary" annual tribute from his subjects. According to an agent of the company, this enabled Kwet aPe to rapidly raise sufficient income to buy a significant number of guns in return for slaves and rubber from small caravans at spots just across of the Middle Kasai River, and even from traders at Luebo. Ultimately the guns still came from Angola both directly and through various intermediaries. This arms traffic was going on under the noses of company agents and state officials in the area, but all of them would later claim that they had been wholly unaware of it. However, whether the king acquired all his guns in this fashion or whether he obtained some or all of them directly from the company as was alleged by its detractors, the effect was the same. Already in 1907 he disposed of an armed and uniformed militia composed of some seventy soldiers apparently recruited among "Tetela," that is, veterans from the colonial army. This was a force sufficient to subdue any recalcitrant village, and indeed he would soon be accused of using his soldiers to enforce extractions of rubber as "tax" whenever agents of the company requested it.

Less than six months after the rebellion and in spite of the sorry state of the country, the Compagnie du Kasai fully resumed its practices as before but with dire results. The pressure to produce prevented villagers from growing enough food crops to overcome the severe shortages of 1905 or even to decently reconstruct their houses. Reports about Kuba villages virtually in ruins continued to be heard all over the country during the following years from the vicinity of the Sankuru River in the north to Luebo in the south. Thus a state agent casually noted in 1907 about the Kete village of Kabaw that "the village is falling to ruins as most others are I saw on the way," a circumstance he blamed on the smoking of hemp.[9]

---

9. William Phipps, *William Sheppard: Congo's African American Livingstone* (Louisville, 2003), 468; Martens, "A History of European Penetration," 278.

Given guns, greedy agents, and vengeful capitas, the company system inevitably led to horror: abject living conditions, occasional atrocities, passive resistance, a few desperate attempts to counterattack, and eventually an impassionate denunciation of the system. In exceptional cases passive resistance worked, as in the case of most Kete villages close to the state station at Luebo. But they were under state, not company, control. They managed to evade both forced labor contributions and most taxes until as late as 1908. It is striking that when the state agent required "tax" in palm oil for Luebo the assessment was paid, but when the company required rubber it was not.

Most villages were not so lucky. Where the company ruled, exploitation became more and more efficient and more and more ruthless over time and slowly slid into outright thuggery albeit with two exceptions, the immediate vicinity around the Presbyterian station near Ibanc and the capital. No rubber at all was levied from the aristocrats in the capital itself, although they were no longer able to rely on corvee labor for reconstructing Kwet aPe's capital nor were they able to obtain food supplies from the crown of villages around the town.

During 1905 requirements for reconstruction of the company posts and the mission stations after the uprising explain a dip for Kasai in rubber exports of some 6 percent compared to the previous year. The following year, however, exports rose by 21 percent, a level that surpassed the highest previous figure (1903) by over 14 percent. This is a measure of the increase in the efficiency of exploitation of the population, an increase that was further accompanied by a steady rise in company profits per pound of rubber year after year until 1906, just before the demand for rubber in the United States almost crashed in 1907. Obviously the Kuba were more intensely exploited in 1906 than before, despite the still unrepaired ravages of the war, but the breaking point was not yet reached. The next year it was, as managers and capitas strained their utmost to increase the volume of rubber produced, in a frantic effort to make up for the falling prices on the world market. As a result a series of violent incidents broke out all over the kingdom. To illustrate the variety of such incidents we briefly cite three clashes.

The most notorious incident was the murder of Father Polet. The Catholics had opened a mission station at the capital in 1906, a station that the governor general himself understood to be but an extension of the local company post for whom the fathers still worked. When Polet was passing through Baambooy on "apostolic itinerance," the local capita of the company asked on April 16, 1907, for his assistance to obtain payment in rubber for a debt due by the headman of the village, probably a debt resulting from an advance of trading goods. The father, who was still on the payroll of the Compagnie du Kasai although he was no longer stationed at Bena Makima, obliged in his capacity as a rubber collector. He managed to catch the headman, Myaan, when the latter was trying to run away. Myaan panicked, cried out "I am dead," drew his knife, and wounded Polet with it. At that moment one of Myaan's relatives came to the rescue and struck Polet in the back. But when the villagers saw that the priest was dying, they laid him in a hammock strung between two trees well outside of the village. Horror-struck, they turned on their headman and threw him out of the village. So Myaan went to the capital.

As soon as the murder was known, King Kwet aPe traveled to Baambooy with the bulk of his soldiers in the company of the missionary companion of Father Polet. The king conducted an enquiry, arrested Myaan, and brought him to Nsheng. Only then did a state agent arrive from his post on the Sankuru to conduct a formal enquiry. This done, he simply returned to his base and astonishingly left the whole case in care of the king. That was all the more surprising because the case concerned the murder of a European. The king then promptly condemned Myaan to six months in the local jail at the capital, a brand-new institution set up by the Compagnie du Kasai but run by the king.

The whole episode suggests that the authorities wanted to hide the details of the case from the public, and that Myaan was not all that much to blame. How exceptionally lenient this sentence was appears from Morrison's comment on the occasion of the murder a few months later of another company agent: "From what I have heard the natives have never been sufficiently impressed with the enormity of the crime in the killing of the Reverend Polet. The trial and the execution ought to have taken place at the place of the crime. Otherwise the natives will not be much impressed."[10]

This is an odd statement indeed to come from a renowned humanitarian usually well known for his defense of Africans against this very same company: it breathes vengeance rather than justice with its summary sequence of trial and execution as if the whole proceedings were a foregone conclusion.

10. Martens, "A History of European Penetration," 300 n120.

The second case began during the sowing and planting season in the fall of 1907 with the refusal of the villagers of Mwek, a large village with its own capita, to collect any more rubber because their capita Mokendji had ill-treated them. He prevented them from cultivating their fields and from hunting, he forbade them to carry traditional weapons, and he forced them to build a house for him and to provide him with chickens and goats. He also beat and held their women as hostages until sufficient rubber was gathered, and one day he caused a pregnant woman to abort by kicking her. In September or October, Mokendji complained to the king as instructed by the company manager at Ibanc, whereupon Kwet aPe with an escort of sixty of his fusiliers went to Mwek to investigate the matter. According to the king's deposition, he found the village deserted and was later met with a shower of arrows from the surrounding forest while the villagers shouted that they no longer recognized him as their king. Rather, Sheppard was to be their king: they worked for him, and they prayed for him. After his soldiers had looted the village, the king withdrew to another village nearby and summoned both the company manager from Ibanc and Sheppard. The manager came, but the missionary did not.

The upshot was that the manager paid compensation for the looting but then placed an armed capita in the village. Sometime later Mwek's titleholders, wishing to make amends, offered tribute to the king, who refused to accept it until one of those who had shot arrows at him was handed over to him. This was done, and the man was kept in jail for six weeks until Sheppard secured his release. There was nothing exceptional to this case. As Sheppard later testified, many of the king's prisoners were people referred to the king by company managers or their capitas for refusal to work.

Mwek is but one example of a whole string of such cases. It illustrates the kind of pressure backed up by the threat of violence that was brought to bear on Bushong villages, but it also demonstrated the limits of such behavior. Too close an alliance of king and company would destroy the kingdom altogether because it would lead villagers, like those of Mwek, to denounce the king's breach of the mutual social contract that ensured his protection for the villagers in return for their tribute. They would then obviously cast about for another protector: in this case the Presbyterian mission at Ibanc.

A third series of disturbances involved fights over food among Kuba villages. According to a story remembered by the Kete villagers of

Kashia, there was a capita in the large Pyang villages of Tyeen Mashepy and Kin aMboom not far from their settlement. This man made these villagers work so hard at collecting rubber that they had been unable to plant enough food crops. So when their food was running out they began to steal groundnuts from the fields near Kashia. A fight in the fields followed, and a man from Kin aMboom was killed, whereupon the men of Kin aMboom returned to their village and began to prepare for war. But those of Kashia sent a message to the king, who came with the company manager from Ibanc to settle the question. The storytellers further speculated that the headman of Kin aMboom had probably been killed as a result of the fracas. It is very likely that this incident happened in 1906 or 1907 because the Pyang had been left alone until 1905 after the invasion by the Zappo Zap in 1899.

This case was certainly just one of a series of small-scale clashes over food among various Kuba villages, and it tells us that by the fall of 1907 the very limit of Kuba endurance had been broached. This and similar incidents also show that the whole society threatened to fall apart in a frantic struggle for food. Yet such incidents exerted no impact at all on the company's conduct of its business. They did, however, reduce the support the company received from the district commissioner's office. When the manager of the company station near Bakwa Kenge, in the extreme southeast of the kingdom, reported in July or August 1907 that he had been fired upon by Pyang villagers and asked for help, the district commissioner in Lusambo merely blamed him for provoking the incident and refused any assistance. But still, the rubber juggernaut rumbled inexorably on for nearly another two years.

From Protest to Recovery

On the first of January 1908 the *Kasai Herald,* the local journal of the American mission, published an article by Sheppard entitled "From the Bakuba Country" in which he wrote of the happy state of the Kuba until "a few years ago" and then contrasted this as follows:

> But within these last three years how changed they are! Their farms are growing up in weeds and jungle, their king is practically a slave, their houses are mostly half-built single rooms, and are much neglected. The streets of their towns are not clean and well swept as they once were. Even their children cry for bread.
>
> Why this change? You have it in a few words. There are armed sentries [capitas] of chartered trading companies who force the

men and women to spend most of their days and nights in the forests making rubber, and the price they receive is so meager that they can not live upon it.[11]

This proved to be the opening shot in the last phase of the great media campaign of the Congo Reform Association coordinated by E. D. Morel in Great Britain, a campaign that had already resulted in the pending takeover of the Congo State by Belgium. The article itself was not a momentary flash of frustration by an irascible missionary destined for their local newssheet but a well-thought-out piece. It seems that Morrison had asked Sheppard to write it and then carefully edited it himself before publication. Still, even if it was less spontaneous than appears at first, even if its rhetoric is slightly overblown, and even though one wonders why it took Morrison and Sheppard so long to protest against such a brutal and destructive regime, nevertheless these accusations were all true, as we have seen. Upon publication of the article, Morrison called for a consular investigation by Great Britain, which represented the United States in Congo at that time.

When word of this reached the director of the Compagnie du Kasai, he retaliated by launching a court case for slander against both missionaries. Guided by Presbyterian missionaries, Wilfred Thesiger, the British consul to Congo, traveled through Kuba country in June and July 1908. He first stayed a week at the mission of Luebo (June 19–25) and then pursued his enquiries inland with Sheppard as his guide and interpreter. They went to Nsheng and came back by a different route. Thesiger took notes, wrote his report, and mailed it in September. Its contents were almost immediately leaked to state officials so that its publication as part of the White Book Africa No. 1 published by the British Foreign Office in early 1909 came as no surprise to them. Still, politically this publication came at a highly sensitive time. In the spring of 1908 the Congo question had been the main issue in the Belgian elections that had resulted in a moderate majority for the parties that proposed to annex the colony. After a follow-up discussion the Belgian Parliament had voted the annexation on August 20, to become effective on November 15, 1908.

11. Robert Benedetto, *Presbyterian Reformers in Central Africa: A Documentary Account of the American Presbyterian Congo Mission and the Human Rights Struggle in Congo, 1890–1918* (Leiden, 1996), 281. "Armed sentries" was the usual expression for armed capitas in the literature of the Congo Reform Association.

So when Thesiger wrote his report the country was still the Congo Independent State, but by the time it was published the colony had become the Belgian Congo. That timing explains its importance. It came at the moment when Great Britain had to consider whether or not to recognize the takeover by Belgium. Under pressure from the Congo Reform Association the British government decided that recognition would be given when and only when obvious reforms had been undertaken. Hence the Thesiger report and Kuba affairs became of crucial importance for the Belgian government.

E. D. Morel, who directed the Congo Reform Association, immediately reprinted the Thesiger report in pamphlet form. Its headline shrieked: "The Enslavement and Destruction of the Bakuba by the 'Kasai Trust' in which the Belgian Government holds half the Stock, and whose directorate it controls." In his foreword he correctly underlined that the Compagnie du Kasai was essentially using the very same system of exploitation that his association had denounced for so many years when it was practiced by other concessionary rubber companies. Once again Morel swayed public opinion, and this time his publication inspired Conan Doyle, the famous creator of Sherlock Holmes, to publish *The Crime of the Congo* in the same year.

In his report Thesiger proffered the following main charges: that the rubber vines were cut rather than tapped in order to obtain more rubber, that the villages were taxed in rubber, that there were armed sentries [capitas] in the villages, that villagers were flogged, that the king enforced the rubber "tax" for the company, that villagers had no time to produce food or take care of their houses, that the Kuba were dying, and that there was starvation in the land. He further noted that several "younger officials" wished to put an end to this state of affairs but were powerless in the face of central authority and that the abolition of tax payments in copper crosses in 1906 had not changed anything.

Although the report was published in early 1909, the Belgian cabinet minister of colonies was already able to deny most of its specific charges by December 1908 since its contents had been leaked from late September onward. The state and the company had had time to react. The director of the company and the state agent at Luluabourg rushed to investigate the specific charges and were already able to correct them by late October and November, just around the date when Congo officially became Belgian.

Indeed for the king and his court at his capital the last months of 1908 were a tense turning point. The times were already difficult as people went hungry while their houses fell into ruins and the capital became dilapidated for lack of maintenance. Under these circumstances, to lodge and feed even one European visitor and his porters or to provide carriers for their luggage was quite an effort. The harbinger of trouble was the arrival on July 1 of Sheppard. Only a few months earlier he had falsely accused the king of having sacrificed a number of slaves on the occasion of the death of his sister, an accusation based as usual on rumors propagated by Luba and Lulua around Ibanc. So his arrival was unexpected and seemed to spell further difficulties. He was accompanied by Consul Thesiger, whom he presented in ominous terms to Kwet aPe as the emissary of an adversary of Bula Matadi who was much stronger than the latter, and he said that when Thesiger returned to Europe with his report Bula Matadi would be in great trouble.

In late September the Catholic missionaries abandoned their station on instructions of the company, which needed staff for a new mission and rubber post elsewhere downriver. Thus King Kwet aPe lost a missionary adviser whom he had befriended after the murder of Father Polet. During the same week, on September 24, there arrived Emil Torday, a Hungarian who had been a state agent before he became an agent of the Compagnie du Kasai, but who recently had turned into a professional ethnographer in charge of an expedition to gather objects for the British Museum. Hilton Simpson, an English adventurer and big game hunter, accompanied him. They remained in Nsheng for nearly three months until December 21 but with an interruption when the lack of available food forced Simpson to go hunting and foraging in the countryside. Torday spent his time studying the main political institutions of the kingdom, gathering ethnographic collections, and documenting them. He had brought interesting gifts for the king, including a live eagle. Soon both were on friendly terms even though Torday was equally quick in pestering the king to give to him some of the revered ancient statues of former kings known as *ndop*. In spite of the bitter opposition of the majority party in the councils, he eventually obtained four statues, helped no doubt by the troubled political climate at that moment.

For on October 9, barely two weeks after Torday's arrival, the director of the Compagnie du Kasai arrived with his secretary to investigate Thesiger's charges about abuses committed by his managers and capitas and to redress them wherever necessary. As part of this he was investigating Kwet aPe's stance in the lawsuit between the company and the Presbyterians and his role in the collection of rubber. A mere five days later the ranking state official for central Kasai, Count Fernand de

One of the foremost titleholders displays a *ndop* to Torday, 1908 (Hilton-Simpson, *Land and Peoples of the Kasai*, 1912)

Grunne, also appeared in Nsheng, intent on questioning Kwet aPe about his militia, his subsidy from the Compagnie du Kasai, and his use of force to raise rubber in recalcitrant villages.

Soon after de Grunne's departure news arrived that the Ngende chiefs in the east were rebelling against the king, very likely because of the imposition in rubber. Perhaps it was news of this development that prompted Morrison in Luebo to then send the following demand to de Grunne, who was also operating in the Ngende area: "In the name of the traders and missionaries both Protestant and Catholic who live in the region, I demand that you hold yourself in readiness for a reprising [uprising] on the party of the Bakuba people."[12] The message went all around central Kasai until a note from Torday in Nsheng to de Grunne in Ngende country quashed the rumor. For meanwhile both Kwet aPe and de Grunne separately set out early in November to quell the uprising. De Grunne met the king in Ngende country, and together they subdued Bwaall, one of the major Ngende settlements, and then declared victory.

Finally, to crown the sequence of visitors to the capital that fall, a Belgian journalist, Fritz Van der Linden, arrived there later in November to report on the Congo's transmutation into a Belgian colony and on the truth of the charges leveled at the company. As part of his task he interviewed both Kwet aPe and Torday about Thesiger's charges. Both exonerated the company, and so did the journalist. The king, who had no idea of what a journalist actually was, seems to have cautiously given the expected answers to the loaded questions he was asked. But he remained suspicious and enquired afterward whether the man had come to Nsheng to remove him from office in favor of the pretender to the throne. Torday praised Bushong art and political institutions but also had the gall to conclude the interview as follows:

> Frankly I do not believe that the work of gathering rubber has had any unfortunate influence on the social life of the Kuba.[13]

---

12. Fritz Van der Linden, *Le Congo, les noirs et nous* (Paris, 1909), 206.

13. Van der Linden, *Le Congo, les noirs et nous*, 227. Before he set out with his expedition, Torday had promised the Compagnie du Kasai that he would not make any unfavorable "political" comments. See Compagnie du Kasai, *Dima files*: letter by Torday, August 7, 1907, and orders from the director general in Brussels to the director at Dima of October 2, 1908. In return for this promise and for the promise to gather ethnographic objects for the company, Torday was granted a subsidy of 5,000 francs outright, free passage onboard the company steamers, and local credit for another 5,000 francs.

This statement was obviously false. But then Torday's voyage was partly funded by the company, he was its former employee, and his expedition depended on the company for transportation by river and on its stations for his supplies. Van der Linden's loaded questions were obviously intended to exonerate the company and are explained, at least in part, by the politics of the newspapers for which he wrote and his dependence on the company during this portion of his travels.

According to the journalist the king must have been totally bewildered.

> How often has his mind not had to run up against problems without solution, when he has wanted to fathom the disputes that arise between the State, the Compagnie du Kasai and the missions! It is not surprising that he tends to be melancholy and discouraged. The "elders" [titleholders] reproach him to be too benevolent towards the whites. He has understood that his good intentions to be friendly towards everyone have not prevented him from playing an important and dangerous role, in palavers without end![14]

He and his court may well have been bewildered. What was evident to them was that all these visitors, like the Bushong themselves, were enemies of the Presbyterian mission, and that they were probably more powerful. That was reassuring. What was troubling was that the state had obviously turned against the company and was no longer willing to leave the governing of Kasai solely to the latter's discretion. So whose side were the king and his court to take? The Kuba councils obviously disliked both the company that exploited the country and the state that had subdued them. The king had benefited from the company's subsidies and had been able to set up the militia that had given him the upper hand over his titleholders in addition to the advantage over his councils that he had already gained after the failure of the rebellion. Yet he also was well aware that his role as enforcer for the company ran contrary to his obligations toward his subjects and was alienating them. That could easily lead to a breakdown of the kingdom—witness the latest Ngende revolt. Since his stay at Lusambo in 1905 he also knew that in the last instance the state was the real power. As long as the company ruled he had not been forced to choose between the two. But now that de Grunne challenged the company, he had to take sides.

---

14. Van der Linden, *Le Congo, les noirs et nous*, 230–31.

Despite the company subsidy, the king decided to back de Grunne, and he succeeded in laying all the blame for the coercion he exercised on the company managers—did they not represent the state after all in his kingdom? His councils backed him because the gross abuses perpetrated by the agents of the company were involved and because de Grunne required the dismissal of the organized royal militia. In return the king received almost instantaneous support from de Grunne in the Ngende incident, and that truly clinched the issue. Henceforth the Kuba king was to be the state's man.

As early as February 4, 1909, that news sufficed to bring the rebellious Ngende and Pyang chiefs back into line. De Grunne also warded off several attempts by company managers and agents after the meetings of October to destabilize the kingdom by stirring up rebellions against the king, and on March 25, 1909, he left a set of instructions for Kwet aPe and his councils that read like a treaty or a blueprint of indirect rule. These included the following eight points: the king could not oblige his subjects to work for private business, only encourage them to do so; he could not dress his messengers or envoys in uniforms resembling those of the army; he had to suppress the poison ordeal; he had the right to arrest troublemakers, but when this occurred he should inform the state official at Luebo immediately; he had to assist with the equitable recruitment of young men from all villages for the colonial army; the state backed the king fully by requiring that his subjects undo the ravages of the rubber regime, increase the cultivation of crops, plant more manioc, reconstitute their herds of small stock, clean and maintain the roads, and rebuild the villages; in the same context the king should report all abuses committed by agents for private business to de Grunne and not to listen to their solicitations; in general he should be convinced that the state was his *only* protector and should avoid transmitting his complaints and desires through private intermediaries who might distort his words.

De Grunne completely routed the company. Between April and November 1908 it had handed over only nine capitas to the state for trial while de Grunne summarily arrested another seven during his enquiry. Still that only came to sixteen arrests (including Mwek's Mokendji) out of 285 capitas for an area that included most of the kingdom. Hence in November he spelled out what was inadmissible behavior for the company's agents. Returning to the fray in March and April 1909, he documented a long new series of specific misdeeds and referred the accused and their files to the judiciary for legal prosecution. His reports and letters to managers of the company underlined African complaints about forced advances, the forced provision of houses as living quarters for capitas, the fall of prices paid for rubber, and the cutting of rubber vines. In particular he castigated the abuses committed in the company's sector ten, which covered most of the kingdom, and cited three specific incidents that had occurred there since November: namely, the arbitrary arrest of a chief, the murder of one capita, and the wounding of one of the company's messengers.

Such warning letters, further arrests of capitas, and the indictment of European agents began to convince even the company's employees in sector ten that this concern about Africans might not be a passing fashion. Still it was only when the minister of colonies appeared in June 1909 to personally inspect the Compagnie du Kasai that they saw the handwriting on the wall, especially after the minister met Kwet aPe at Bolombo on June 24. To cap it all, in September the company lost its case against Morrison and Sheppard in Léopoldville after a trial that had drawn very unwelcome and considerable international attention to its misdeeds.

Times of Transition: The Coming of the Belgian Congo

November 15, 1908, the date Belgium took over Congo, went by totally unnoticed in Kasai and in the Kuba realm. Even the journalist seems to have forgotten it. On that day, which was also the official celebration of the royal dynasty, he wrote only "Day of the king . . . November 15 looks very much like all other days . . . , perhaps only somewhat warmer."[15] No wonder then that this transition is usually believed to be unimportant and is merely credited with a few reforms to prevent further abuses. In fact, though, within a few years the whole colonial situation especially in Upper Congo was transformed almost beyond recognition.

First, as of January 1, 1909, the state fixed the rate of taxation everywhere in Congo at 12 francs as an initial step to put an end to the era of arbitrary levies by state or company agents alike. Not much changed yet for the Kuba or in Kasai because there still was no money in circulation and therefore taxes continued to be paid mostly in rubber that was valued in francs at a very low exchange rate, so the Compagnie du Kasai was initially not much affected.

---

15. Van der Linden, *Le Congo, les noirs et nous*, 207.

Then on July 1, 1910, the franc became the only legal tender in large parts of Congo, including Kasai, which really did away with arbitrary taxation. On the same day the Compagnie du Kasai lost its trading monopoly, and within months several Portuguese traders began to compete with it.

In the fall of the same year the state finally assumed its full responsibility toward the Kuba realm and founded a state post at its capital, thereby ending the period of company rule. Early that year a new decree on chiefdoms had been passed that formed the basis for a new administrative framework. Vice Governor General Eugène Henry came to Kasai to enforce this and delimited the Kuba "chiefdom." In doing so he excised the portion of the kingdom that lay east of the Labody (Lubudi) River and also amputated the Kete villages north of Luebo from it. Those villages, however, absolutely refused to accept their excision and continued to bring both their tribute and their palavers to the Kuba capital. Obviously at that point Kwet aPe had recovered his prestige in their eyes, and his rule was now preferable to any other.

Next the Belgian Parliament ordered the state to divest itself of its shares in the Compagnie du Kasai, and the state complied in February 1911. The Compagnie du Kasai was now reduced to the status of any other private company, even if its size ensured that it still remained one of the main players in the commerce of Kasai. Nevertheless the disengagement of the state finally ensured that there never could be a recurrence of the systematic abuses that had made the company infamous in earlier years.

In March 1912 the whole territorial structure of districts in Congo was reformed. In Upper Congo they became somewhat smaller. They were also divided into new units called *territoires*, each of which usually encompassed a number of chiefdoms. The huge old district of Kasai was now divided into two smaller ones: Sankuru and Kasai. Luebo became the capital of the new Kasai with all the attendant administrative and judiciary offices. Part of the new Kasai district, the Kuba realm now formed a *territoire* all by itself, perhaps the only "chiefdom" in the colony to do so. No doubt as a result of their protests the Kete villages in the south were now restored to it, but the lands across the Labody River went to Sankuru district. With this and the division of Congo into four provinces early in 1914, the new administrative framework was completed. It was to last throughout the whole remainder of the colonial period, and so was a large array of diverse and subsidiary arrangements from taxes to rules about the placement of mission stations.

While this achievement may seem to be of limited interest today, at the time it was perceived as a revolution. For the best kept secret of the former regime was well known there—namely, that in practice there had never been any government worthy of the name at all in Upper Congo upstream of Léopoldville. In the early years all foreigners from overseas, whatever their status, had acted in any way they wished and only lost a little of their freedom of action later on. Even as late as 1905 district commissioners still did not, or could not, rein in the autonomy of their subordinates in all but military matters, and the Compagnie du Kasai did not even attempt to control its employees. The government of the Congo Independent State was a ponderous and bureaucratic reality in the Lower Congo but not beyond. Therefore, what happened between 1909 and 1914 almost amounted to the creation of a brand-new colony, although this creation was in large part inspired by the earlier experience gained in the Lower Congo.

During these years Kuba country recovered from the regime of terror. When another British diplomat, Vice Consul E. W. P. Thurstan, visited the region in November 1910 to check on how far the charges made by Thesiger had been remedied, he heard only about a few cases of petty acts of violence and found no evidence of company agents or capitas flogging people or jailing them anymore. Although he found that the rubber vines were still cut rather than tapped, this was now legal. The king's militia had been disbanded, and the inhabitants were no longer forcibly compelled to produce rubber. Indeed, most Kuba were now making no rubber at all. Still, he worried about the survival of the advance system with its obvious potential for abuses and about the company's continued payment of a commission to the king, now calculated per ton on all rubber collected in the realm either by Lulua or by Kuba. Yet he also found that while the king still encouraged villagers to produce rubber, he advised them "to make a little rubber every day, but not too much," which was his interpretation of the instructions given by de Grunne and later by the vice governor general. His conclusion: "The Bakuba have now at least a sufficiency."[16]

Despite the vice consul's optimism, one still gathers from his report that all was not well. The recovery remained uneven. Once again people could and did hunt, carrying "traditional" weapons, and although there

---

16. E. W. P. Thurstan, *General Report on the Kasai District . . .*, Command Paper 65860 (London, 1911), 43–46.

was no longer any evident scarcity of food in the country, there were still plenty of dilapidated houses, and details show that the quality of the food supply had not yet recovered. Furthermore, there had been trouble with capitas until early 1910, and payments forcibly extracted for an advance were still extortionate. The village of Mwek complained that its capita had seized a goat and some camwood to make up for a shortage of rubber worth far less and moreover that these things were seized from someone who was neither the debtor nor even a relative of his. In any case, one becomes truly suspicious of an observer who begins his report by claiming that the Kuba are untrustworthy liars and were to blame for the abuses—"It is this inveterate aversion to work of an unaccustomed nature, which has been at the root of all trouble in connection with the rubber." Obviously Thurstan's sympathies lay with the colonialists, not the Kuba.

Only Vice Consul H. H. Castens's report from January 1913 provided conclusive evidence that the abuses had really ended, even though the advance system was still being practiced. By then the Kuba had fully recovered. They had plenty of food, although the inhabitants of the capital were still obliged to farm for themselves; Bushong and Kete houses were of adequate size, even though they were still less well made and ornamented than they had been before the company's regime of terror; and villages were cleaner and more prosperous in appearance. Still, the recovery was limited by the prevailing colonial circumstances. The people still had to spend too much time on earning their tax in money and providing tribute for the court. Although forced labor had been abolished in 1910 and villagers could not be forced to gather rubber, they still lost time on corvee labor for the king and were still occasionally forced to act as porters for European officials or traders, even though such services were now paid. Nevertheless, Castens's report along with several others convinced the British government that the era of abuses was really over. It formally recognized the takeover of Congo by Belgium in 1913.

After 1912 most Kuba did not gather rubber anymore, not even to pay their annual tax in money. But because "Kasai red rubber" was of exceptional quality, the Compagnie du Kasai was still trading in some rubber. The product was now gathered by Lulua or Luba who supposedly resided there only temporarily to harvest the product and no longer by people who settled in the kingdom. Nevertheless what remained was a large proportion of all the rubber still sold in Europe. Many of these Lulua or Luba were probably former Kuba slaves who had been freed by the very first decision of the first official agent of the administration to staff the post at Nsheng in 1910. Most of these people had no other place to go to and remained in the kingdom. In addition to migrant labor, all permanent paid workers for the foreign establishments were also Luba and Lulua. In the future this situation was bound to lead, once again, to strained relationships between the Kuba and Luba immigrants, especially over land tenure. At the time it was already creating tensions because most Luba and Lulua did not recognize the king's territorial authority over them. Moreover, these immigrants, especially the Luba, strove to imitate European dress and deportment as much as possible. Many among them became literate so that the contrast between them and the Bushong became more pronounced than ever and turned into a colonial cliché that opposed such progressive modernizers to the local backward-looking conservatives in spite of the fact that the Kuba kings wanted to and did send some of their kinsfolk to school.

Meanwhile the Bushong and Kete who did not gather rubber still somehow had to find the wherewithal to pay their taxes. After 1905 some Kete villages were taxed by the government official of Luebo in palm oil, and as this became a commodity for export from Luebo they continued to do so thereafter. Other Kete villages seem to have produced mostly foodstuffs although some among them, and some Bushong villages as well, also sold enough mats, textiles, and curios to cover their taxes so that they only occasionally needed to work as porters. But it still remains unclear how the bulk of the Bushong earned the funds to pay their taxes. They stubbornly resisted porterage whenever possible and worked very little rubber. One suspects that they now sold foodstuffs to the Luba and Lulua migrant laborers in return for rubber with which they then acquired the money for their taxes. It is worthy of note that like most Bushong, many other Congolese seem to have found ways to pay their taxes in the climate of freedom and competition that flourished after 1910 without having to work for ill-paying and oppressive companies. Indeed, so many succeeded that the government and the major companies eventually began to worry about their supply of labor.

At the same time as these reforms were being carried out by the new Belgian administration, they also attempted to lessen the competition between the Catholics and the Presbyterians by keeping the mission stations far apart. Yet at the same time the government tended to side with the Catholics. The minister of colonies wanted a Catholic mission at Nsheng, but it was not until 1915 that the missionaries of Scheut reluctantly founded one there. Meanwhile dissension among the Presbyterians had led to the foundation of a new station the year before among a

The Oil Palm and the Raffia Palm

Coming upstream by boat on the Lower Kasai River, many early colonials delighted in describing the frequent scattered stands of tall oil palms in Kuba country as they steamed along its shore. Yet none of them mentioned the dense orchards of raffia palms around practically every Kuba village, almost as if they were invisible to the colonial eye. In partial contrast the Kuba gaze registered the raffia trees first before it recorded the oil palm. Why were these colonial and Kuba perceptions so different? Let us explore the answer.

The oil palm (*Elaïs guineensis* Jacq.), a relatively tall palm tree, grows spontaneously on deep, well-drained, and well-watered soils in sunny spots all through the subequatorial savannas of West and Equatorial Africa, but especially near the margins of the rainforests that stretch from Gambia to Angola. For at least four thousand years Africans have appreciated the tree for its sap and its fruit. The sap produces palm wine, and the nuts yield palm oil. For uncounted ages men have climbed the tall mature trees (from well over thirty feet to one hundred feet at most) every morning to tap the sap from a place just under its crown and let it seep into a calabash to be collected in the evening.

When the fruit was ripe men were in the trees to cut bunches of fruit near the crown. Each bunch weighed between ten and thirty-five pounds and contained hundreds of reddish nuts, and each nut consisted of outer skin, a mass of oil-filled pulp, and a hard-shelled kernel. Palm oil was obtained by pressing the oil out of the pulp by various techniques. Most of the resulting buttery and reddish-yellow liquid was used as a sauce for almost every meal, but some of it was also rubbed on the skin as a conditioner and a beauty product. The hard-shelled kernel contains another kind of oil, finer and of a different composition than palm oil. But the shell is so hard to crack that many Africans including Bushong and Kete have not found it worth the effort to extract the oil. Usually they made no use of palm kernels.

After the abolition of the slave trade and just at the time when industrialization in Europe was growing rapidly, Europeans along the West African coast found new uses for palm oil and

Climbing an oil palm tree (photo by author)

palm kernels. Palm oil exports to Europe began as early as 1790, first to make soap and fashion candles. The demand soared from the middle of the nineteenth century onward when palm oil began to be used to keep machines lubricated, to process the tinning of iron, and later still for other industrial uses such as the fabrication of linoleum. Eventually it was found that palm oil was ideal for making margarine. Kernels then began to be imported whole, and the oil was extracted in Europe. It was converted almost exclusively into margarine or vegetable oil for cooking. The export of palm products from the West African coasts including the Lower Congo had reached impressive volumes by the 1880s so that it is not surprising that the colonials who ascended the Kasai River immediately noticed the oil palms in Kuba country.

The exploitation of oil palms upstream from Kinshasa began in earnest only after rubber exports plummeted in 1910–13. From that time onward the export of palm oil and of whole kernels grew rapidly, especially after 1917, when most inhabitants in the province of Equateur, in Kwilu, and among the Kuba began to be obliged to gather palm fruit and to produce both palm oil and kernels. This was followed from the early 1920s onward by the creation of regular oil palm plantations and the development of new and more fruitful varieties of trees. By that time the oil palm had become an emblem and a major pillar of its rural colonial economy.

The raffia palm (*Raphia textilis* Welw.), a much shorter tree (about thirty feet), grows under conditions generally similar to the oil palm. It is especially appreciated for its wine (preferred to any other among the Kuba) and for the raffia strands within its leaves, which are converted to fibers for weaving cloth. But among the Kuba the raffia tree has far more uses even than this. They found a use for absolutely every part of the tree, be it for construction, for roofing, for crafting furniture, as strong string for sewing, as tinder, and even as a medium from which to harvest edible grubs. No wonder that they carefully planted and tended raffia trees in orchards all around their villages.

The most essential and irreplaceable of these functions for the Kuba was to provide the raw material for clothing. Three times a year all adolescents and adults needed two new costumes, containing some five standard lengths of raffia cloth each. As there were around twenty thousand Bushong and Kete adults plus adolescents, some six hundred thousand lengths of cloth had to be produced per year, and that total does not include raffia cloth for other uses such as velvet or embroidered lengths used at funerals, for making dancing costumes, or for export. The volume of required lengths of cloth diminished only slowly over the course of the colonial period because the demand for imported cloth grew quite slowly among the Kuba: even as late as the 1950s at least two-thirds of all the clothes worn by them were raffia costumes. No wonder then that the raffia tree was so prominent in Kuba eyes.

But there was little demand for raffia in Europe. Annual exports from all of Congo stagnated around one hundred tons except during World War II when it was used for the manufacture of

large Protestant Kete group at Baancep (Bakwa Nzeba) that was competing with a large Kete Catholic group nearby, and in 1915 Ibanc was abandoned.

The new station was called Bulape after a converted Bushong princess. Henceforth it became the major Presbyterian presence in the kingdom. But the Protestant missionaries did not give up their hope of establishing a station one day at the heart of the capital itself. Meanwhile, though, they continued to thoroughly alienate Kwet aPe by their wild charges. Only a few months before his death in April 1916 they were still accusing him of plotting rebellions, a charge that was once again based on vague rumors spread by neighboring Luba and Lulua who were still afraid of him. Presbyterian relations with his successor remained just as bad, and it was not until 1920 that success for that mission finally seemed to be around the corner.

Toward an Era of Indirect Rule and Captive Labor

The form of government that the colonial administration had gradually developed to govern the Kuba kingdom by its improvisations between 1908 and 1910 was stable and well established by 1912. What had emerged was an indirect way to control the country. Rather than installing its own officers in the country and assuming direct command over

---

ammunitions. In 1942 production even reached 650 tons. But from the perspective of the Kuba, the export of embroidered or velvet cloth to outsiders from overseas was much more important and occurred in quantities that were not negligible to them. The production and sale of such objects for the European market began shortly after 1885, and the demand never abated so that by the later 1930s lengths of cloth for export began to be made on order, especially at Nsheng. To the Kuba such sales were important because they brought them more personal freedom by allowing people to earn money with which to pay their taxes outside the exploitative system set up by the colonial authorities. And so it came about that in contrast to the oil palm, an emblem of colonial exploitation, the raffia tree became an emblem of how to evade its impositions.

the local people, the colonial government co-opted the Kuba king and his government as agents to carry out most of its administration. Such a form of governance is known as indirect rule. Three years later the district commissioner of Kasai formalized what had hitherto been a rather informal relationship. He ordered that the king be treated as if the monarch were a ranking territorial official and he seconded him with a European adviser. To the Bushong and Kete villagers this solution must have looked like a total vindication of their king and a proof of his continuing power.

Much of the credit for this successful transition from independent kingdom to what now looked like a sort of protectorate must go to the policy choices of Kwet aPe. When he died in April 1916, this kind of rule had struck root and variants of it would prove sturdy enough to last throughout the remainder of the colonial period. Thus the maintenance of the Kuba kingdom remains a prime example of the importance of African actors in creating colonial Congo.

The outbreak of World War I brought any further evolution of the colony to an abrupt halt. The urgent and imperative demands of a war that was also fought in Africa around Congo with the participation of Congolese troops took precedence over anything else and completely reversed the trend toward a form of colonial government that largely respected African economic freedom in favor of renewed coercion. Even so, it was not until February 1917 that the government dared issue a decree that established a certain amount of compulsory labor per year—hypocritically justified as an effort to civilize the Congolese. Hence, the decree was entitled Travaux d'Ordre Educatif, "Labor of an Educational Nature." Possibly the war provided an opportunity to publish a decree devoutly desired by the main colonial companies in the absence of a Parliament that otherwise might not have approved it. Be that as it may, to a certain extent World War I itself must be blamed for the momentous decree it spawned.

FURTHER READINGS

See also chapters 2 and 3.

Castens, H. H. *Tour in the Bakuba Country*. Command Paper 118427. London, 1913.

Harms, Robert. "The World Abir Made: The Maringa-Lopori Basin." *African Economic History* 12 (1983): 125–39.

Hilton-Simpson, M. W. *Land and Peoples of the Kasai*. Chicago, 1912.

Morel, E. D., ed. *The Enslavement and Destruction of the Bakuba . . .* London (Congo Reform Association), 1909. This contains a reprint of the Thesiger Report.

Thurstan, E. W. P. *General Report on the Kasai District . . .* and *Report on the Bakuba and Lulua Sections.* Command Paper 65860. London, 1911.
Torday, Emil. *On the Trail of the Bushongo.* London, 1925.

5

Were the Kuba
Nearly Wiped Out?

> Considering that the population of Congo . . . is continually falling
> since the onset of the European occupation . . . it is not exagger-
> ated to say that on the whole it has been reduced by half.[1]

This urgent warning from the Permanent Committee for the Protection of the Natives is the most explosive statement ever made about
the early history of Congo. It is so because all history is about people,
and what happens to their numbers is of fundamental importance for
everything else. That is the main reason why a whole chapter is devoted
to this issue. Moreover, the veracity of this declaration has been and still
continues to be bitterly contested between those who accept it and those
who do not. The ongoing polemic about the death rates during Leopold
II's regime in Congo revolves around the question of whether or not it is
to blame for this supposed loss of half its population. The most damning
indictment of those who denounced the terror practiced in the Independent Congo State at the time had been the charge that these practices
had caused a massive decline in the population on such a scale that a
very large proportion of the Congolese population fell victim to it, something close to what is called a genocide today. The defenders of the state
denied this accusation just as indignantly and vigorously as it was

---

1. Warning from the Permanent Committee for the Protection of the Natives to
the Government, 3d session 1919. In *Bulletin Officiel du Congo Belge* (1920): 636.

propounded by its accusers. For them the number of deaths that could be attributed to colonial rule and exploitation was actually quite small.

Recently the whole debate flared up once again, and the Permanent Committee's estimate is once again very much in question. There are actually two issues in contention: whether or not there was a massive decline in population and what, if anything, early colonial practices had to do with this loss. On the first issue one set of scholars holds that we cannot know how many people died during the period for lack of accurate data. All the numbers proposed are sheer speculation because no systematic population counts, let alone censuses, were undertaken until well into the 1920s. On the second issue the same scholars argue first that documented atrocities caused only a small number of deaths in excess of the high level of mortality that is usual among populations in tropical environments and that epidemics rather than direct violence caused most of the drop in population. For them the colonial situation was not to blame except perhaps for a small number of deaths from avoidable violence. In reply to this the opposing set of scholars now holds on the first issue that whatever the exact numbers of deaths and the decline of the population were, both must have been very large, and on the second issue that the colonial situation was responsible for death from deprivation and epidemics.

Rather than pursue the various arguments in an abstract way, let us focus on a single case in order to examine the nature of the available evidence. Only when that is appreciated can one evaluate the reliability of the deductions that can or cannot be drawn from it and whether the evidence adduced or the arguments used suffer from any fatal flaws. As it happens, the Kuba are a good test case. Hence we closely follow the common pattern of reasoning adopted by both sides in the debate.

To find out whether there was a population decline we first try the most direct way of doing this by establishing the size of the Kuba population in 1885 and compare it with its size as indicated in the first official results of a population count in the 1920s. Because that exercise suggests a considerable loss of population, we then look at data from this period that betray a general awareness that the population was in decline. Next we turn to the evidence that exists about the specific causes for the number of deaths directly or indirectly caused by the exploitation of rubber as contrasted with the number of deaths caused by epidemics. Finally we indicate what can be said about the growth or decline of the Kuba population between 1880 and 1920.

A Dying Population?

Arriving in the first Kete village he entered within the kingdom, celebrated Portuguese trader António Ferreira da Silva Porto was struck by the great number of children he met there, and when he reached the market of Kampungu on August 13, 1880, he exclaimed:

> It [the population] exceeds 3,000 individuals of either sex belonging to the two tribes [Kete and Bushong]; and what generally strikes the traveler who crosses such settlements is the large number of the people of a tender age who swarm within them, and who follow him everywhere, as happened to us in the village of Besia-Calunga [Buya Kalunga]; in another village that we passed and visited on that occasion the same peculiarity was to be observed; and today the site of the market of Loquengo [the Kuba king] proves it to be general and no doubt due to the clemency of the climate.[2]

According to his observation the population was then obviously expanding at least in the southern Kuba region. Five years later Wolf, using a technique much used in his day (see "How Wolf Calculated the Number of Kuba in 1885"), put the population of the kingdom at eighty thousand. His figure is much lower than the guesses made by various Presbyterian missionaries in the 1890s and 1900s. Those range from as improbably high as 450,000 to as low as 250,000. All of these figures and other high numbers, such as the official estimate in 1920 of 150,000 to 200,000 cited by the minister for colonies during an interview, may be dismissed as guesswork for propaganda purposes.

Still, even 107,000, the lowest number extrapolated from Wolf, stands in stark contrast with the total for the 1926 administrative count at 58,452. But how reliable is that figure? The count yielded 16,718 Bushong at that time, yet three years before a traveler was told that there were only about 8,000! Moreover, the government believed its own

2. António Ferreira da Silva Porto, "Novas jornadas de Silva Porto," *Boletim da Sociedade de Geographia de Lisboa*, 6a series (1886): 538. Yet in the very next paragraph he confesses that the abundant palm trees at Kampungu made it so lugubrious that he was oppressed by it. So much for the benign climate. In 2007 Kampungu was the site of a joint outbreak of three epidemic diseases, one of which was the dreaded hemorrhagic fever known as ebola.

1926 count to be a severe undercount and suggested raising it by 20 percent to obtain a more reliable figure. Four years later the government official in charge of a study about the labor pool in the territory of the Bakuba cited a population of 134,000, a figure that excludes another 2,665 at Ilebo (Port Francqui), but he also believed that these figures were completely unreliable. By 1932 there were supposedly 115,000 Kuba, but this time excluding the Kete. One must conclude that none of these figures can be trusted. As late as the middle 1930s the counting seems to have been haphazard. Moreover, most of the resulting figures are not comparable with each other because they refer to different sets of people: some count everyone in the territory (including Luba and Lulua immigrants), some are restricted to the same population but minus the inhabitants of the towns of Mweka and Port Francqui, some

How Wolf Calculated the Number of Kuba in 1885

Wolf arrived at his total of eighty thousand Kuba in the following manner. First he estimated the population size for each village through which he traveled, but he does not tell us how he did that. He seems to have used the size of the village rather than a count of all the houses and estimated a number from that size. With these data he calculated the total number of people he had met along his line of travels per square German mile. That yielded a density per square mile that was then extrapolated to the calculated total surface of the kingdom as deduced from longitudes and latitudes. Eighty thousand was the result.

But his figures need to be corrected as follows. His estimate of the extent of the kingdom at four hundred square German miles (*Quadrat Meil*) was barely half of the real size, since he wrongly defined the extent of the kingdom as the lands between 5°10′ and 4° South by 21°10′ and 22°20′ East, which is only about half of its real size. His population estimate is too low. On the other hand, the surroundings of the market town of Ibanc through which he traveled were savanna (with good visibility), and he counted at least two hundred people per *Quadrat Meil*, which yields eighty thousand people [200 p × 400 M²] and gives a population density

refer to all the people in the kingdom within Kasai district (and the boundaries of both change over time), and some count the Kuba minus Kete or minus the Cwa. Obviously these figures are no more reliable than the figure for 1885.

Indeed, one can deduce anything one likes from them. For instance, take the 136,665 total (Kuba + Ilebo) from 1930, and you can argue that the Kuba population remained stationary between 1885 and 1930 or even that it increased a bit. Take the 1923 estimate or even the 1926 figure, and there was a dramatic loss. The inescapable conclusion to all of this is that the evidence cannot tell us, even approximately, by how much the population declined nor indeed whether it even declined at all. Nor is the Kuba situation in any way exceptional. Similar exercises reach similar sad conclusions in most of Congo.

---

of eight people per square kilometer [1 *Meil* = 5 km; 1 *Quadrat Meil* = 25 km^2; 400 M^2 = 10,000 km^2]. That density is not out of line given that it is as high as the highest densities for the same region found in later colonial times while it is lower than the densities in postcolonial times.

However, since his estimate of the size of the kingdom is too low by half, we can multiply his total by two to arrive at 160,000. That is not correct, though, because the population density was not uniform over the whole kingdom. From the scant data available for all periods one knows that few people lived inland from the Sankuru both in the far east and in part of the far northwest of the realm, while even elsewhere in the northern half of the realm the population may have been significantly smaller than in the southern half. Nevertheless it is just possible that the lesser density in the north was itself the result of a murderous smallpox epidemic that occurred in 1893–94.

Hence to multiply Wolf's total by two is probably too much. From projecting variations back to 1885 in densities in different places known from later times one might estimate that between one-third and one-half of Wolf's eighty thousand should be added to it. The total number would thus lie somewhere between 107,000 and 120,000.

Could one perhaps do better in the Kuba case by looking at other figures, such as the number of villages and the number of houses or inhabitants per village? For 1912, a number of villages is known to be based on an actual count established by the manager of the Compagnie du Kasai at Nsheng. He reported approximately 164 villages in a twenty-to-thirty-mile radius of Nsheng with an average of 30 adult men per village, for a total of 4,920 men. Assuming a stable demographic balance at four persons per adult male, this yields 19,680 people (at 4.5 persons we arrive at 22,140 people).

Let us then add the population of Nsheng, which was estimated at around 4,000 in 1912, up from around 2,000 in 1908 and 1909. The total for the stable population balance becomes 23,680 people with the 1912 estimate for Nsheng or 21,680 with the estimate for 1908. Those figures allow us to calculate the population density per square kilometer of a circle around Nsheng with a 40-kilometer (25-mile) radius. That gives us 5,027 square kilometers and 4.71 persons per square kilometer for 23,680 people (or 4.31 persons per square kilometer for 21,680 people). Compared to eight people per square kilometer in 1885, this density is down 41 to 46 percent but it is still somewhat higher than the one calculated for the 1950s.

This result looks plausible but it does not necessarily reflect the extent of the population losses because one expects that some people fled from the area counted by the manager of Nsheng to regions, especially to the west, less ruthlessly covered by rubber collectors. So the calculation only tells us that if there was a population loss between 1885 and 1912, it was less than about 46 percent.

Besides the figures on which the calculations above rest, still other figures can be obtained, such as the number of houses in a village or a direct count of people in a few villages. Such figures allow one to show that the size of individual villages ranged between about ten people to almost four hundred—and thereby warn us how precarious the notion of an "average" village really is. It soon becomes evident that any calculations derived from such data require so many extrapolations and are fraught with so many assumptions that whatever results they yield will be worthless. For example, we are told that in 1908 there were 285 capitas in the whole Compagnie du Kasai sector ten. Even assuming that there was one capita per "average" village and that the average village was as large then as it was in 1912, we still need further assumptions because sector ten included places south and west beyond the Kuba realm and excluded Kuba lands north of the Lacwady and east of the Labody

(Lubudi) rivers. In other words, too many unknowns and too many extrapolations in such calculations make any detailed results completely implausible.

Contemporary Awareness of Population Decline

Yet calculations like the ones above are not wholly useless. Most of them leave the impression that there truly was a sizeable demographic decline even if the numbers themselves are unreliable. That impression should be tested by other means. A first line of testing is the following. If there had been so many extra deaths as to lead to a huge decline in population, one would expect a general awareness that it was happening. The first author to report such a population decline was Consul Wilfred Thesiger in 1908, no doubt inspired by his Presbyterian missionary guides. But he was followed a few months later by the anthropologist Torday, who seems not to be aware of such a decline.

As to the Bushong themselves, we have seen in previous chapters that they were alarmed first by the spectacular mortality and the lack of births in the royal dynasty, which they attributed to the charm of Kwet aMbweky. That, however, was soon followed by a general awareness of population loss due to an exceptional mortality overall as indicated by the following Bushong reminiscences of the 1950s:

> In the old days they had a charm consisting in a bunch of palm-nuts; if you eat something that does not belong to you they will make these charms: they took a bunch of unripe palmnuts and hung it up [on a string] between two poles. When these nuts had ripened the man who had asked for the charm was informed, the maker of the charm returned and shook the poles supporting the bunch: if two nuts fell, then also two people die, if twenty fell then twenty people will sicken and die.
>
> When king Kwet aPe saw this he gave his official spokesman instructions to forbid this practice. The spokesman told everyone "if you continue with this we will all perish and if someone continues with this despite [this order] the king will kill him." So the practice was then abandoned.[3]

A general consciousness of a demographic decline is also very evident in many village histories. These record the fusion of several villages

---

3. Vansina Files, *nyim—before 1920:* Kwete Gaston, *Charms to Kill People.*

Children at play (photo by author)

into a single settlement as the result of population losses, which at that time were not induced by any sizeable emigrations. Indeed, the very landscape helps villagers remember such fusions because the village domain is the sum of the domains of all the villages that coalesced into a single settlement, and hence all the abandoned sites of each of the former villages were carefully remembered as proof of ownership of that domain. Sometimes even the remembered names of such abandoned village sites commemorated population losses. The village site of Labaadibaam, named "the village of the corpses," speaks for itself. We also know enough about the contexts to be certain that neither out-migration nor forced relocation is to blame for the shrinking and the subsequent fusion of villages before the 1930s.

There is no doubt then that local people had the impression that the population was declining and that the death rate was very high, and there is plenty of anecdotal evidence to confirm this. But whatever the amount of such anecdotal evidence, all of it still remains far too vague to test the assumption that the population declined by half or even more between 1885 and the early 1920s as the result of the deaths of very large numbers of people. That judgment, though, is a quantitative statement that can only be tested by quantitative means, even if these can only yield an order of magnitude. Can such evidence be found by focusing on specific causes that would document and account for such a population decline? Is this due to a truly extraordinary number of deaths?

The participants in the wider Congolese debate thought so. Let us continue to follow their example and now focus narrowly on the numbers of dead. We consider first the number of deaths that can be attributed directly to war or violence, then population losses caused by the malnutrition and general deprivation that accompanied the gathering of rubber, and finally losses caused by epidemics.

Fatalities from Violence and Deprivation

The conquest of 1899–1900 followed by the insurrection of 1904–5 caused most of the losses in warfare. There are contemporary estimates of fatalities for most major incidents, but they are neither precise nor reliable enough to yield more than an order of magnitude. The estimates for the 1899–1900 conquest are based on the following: during the first raid on Nsheng four hundred were killed, according to Schaerlaeken; during the Pyang raid, as reported by Sheppard, eighty-three right hands were gathered and additional fatalities occurred both before and after he visited the Zappo Zap camp; there is no estimate at all for Henrion's operation during which he fought several skirmishes, and his soldiers then operated for several days out of his sight. Missionaries of the American Presbyterian Christian Mission (APCM) spoke only of "hundreds of dead," "many," and "a great number." Although the number of fatalities he caused seems to have exceeded those inflicted by Schaerlaeken, we might merely assume that it equaled them.

Moreover, all the figures concern only the number of dead left on the field, not any bodies that had been carried away, nor the wounded who died later on. In general, the number of wounded in such engagements tends to be up to ten times the number of outright fatalities, and until very recently the number among them who eventually died from their injuries usually exceeded the numbers who were killed outright.

But let us accept that it only equaled that number. With all these assumptions we come to eight hundred fatalities, mostly men, in the first operation and another eight hundred, mostly men, in Henrion's attack, to which we add some two hundred or so men and women for the Zappo Zap raid, to reach a very rough total of 1,800 fatalities. This figure is only intended as an order of magnitude. According to the probable size of the whole Bushong and Kete population, these losses might perhaps amount to between 1 and 2 percent.

During the rebellion and its repression the totals reported by De Cock and by the APCM militia add up to 185 apparently counted fatalities. In addition, an unknown but substantial number of warriors were killed or wounded when they stormed the various company stations, including the Catholic mission at Bena Makima. The population fled into the bush after skirmishes with the soldiers and stayed there for weeks or even months. Losses due to lack of shelter and food certainly mounted among the injured, the old, and the pregnant. But apart from the certainty that the number of dead substantially exceeded the 185 reported, one can only guess at how much more. For the sake of calculation we assume that in this case three or four times that number is not implausible, which yields a total of 555 or 740 fatalities. This order of magnitude would then include approximately .5 to .75 percent of the whole population. If fatalities from all military operations are then added, the total still remains well under 5 percent of the Bushong and Kete populations, at least in most estimates. It follows that these outbreaks of violence cannot be the main source for a dramatic overall decline of the population.

The main contention of the Congo reformers was that the population was dying from lack of shelter and hunger. Thesiger also speculated that fatal accidents were common when men fell out of tall trees where they had been cutting the rubber vines, but considering the Kuba experience in tapping palm wine just under the crown of tall oil palms, one can dismiss this speculation out of hand. Most of the deaths stemmed from shortages of food, outright malnutrition, and lack of adequate shelter in the forests, all added to the sheer fatigue of incessant work. This, in turn, weakened people's resistance to endemic diseases such as malaria or respiratory illnesses. A woman from the village of Ibunc summed up the situation as follows in 1908: "The men go out hungry into the forest; when they come back they get sick and die."[4]

4. E. Morel, *The Enslavement* (London, 1909), 13.

Once attention is drawn to food shortages, there are indications that such shortages occur in nearly every account for the years 1904–9, including those of the Frobenius and Torday expeditions. At one point in late 1908 the latter group was so hungry that Hilton Simpson had to leave Nsheng to go on a long hunting and foraging expedition. In 1905 Frobenius was well aware of the latent famine in the Bena Makima area but had apparently forgotten all about this when he arrived at Ibanc and expected a substantial welcoming present in food from the queen mother that befitted her exalted status. She could only send him a tiny little goat, which he mockingly pretended to be only an appetizer. In order not to lose face she was then forced to send him three additional large goats that may well have been the last of her herd.

Even as late as March 1909 the situation was still so bad that de Grunne found it necessary to include the following in his set of orders to the king just before he enjoined him to denounce abuses by "private companies or their agents":

> 6. He must force his subjects to enlarge their fields and to vary the crops they produce (mainly to cultivate manioc), to raise small stock, to clean and maintain the roads, and to better build their villages.[5]

Hunger, overwork, and deprivation for almost five years probably killed a great many people, but we cannot know how many. At least we do know that these calamities affected practically all the Kuba settlements and probably caused some deaths in every village. This number obviously greatly exceeded the number of deaths caused by direct violence, even if one can argue that in many cases deprivation merely hastened a death from disease. That makes it nearly impossible to even guess how many deaths were caused by this scourge and hence how large their proportion was in the overall death rate for the period. It was certainly large, but likely still far less so than the toll taken by epidemics.

Epidemics

Between 1885 and 1920 several hitherto unknown or rare diseases appeared in the Kuba realm as byproducts of colonial agency. Most of

---

5. Fernand de Grunne, annex 1 to letter of April 12, 1909, to district commissioner. A copy of this letter can be found in Vansina Files, *Mweka to 1917 minus APCM.*

these swept with epidemic force through the region and killed more people than any military action or general violence did. The most important ones were smallpox, sleeping sickness, venereal diseases, amoebic dysentery, and the swine influenza.

The first physician to practice in Kasai arrived at the tail end of Leopoldian rule in Congo. Dr. Coppedge, a Presbyterian, opened a mission hospital at Luebo in 1906. The first laboratory able to identify specific diseases would not be established there until many years later. Yet despite the lack of any government provision for the health of Africans in Kasai, on a trip to Nsheng in 1909 the state officer in charge of Luebo found no better example for extolling the quality of European civilization to the heir of the throne than to vaunt the benefits of the European medicines and physicians who fight smallpox and sleeping sickness. Naturally he was then asked for medicines the Kuba already knew about, mostly from the Presbyterian missionary dispensary in Luebo. The heir to the throne even inquired after a set of remedies that may well have referred to some of the main diseases that plagued the Bushong at the time, namely iodium to treat wounds, quinine against malaria, Epsom salt against intestinal disease, and what the Europeans thought was an aphrodisiac but may have been medication for venereal disease. But of course the bragging officer could not provide them. Indeed, as late as the fall of 1923 a journalist remarked that there still was neither a pharmacy nor a dispensary at Nsheng. So much then for the supposed medical benefits of civilization.

Smallpox was the first killer. The dreaded disease appeared first in Kasai near Lusambo in 1887–88, where it seems to have been introduced by caravans either from Angola or from the East African coast. On that occasion the Kuba region seems to have been spared. It suffered its first dramatic outbreak in 1893 when the disease was carried from Kinshasa to the Lower Kasai and the Sankuru River on the riverboat *Stanley*. This scourge produced a huge number of victims, considering that mortality among the stricken sailors had been 41 percent. That four out of every ten patients died is not exceptional for a first outbreak of this disease (*Variola minor*) and is in line with fatalities during a less virulent but recurrent outbreak in eighteenth-century France. There 33 percent of the stricken died—including King Louis XV. As at least eight out of ten people exposed to the disease were estimated to have caught it, the mortality rate in eighteenth-century France stood at 26.6 percent of the whole population in the region in which the disease raged. It is therefore not unreasonable to estimate that just under one-third (32 percent) of the people in the Sankuru valley portion of the Kuba kingdom died during the more deadly first outbreak of the disease. That might well explain why the population density in this region was later so much lower than elsewhere. Note, however, that at most half of the whole Kuba population was exposed to the disease, and hence the overall mortality from smallpox would have been about 16 percent.

The next epidemic struck the center of the kingdom from 1900 to 1902, when it felled King Mishaape, his two successors, and many other people. Whether or not this plague was smallpox is unknown, and the evidence is too vague to allow for any quantitative estimate of the losses. Later still, several new and less devastating outbreaks of smallpox occurred until Jennerian vaccinations began to be undertaken (from 1923 onward in this region), and the number of deaths declined dramatically. Thus in 1926 yet another epidemic of smallpox came from downstream and broke out in the Sankuru region, but it caused only 653 deaths out of 7,635 cases (8.55 percent of the afflicted). The last known outbreak that struck Nsheng in 1939 also caused only a modest mortality.

Nearly a decade after the smallpox outbreak of 1893 two sets of new diseases were reported that started on a small scale and later became epidemic: sleeping sickness and venereal diseases. Sleeping sickness is caused by microorganisms called trypanosomes, transmitted by the bite of the dreaded tsetse flies (*glossina palpalis*). Those flies flourish along partly shaded riverbanks. Hence people catch the disease when they fetch water, fish near the river bank, or harvest salty grasses in the marshes for extracting salt. People who live on or near the main river-banks are the most vulnerable.

Before about 1905 the disease either did not exist or was extremely rare in Kuba land, so rare that it was not even mentioned. The first mention of someone affected by it dates to 1905, the second to 1907, although a year later British consul Thesiger could still assert that there was no epidemic of the disease. But in 1911 an outbreak of sleeping sickness was reported at Bulape, and two years later the disease seems to have become endemic mainly along the banks of the Labody River and along some salt-making sites nearby. In consequence, a number of villages moved to higher ground, away from places infested by the tsetse flies along the river banks. In stark contrast to some other parts of Kasai, however, the outbreak among the Kuba affected only a dozen or so villages, and even though nearly every person stricken by this disease died of it, the extra number of deaths did not greatly affect the overall rate of mortality for all Kuba. Hence one can disregarded sleeping sickness as a significant contributing cause to any population decline there.

That unfortunately is not the case with the venereal diseases syphilis and gonorrhea. Because they do not kill their victims on the spot and because of the lack of any medical personnel before 1906, these diseases were not mentioned when the first surge of infections must have occurred. They may perhaps have been present in the region from before the onset of the colonial era, but if so they were rare. Regardless, the first years of colonial contact caused a strong outbreak of these diseases

The *Stanley* Brings Smallpox

In his travels the Catholic missionary De Deken records the following episode.[6] In January 1893 smallpox broke out on board the riverboat *Stanley* during its trip from Kinshasa to Lusambo when the ship was steaming up the Lower Kasai and threatened to strike all those on board. At this point it was decided:

> Among two ills one had to choose the smallest, and to land all the sufferers from smallpox ashore. One left them a sufficient quantity of commodities for trade so that they could buy everything they might need for their maintenance for three months at least. The ship was to pick them up on its return from Lusambo.
>
> This sad parting caused as much painful grief among the blacks who remained on board as among the whites. For among them were their fellow workers, compatriots with whom they hoped soon to return to their native region; and the small one from the Bangala tribe, who cooked for all of them. How much did these poor blacks sob when sixteen of their comrades were put ashore, several among whom seemed to be near death. But we had to leave with hearts full of fear and sadness.
>
> Alas! We were not yet at the end of our misery! Four days later we again had to put eleven men ashore; and among them were several whom we absolutely needed to sail the ship.

Eventually the *Stanley* reached Lusambo and returned.

6. Citations from C. De Deken, *Deux ans au Congo* (Antwerp, 1900), 138–41, 142.

among the Kuba around 1900. The infertility of the royal princesses from 1900 onward that the Bushong attributed to the charm of Kwet aMbweky may have been caused by these diseases. These soon became entrenched but were only first reported as a major problem in 1910. Then silence again until we accidentally learn that King Kwet aPe died in his forties in April 1916 from the effects of an old venereal infection. The following year a short note states without any elaboration that there were many cases of venereal disease among the Bushong, less among the Ngende.

Later we learned that on the return of the Stanley to Léopoldville they had only found sixteen blacks alive of the twenty-seven that had been put ashore. The survivors returned with the ship to their country. And when we returned by the same way after our stay at Luluabourg we learned that there had been more accidents.

The inhabitants of the region, attracted by the goods which we had left with our patients, had been in contact with them and had thus carried the infection into their own villages. A year later small-pox was still raging in the Sankuru region, ten thousand Africans had succumbed to it, whole villages had been abandoned and burned by their inhabitants, who later moved to the shores of lake Leopold [II]. And when I passed along that way on the same steamer, the *Stanley*, with the nuns whom I had to accompany from Léopoldville to Luluabourg as I will tell later, the ship was immediately recognized and we were attacked with arrows and spears on the pretext that the ship had brought the plague into the country. We had to flee with all speed; but before he returned to Leo the captain found a remedy that completely succeeded. His boat had always been gray; now he had it painted black. Misled by that new dress the Africans now let the *Stanley* approach their coast to gather wood and foodstuffs without any hinder.

The mortality rate among the abandoned crew had been 41 percent. The "ten thousand" victims along the Sankuru are but a figure of speech to suggest very large numbers. The text thus tells us that in 1893 the plague had struck Kuba territory all along its northern border, the Sankuru. It is not likely, however, that the Kuba survivors, unlike the semi-nomadic fishing folk also found along the Sankuru River, fled all the way to Lake Leopold II.

The cultural patterns of their sexual relationships indicate why so many Kuba became afflicted in comparison to other societies. Divorce rates among them were so high that most women expected to be married up to seven or eight times during their lifetimes, a condition known as serial polygamy. Yet, whatever the reasons for the high prevalence of these diseases, more attention should have been paid to them because gonorrhea causes infertility and syphilis causes stillbirth. By lowering the birthrates they exert a considerable impact on population growth. That was exactly the point made by the next known commentator about these diseases. During an interview in 1923 the superior of the Catholic Scheutist missionary at Nsheng casually prophesized the extinction of the Kuba as the result of a falling birthrate caused by venereal disease induced by their own immorality: "He estimates that the Bakuba race is condemned to an imminent disappearance."[7] The ring of ineluctable fatality of the prophesy is shocking, but the very fact that the journalist who reported this did not deem this worthy of any further comment is even more so.

In 1918–19 two severe epidemics struck the Kuba realm, one shortly after the other and both spawned by World War I. This war was fought in Western Europe for four long years, while in Africa most of the German colonies including the Cameroons were rapidly overrun. Most, but not all. German East Africa, which encompassed the mainland part of Tanzania, was the exception. In and around this territory the war lasted as long as it did in Europe. One epidemic, dysentery, broke out among the legions of porters in that theater of war as the result of the unsanitary conditions that prevailed there. The second one, a pandemic of the swine flu, seems to have appeared first in a perennially overcrowded British army base in France. Because large numbers of troops continually moved in and out of the base, conditions there were extremely favorable for the uncontrolled spread of a new mutation of the influenza virus, first in the theater of war and later across the world.

In Kuba country there was first a sudden and deadly outbreak of severe dysentery, whether amoebic or bacillary we cannot say. Amoebic dysentery was the form reported as early as 1916 among the workers along the railway from the Upper Congo to the Great Lakes, a labor force then engaged in the provision of ammunition and other supplies for the military operations of the Congolese army in what was then still

---

7. Chalux, *Un an au Congo Belge* (Brussels, 1925), 247.

German East Africa. In that outbreak the mortality rate among the known stricken was about 17.5 percent, but the real rate was certainly higher. In the same year the mortality rate for all cases known in Congo was 18.9 percent. This was considered a success due to a new medication that had cut a rate of 30 percent among those treated in hospitals as late as 1915, compared to rates estimated at between 30 and 60 percent overall in 1913.

The outbreak among the central Kuba populations in 1918 followed an earlier outbreak of bacillary dysentery in Sankuru district that also seems to have come from the railway area. Carried by returning porters, the disease struck the central Kuba suddenly, although it traveled slowly from village to village. As reported by the missionaries of Bulape, absolutely everyone died in two villages while elsewhere an estimated 50 percent of the population died. In order to fight the epidemic the mission nurse organized a hospital camp to treat the afflicted, while the missionary Hezekiah M. Washburn was sent out to every village "within fifty miles" to teach people how to take care of themselves and to send the sick to the camp.

The situation worsened even more a few months later, when by the very end of 1918 a swine flu pandemic struck the region as well. That inflicted all the more fatalities as it found people already much weakened by dysentery. At this point the king lost his nerve, abandoned his capital, and fled to a distant village, but his entourage carried the infections with them. Meanwhile the epidemic became "really bad" at the capital. Some seven hundred people died there within a very short time. Panic set in, whereupon the queen mother took matters in her own hands. She called in the missionaries and obliged the king to surrender his well-known ankle ring as a token of royal authority and gave it to Washburn. Thereupon the king returned to the capital, where he fell ill from either the dysentery or the flu. He died in February 1919. During the following months both epidemics burned out.

How many people died? In the makeshift hospital organized around Bulape, where medicine was available, the mortality rate was said to have been down to 4 percent. Washburn's vague estimate of 50 percent of the whole untreated population must apply to both epidemics and is not completely out of the question. Based on the then current estimates by the health service, the mortality rate for dysentery elsewhere was estimated to have been between 30 percent and 60 percent, and the disease affected 80 percent of the population. The official estimate for the swine flu was a 4.8 percent death rate for the whole population in

Congo. But the combination of both epidemics among the Kuba means that the death rate for the flu was higher there. Given the known figures and combining both treated and untreated cases of dysentery at 30 percent of the estimated 80 percent stricken plus adding 5 percent for the flu, one arrives at around 29 percent mortality for the whole population.

Rushing to a False Conclusion

From the evidence adduced it is evident that the alleged atrocities and abuses among the Kuba claimed by the Congo Reform Association really did occur. The allegations are true, and it has also become clear that not all scandals of this nature were denounced. The situation in 1899–1900, for instance, was actually far worse than what was reported abroad. It is also evident that war and direct killing are not responsible for the most severe losses of life. Those are due to deprivation, hunger, and malnutrition, aggravated by a set of epidemics that signaled the introduction of new diseases.

What does it all add up to? We begin with 5 percent of deaths caused by the wars of conquest and the rubber regime and add the smallpox epidemic in 1893 that killed about 16 percent of the Kuba and the epidemics of 1918–19 that killed another 29 percent of them. Hence between 1885 and 1920 these factors combined to kill 50 percent of the population, and that does not even include those killed by a recurrence of smallpox or by sleeping sickness. Does this mean then that Kuba population fell by half between 1885 and 1920, presumably as a result of the introduction of colonialism, and that the declaration of the Permanent Committee was indeed accurate?

Absolutely not. The reasoning that I have followed to arrive at this conclusion is completely wrong. To begin with, one must remember that changes in the size of the same population are caused both by biological growth, which depends on mortality rates versus birthrates, and by immigration or emigration. Hitherto we have exclusively focused on unusual mortality rates and have been blind to all the rest as if the "usual" death and birthrates were exactly identical and thus canceled each other out to keep the population in balance, and as if the "extra" deaths did not include anyone at all who would have died during the current year anyway, whereas it is more than likely that most of those who were already quite fragile because of age or potentially life-threatening diseases simply lacked the biological resistance necessary to survive. Moreover, one cannot simplistically add up percentages of population losses from year to year to a grand total because the percentages refer to different total populations from year to year and because such a procedure presumes that nothing but the death rate affected population totals from year to year, as if no one was born, no one immigrated, or no one emigrated.

We can now see how those who denounce the human slaughter in Congo came to the conclusions they espoused and how they were misled. They were misled by focusing exclusively on deaths caused by violence or epidemic disease without considering any other demographic forces at work. However, that does not validate the claims of their opponents who hold that the abuses were only sporadic, exceptional, and temporary so that overall numbers of such deaths remained rather low. These opponents arrived at their conclusions by excluding most fatalities of deprivation as accidental and epidemics as irrelevant to the number of deaths. According to them these deaths—and we have seen that they were by far the largest numbers of fatalities—were irrelevant because the colonial situation had nothing to do with this. They are wrong. In part, colonialism and colonialists were involved in the spread of all the epidemics. True, the latter epidemics (smallpox, venereal disease) would have struck in any event when contacts with the outside world increased and other epidemics often concerned diseases such as sleeping sickness that were of African origin anyway. Since these diseases caused most of the fatalities, were the early colonialists uninvolved? Not according to their opponents. They correctly point out that early colonial activities are in fact the main cause for the spread of these epidemics, and that colonialists facilitated them through negligence or a complete indifference to what was happening. Indeed, it is striking to observe that all the major epidemics in the Kuba realm can be linked to colonial activities and that their spread was often facilitated by the sheer callousness of colonialists and their indifference as to the fate of Africans. The case of the *Stanley*, the demobilized porters who fell victim of dysentery in 1918, and the spread of sleeping sickness from the Lower Kasai River upstream by means of boats harboring infected tsetse flies all attest to this. Finally let us also not forget that both dysentery and swine flu were introduced in Congo by Belgian participants in World War I since the first illness incubated among army porters in East Africa and the second among British soldiers camped on French soil.

A Demographic Scenario and Its Findings

In order to correct our erroneous conclusion we must now pay attention not just to death rates but to the whole demographic panorama: birthrates, death rates, immigration, and emigration. Granted the evidence to do this is very thin and does not permit any valid quantitative findings, but the data do allow one to construct a very rough demographic scenario that leads to a more realistic conclusion. We start with a finding shared by all demographers: namely that pre-industrial tropical populations, and that includes the Kuba, were characterized both by very high birthrates and very high death rates and also by an unstable equilibrium between the two, which accounts for an alternation between booms and busts of population. Our scenario starts from this point.

Between the late 1870s and 1900 large numbers of slave immigrants swelled the Bushong and Kete populations. A majority of these were female slaves (some 6 percent of their population in the 1950s descended from them) who bore children for their masters. As a result the annual birthrate rose, as Silva Porto observed, while the death rate, although high, remained stable in most years, and the population grew from year to year.

But the trend was checked in 1893 when smallpox killed about 16 percent of the population. Because this certainly included many of the otherwise expected deaths as well, the death rate probably did not exceed the rate for the preceding or following years by that high a percentage, although the excess was still greater than 10 percent. Even though the high birthrate was not affected, the population fell during that year. But the earlier conditions returned from 1894 onward, and the continued immigration of slaves (although somewhat in decline as the result of anti-slave trade activity), allied with a very high birthrate, created a population growth that erased part and perhaps even all of the losses that occurred in 1893. Regardless, the Kuba population reached its peak in 1899.

The events from 1899 to 1910 led to a sharp drop in the immigration of slaves within Bushong and Kete communities while some Bushong and Kete also seem to have fled temporarily from central Kuba land. It also led to a drop in the birthrate as there were fewer slave women available and as a result of war, malnutrition, and abuse after 1904. Meanwhile the death rate obviously increased so that the population balance became negative in most years until and including 1909, and the population declined. The freeing of slaves in 1910 and the emigration of many among them out of Bushong and Kete communities probably caused a negative population balance for that year as well.

Between 1911 and 1917 migration does not seem to have played much of a role because of the relatively modest number of porters drafted for the army in East Africa between 1915 and 1917. Death rates seem to have stayed at a moderately high level due to a certain influence of sleeping sickness. But the birthrate was probably still falling as the result of venereal disease, despite a small influx of Luba pawn women concubines, and the population balance was slightly negative. Losses from the previous decade were certainly not completely recovered.

Then in 1918 and 1919 dysentery and the flu killed about 28 percent of the whole population. Given the nature of these diseases, the fatalities certainly included most of the deaths that would have occurred anyway. The birthrate also fell because of the deaths of so many women of childbearing age and because venereal diseases were still spreading. On the other side of the ledger, some porters returned home in 1918 from the war in East Africa, but they were the same ones who carried the epidemic of dysentery into the country. All in all, there is no doubt that the population declined dramatically—perhaps by as much as a quarter. No doubt either that by the end of 1919 the population had reached its lowest point since the onset of the colonial period around 1880.

How much lower was the population by the end of 1919 than it had been in 1880? We don't know, but the scenario shows that, contrary to expectations, the Kuba population was actually rising rather than falling during the first two decades of the colonial era. The decline began with the conquest in 1900 and then continued to 1919. One can only guess at exactly how great that decline had become by the end of 1919. One must also realize that the birthrate must be deducted from the calculated death rate of about 29 percent to obtain a population balance. Furthermore, although the losses between 1900 and 1910 were not completely made up before 1918, one could only include a fraction of the estimated 5 percent loss of that decade in the total decline of 1919, a fraction probably too small to matter much. Clearly there are too many unknowns or approximations to come to anything better than a rough estimate: in 1919 the population was perhaps as much as 25 percent less than what it was in 1900 and it was approximately 15–19 percent lower than it had been in the late 1870s.

Between 1919 and 1960 the dominant feature in the evolution of the population was no longer a very high mortality but a very low natality resulting from venereal disease. After the prediction by the superior at the Catholic missions in Nsheng in 1923, similar observations were regularly made by missionaries and administrators alike. For instance, in his report for 1927–28, the administrator of the territory remarked that Nsheng children were rare and that the demographic situation was pitiful, while shortly after World War II another Scheutist missionary wrote a polemic article about the same subject.

Actually, no one during all these many years really knew what was happening to the population for lack of accurate administrative counts. Such counts began in the 1920s, but until the very end of the colonial period they were obviously flawed, inconsistent with each other, internally contradictory, and inaccurate enough to be useless. Nevertheless, despite the unreliability of their data, the European administration in Mweka remained convinced from the 1920s to the late 1950s that the Kuba population was continually declining only as the result of a low birthrate. Thus the Belgian senators who visited the territory in 1947 were told that six out of every ten Kuba women were childless. Eventually a sample demographic study was ordered and carried out in 1951. It calculated an annual rate of population loss of .08 percent as a result of the difference between a raw death rate of 2.38 percent and a raw birthrate of 2.3 percent per year. Most worrisome of all was that there were only 75 children per 100 women, which accounts for a net birthrate of only 1.4 percent. As soon as they were known, these results were then accepted as proof of a severe population decline among the Kuba.

Could we extrapolate these figures backward to 1920 and thus obtain rough figures for the years between? No, first because this approach once again omits any consideration of either mortality rates or the changing balance of migration. Second, it is not likely that the falling birthrate remained steady over the thirty years in question. It is more likely that over time the rate of decrease increased—that is, the birthrate decreased ever more from year to year—as an ever higher percentage of women were stricken from a continually shrinking total population.

Is this whole demographic investigation worth the effort just to reach such tentative conclusions? Actually, yes. First, the evolution of a population is fundamental to its history, so it is always worthwhile to study it. Second, the investigation allowed us to expose the main flaws in the arguments used by scholars on both sides of the polemic about the Congolese demographic disaster. Moreover, in spite of being only approximate, the findings are clearly an advance over the conclusions of those authors who reject all figures in principle as unreliable—and yet then paradoxically assume that the genuine numbers of deaths must be lower than any of the figures cited. The findings are also preferable to the conclusions of those who claim that numbers do not matter anyway. After all, the findings yield at least an order of magnitude, and the scenario technique trains the spotlight onto other possible but hitherto neglected avenues for future research.

FURTHER READINGS

Fetter, Bruce, ed. *Demography from Scanty Evidence: Central Africa in the Colonial Era.* Boulder, 1990.

Gewalt, Jan Bart. "More Than Red Rubber and Figures Alone." *International Journal of African Historical Studies* 39 (2006): 471–86.

Hochschild, Adam. *King Leopold's Ghost.* Boston, 1998.

Lyons, Mary-Inez. *The Colonial Disease: A Social History of Sleeping Sickness in Northern Zaire, 1900–1940.* Cambridge, UK, 1992.

Wharton, Conway Taliaferro. *The Leopard Hunts Alone.* New York, 1927.

6

Fifty Years of Belgian Rule

An Overview

Once Belgium had taken over Congo and organized its administration in Upper Congo, further developments of the colony often seem to have been so gradual, at least until the last years before independence, that the entire half century is often perceived as a single, rather uneventful era. Indeed, some authors speak of the unfolding of events during those years as a "placid river." Yet it was not. From the perspective of 2010, one set of events stands out from all the others in Kasai between 1910 and 1959 in that it produced permanent change whereas the others did not. That event was the building of the railway from 1923 to 1928. When one then takes a closer look at the flow of time, one also finds a succession of other lesser trends. After the first years of the takeover came World War I and its sequel (1914–22). After the building of the railway came the Great Depression (1929–39), followed by World War II with its aftermath (1940–47), and then the Age of Welfare (1947–57) before the final run-up to independence. But none of these lesser trends were comparable to the two decisive turning points: the railway and the coming of independence.

Clearly one should not handle the fifty Belgian years as a single era, because that completely erases the role the railway played in Kasai's history, a role so crucial that it cannot be overlooked. Second, that also erases the nuances in the colonial experience that both colonized and colonizer underwent as the periods succeeded one another during this half century. Hence, and in spite of the importance of a thematic approach to colonial history, one also needs a general chronological overview for the history of the Belgian Congo in general. This chapter does that, and therefore the Kuba do not occupy center stage in it. But the chapter focuses on the colonial context overall as a prelude for the following five thematic chapters that are devoted to Kuba experiences during the same period.

The Coming of the Railway

Years before Belgium took over Congo, the vast mineral wealth of Katanga and parts of Kasai had been recognized, and several well-financed companies were set up in 1906 to exploit it. They represented the decisive investment in the colony by some of the great international holdings. Belgium's own holding in that league, the Société générale, launched not only the Mining Union for Upper Katanga to exploit Katanga's minerals but also the Bas-Congo-Katanga (BCK) Railway Company, as it had been appreciated from the start that a railway from Katanga to Matadi was needed in order to export the minerals along a wholly "national" Congolese route rather than to depend on routes running through other colonies. The BCK's job would be to build and run such a railway.

As a result of these financial commitments in 1906, the landscape of Upper Katanga was completely transformed during the 1910s: its first cities appeared, its first industrial scale mines were opened, and its first railroads were built. Still the BCK project was a huge job, so big that the state and the BCK soon decided to build the railway in two stages. A first section was to connect Bukama temporarily to a point on the Kasai River from which freight could be transferred all year round to be shipped to Kinshasa. That section would carry both food and labor from Kasai to the industrial belt and was expected to be immediately profitable. Once this was finished, the second section from that point on the Kasai River to the Lower Congo would follow. But the outbreak of World War I directed Belgian priorities elsewhere, and plans for the BCK railway were put on hold except for further prospecting to find the most appropriate line of rail.

After the war, prospecting resumed. By 1922 most of the railroad line had been set out, but Odon Jadot, the engineer in charge of the prospecting team, was dissatisfied with Djoko Punda (Charlesville) as the provisional terminus on the Kasai River, because he questioned whether the water would be deep enough for shipping all year round.

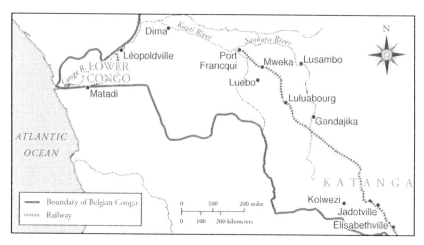

The Bas-Congo-Katanga Railway

Up to that point none of the projected railway lines had even come close to the Kuba kingdom, let alone run through it. Now, however, Jadot prospected a new route from central Kasai to Ilebo (soon to be called Port Francqui) near the junction of the Kasai and Sankuru rivers. But when he came from the southeast to the Kuba lands he found himself confronted by almost two hundred miles of lush equatorial forests. Nevertheless he persevered, and by year's end it was this route that was adopted by both the government and the company. Thus the railway line ended up bisecting the kingdom from its far southeast to its furthest point northwest.

Building a railway was a major enterprise that had to be very carefully planned. It required the recruitment of large numbers of workers who had to be brought to the site, housed, fed, and provided with some medical care. Planning errors were bound to result in huge cost overruns and in large numbers of fatalities as had happened on other railways. Moreover, at the same time access roads had to be built all along the rail line, including one from Luebo to the railway, while planners also had to take into account the requirements of the other large modern company in the region, the Forminière, which exploited diamonds at Tshikapa south of Luebo. Hence close cooperation was required between the territorial administration and the railway company in order to achieve the goal. The administration collaborated wholeheartedly.

As a result it took only five years to build the railway and it was built without major loss of life. It was remarkable at that time, for instance, that right at the outset in 1923 an outbreak of smallpox in the camps for laborers at Ilebo and Mweka could be immediately controlled and that it was followed without delay by vaccination campaigns among the navvies (unskilled laborers), a campaign efficient enough to prevent any further recurrence of the disease during construction later on. And yet very large numbers of people were involved. To begin with, most of the work was carried out by teams equipped with only hand tools and wheel barrows without benefit of heavy machinery. At the height of the operations one counted fifteen thousand laborers. In addition, large numbers of other people were called upon to carry foodstuffs to the railroad line, while still others were drafted to build the necessary access roads. And yet, there were no further epidemics, and contrary to what had always happened earlier during the construction of other railways in Congo, there were no losses from malnutrition or exhaustion.

In the Kuba area the job consisted of three different and successive operations: to clear the forest, to prepare the railway bed and build earthworks as required, and to lay the rail. Each of these operations was to be carried out by different teams. It was obvious that the Kuba king could not refuse to provide labor, but it was also obvious that if he did so efficiently he would benefit from it. So the king—and his councils no doubt—negotiated the following deal. He would provide all the lumberjacks needed for clearing the forests, and in addition the Kuba would grow and deliver enough surplus manioc and maize to feed the whole labor force very cheaply. In return, they would be exempt from providing any additional labor for any of the other operations on the railway. That was the agreement, and it was carried out as stated.

Yet in addition to this the Kuba continued to provide whatever labor the state required in order to build or maintain roads, rest houses, and even auxiliary airfields. On top of that they still had to provide palm oil and kernels or other products for sale to trading companies such as the Compagnie du Kasai in order to earn the money with which to pay their taxes. The overload brought by the building of the BCK during these years was huge, and villagers everywhere were under a great deal of stress as they struggled to meet colonial expectations, a stress that sometimes led to open rebellion but more often found expression in the creation of movements to restore harmony. No wonder then that any further impositions, even relatively minor ones, could push villagers beyond the limits of their endurance and into rebellion, even though such uprisings remained rare, sporadic, and minor.

The uprising in the Kete town of Kampungu in 1926 is a case in point. The administrator of the Kuba territory tells us that it was triggered when a state agent acting on behalf of the state official delegated to the BCK suddenly appeared to demand lumberjacks for the clearing of the path of the railroad. The villagers retorted that they would no longer obey orders from the authorities in Nsheng. They were especially exasperated by the extortions of the king's envoys there, and they reeled under the never-ending demands by state agents for raw construction materials destined to the construction of houses in Luebo, and by European traders there who continually wanted to obtain more palm oil and kernel. First the palm fruit had to be cut by the men, and then the oil and the kernels were extracted and processed by women. That was a time-consuming task for which women had to find extra time despite their other responsibilities, including the growing and processing of extra food crops. Still, this task was essential because it provided most of the cash with which to pay the state's taxes.

Indeed, the burden was so heavy that wherever possible Kete youth fled to the refuge of mission stations to be exempt from such demands while some Kete villages around Kampungu proposed to declare themselves to be the exclusive dependants of one or another expatriate trader in Luebo and thereby to free themselves from all other obligations. This uprising was rapidly quelled, and after negotiation the Kete again began to provide construction materials, as well as to build guest houses in their most important settlements and to repair the road from Luebo to Mweka. But they don't seem to have sent more lumberjacks to the railway line.

The clearing of the forest for the rail line was hard and dangerous work that resulted in the creation of a huge straight-edged gash of some 120 feet wide, exposing a completely bare soil that ran like a trench through the closed canopy of the rainforests for almost two hundred miles. Visitors found the site so impressive that they often photographed it, yet no one at the time seems to have given any thought to what this did to the local environments. In the next two decades intensive agriculture along the rail line was to widen the gash to a mile or so of nearly exhausted soil while at the same time parts of the adjacent forests were practically clear-cut for timber with very little replanting. In the early 1950s the colonizers finally became aware of the problem, but by then the damage seemed irreversible. Today even high-altitude satellite

Deforestation caused by the railway (HP.1961.5.201, collection RMCA Tervuren; anonymous photo, © RMCA Tervuren)

pictures show the effects. The trench in the unbroken canopy of the forest has become a wide channel of open country dividing the still impressive forests to its north from its remaining shreds to its south.

The completion of the railway in 1928 was considered to be such an important feat that Albert and Elisabeth, the king and queen of Belgium, traveled to Congo to inaugurate the line. There they stopped at the station of Domiongo (Ndoom aIyong) near Nsheng to receive homage from King Kwet Mabinc and his court. On that occasion the king claimed that he had built the railway. While colonials scoffed at the idea, his people knew exactly what he was talking about. King Albert was impressed, thanked him, and shook his hand, a highly significant gesture in a racist colony.

Although the railway certainly was the decisive element in the transformation of Kasai from backwater to the granary and labor reservoir of Katanga, it was not the only one. During that decade international business was booming, and companies such as the Compagnie du Kasai were making money hand over fist, which in turn brought much tax revenue to the state coffers. All this allowed for expanded investment. The first modern roads appeared in Kasai and along with them the first cars and trucks. The Presbyterian missionaries introduced the first motorbikes in 1919 or 1920. In 1923 the district of Kasai boasted only one car and one road for it to travel on, but by 1926 there were trunk roads while cars—Ford Model T's for the most part—and trucks were becoming common. By then porterage began to be outlawed along the major highways. In 1925 the first regular airline from Léopoldville to Elisabethville was launched when the planes reached Luebo.

The state was able to hire more territorial and agricultural personnel and carry out its plans for the definitive organization of the local courts and the setting up of local treasuries. Thus by January 1929 the territory of the Bakuba boasted six territorial agents and one agronomist. It had just set up a principal tribunal at Nsheng and was ready to start three lesser ones at Mweka, Port Francqui, and Bena Makima, while it was also on the verge of launching a chiefdom treasury in Nsheng.

However, the state continued to leave education in the hands of the religious congregations, with particularly unfortunate results for the Bushong. The district commissioner forced the Protestants to abandon their planned mission at Nsheng in 1923 because of the sharp rivalry between Presbyterians and Catholics there, a rivalry that was threatening the peace at the capital. Because there already was a Catholic mission in town, the proposed Presbyterian establishment was banned. Then in 1927 the Catholics also abandoned their mission at Nsheng supposedly because of the lack of converts but actually because of continuing quarrels between the missionaries and the king. Moreover, Tshiluba was the language used by the Catholic mission for all its teaching, while Bushong was only used for the most elementary grades by the Protestants. This constituted a handicap for speakers of languages other than Tshiluba, such as Kete, and it was especially difficult for Bushong children whose own tongue was quite different from Tshiluba. Thus this language policy greatly hindered their access to even elementary levels of Western-style education.

General health care was also left to private initiative, in this case religious congregations and the major industrial companies, while the state only set up mobile medical units to fight sleeping sickness and later other endemics such as leprosy. Although there had been a full-fledged Presbyterian hospital at Luebo since 1916 within the Kuba realm proper, a dispensary at the Presbyterian mission in Bulape only became a true hospital in 1932–33. At Nsheng there was not even a rudimentary dispensary until the late 1920s. While the hospitals gave many Kete at least some access to Western health care, it left most Bushong and other Kuba to their own devices and their own initiatives.

The Great Depression

Barely a year or so after the triumphal inauguration of the railway, Congo was suddenly hit by the worldwide Great Depression of 1929, which reached its nadir in 1934. Thus its impact occurred almost simultaneously with the momentous social and economic effects of the new railway and combined with it to create a wholly different climate from that of the booming 1920s. We first discuss the lasting effects of the railway before we turn to the impact of the Great Depression itself.

The railway was the major turning point in the colonial history of both Kasai and the Kuba kingdom in particular because it decisively rearranged the geography of these lands. In earlier times this whole region had been oriented toward Kinshasa. From 1886 until 1928 travel from Kinshasa to southern Congo had been by river as far upstream as Lusambo or Luebo and then overland by caravan. The cost of carrying freight by water was but a fraction of its cost by caravan, and it usually took about as much time to travel from industrializing Katanga to Lusambo or Luebo as it took to travel there from Léopoldville. The railway changed all of that. From 1928 onward Ilebo (soon to be Port Francqui) was suddenly only three days away from Elisabethville, five times closer than it was to Léopoldville, and thus all of Kasai became the hinterland of Katanga. Thanks to the railway the Kuba region turned into a major granary for the copper belt there while central Kasai became its main reservoir of labor. Within the Kuba lands the BCK created a major station for the control of traffic and for repairs at the European post called Mweka near the Bushong village Mwek.

Only one and a half years after the opening of the line the European post at Mweka had become so important that the capital of the territory of the Bakuba was moved there from Nsheng, and soon Mweka began to rival Luebo. Meanwhile further south a new Luluabourg was founded along the rail line and steadily grew into a city of major importance at the expense of Lusambo to the point that in 1949 the capital of Kasai province was moved from Lusambo to Luluabourg. Elsewhere also and all along its whole length the railway reorganized space everywhere in Kasai, and today the imprint of that reorganization of space is still more evident.

The construction of the line had absorbed all available Luba and Lulua labor in and around the Kuba lands. Once the job was done, the navvies settled all along the rail line while the inhabitants of what had

Inauguration of the railway at Mweka, July 7, 1928 (HP.1961.8.120, collection RMCA Tervuren; anonymous photo, © RMCA Tervuren)

earlier been the main Luba/Lulua enclaves in the south resettled along the road from Luebo to Mweka. By 1929 the administration discovered that all of a sudden there now existed a ribbon of 123 almost contiguous Luba or Lulua settlements strung out along the railroad from the southeast border of the territory nearly to Port Francqui and along the motor road from Mweka to Luebo as well. These new settlements formed a huge letter T right across the southern half of the whole territory. At the same time nearly all the older small Luba/Lulua agglomerations scattered elsewhere in Kuba land vanished as their inhabitants migrated to the rail line. From 1930 onward this T became the commercial and economic backbone of the whole territory. Nearly all the new commercial centers arose along the T, and all the former roads or paths within the region were reoriented in relation to it, so that the human geography of the territory became completely different after 1928 from what it had been earlier.

In effect, the Luba/Lulua were now almost completely separated socially and culturally from the Kuba and were no longer influenced by them as they had been in earlier days. By now they not only differed from the rural Kuba villagers in their language (Tshiluba) and in some

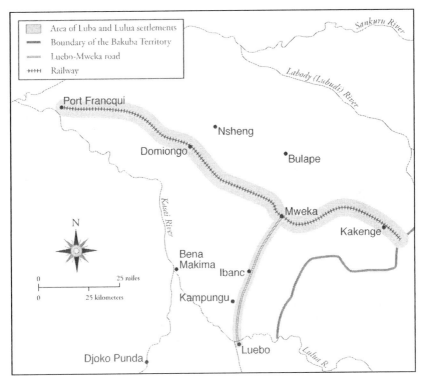

Luba and Lulua settlements in the kingdom, ca. 1930

of their customs, as had been the case in the past, but their new aspirations quickly led them further away from the Kuba way of life. Under the motto *"Lupetu lulue!"* (Let wealth come!) these people sought to be fully integrated into the money economy as wage laborers whenever possible and otherwise to earn money as cash-cropping peasants or petty traders. They did not organize themselves into agglomerations with a stable population and with their own institutions of collective governance. They were far too individualistic for that. They easily converted to Christianity, accepted leadership from Catholic catechists or Presbyterian evangelists, and consequently had access to schools. Eager to learn, they strove to imitate the colonizer's daily lifestyle as much as they could afford. While the colonizers thought of them as "uprooted" or "living in anarchy" and deplored the situation, these people made themselves at home in the new colonial world of the railway and the main motor road with its monetary economy and its fluctuating labor requirements.

"Administrator at Work" by Djilatendo, 1930–32 (Thiry, *A la recherche de la peinture nègre*, n.d.)

In contrast, the rural Kuba continued to live in their still well-organized villages of farmers and local artisans. To cope with common problems they continued to think and act as members of various collectivities ranging from clan section to village, chiefdom, and kingdom, rather than as individuals. In economic terms they eschewed wage labor as much as possible, and wherever feasible they stuck to the production of food crops and local crafts such as raffia cloth, pottery, carved objects, or metal products, which they exchanged at local markets or sold for money as curios for foreigners. They were not much attracted by the missions, nor were most of them targeted as converts by the missionaries. Hence there were not all that many village schools either. All of this earned them the reputation of being "backward people." Yet, actually, they were able to keep their distances from the modern world in such great numbers only because the Luba/Lulua immigrants in their midst fulfilled nearly all the needs for wage labor in the region.

Already from the early 1930s onward the great difference between these two populations was so evident that most lower-rank territorial officials in Mweka were assigned to one of the populations rather than the other. Moreover, they reacted very differently to Kuba and to Luba/Lulua. For instance, agent Raymond Beeldens, who worked in the Kuba milieu and at the capital, continued to value and collect Kuba art objects and even managed to obtain a royal *ndop* statue early in 1934. Meanwhile agent Georges Thiry, who worked at the post of Mweka in a Luba/Lulua milieu, "discovered" Djilatendo, a Luba/Lulua tailor and painter living near Ibanc in 1930, became his patron, and promoted him as one of the two earliest artists to produce modern Congolese painting. The separation between both populations, even at this early date, was already so extreme that no one at the capital seems to have been aware of Djilatendo's existence, while the latter never represented anything Kuba in his figurative painting although his geometric art was inspired by some of the less complex Kuba decorative patterns.

While the effects of the building of the railway were becoming apparent, the Great Depression was upsetting all the usual routines. To show its impact let us start with the diary of the Compagnie du Kasai at its headquarters in Dima that recorded the movements of company ships and of notable personalities on the Kasai River. Although the stock market in New York crashed first in September and then decisively in October 1929, the first reference to such events occurs here only on March 31, 1930, when the diarist suddenly departs from his usual routine to record market quotations and does so in red ink. He then

Djilatendo and
the Colonial Situation

Djilatendo was a Lulua tailor who left Luluabourg to settle at
Ibanc in the later 1920s.[1] His specialty was the manufacture of
small aprons approved by the Catholic missionaries as decent
wear for the otherwise scantily clad Lulua women. He had decorated the outside wall of his house along the road to Luebo with a
painting of soldiers on the march. In 1930 this drew the attention
of Georges Thiry, a territorial agent recently posted at Mweka
who fancied himself as a "explorer-poet" in search of artistic tal-
ent, rather than as a mere bureaucrat, and even though his writings betray the arrogant and racist attitudes of his fellow colonialists so common at the time, Thiry was so impressed by the wall
painting that he became Djilatendo's patron. He provided him
with paper and paints, encouraged him to paint some modern
things, and bought all his finished works, figurative or not. He then
sent the paintings to a friend in Brussels for exhibition and sale.
But at the time they did not attract much attention. All but forgotten, Djilatendo was still living at Ibanc in 1953. He was then exhib-
iting paintings on long strips of cloth that were replica's of Kuba
geometric designs, but he was not selling anything. Today, however,
he is hailed as one of the first two painters who created modern
Congolese art.

Djilatendo painted both geometric panels and figurative
scenes. Some of the latter works are the result of Thiry's suggestions about modern scenes. They show contemporary items such
as a car, a riverboat, a plane being serviced at Luebo, a bicycle, or
a sharp-nosed foreign lady with high heels and an umbrella—all
sorts of things he had seen—but no train! The precise way he
interprets such items fascinates the historian because it tells a

---

1. Georges Thiry, *A la recherche de la peinture nègre (Les peintres naïfs congolais Lubaki et
Djilatendo)* (Liège, 1982), 25–45 (citation 31); for a full catalogue of the works see Kathrin
Langenohl, *"Repeat When Necessary": Zum Verhaltnis von Tradition und Moderne im Malerischen
Werk Tshelatendes (Djilatendo), Belgisch Congo* (Frankfurt, 1999).

good deal about the impression these products of the most modern technological creations left on those who aspired to be part of that world. His specific interpretations of the colonial activities around him are particularly telling: works such as the massive bearded Catholic missionaries smoking huge briar pipes, administrators crouched over a typewriter or chatting over drinks, sharp-nosed men and ladies walking arm in arm (probably Protestant missionaries), a state post with a flag, and a column of soldiers. While he obviously pokes some fun at the weaknesses of different sorts of colonial personages, there seems to be some underlying admiration, while none of the portrayals, not even the military scenes, seem to criticize colonialism in any way. But how could it be otherwise?

Moreover, his view of *modern* was not limited to such topics: all the personages in his paintings wear modern clothes (an advertisement for his tailoring?) and accessories with the exception only of a few mythical heroes. By these signs they all reveal themselves to be Luba or Lulua. In his whole work no person wears anything that would identify him or her as Kuba. One might imagine that even in Ibanc Djilatendo never saw any Bushong or Kete at all, were it not for his geometric pieces. Even so, his art does document the then-still-novel abyss between the world of the Kuba and that of the Luba/Lulua. Djilatendo's oeuvre thus portrays the quasi-urban modern lifestyle in the region and illustrates Thiry's off-the-cuff remark about Mweka: "The Lulua peoples who live in this region."

Thiry was also responsible for one of the earliest modern literary works from Congo: Badibanga's collection of stories illustrated by Djilatendo and published as *The Elephant Who Walked on Eggs* (Brussels, 1931). Badibanga was a Luba tailor from Luluabourg, educated by the Catholic missionaries there who had just settled at Mweka. At Thiry's suggestion, he started to collect stories ("fables") among the local Luba and Lulua settlers. Several clerks from the administration and even Thiry's mistress soon joined the quest. Again it is striking to note that despite the location of Mweka near Bushong and Kete villages, only one of these stories was gathered among them by Badibanga and his friends. Nearly all of them stem from the almost brand-new Lulua or Luba settlements along the rail line or the road to Luebo.

continued to do so fairly frequently at later dates to record falling prices. Here are the first such mentions:

> 31 March: Cable A. C. palmkernels 14 £ Antwerp; palmoil 16 £ Léo[poldville]
> 10 May: Cable A. C. palmkernels £ 14.15 Antwerp; palmoil £ 16 Kin[shasa]
> 11 June: Cable A. C. palmkernels Antwerp 13£; palmoil Kin[shasa] £ 12. Stop all bulk purchases of palmoil.
> [. . .]
> [and the following year]
> 19 May 1931 Palmoil 5£ 16s, palmkernels 9 £ 15
> [. . .]
> [and finally]
> 14 April 1933 at Antwerp palmkernels francs 975 and palmoil francs 1375 at Antwerp (delivered at Kin[shasa] francs 740). What a disaster![2]

The prices continued to fall right through October 1933 before hitting rock bottom. At first the company tried to cope with falling prices by buying less and cutting costs. They used fewer ships, dismissed some of their European personnel, and paid less to African producers. The latter reacted with a boycott with the inevitable result that they did not have the wherewithal to pay their taxes. Then the company began to rely on state agents to force Africans to produce more palm products than before and at lower prices to make up in volume what was lost in value. State agents, eager to collect taxes, obliged. Among the Bushong and the Luba/Lulua at Domiongo on the rail line, sabotage was the answer. The diarist of the company notes on July 24, 1931, that 57 percent of palm kernels were defective and 48 percent of the palm oil was spoiled. In the Kwilu area to the west the reaction was worse. There a large-scale revolt had broken out by June 1931, a revolt caused in large part by the ill treatment of palm fruit cutters by the Huilever Company (HCB). Its brutal repression was followed by a general malaise not only in Kwilu but in large parts of Kasai as well.

At the same time attempts were made by state agronomists to multiply large artificial palm groves and to have the company disseminate oil presses for producing palm oil, both of which greatly improved productivity per worker. In addition to this the administration was also

2. Compagnie du Kasai, Dima Archives: *Memento* 1930, 1931, 1933.

mobilizing the local populations to build more local roads in order to re-move the palm products more efficiently by truck rather than by porters.

As prices continued to fall, the son of the company's president passed through Dima on October 18, 1933. From his indiscretions the diarist learned that the district commissioners in whose territories the company operated complained that it did not pay enough to its palm fruit cutters, that it did not keep its promises, and that it quarreled more and more with its own European agents. The district commissioners had jointly complained to Brussels, with the result that the president of the company had recently been summoned three times by the minister of colonies about these questions. This was the bottom, however, for from 1934 onward the prices paid for palm products stabilized and then slowly began to rise.

The Great Depression caused similar ravages everywhere else in Congo as prices dropped not just for palm products but for every single commodity except gold. The reactions of other companies were gener-ally similar to those of the Compagnie du Kasai: cutbacks in produc-tion, a steep decline in prices paid to African producers, a subsequent boycott by the producers, followed by the threat or the use of force to compel Africans to steadily increase production in order to make up for falling prices. This trend was accompanied by attempts to increase pro-ductivity, especially the construction of roads to transport cash crops such as cotton instead of continuing to rely on porterage as well as re-placing the gathering products with raising them on plantations. Mean-while in industrial Katanga the depression caused layoffs on a large scale and during a few years the process of urbanization there reversed itself and then stagnated almost until the outbreak of World War II.

The administration suffered nearly as much as the companies did be-cause its income from taxation fell dramatically. Hence, it also dismissed some European personnel and exploited local Africans as much as pos-sible. Then in 1933 it reorganized all its territorial, judicial, and financial institutions in a drive to cut expenses. The very creation of a province of Kasai in that year was part of that drive. Still it was typical for the terri-tory of the Bakuba that the territorial reforms of 1933 were not formally applied there until twelve years later. Only in 1945 were the Luba/Lulua immigrant populations along the rail line finally detached from the Kuba chiefdom and organized into three separate sectors of their own.

During the Great Depression and the recovery that followed, the tenor of the overall colonial climate was very different from what it had been in the confident 1920s. The accent now lay on the ruthless exploitation of rural villages to raise the production of cash crops under the immediate supervision of agronomists rather than territorial agents. Yet, at the same time, the higher echelons of the administration continually feared widespread insurrections by frustrated villagers organized

---

An Agronomist's Report
for December 1935

The following is a monthly report about the tasks accomplished by the adjunct agronomist H. Marien during the month of December 1935.[3]

> During the month of December part of my sector [Mweka] and a part of the sector Kakenge have been visited:
> The roads of Mweka-Bwa [=Bakwa] Loshi (Luebo) 40 km, Mweka-Bwa Kashi (Kakenge) 30 km have been cleared from vegetation by the natives of the villages over a few km [each village].
> The Luebo and Domiongo roads have been widened to 6 meters by the road workers.
> 38,980 small one year old palm trees, from Mweka's nurseries have been divided between the villages along the roads of Luebo and Kakenge, each of which in this way own their small nursery of "FUTSHI" palm trees.
> [There follow two paragraphs listing the villages and the quantities of trees given to them. All these villages are along the railway and seem to be inhabited by Luba or Lulua.]
> 110,000 seeds of palm trees have been sown at Mweka of which 90,000 seeds of "FUTSHI" palm trees and 20,000 seeds of improved palm trees VAR/TENERA stemming from INEAC [National Institute for Agricultural Research].
> From the 10,000 seeds of palm trees from Yangambi, INEAC sown in January 1935, only 700 had sprouted.
> From the 100,000 seeds of "FUTSHI" palm trees gathered in the forests by the natives from the vicinity of Mweka and sown in December 1934 about 6,500 have sprouted. Those are the young palm trees that have been distributed to the villages of the Mweka Sector.

---

3. Province du Kasai, *Dossier sectes secrètes: Lukoshi.* H. Marien's monthly report, December 1935.

by shadowy secret societies under the mask of religious revivals. But whereas religious revivals were common, active anticolonial organizations were quite rare. See "An Agronomist's Report for December 1935" for text that is typical for the climate during these years.

The forest clearings for plantations of palm trees in the villages on the Luebo road are finished, which brings the number of Ha [hectares] cleared to 240 [about 500 acres].

There have been delimited at Bna [Bena] Longo 100 Ha, Bwa [Bakwa] Nongo One 100 Ha, Bwa Nongo Two 160 Ha, Bwa Kashi 60 Ha for man made plantations of palm trees.

The lands for the immigrated villages have been provided with boundaries, Bakwanga 3,680 Ha, [of which] $^9/_{10}$ in savannas, Bwa Mulumba 1,840 Ha, Bwa Loshi 1,600 Ha.

Delimitation of the parcels for artificial plantations for palm trees in the villages Bakwanga 76 Ha, Bwa Mulumba 60 Ha, Bwa Loshi 60 Ha.

The construction of three guest houses has been started, 1 at Dibanda, 1 at Bwa Nongo, 1 at Bulongo (Kwadi).

I have launched an enquiry in the Bakuba [Bushong] villages of Sonombuie [Shoong aMbooy], Bulongo [Buloong], Ngete [Nget], Yengembana [Yeeng iMbaan?] about the Bwanga [charm] "LUKOSHI" [Lakosh]. They all admit to have adopted it.

Taxes: 69 counters IC [direct tax] 1925, 14 counters IS [supplementary tax] 1935, 4 counters IC 1934, 6 counters IS 1934, 9 PPA [main tax].

There follow three paragraphs about amounts of palm seeds gathered, distributed, and planted in various villages, about young "FUTSHI" palm trees from the Budimbu nursery distributed to a long list of villages along the railway line, and about 1,300 hectares of forest set aside for future plantations of palm trees in the same general area. The report then mentions the clearing of a road and ends with another four paragraphs detailing amounts of palm seedlings distributed in the east of the territory from two nurseries there. However, Delcroix, a local Belgian settler there, illegally took most of the plants from the nursery that Marien had established in 1934. Then unbeknownst to Delcroix the villagers of Muango had planted manioc in the forest he had cleared for establishing his palm tree plantation.

Although economic recovery was very slow, Africans in the territory of the Bakuba as well as colonialists were quite conscious of it by 1936. In that year Congo's exports doubled in quantity compared to 1932, and by 1939 they were close in value to what they had been ten years earlier. But there was no letup in the demand for cash crops or labor, mainly for the roads, and hence the rural climate did not change. Thus in the territory of the Bakuba cultivation of cotton, which had been imposed during the depths of the depression and had produced a first crop in 1933, continued to be imposed without any letup for the next nine years. Still, the improving conditions allowed colonial organizations to take a few modest initiatives after 1934. For the Kuba the most important one was the reopening of several mission stations in their territory by the Josephite order, especially the one at the capital in 1937, and the arrival there a year later of a group of nuns of the order the Canonnesses of St. Augustine to set up a health service and open a girls' school. From then on the children in the capital finally had access to six years of primary education including the teaching of French by members of an order whose specialty was teaching.

World War II and the Congo

On September 3, 1939, World War II broke out. It immediately made communications with Belgium quite difficult. After Belgium was overrun in May 1940, Congo's governor general decided to continue the war, and all links between the metropole and the colony were severed except for communications with a rudimentary Belgian government in exile in London. As a result a number of Belgians in the colony were called up for military service while most of the others were blocked in the colony without any home leave during the whole war from 1940 to 1945. Nor were there any new recruits. On top of that, this smaller number of agents soon had to cope with exceptional demands of the war effort.

In practice Congo became an Anglo-American dependency for the duration of the war. One expeditionary force of the Congolese army joined British troops in the conquest of Ethiopia from the Italians, while another unit was sent first to Nigeria and then to North Africa. Some Bushong soldiers, for instance, were stationed for a while in Jerusalem. A small number of Congolese even reached Burma.

Congo's main contribution to the Allies did not really get underway until 1942. It was an all-out war effort to produce ever more essential commodities for the war such as rubber for tires, copal, copper, and groundnuts for munitions, uranium for the atom bomb, as well as cobalt, palm oil, cotton, and foodstuffs. Most of the effort and stress that accompanied it fell on the African populations. Usually they were simply ordered to produce this or that, whether or not they had done so earlier. The Bushong, however, were given a choice between cotton or rubber plus groundnuts. Despite the painful memories about rubber, they chose this option as the lesser of two evils. While exports rose as a result of such impositions, imports for consumption became less abundant and were often of lower quality than before, and their prices rose sharply.

A Soldier's Letter to the King

In the Field 26 June 1942

To My Chief, LUKENGO, Bope-Tshuala.

Many greetings to you and to MINGASHANGA-BEKI, many greetings to him from all of us in Mil .53B.M.[1] Our status is *that we are* those from Mweka first regiment, all those who are soldiers [from first] battalion from Mweka, second battalion from Lulua-bourg, eighth battalion from Tshoko—Punda [Djoko Punda was west of Luebo]. I am telling once more: why is it that we sent letters to you and have received no letter [in return]? No news has reached us until now. Finally it is very discouraging . . .

Accept many greetings from

Me

B O P E Alphonse

Mil 53 B.M.[1]

[signed]

I am sending you two newspapers, one photograph of a battle.[4]

As was their practice, military censors probably destroyed the papers and the photo.

---

4. Hymans Papers of King Bop Mabinc maKyeen, 1942 (available at the Memorial Library of the University of Wisconsin–Madison). Idiomatic Tshiluba and French. Slightly damaged. Dots indicate a gap in the text, and italics indicate reconstructed words.

In this climate of stress and censure generated by the unusual circumstances, panicky rumors of all kinds flourished among both colonizers and colonized. Europeans believed that Africans were planning to massacre all of them, while African soldiers believed that vaccinations were being used to kill a number of them so they could then be turned into tins of corned beef. From industrial Katanga rumors spread all along the rail line in Kasai about so-called Mitumbula, African servants of European cannibals who were lurking about at night searching to kidnap Africans to be fattened up and eaten. Even after the conclusion of the war and almost until independence, fear of these Mitumbula continued to spread among villagers in the countryside, including most of the Kuba country.

After Congolese noncommissioned officer veterans returned to Katanga and Kasai and saw how badly they were treated by the colonial officers, they plotted a rebellion that was to break out in every major city along the railway from Luluabourg to Elisabethville. They even contacted the "main chiefs" to gauge their support for an insurrection and more than likely included the Kuba king. None of the chiefs betrayed the plotters, even though none seems to have promised them much support. Eventually only the troops at Luluabourg rebelled in early February 1944, and it was a bloodless sort of rebellion that looked more like a strike than an insurrection. Nevertheless, the whole affair shook up the government's complacency and provoked boisterous warlike martial posturing by the Katangese settlers, while in Kasai the rumor flew around that the American Presbyterian Christian Mission (APCM) had suddenly decided to import African American missionaries in order to survive a general takeover by Africans.

The earliest known expression of modern Congolese nationalism was part of the planned uprising in Elisabethville. It is found in a letter addressed to "the representative of the U.S. army in Congo" written by Lievin Kalubi, a clerk of Luba Kasai origin on behalf of the noncommissioned veterans. Some of the most relevant passages follow.

> This is why Mister representative we address your person to ask by means of this short report whether the Black of the Congo does not have the human right like any other race in order to defend its cause and its common interests without of course causing injury to any other race. Ever since the onset of this cruel worldwide conflict the great powers of Europe and America have always spoken of the freedom of the nations and of the individual in all domains without distinction of race nor color in the whole world. The

Atlantic charter signed by the high great representatives of the two nations, England and the United States, gives to understand that this war is a war for freedom for the strong and for the weak, yes even for the least human being who cannot yet manage on his own. This freedom which is summarized in four main points which you know best, Sir, does not seem to be made for the Blacks, particularly for those of central Congo, because for the least objection made by him, even if justified, the Congolese native deserves the most severe punishment as it is said that the Black person has no right to speak. . . .

If the Black of the Congo is not a person like anyone else, why then ask him to cooperate to the war effort be it the agricultural or the industrial one? Why mobilize him to be a soldier, to build, to create airfields for warplanes, to care for and to transport the wounded? why?

Despite all of this a person has no value, remains without any dignity or any consideration in the eyes of the European who calls him monkey, imbecile, idiot, for whom there is neither law nor justice. Yet we do know that our war effort is required and appreciated by all the nations allied against the Nazi regime and its satellites. If ever the native of the Belgian Congo refuses to work for this necessary endeavor this would have serious consequences for all the nations, including England and the United States to the detriment of the rapid liberation of the mother-country, Belgium.[5]

Thus by 1943 the war had spawned the first stirrings of pan-Congolese nationalism. As could have been expected, Congolese nationalism developed first in the army because soldiers coming from all over the Congo served together and were moved from post to post all over the country as well. When returning veterans realized that nothing in the colonial relationship had changed despite all the promises made during the fighting, their grievances burst into protest. Besides this the whole episode also made it clear to colonial consciousness that there now existed a whole class of Western-educated Congolese (*évolué*) in the country, a class that could no longer be ignored but had to be won over.

Meanwhile the failure of the plot did not relieve the general malaise and stress among civilians, as wages remained low, essential clothing

5. Jean LucVellut, "Le Katanga industriel en 1944: Malaises et anxieties dans la société coloniale," in *Le Congo belge durant la seconde guerre mondiale: Receuil d'études*, ed. Jean Stengers (Brussels, 1983), 504–6.

and tools were lacking in the shops, and inflation rose rapidly. Reports by district commissioners concerning the main towns in Kasai, including Luebo, made clear the discontent of the urban population as well as their clamor for relief. In Lower Congo the tension led to a general strike by Africans at Matadi in 1945. The war effort only ended in the fall of that year. Only then could the exhausted country begin to recover, as most of the old guard returned on leave to Europe, and a new generation of colonials took over while economic conditions gradually improved before entering a new boom.

Toward a Welfare State

When Congo emerged from the shadows of World War II, it was no longer the old place but a new sort of colony. First, the usual composition of the Belgian governments changed as the traditionally anticolonialist socialist party participated in several government coalitions. Second, modern aviation revolutionized communications with the metropole, so that a committee of the Senate in 1947 could travel by plane to the colony and investigate for themselves conditions there. Third, the mindset of most newcomers to the colony was drastically different from that of the old-timers because of their experiences during the war. They no longer automatically accepted that they had a natural right to boss the Congolese around as one of the lesser races, and a few among them even began to see their task as a mission to teach the Congolese the necessary technical skills so that they could eventually take over.

Yet at the same time a fresh wave of settlers seeking a better life also arrived in Congo, most of whom settled in the healthier climates of Kivu and Katanga. Only a mere handful of them arrived in Kuba country, where all old and new settlers together reached a peak of only thirty-six in 1957. Most of them exploited modest oil palm plantations with oil-processing plants, owned sawmills, or were traders in maize (corn), and most also operated a string of general stores. With the exception of a few bush traders along the Sankuru River, newcomers settled along the rail line and used Lulua or Luba labor. Compared to the older and bigger companies such as the Compagnie du Kasai, the cotton companies, or Exforka, a huge sawmill concern at Kakenge owned by the railway company, most of the other businesses remained small, and their impact on the Kuba villagers was slight. The new settlers began to be joined by Kwete Mwana, a son of King Kwet Mabinc maKyeen and now a businessman, and by a steadily growing number of local Luba/Lulua traders and shopkeepers and later still by some other Bushong. By 1947 Kwete Mwana had even acquired a pickup truck, and in 1952 Kwaakong, a younger relative of King Mbop Mabinc maKyeen, became the first Bushong trader at Nsheng itself to own and operate such a truck.

The new style of government included a brand-new Stalinist-like faith in social engineering and planning. It published a detailed ten-year plan for development in 1949, mostly financed by the government. This was actually carried out over the next ten years and on the whole was a success. Congo's infrastructure developed rapidly, and the colony became much more industrialized during the 1950s. Despite efforts to slow its pace, urbanization exploded. The administration finally recognized the social realities in the Kuba region and created a wholly separate administration for the Luba/Lulua settlements along the rail line but still within the same territory. As a consequence the latter's name was changed from Territory of the Bakuba to Mweka Territory.

While many rural Kuba were still required to maintain or build secondary roads within the revived economic framework, their main task now was to produce palm oil and palm kernels, to start plantations of improved palm trees, and to grow maize in place of cotton. Both Kuba and Luba/Lulua components of the population liked maize and produced ever increasing quantities of it, so that Mweka soon became the main exporter of corn for Katanga's industrial belt. Hence the ten-year plan budgeted silos at Mweka's railway station. By the mid-1950s, however, the intensive production of maize along the rail line resulted in expanding swathes of wholly exhausted soil and was causing considerable environmental damage. The plan had also not foreseen the subsequent rapid growth of the town of Mweka, a growth so rapid (from well under ten thousand inhabitants in 1950 to almost twenty thousand in 1958) that it forced the administration during every year from 1950 onward to develop its infrastructure in one way or another.

As part of its program for modernization, the ten-year plan also aimed at integrating rural Africans into the new economy by turning them into a genuine peasantry. They would be taught to raise a multi-year sequence of food and cash crops on the same fields thanks to inputs of improved seeds, pesticides and fertilizers, and a scientific sequence of crops on the same field. The program was officially known as the peasantry system (*paysannat*), but in Kasai they called it *mpiki* after the sticks (French: *piquet*) with which the parcels of land were delimited. Once the *mpiki* were producing well, they would then become the private property of those who cultivated them. Thus a new class of yeoman farmers, whose members would earn a handsome income from their crops, was supposed to arise. Meanwhile, however, the sale of the crops continued mainly to benefit the existing big companies that bought the palm products and the cotton for sale overseas and the smaller businesses that traded in maize to be shipped to Katanga. This peasantry scheme was a Utopian vision bound to fail for different cultural, technical, and financial reasons, and yet, incredibly, at the time of independence it was working well in one small corner of the province among the Luba Kasai of Gandajika. Elsewhere it became the most hated part of the colonial order. The never-ending interference with people's daily lives, the constant instances of coercion, and the dismissal of all tenure rights over land were resented by all and fueled a rural radicalism that surprised nearly all colonials in the run-up to independence.

For the first time ever the government accepted direct responsibility for education and health after World War II, rather than relegating these domains almost exclusively to missions, to companies, or to a few charitable institutions. From 1950 funding in Kasai began to be forthcoming for official clinics, dispensaries, and hospitals for the Congolese. In the Kuba region the main contribution of the ten-year plan was the construction of a hospital at Nsheng that opened its doors in 1957.

The provision of schools was a much more contentious matter. In Belgian politics, schools were political dynamite and a cause of eternal tension. The country had essentially two parallel and competing networks of official education, one run directly by the state and the other by the Catholic Church. During the whole twentieth century, schools remained a bitter bone of contention as the conservative/liberal and socialist parties supported the state schools while the Catholic party supported the religious system.

From the outset the Congolese administration had left nearly all officially recognized schools in the hands of the "national missions" and paid a large part of their costs. Nearly all of these were Catholic. There also existed another unofficial network of Protestant schools. In practice this system meant that schooling was actually denied to all children in regions where missions were not welcome, or to children elsewhere whose parents were not becoming Christian. Kuba country was a notorious instance of this situation. Between 1920 and 1937 the Catholic mission was not welcome in Nsheng, and the APCM was not allowed to open a mission there. At Bulape the APCM had a set of nonofficial schools, but without French. Both confessions had schools in Luebo and along the rail line, but all the available places in these establishments were taken by good Christian Luba/Lulua pupils. That was the background when the first Belgian senatorial commission of enquiry arrived at Luebo in 1947 and was serenaded by a group of welcoming Africans. To their amazement at one point the song suddenly went: "Moreover the Congo asks from its dear Belgium / a lay school for its boys and its girls."[6]

And so as soon as a Liberal politician became minister of colonies in 1954, the first network of lay schools was introduced. Luluabourg opened the doors of its first lay school in 1954, and Nsheng followed only a year later. Finally the Bushong had their own full-fledged primary school. In the following years Catholics and anticlerical people vied with each other in Mweka territory to "capture children" by founding all sorts of technical schools, including an art school at Nsheng that was no doubt also supposed to counter the attraction of the lay grade school. Thus, albeit long after the Luba/Lulua, most Bushong children finally got a chance to acquire a solid, Western-style education during the waning years of the colonial period.

After Word War II the colonial government could no longer ignore the Congolese elites. These persons were becoming modern leaders in the main cities at the time when the cities were becoming more and more pivotal as the arena in which a new Congo was taking shape with its own society, culture, and arts. Faced with the political importance of the cities, the administration made fruitless attempts to stem a tide of uncontrolled immigration, but at the same time its policies privileged the cities and their elites at the expense of the countryside. Apart from rural flight another result was the emergence of a great deal of resentment against city slickers on the part of both African and European rural folk while urban dwellers poured a great deal of scorn on the country yokels. Moreover, despite appearances, the elites were not won over, and the notion of self-determination did not disappear but continued to be debated among intellectuals. Indeed, even in Nsheng, this unimportant backwater on the Congolese scene, by 1953 a small handful of intellectuals were already debating among themselves whether, when, and how they could become independent.

6. Jean Stengers, "La Belgique et le Congo," *Histoire de la Belgique contemporaine*, 1914–1970 (Brussels, 1975), 401 and 438 n8. "Le Congo demande encore à sa Belgique chérie / Une école laïque pour les garçons et les filles."

As the population in the cities ballooned, tribal associations based on the common rural origins of their members appeared there as a major means for immigrants to adapt to city life. They soon became "natural" constituencies for elite leaders and a vehicle for their political ambitions. So when tension began to rise in the Katangese cities and in Luluabourg between Western-educated Luba Kasai and Lulua, the latter founded a common action group, Lulua Frères (Lulua Brothers), that became more and more active by the mid-1950s. Although a feeling of being excluded by the Luba from access to attractive jobs in Katanga contributed to their dissatisfaction, the main Lulua grievance was that immigrant Luba Kasai had taken over most of the Lulua land in central Kasai. The Luba reacted by creating their own organization. A series of ever growing political and then armed clashes between the two groups finally flared into open warfare by mid-1959. The colonial administration was unable to contain it, and civil war engulfed the whole of central Kasai.

Thanks to stern directives from King Mbop Mabinc maKyeen, the Kuba stayed out of the conflict despite a few incidents that affected some of their villages in the southeast. By the end of 1959 the king was co-opted by the Belgian administration to mediate between the warring sides. At that same moment, though, stress in the Bushong villages about an uncertain and hence insecure future as independence loomed found an outlet in a fierce and deadly outbreak of witchcraft accusations. The king, rather than the administration, finally managed to bring the situation under control during the spring of 1960.

The first open discussion about decolonization dates from early 1956 in Belgium. By July of the same year a number of Congolese intellectuals followed by demanding "a progressive but total emancipation." Two years later, in August 1958, the same group led by Patrice Lumumba proposed a program of decolonization, and in October Lumumba founded his National Congolese Movement (MNC) in Kinshasa and formally demanded independence. As his party's platform favored a strong central government, it was immediately opposed by federalist movements. The Association of the Bakongo (ABAKO), the oldest and the most influential of these in Kinshasa, led by Joseph Kasavubu, instantly matched Lumumba's demand. From then on both parties began to bid against each other by clamoring for an ever closer date for independence until they all wanted "independence now." Various government attempts to retain the political initiative during 1958 backfired.

The crucial turning point came on January 4, 1959, when a large and rowdy ABAKO rally clamoring for independence in Kinshasa was dispersed by the army at the cost of about a hundred casualties. This provoked a furious uprising that lasted several days. By then, and despite its belated promises for a speedy independence, the colonial government had lost the initiative. Soon the administration lost control over several important parts of the country one after the other, including central Kasai, which was now descending into civil war. The pace of decolonization was now dictated by the rivalry between the centralist Lumumba and the federalist Kasavubu. After an extremely short period to set up the machinery for a parliamentary democracy, elections were held, and Congo became an independent republic on June 30, 1960, with Kasavubu as president and Lumumba as prime minister. Less than a month later the country nearly disintegrated as it fell prey to political and military chaos.

FURTHER READINGS

Anstey, Roger. *King Leopold's Legacy: The Congo under Belgian Rule, 1908–1960.* Oxford, 1966.

Fetter Bruce. *Colonial Rule and Regional Imbalance in Central Africa.* Boulder, Colo., 1983.

Hunt, Nancy. *A Colonial Lexicon of Birth Ritual, Medicalization, and Mobility in the Congo.* Durham, N.C., 1999.

Jewsiewicki, Bogumil. "Belgian Africa." In *The Cambridge History of Africa,* vol. 7, *From 1905 to 1940,* ed. A. D. Roberts, 461–93. Cambridge, 1986.

7

A Kingdom Preserved

The rulers of colonial Africa have been famously divided over how best to govern their dependencies. What was better, direct rule or indirect rule? Was direct rule better in which the colonial overlord created territorial units and imposed any person of their choice to head them, or was indirect rule better in which the overlord recognized the preexisting territorial groups and strove to rule through the legitimate leaders they found, provided that they could obtain the cooperation of these leaders? Most French and Portuguese colonies adopted the first approach, while most British colonies adopted the second one. In theory the rulers of Belgian Congo preferred indirect rule, but in practice they found nearly all the larger kingdoms in Congo in ruins, or they destroyed them during their conquest, so that they actually recognized only chiefs over small chiefdoms whom they named and deposed at will. Hence their indirect rule often came very close to direct rule. By its very size, however, the Kuba kingdom was one of the rare exceptions to this situation.

The colonial experience of the Kuba during Belgian times was mostly shaped by two major laws: the decree of May 2, 1910, about chiefdoms (that is, governance) and the decree of February 1917 about compulsory labor. This chapter is devoted to the effects of the first decree since the preservation of the kingdom and its governance by indirect rule derived from it and thus created a striking anomaly in the administrative practices of the Belgian Congo. This was the only precolonial kingdom to survive nearly intact, the only territory of its kind and its size encapsulated in the colony's administrative grid like a fly in amber, large enough to be effectively governed by indirect rule and yet small enough to fit in the colony's standard territorial grid as a "territory." After relating how this case of indirect rule took shape, we follow the political history of the kingdom until independence wherever we can from the perspective of Kuba experience. In this chapter that means, first, what the kings and their councils did or what happened to them, but also the influence of the village constituencies as represented by their titleholders at court.

The Imposition of Indirect Rule

In chapter 4 we saw that it was only after the takeover of Congo by Belgium that the foundations of a genuine colonial administration based on the rule of law were laid down in Upper Congo, that is, in the whole of the colony upstream of Kinshasa. The 1910 decree on the chiefdom was the lowest but most fundamental element of a territorial system that was completed two years later. By then Congo was organized in districts, which included a number of territories (*territoires*), themselves composed wherever possible of chiefdoms and otherwise of an unstable aggregate of even smaller units such as villages or clans, called sectors. Yet even though districts existed in Leopold's Upper Congo, the state had actually abdicated its powers on the ground to the Compagnie du Kasai over a very large portion of that district, including the Kuba kingdom.

In contrast to this situation, however, as soon as the Belgian decree on chiefdoms became law in 1910, it was realized on the ground among the Kuba. In that same year no less a personage than Vice Governor General Eugène Henry visited the region and personally fixed the boundaries of "the Kuba chiefdom." Although he amputated several peripheral portions of the realm, including one in the south toward Luebo, most of the kingdom stayed intact. Somewhat later in 1912, when the new district structure was decreed in Congo and the districts were divided into territories, a new smaller district of Kasai was created and territories were set up within it. But the Kuba "chiefdom" was so large that it became the territory of Mushenge all by itself, and when its boundary with the adjoining territory of Luebo was traced anew, the kingdom recovered all the land it had lost two years earlier in that direction, except for the town of Luebo itself.

To complete the new organization of the Belgian Congo and supposedly to decentralize the administration, the country should have been divided into provinces beginning in 1914, but by that date only three provinces had been set up. This measure was actually taken so as to provide for more oversight over the district commissioners and hence to centralize the government. But World War I intervened, and Kasai was not included in any of the three new provinces that were set up. After the war in 1919 the remainder of the country was simply proclaimed to constitute a single province called Congo-Kasai, of which Kasai was one half. One effect of this, however, was that the district commissioners in this province retained nearly all of their former autonomy.

The decree of 1910 on chiefdoms foresaw that the chief, appointed by the state, was to be a mere cog in the administrative machine, in charge of carrying out its routine tasks at the command and under the supervision of the local territorial agent. Chiefs were not expected to act on their own initiative. Most chiefdoms were so small that the system worked as planned, and most chiefs did as they were told or else they were replaced. But the Kuba kingdom was different. Here the realities were its large size, the considerable authority of its king, Kwet aPe, over most parts of the kingdom, the existence of an effective Kuba administration, and the brute fact that the one territorial administrator in the territory simply did not have the means nor the armed men to take over the day-to-day government of the country.

That was the existing anomalous situation that the district commissioner, N. Gelders, found necessary to clarify in late November 1915, not long before he left office on March 1, 1916, and shortly before Kwet aPe's death in April 1916. Gelders correctly read the decree of 1910 as a blueprint for indirect rule: using his own initiative, the king would administer his kingdom as he saw fit within the overall guidelines provided by the administration and according to its requirements. Using this interpretation, Gelders then wrote a set of instructions for the administrator in charge of the now merged territories of Mushenge and Luebo.

According to these instructions, that official was to acknowledge and maintain the authority and the prestige of the king, who was to be treated as an adjunct territorial administrator in chief—that is, someone of a higher rank than any ordinary subaltern European agent. Next the commissioner dictated what the king was forbidden to do, followed by what he could and should do. To round off his instructions Gelders then ordered the administrator in charge to consider himself to be a superior adviser to the king, while leaving the latter every freedom of action whenever possible. A European subaltern territorial agent was provided to assist the king (someone needed to do the paperwork) and at the same time also to check that he used his power only for the general welfare. In sum, the Kuba king was to rule his realm in the name of the government and could do so as he pleased barring only a few judicial matters. Obviously such instructions amounted to a form of rule halfway between a protectorate and direct rule, but Gelders did not label them as such.

Four years later, however, on the occasion of the installation of a new king, Kwet Mabinc maKyeen, the new adjunct commissioner of the Kasai district, Lode Achten, carried out a thorough and detailed examination of the kingdom's political and judiciary institutions in order to reevaluate the whole situation. This study resulted in the renewed creation of the territory of the Bakuba on February 20, 1920. Barely a few months later the new minister of colonies, Louis Franck, visited Luebo, enthusiastically endorsed Achten's work, and formally attached the label "indirect rule" to the Kuba situation. When interviewed on September 29, 1920, while still in Congo, the minister gave a brief exposé of his views on native government and used the Kuba case as a paradigm of indirect rule in the following comments:

> The region of the Bakuba is interesting because it is one of the last in which a great chiefdom still exists. The great chief has some 150,000 to 200,000 subjects.
>
> We wish not to let the indigenous organizations be broken up. When they disappear there remains usually only small chiefdoms; authority is scattered; the chiefs lose all genuine authority; this situation already exists in many other regions of the colony; one of the great problems for tomorrow will be to remedy this, for we don't want to be faced one day with a true indigenous anarchy.[1]

Indirect rule now became official colonial policy, and the Kuba realm was to serve as its paradigm to be achieved wherever possible. However, all other large African political entities in Congo had already collapsed or had been broken up by then and could not be completely reconstituted. Hence Franck's policy was never fully implemented, although the colonial government did not admit this before 1933 when it abandoned the policy, except among the Kuba and in a very few other

---

1. Interview with Louis Franck in *Mouvement géographique* 37 (1920): 521.

cases. Thus the kingdom became a glaring rarity rather than the expected exemplar.

This account, however, is far from the whole story. Why had the Kuba kingdom, unlike all the others, escaped destruction before 1920? What had repeatedly convinced the colonial authorities, from the governor general in 1905 to the minister of colonies in 1920, that the Kuba kingdom should be preserved? They all seem to have been convinced that, unlike any other Congolese society, the Kuba were the heirs of a true ancient civilization. Already in 1885 Ludwig Wolf had deduced this from their industriousness, their technical know-how, the beauty of all the objects they made, and the art of their dancing exhibitions, combined with the considerable authority of their kings. Kuba art was greatly appreciated in Europe from the very beginning, especially by the avant-garde artists who launched art nouveau. As early as 1897 they had organized the first exhibition in Belgium about Congo, decorated the hall of honor with embroidered Kuba textiles, and celebrated Kuba sculpture elsewhere in their exhibition. By then it had become commonplace among well-informed colonials to believe that the Kuba were somehow heirs to the old civilization of pharaonic Egypt.

A few years later and despite the failure of the Kuba rebellion, colonial authorities were impressed with the Kuba ability to mobilize in an orderly fashion, their political unity, and the talents of their ruler, Kwet aPe. That explains the decision of Théophile Wahis, the governor general in 1905, to maintain the kingdom for the time being. Then came the events of 1908. The very denunciation of the king by Consul Thesiger brought the king and his realm to the attention of the Congo reformers and the highest Belgian authorities alike. This awareness of the Kuba implied that any tampering with the kingdom might well raise an international hue and cry. Moreover, Thesiger's accusations forced the king into a stronger alliance with the state, an alliance that was then sealed a year later when the minister of colonies, Jules Renkin, met with Kwet aPe. The message to the local colonial officials was loud and clear: the Kuba monarchs were now under the direct protection of the metropolitan authority.

Moreover, around this time Emil Torday's publications were causing quite a stir in Europe. He claimed that the kingdom was older than any of its European counterparts, he described a sophisticated political system that included over one hundred specialized officials as well as trials by jury, and the British Museum joined him in hailing the Kuba royal statues as the pinnacle of all African art. The conclusion in the colony was that the Kuba were obviously civilized and could rule themselves, and that one should remember that the young Belgian Congo might well be judged abroad by what happened to this realm. When district commissioner Achten fully confirmed and even elaborated on Torday's findings, the die was cast. The kingdom was preserved and encapsulated whole into the new Belgian colonial order.

Just as relevant to this outcome were the policies pursued by the Kuba kings. Kwet aPe quickly grasped that he was no match for the colonial establishment and that his kingdom could only be preserved by fully collaborating with the powers that be. He therefore nurtured personal relationships of political importance with foreigners from overseas and pursued a careful policy of graded gift giving as an instrument of rule, a common practice among the Kuba themselves. The point was to give, whenever possible, a gift of higher value to any donor than the gift that was received so that the donor would remain beholden to the king.

Torday had insisted that Kuba art was highly appreciated in Europe, that museums craved such objects, and hence that gifts of textiles and carvings to foreigners from oversea were highly appreciated. By his behavior he also proved that the rare official royal statues of former kings were supergifts, the richest possible things that the Kuba court could bestow. From then on Kwet aPe and his successors gave art objects of appropriate quality to all foreign visitors and especially to administrators for services rendered. In 1919–20, for instance, the territorial administrator Blondeau received a genuine royal statue for his services most likely because he backed Kwet Mabinc maKyeen, the successful candidate to the throne, despite the paralysis that had incapacitated him years earlier. This was remarkable because this circumstance had prompted many Kuba and some European officials to back Kwet's younger brother Mbop for the position until the governor general himself decided otherwise.

The Kuba kings were also well aware of the positive effect created by their artistic dance performances. The photographs by Queen Elisabeth of Belgium of such a display in 1928 were published in the following years and especially enhanced their reputation in this regard even further. Later the portrait of Mbop Mabinc maKyeen in full regalia made by the photographer Eliot Elisofon in 1947 for *Life* magazine became the most celebrated icon of Kuba kingship (this portrait is reproduced later in this chapter). Elisofon was struck by the professional way in which the king took his pose and by his obvious experience with photo opportunities: he even used a full length mirror to check his appearance.

It is clear from the plethora of published photographs and films con-
secrated to them and their court that the Kuba kings worked hard to
project an aura of majesty, power, and competence. In retrospect it is
evident that they were hugely successful in doing so, for indirect rule endured, contrary to every expectation and despite severe challenges.

From time to time outside observers announced its imminent collapse because the system jarred so much with administrative practice
elsewhere, but they were always wrong. The most common complaint
by expatriates was that the Kuba were arrogant, haughty, and often on
the fringe of rank insubordination. They lacked proper respect for colonials, were not easily overawed, and set a bad example for other Congolese. They cramped the style of many officials and missionaries who
were used to giving peremptory orders rather than convincing or even
negotiating for anything they wanted done. The Kuba had an attitude,
colonials said, and they all blamed indirect rule for it.

Despite this the system endured because it worked, because it enjoyed
the protection of Belgium's ruling circles, and because it continued to
have an excellent reputation in Europe. The lure of "traditional" Kuba
kings and their artistic court was fascinating enough to attract high-brow
tourists during the whole colonial period—including nearly all the members of the royal family of Belgium. Finally the Kuba were also lucky
with their politics of personal relationships. As it happened, only two
kings, Kwet Mabinc maKyeen and his younger brother Mbop Mabinc
maKyeen, ruled between 1919 and 1969, while their most significant
counterparts in the colonial administration also remained in place for
unusually long stretches of time. Thus the same players usually shared
considerable experience with each other and shared the common goal
to make indirect rule work.

Theory and Practice of Indirect Rule

In theory the colonial administration expected all chiefs, the Kuba king
included, to fulfill the following main duties: to combat so-called savage
customs such as trial by poison ordeal; to maintain law and order and to
punish crime as defined in Belgium; to maintain villages, roads, and
bridges in good repair; to count their subjects and raise taxes among
them; to inform the administration of any threat of uprising or unrest;
to supply labor to the state when needed; to raise recruits for the army
as needed; and to compel their subjects to raise and sell designated
crops as required by the 1917 decree on compulsory labor. In return for

their cooperation, both Kwet Mabinc and Mbop Mabinc understood that the realm would be restored to its full territorial extent and that the kings would rule their realm without colonial interference. They would levy tribute and corvee labor as needed, and their tribunals would carry out justice as they were wont to.

The colonial administration liked this arrangement because it provided considerable savings in personnel, whereas the Kuba government and the inhabitants of Nsheng liked it because it gave them a great deal of autonomy. As to the rural villagers, at times it made their king look like a stooge—for instance, when he ordered each village council to identify a certain number of men for the colonial army—while at other times he looked like a savior—for instance, when he managed to avoid the compulsory cultivation of cotton in 1942 as the Kuba contribution to the war effort.

The official colonial view was that indirect rule worked because the Kuba king retained legitimate and absolute authority, and therefore it backed him up with its administrative and military powers when needed. The early territorial administrators believed that this was a divine kingship in which subjects slavishly obeyed their rulers, and they were not interested in its details nor curious to know how exactly royal authority was exercised. Their view was not wholly fanciful since many Kuba believed that the king protected them by upholding the natural order of society and the world and could withhold fertility to those groups who did not please him. As late as 1954, a young Bushong intellectual still dreamed one night that the sun had miraculously but actually set in the king's house. Still the administrators were wrong in that such beliefs were only one of five different strands that shaped a king's authority.

The second strand was fear induced by force. As Kwet Mabinc told Minister Franck, who complained that royal authority seemed to be sometimes flouted: "Restore the rights of my forebears. Allow me to punish rebels the way they did and I assure you that my authority will be respected."[2] Those punishments were sometimes gruesome. Thus Mbop Nnop, the headman of the village of Kosh, was blinded and nearly starved in 1917 because he and his village had converted to Presbyterianism without permission to do so. But this was exceptional. In general, the king's power was limited by the authority of the councils. In

2. Louis Franck, ed., *Le Congo Belge*, 2 vols. (Brussels, 1930), 1: 286–87.

the 1950s a hunting net hung on a wall of the square where the councils
of notables met with the king. It symbolized the fate of a catch and referred to a saying that summarized the following incident:

> In the year 1921 [*sic*] the *mwaanyim* [title: son of a king] Tula Ncedy
> aMing was caught with a wife of king. King Kwet Mabinc sent his
> slaves to check on his wife. They caught Tula Ncedy and the king
> ordered to beat and tie him up. They struck him, they stuck a
> wooden arrow through his penis. The *mwaanyim* stayed like this for
> many days. He slept in jail for 200 days. The Bushong [notables]
> ruled at court in his favor and the king pardoned him. The Bashi
> Bushong coined a saying "Be caught by the king, don't be caught
> by the Bushong": If you are caught by the king, the Bushong can
> rule in your favor; if you are caught by the Bushong who will ab-
> solve you?[3]

Perhaps more important still than fear for the clout of royal authority were patronage and wealth. Until the creation around 1928 of an independent treasury in the kingdom, the whole Kuba administration, including all the notables and judges, was paid for by the king. But he did
not have the power to appoint the most important officials. They were
chosen by the royal councils, which did not always favor the king's can-
didates despite the latter's considerable influence. But the monarch appointed and dismissed secretaries, messengers, and police as well as "the
king's men" — that is, his sons, his slaves or servants. They were his emissaries to collect taxes, oversee corvee laborers, and gather tribute for
designated villages or chiefdoms. After 1928 he no longer paid the notables, judges, other officials of the tribunals, messengers, and police, but
he still paid secretaries and "the king's men" so that his influence and his
power of patronage remained almost as substantial as before.

It follows from the above that royal income and wealth were crucial
for the government of the realm. As an agent of the state, the king was
paid an annual salary linked to the estimated number of adult and
healthy men in the realm. Between 1910 and 1923 this was roughly estimated to be a sum of 60,000 to 70,000 francs, which is a large six-figure
sum in today's dollars. In addition, he also received a tiny portion of
every household tax collected in his realm. On top of that he was still
paid a yearly stipend by the Compagnie du Kasai for promoting the
cutting of palm fruit among his subjects and the promotion of whatever

---

3. Vansina Files, *nyim—after 1920*, text by Mbop Mbanc.

The Chase for Money

Early in 1940 Mbop Mabinc maKyeen baptized his new capital "the Chase for Money," and in a speech on July 8, 1953, he commented on this choice as follows:

> If you chase money fast, may the money not hear you. If you wait for money seated down, may the money not hear you muttering. If you chase money fast, if it hears the noise, you will chase it far away. If you wait for money seated down, if it hears you muttering, you will chase it far away. Money, if you look for money, you refuse to be on good terms with people. Money, if you look for money, you despise the clans.
> [After an interruption for a shout of approval by the audience, he continues.]
> If you look for money, if you go out to search for money, you must search for a means to be on good terms with people. If you deal in money, if you look for money, you are looking for the clans. If you are the owner of money, and if you search for money, you are a proud person. If you are a person who looks for money, you are a person who does despise people.
> [After an interruption for a shout by approval by the audience, he continues.]
> If you have no money, you flatter people. Money makes the proud person; poverty is the place for flattery. If you cannot flatter, will a person let you in his/her house? If you come empty-handed and you have not flattered, will a person let you in his/her house?

In the last two sections of this text the king was contrasting those who need money and those who have money: the first group look for support among their social networks ("look for the clans") and have to flatter those who have money, while the second group can ignore their social network and be full of pride.[4]

4. John Jacobs and Jan Vansina, "Het koninklijk epos der Bushong," *Kongo-Overzee* 12 (1956): 34–35. This is a transcription and a translation of a public address by the king.

rubber was still being gathered. Beyond this he collected "customary" tribute in kind (which included some valuable ivory), and he disposed of obligatory labor for the upkeep of his capital. To cap it all, he received part of the fines paid to the tribunal at Nsheng, all the income from the sale of goods produced by the slaves attached to his office and by his hundreds of wives, and more income in kind stemming from the labor or goods of specified servile villages. All in all, his yearly income was quite considerable, and his subjects believed that he was unimaginably rich.

A good deal of this income was spent to run the kingdom. Some funds were used to compensate "the king's men" as well as his personal emissaries, who usually extorted rather more than the specified amount in taxes and customary tribute from the villages. Other funds went to cover the costs of the households of his successors, as compensation for the titleholders at his court, and as recurring payments for the sculptors, smiths, jewelers, tailors, and other artisans who worked for the court. Then there were political gifts. Some of these went to chiefs, subchiefs, and notables; some others in kind were used to compensate chiefs or villages that brought in their annual tribute. Still other funds were used as countergifts for administrators, officials from the Compagnie du Kasai, and other visitors, whether Congolese or from overseas. Thus much of

Demand of Tribute

Office of the Bakuba Chiefdom[5]   Mushenge 26/1/43
I the signatory Lukengo M Bopé-Mabintshi Makena King of the Bakuba (Bushongo etc.) declare to have designated the inhabitants of the village of Shingteke [Shin a Ntek], Bakele tribe these folk must give me the tribute [of the Bakuba chiefdom]. See the tribute as follows:

Lengths of raffia cloth   The Nyimi Bushongo
Packets of fish   Lukengo [signed] Boppe Mabintsh
Once a year

5. Hymans Papers of King Bop Mabinc maKyeen, 1943, number 2 Outgoing (available at the Memorial Library of the University of Wisconsin–Madison).

the king's income was spent in patronage and to lubricate the political relationships that made indirect rule function and that perpetuated it. At the time there seemed nothing wrong with this since this was the usual Kuba technique for governing. Today, however, such practices, which are still common, are called corruption.

Laissez-faire Indirect Rule in the 1920s

When formal indirect rule was being set up in 1919, the main political actors were the then adjunct district commissioner Achten, King Kwet Mabinc, and his presumed successor Mbop Mabinc, who traveled all over the kingdom in place of his lame brother. This was an anomaly because usually successors were kept well away from any real power. But then the whole situation was an anomaly. Although Kwet Mabinc was paralyzed he had still been chosen by the Bushong and the colonial authorities to succeed, but at the price of letting his brother carry out much of the work involved. This arrangement provided Achten with considerable leverage into Bushong politics and Kwet Mabinc with effective means to supervise his notables in the countryside without actually having to travel much. In the beginning the main issue still was the interference of all sorts of Europeans. Kwet Mabinc complained to the minister of colonies in 1920 as follows: "At the very least there should be only two authorities here, yours and mine—mine after yours. Yet today any white person whatsoever delivers written commands and believes that he/she is a judge."[6]

He was mainly alluding here to the behavior of officials of low rank and of competing missionaries whose rivalry triggered the first challenge to indirect rule. Only about a month earlier Robert Bracq, a Catholic cleric at Nsheng, had brandished a revolver in the face of the king in his palace, while Hezekiah Washburn, a Presbyterian cleric of Bulape, ordered Protestant headmen to inflict fines on their villagers for purely religious reasons, such as working on Sundays or making a hunting charm. At the same time, Washburn attended council meetings as if he were an initiated Bushong notable, while Bracq retaliated by behaving as if he were a Kete notable. Achten finally intervened forcefully to resolve the incendiary situation after Kwet Mabinc sent him further exasperated messages about Bracq. In a scathing letter to Bracq's superior

6. Franck, *Le Congo Belge*, 1: 286–87.

Achten requested and obtained the removal of that cleric from the Kuba realm.

Achten then moved further and this time very much against the wishes of the king. As soon as Kwet Mabinc, who wanted a decent school, was elected in 1919, he called on the Presbyterians to found a mission station at Nsheng. At first they sent only a few evangelists, so when the king traveled to Luebo in January 1920 he urged the congregation to hasten its arrival. Meanwhile, the Presbyterian evangelists at the capital were meeting with considerable success, to the dismay of the Catholic mission. The following year the Presbyterians sent a missionary to Nsheng and formally applied for permission to open a station there. Achten, by now the district commissioner in charge, refused to do so on the grounds that two mission stations at Nsheng threatened the maintenance of public order.

He certainly had a point. Ever since 1905 Catholic and Presbyterian congregations had been vying with each other for converts in the same localities, and of late there had been several serious clashes among their followers. Because there was an approved Catholic mission station at Nsheng, Achten refused permission to implant a Presbyterian mission station there, just as he had refused a Catholic mission station near Bulape, where the Presbyterians had one. For good measure he then told the king what his duties were regarding the practice of the religious cults.

Thus Kwet Mabinc and his court discovered that there were limits to their autonomy even in a matter of importance for the welfare of the Kuba, since the results of Achten's ruling were that the Protestants permanently gave up any attempts to settle new stations with their attendant schools and dispensaries anywhere in Bushong country or indeed elsewhere in Kuba country, while the Catholic missionaries never healed the rift with the king caused by Bracq. They abandoned Nsheng in 1927, supposedly because of a lack of conversions, and took their school with them. For the next ten years and in spite of the constant demands by the Kuba court, there was no school at the capital.

Apart from religion the other major challenge to indirect rule in the 1920s was the restoration of the whole kingdom under the authority of its king. When Kwet Mabinc came to power, several older small-scale conflicts between the center of the kingdom and several groups of Kete and Coofa to the southeast were still ongoing, while the chiefdoms east of the Labody (Lubudi) River were not even part of the district of Kasai. Yet already in 1924 those chiefdoms were reintegrated into the territory of the Bakuba, and their Ngongo chiefs accepted the king's overlordship without further ado after he made an intimidating formal tour to their main town of Misumba early in the following year. Both the recuperation of the lands across the Labody River and the ravages of a subsequent epidemic (probably sleeping sickness) were remembered as follows in the 1950s:

> In 1925 King Kwet Mabinc went on *kidy* [a formal royal trip] to Misumba of the Ngongo. The chief of the Ngongo said that the king had spent many days in his town and all the Ngongo were complaining. King Kwet Mabinc had a charm in a pot. It contained human hair, human nails, the loincloth of the sorcerer, and bones from dead witches. That was his charm.
>
> People were not supposed to criticize him; if they did, they died. The chief of the Ngongo had remained in the village and he had died. Many people died and the Ngongo came to the king and told him that they were being exterminated and the king accepted their surrender.[7]

The ease with which this reintegration happened owed perhaps as much to a then ongoing struggle for the succession between two branches of the Ngongo ruling dynasty at Misumba as to the Ngongo belief in the supernatural powers of the king. Still, as late as 1956 a Ngongo chief declared that he obeyed the king only because the latter's spiritual power was greater than his own.

Whatever its reasons, the ease with which the chiefdoms across the Labody River submitted to the king's rule stands in sharp contrast to the effort and the time it took to overcome the resistance of populations that were not organized in chiefdoms but only in individual villages or camps. Several rebellions broke out among such groups, and the exactions of royal emissaries as well as the obligation to pay tribute on top of the state taxes played a prominent role in all of them. A typical succession of events is well illustrated by the following case of the Kete villages north of Luebo.

In 1923, the year when construction on the railroad began, Kampungu (Kapoong) rebelled. Because this town, like the other Kete settlements, was located near Luebo, it was called upon to provide for the needs of the many inhabitants of that town. Hence it was far more exploited than villages elsewhere. On top of those extra exigencies came their obligations toward the kingdom. In earlier times five or six low-level Bushong representatives called *paangl* had been charged with the collection of tribute, but when the Kete towns, Kampungu included,

---

7. Vansina Files, *nyim—after 1920*, text: *Kum angwong.*

were reunited with the kingdom in 1913, the territorial administration insisted on having these *paangl* supervised by a single representative of the king who would mediate between the state and the Kete.

A *mwaanyim* (king's son) was named to this position. He soon chased away the *paangl* and became notorious for his rapaciousness. He demanded tribute whenever he felt like it and took for himself an illegal portion from every fine inflicted in judicial cases by the village courts. When local leaders talked of complaining at Nsheng, he heaped more fines on them for insubordination. *Mwaanyim* succeeded *mwaanyim,* but all of them misbehaved in the same way so that the situation finally burst into open rebellion. Kampungu chased its *mwaanyim* and his minions out of town and refused the king's overrule and hence any payment of tribute or fines. Thereupon the king sent his brother Mbop with a party of policemen to occupy the town while the district commissioner sent a military contingent from nearby Luebo for the same purpose. In 1953 old MboMaloom, a senior aristocrat at the capital, remembered and recounted the story as follows without any mention of the causes of the rebellion nor about any loss of life during the uprising, nor anything about its aftermath:

> In 1922 [actually probably a mix of 1923 and 1926] the Bakete of Kampungu said: "We refuse, we no longer will be subjects of the king." King Kwet Mabinc then sent a message to Mbop the successor. Mbop, the successor, came and Kwet Mabinc told the news that the Bakete refused to submit to him. The successor [then] called Bityet biLoop, Kwakong, [and] Pyem Bushap, the bugle. He [Pyem] sounded the bugle, the royal slaves assembled, Bityet biLoop took the guns [from the royal armory], and distributed them to sixty men. The man in charge of the peace charms went ahead. They [all] arrived at Kampungu. The Bakete said: "Leave our village, we are not the king's people." The successor sent a message to the company commander [of the colonial army]. Sixty soldiers came. When the Bakete saw the soldiers they shot sharp wooden arrows at them. The soldiers killed Bakete. [There were] forty corpses. All the Bakete fled into the bush.
>
> *Shansheeng* [a Kete title] Shyaam came out of the bush. He went to the successor and said: "I am your man." [He surrendered and] all the prisoners went to jail in Luebo. Then the Bakete submitted to the king.[8]

---

8. Vansina Files, *nyim—after 1920,* translation of MboMaloom, *Histoire du nyim K.M.K.*

So the situation returned temporarily to where it was before the outbreak. But two years later a better coordinated rebellion involving all the southern Kete villages broke out. Shamba [Shyaam], one of the notables of the village of Kasenga, just outside the American Presbyterian Christian Mission at Luebo, had taken the leadership of a coalition that wanted to create a Kete chiefdom and detach it from the kingdom to transfer it to the territory of Luebo, once again, because of the exactions of the *mwaanyim*. As we have already seen in the previous chapter, the trigger to this uprising was the order to provide lumberjacks from these villages to work on the rail line for the deforestation teams. The messenger who brought this order was told that henceforth the Kete would no longer obey any orders from Nsheng, and a few weeks later the administrator of the territory was told that they would only pay their taxes at Luebo and not at Nsheng. In late 1925 further talks, in which an aide to the district commissioner also participated, led to a partial payment of the taxes due. Further talks resumed in April 1926 between the same parties, now joined by Mbop Mabinc acting for the king.

But on May 1 the inhabitants of Kampungu arrived with weapons at hand. They threatened war if any of their notables were arrested over this, and they flatly refused to remain in the kingdom. Thereupon the whole region was put under military occupation. Although several villages came to negotiate on the first day of this occupation, nevertheless several armed clashes occurred before a truce was called. Mbop Mabinc then reinstated the *paangl*, the *mwaanyim* was sent packing to Nsheng, and the Kete villages, including Kampungu, began to acquit themselves of their imposed tasks. Shyaam, the Kete leader, was then relegated, that is, sent in exile to a designated place far from his home village. In Congo, relegations of this sort were a standard measure to remove troublesome African political or religious leaders.

In some other cases of rebellion by such groups, additional factors made resolution of the conflict even more difficult. For instance, in the case of the Kete of Bulape and their neighbors, religious rivalry between Protestants and Catholics underlay a whole series of clashes between 1907 and 1931. In the case of the Coofa, language and culture were involved: they were Tshiluba speaking and followed Lulua customs more than those of the central Kuba. As long ago as 1905 they had rejected the king's overlordship and his demands for tribute, and they were only subdued and convinced to pay tribute in 1933. The nomadic Cwa foragers east of the Labody River, who had hitherto been free of any kind of tax, tribute, or corvee labor, were suddenly declared to be rebels by the

King Kwet Mabinc maKyeen (1920–39) (photo by unknown author)

territorial authority in 1928. Actually the real problem was that the Ngongo chief of Misumba, backed by the Belgian administration, wanted to control them, but as foragers and original inhabitants of the land they were directly under the king's own protection. Tensions mounted, and in 1931 they killed a messenger from the Ngongo chief. That triggered a useless military occupation—useless because they simply could not be caught in their wide open spaces. The whole affair ended two years later with a face-saving arrangement that resulted in a victory for the king's party and a retreat by the state, which was forced to abandon its attempt to make the Cwa sedentary.

While the colonial government was reuniting the kingdom and enforcing royal authority, it left the internal politics within the realm strictly alone, just as it was wont to do elsewhere in chiefdoms and sectors. Hence the internal political dynamics continued much as before. Over the years Kwet Mabinc and the royals gradually gained the upper hand over the aristocrats and the councils. The rivalry between the faction of Kwet Mabinc's most trusted sons and favorites and the faction of his successor, Mbop Mabinc, and his followers grew especially in the 1930s. In addition, the new rivalry between Protestants and Catholics surfaced at court from 1919 onward.

Before 1928 the administration remained passive even though the administrators soon realized that much of the resistance they encountered was due to the rapaciousness—and in one case the religious politics—of the *mwaanyim*, who were the king's representatives. But they also soon discovered that the successor Mbop Mabinc was always happy to oblige by having offending *mwaanyim*, all of whom belonged to the king's faction, removed from their posts. And so he gradually became the administration's trusted ally in the internal power politics at court.

Indirect Rule by Order

The year 1928 was both a culmination and a turning point for Congo and for the territory of the Bakuba. The railway was completed, an event deemed so important that King Albert and Queen Elisabeth of Belgium came in July to inaugurate the line and to shake the hand of Kwet Mabinc. But in February of that year district commissioner Achten left his position, and his hands-off style of indirect rule soon came under attack. First the local administration was forced to intervene into local practices. Thus in November of the same year a principal tribunal for the territory of the Bakuba was created at Mushenge as required by legislation dating back to 1926. Because the king was to be its president and Mbop Mabinc a member, the new tribunal played havoc with the system of Kuba checks and balances. It abolished the former tribunals at Nsheng, all of which bar one excluded the king, and all of which insisted that the panel of judges be different for each case and be truly representative of both parties and of the substance of the case. Now the balance of power in general tilted decisively in favor of the king and the successor. Yet ironically the administrator proudly reported in 1929 that the settlement of legal cases was no longer left to the arbitrariness of the ministers!

Around the same time general Congolese legislation also obliged the administration to create a Native Treasury. This was run by the Belgian administrator of the territory, not the king. The treasury's income derived from a portion of the general poll tax, while its expenditures were to be devoted to the improvement of the general population. In practice, the money was spent just as in other territories without much regard for the wishes of the king and his court: no money at all was set aside for health or education, and most of the funds went to local road construction.

The Great Depression of 1929 interacting with the consequences of the completion of the construction of the railway soon hastened change. The geographic reorientation of the Kuba kingdom explains the move in 1930 of the territory's capital from Nsheng to Mweka, and the new main tribunal moved with it. The king lost the eminent judiciary position he had just acquired, and Nsheng was left with a tribunal for Bushong only, which pointedly excluded the new Luba and Lulua settlements along the railway. Two other such tribunals were created for the Luba/Lulua in the vicinity of Bena Makima and Port Francqui (Ilebo). At one stroke the Kuba and their king lost not only judicial control over some 123 settlements but also most of the indirect influence they had exerted until then through daily meetings with the territorial administrator.

On the other hand, the move to Mweka meant that the political activities of the Kuba establishment became less visible to the administration, just as the Depression caused a significant decline in the number of territorial officers. That loosened oversight over the activities of the Kuba court even more and at the same time further increased the role of Kwet Mabinc in the practicalities of the administration. Nevertheless, barely a year after Achten had left, indirect rule came under attack. The annual report to Parliament written in early 1928 included lavish praise for indirect rule. In contrast, the one written in early 1929 contained the following frustrated observation: "The king is impotent, the conservative reactionary caste resists any evolution. The authorities expect much from the successor, who is intelligent and devoted to our interests to return the populations to the road of evolution and to free the subject tribes from the yoke of the king's lieutenants."[9]

This was no expression of a temporary exasperation. Almost two years later the administrator complained to a passing French writer that Kwet Mabinc's insubordination was becoming worrisome. King Albert's handshake had made him so haughty that he affected to refuse to obey the white administrator. So between late 1928 and 1932 the territorial administrators tried to rule some Kuba "subject tribes" directly without any reference to Nsheng. The result was a major insurrection in one case and a tax strike in another: not good for the administrator's career.

A new change of course came with the appointment in 1932 of Emile Vallaeys as district commissioner and René Van Deuren as territorial administrator. Vallaeys had worked with the Kuba court during the building of the railway, and Van Deuren had served in a neighboring territory during the 1920s. Both officials were to hold their new posts for the next decade. In 1933 the colony was reorganized and further centralized. As part of this reorganization the district of Kasai and two others were fused into the larger province of Kasai. As a result the district commissioner lost his direct contact with the ministry in Brussels. In addition, the province set up its own specialized departments, which soon began to compete for influence with the territorial service. That was especially true for the department of agriculture. Nevertheless, the district commissioners still managed to keep close control over all governmental activities in their districts with the exception of the health service.

Once appointed, Vallaeys immediately restored indirect rule in Kuba country, but it was a new brand of indirect rule. The district commissioner bluntly ordered the king around without even appearing to ask for his opinion, and he no longer called Kwet Mabinc "king" but "chief." This was a new style of rule in keeping with the harsh conditions of the Depression. A striking instance of it occurs already in a report from 1933 in which Vallaeys threatened: "He [the king] fully understands that such maneuvers threaten the integrity of his chiefdom."[10]

The result of both the provincial reorganization and the decisions of Vallaeys was a hands-on administration. In 1933, for example, rather

9. Chambre des représentants, *Rapport annuel* for 1928 (Brussels, 1929), 58.
10. Province du Kasai, *Dossier sectes secrètes*, September 28, 1933.

than wholly rely on the Kuba, Van Deuren, the territorial administrator, accompanied Mbop Mabinc, the successor, to the western parts of the kingdom to conduct his own direct enquiries into the activities of so-called secret societies. At the same time, the king lost all control over anything beyond the strict routine of territorial administration. Soon one saw, for instance, Belgian adjunct agronomists organizing the maintenance of the existing roads, collecting taxes, and deciding land tenure questions along the rail line, all in addition to their proper job of setting up nurseries and plantations for oil palm trees and ordering villagers to grow cotton or manioc. They were clearly bypassing any input from the king and his councils, even though they were directly interfering with Kuba villagers and ordering them about. (See "An Agronomist's Report for December 1935" in chapter 6.)

But despite the new style of indirect rule and the economic crisis, internal politics at court continued along the same lines as before and soon induced the main political crisis of the 1930s. Around 1930 the king invited a renowned Lele healer and his slave helper to the palace, unbeknownst to any outsider, in order to cure him of his paralysis. He dismissed this healer five years later when his health began to deteriorate further and when he finally accepted that he would not be cured. With that action he also recognized that his reign was waning, and the struggle for his succession began. A year earlier Mbop Mabinc had helped him to drive the *kikaam* (prime minister) away and thus to incapacitate the councils at the court. But this maneuver had allowed Georges Kwete Mwana, the king's most gifted son, who was literate and knew some French, to dominate the court and to engineer a rift between the king and Mbop Mabinc. In retaliation the latter apparently leaked a few spectacular abuses at court to the administrator. As a result, some courtiers were jailed for extortion, and the following lines appeared in the Annual Report to the Chambers: "In recent years the impotent *Lukengo* [king] had relied too much on the support of a band of slaves, servants, and kin, who without his knowledge but under cover of his authority committed all sorts of abuses. Their influence was so great that they even succeeded in thwarting the customary powers of the great dignitaries of the council."[11]

A few months later in 1936 a new variant of a much feared "secret society" was discovered by chance among the Kete north of Luebo.

11. Chambre des représentants, *Rapport annuel* for 1935 (Brussels, 1936), 9.

This movement had been launched by the slave of the Lele healer mentioned earlier not long after the healer, dismissed by the king, had left Kuba country. When Van Deuren uncovered all of this during his enquiry, he was livid. He denounced the king. He speculated that the king had launched the new movement on purpose. He reinterpreted the recent political infighting at the court so as to implicate Kwet Mabinc in the recent cases of extortion and accused him of thereby adding fuel to the increasing general hostility toward the colonial authorities. But Vallaeys would have none of it, and the whole crisis ended with a reconciliation between the king and his brother.

Vallaeys knew that it would be unwise for the colonial authorities to relegate a person who was so well known abroad. Despite the growing tensions in Mweka, the prestige of the Kuba king, his people, and their art remained unabated overseas. Between 1937 and January 1940, for instance, their reputation attracted a journalist on tour in the Congo, a German art historian, a movie company from New York, and a Belgian artist, while a spectacular exhibition of all known "authentic" royal statues was held in Belgium, followed by a smaller one in New York the following year.

The king died on November 14, 1939, shortly after World War II broke out. Mbop Mabinc succeeded with the backing of the governor general and despite an implicit challenge by Kwete Mwana. A month or two later Kwete Mwana was first forced to leave the capital for Mweka and somewhat later was forced to leave the kingdom altogether for a few years. Thanks to Mbop's fearsome reputation as a ruthless man during two decades of previous experience in government, and the input of an exceptionally able senior territorial agent, Charles Schillings, the transition went smoothly despite the outbreak of the war. Even when extra burdens were imposed on the population starting in 1942 as their contribution to the war effort, the kingdom remained quiet.

The new situation with its losses among colonial administrators and its exceptional demands for the war effort required a novel attitude of close collaboration between the two parties in indirect rule, in which the king and his councils gained more input, as is shown, for example, by the fact that the administration accepted their proposal of crops to cultivate for the war effort instead of its own earlier choice of cotton and manioc. As a result of this new attitude, the two parties collaborated smoothly throughout the following years in spite of everything. Neither increasing war fever, which generated tensions of all sorts expressed in rumors about disasters, human sacrifices, or cannibalism, nor the mutiny at

Luluabourg in January 1944, nor the ever worsening shortages of essential imports such as cloth, hoes, and machetes in 1944–45, nor the major discontent and unrest these shortages caused in the main cities of Kasai, including Luebo, nor the ensuing inflation had any impact on the relationship between Mbop Mabinc and the colonial authorities.

Representative Indirect Rule

It took until 1947 for Congo and Mweka to fully recover from the war. By then a new generation of colonials had replaced worn-out old-timers, salaries had been raised, and shortages had been remedied. The first sign of renewal occurred late in 1946 when a great boom in food crops for Katanga, especially maize, started in Mweka and attracted a few new European settlers. Then in October 1947 the Belgian senatorial

---

Eulogy of Kwet Mabinc by His Son Kwete Mwana

Georges Kwete Mwana wrote this eulogy in French (translated here) as the last entry in a little notebook about the history of the royal dynasty for foreign readers, probably administrators and Catholic missionaries. Some small bits of this text are missing. The lacunae that can be reconstructed are within brackets and gaps that cannot be reconstructed are rendered by ellipses.

No. 35. *Kwet Mabinc.* Our venerated king ascended the throne in 1919 after his brother Bop Mabinc, chief no. 34 on the list [of kings]. He has been . . . considerable from every point of view by his behavior and the [work] for the Belgian Government. He called the missionaries to the Catholic mission of Mushenge known as Bem aNgidy [name of the mushenge of King Kwet Mabinc]. He wanted that all the boys and girls could be taught at school and thus that many others be able to read and write.

When they began to build the railroad—I think that you know this—the Bakuba (Bushong) were afraid to work with the whites; indeed it is he who called them to him to advise them at the same time that he also threatened them.

He knew well how to render justice to the village, he inflicted fines to the . . . in proportion of the evil [they had committed]. Hence

commission visited the capital as a harbinger of the ten-year plan that followed two years later. By then colonial government had once again been reformed. The removal of Kasai's capital from Lusambo to Luluabourg further underlined the impact of the railway but was less important than the reorganization of the institutions of government.

From this point on the provincial offices of the technical departments took over, and within a few years the district commissioners had lost most of their influence. In his report about 1951 to the council of the Kasai province the governor declared that the district level of administration had lost nearly all relevance. Henceforth district commissioners were reduced to mere "inspectors and specialists in native affairs."[12]

This was not a climate favorable to indirect rule. In 1950 Governor Fernand Peigneux raised the issue in the council of the Kasai province to stress both the great loss of authority of most chiefs and also the risks

every Bushong prefers him ... in whatever case one discusses ... one always says that at "... *Beem aNgidy Kwet Mabinc bamaakel ngo, bamaamon ngo*" [translated "Bem aNgidy during the reign of the king Kwet Mabinc he did this and he decided the palaver in this fashion"]. When this or that white man had come such as for instance the administrator or the territorial agent about a matter of disobedience, of theft, of revolt, and so on are decided in this fashion.

Death of King Kwet Mabinc. After 21 years of rule he was stricken by diarrhea for two months. On November 14, 1939, around four in the evening he returned his soul to the Creator. Five Europeans and hundreds of Congolese witnessed it. The body was carried to the house which the chief [Kwet Mabinc] had built where his wives sang the *ngesh* [a traditional song]. After that we accompanied the body to its last dwelling. I myself tried to see the revered coffin as closely as possible [but it] was impossible as there were [so many people].

Kwet Mabinc [was] a brave and generous chief. [He] much [liked] the customs of his country ... and he did many things which I could not [express] very well in French because [I don't know the language well enough].

Signed Kwete Mwana[13]

12. *Conseil de la province du Kasai 1952.* March 25, 1952: 3–5.
13. Vansina Files, *nyim—after 1920,* Kwete Mwana's *Notebook,* pp. 23–24.

Indirect Rule in Action in 1944

The following letter written by the administrator of the territory of the Bakuba is typical for routine business in the territory. First the official reassures the king about a military convoy in order to avoid unrest; then he answers three different queries and complaints by the king. Finally he closes with his completely unofficial private demand for a leopard skin. Note the relevance of the missionary and that the former settler, L. Delcroix, was now recruited as a territorial agent.

Terr. Des Bakuba   Mweka le 8/11/44
Bureau of the Territory
　　　　To the chief Lukengo Bope
　　　　Nyme Bashi Bushongo
　　1. Many Greetings. Concerning the business of the soldiers. They are absolutely not going to Mushenge to fight.
　　2. The business of your villages who ran away from work for you. It is best to bring this palaver to Mister L. Delcroix, the territorial agent for the sector of Mushenge. He will look into this palaver.
　　3. The palaver of your wife Peshanga fille. She is in the village Shuenge [Shweeng], [in] her clan (Bashi Matunga). She had a big quarrel with another woman. She is not a nice small child. Peshanga does not want to be near you and she is in jail [*idiko na bloc*]. I want [*Npilai*] to send her to her mother near you. Even although you do not have to give the bridewealth, [still] bring it very quickly.
　　4. I send your wife Matakaniengi to you with Shamananga. Mon père [the Catholic Missionary] at Bena Makima wants to send her to you for her to stay near you in the enclosure [=women's quarters].
　　What about the skin of the leopard? Send it to me fast.
　　　　Many Greetings
　　　　A. T. P. chief
　　　　Of the Territory of the Bakuba.
　　　　[signed over official stamp] VIIIIe[14]

---

14. Hymans Papers of King Bop Mabinc maKyeen, 1944. Text is in a mixed jargon of Tshiluba and Lingala, hence the intended meaning of the message is not always clear.

involved in upsetting the existing order. Nevertheless, all over Congo, Kasai included, chiefdoms were phased out and replaced by sectors in the charge of "modern" leaders. Inevitably, then, the question of the Kuba kingdom was raised once again in a territory where after fifteen years of further immigration by rail from central Kasai a quarter of the population was now Luba or Lulua.

As early as 1949 the new district commissioner Paul Pierrot involved himself in a thorough study of the issue. He conducted several fact-finding missions in 1950 and 1951 to question the king and the councils in Nsheng before proposing any reforms at all. The opposition to indirect rule ranged from the Catholic missions to officials in Luluabourg and influential settlers. The opponents claimed that indirect rule was contrary to the usual standard practice, that it was responsible for the backward status of the Kuba, and that it did not take the inroads of modernity into account, inroads such as the influx of Luba and Lulua and the rise in the number of Western-educated and Christian residents.

On the other hand, the Kuba kingdom was still a showcase of benign Belgian colonial rule in the Western world. The king and his capital attracted more journalists, moviemakers, artists, photographers, and tourists than ever before as well as more and more art historians and art dealers, while support for the king and his realm remained considerable in exalted circles in Belgium. Hence already in 1947 the king and the capital had attracted the senatorial commission and the king's portrait had appeared in *Life* magazine, and by 1950 Leon Kochnitzky, an American art dealer and art historian, was even pleading to turn most of the kingdom into an ethnographic natural reserve.

Given the pressures for and against indirect rule, the administration became very careful and took its time. Its first reform was to detach Port Francqui from what was now called Mweka Territory—no longer Territory of the Bakuba. Then all the Luba/Lulua settlements along the rail line were excised from the kingdom and organized into three independent sectors of their own. Finally, in 1951 it was decided to maintain indirect rule but to reorganize it. The new regime should be representative of all the populations in the kingdom, not just the Bushong. A new "traditional," "national" Kuba council would be created with delegates from every single Kuba chiefdom or grouping, and it would meet once a year. The king was to be removed as judge from the tribunal at the capital, and the old tribunals with trial by a jury of judges were to be reinstated. Royal tribute, which hitherto had caused the greatest discontent among all the Kuba but especially those in the outlying chiefdoms, was scrapped

King Mbop Mabinc maKyeen (1939–69) (photograph by Eliot Elisofon, 1947, Eliot Elisofon Photographic Archives 22923-P5, #10, National Museum of African Art, Smithsonian Institution)

and replaced by a small tax to be paid in money to the kingdom's treasury, which would be administered by his special adviser—for a senior territorial administrator was now to be appointed as the king's mentor and special adviser.

Once approved, the reforms began to be carried out immediately by Schillings, who was appointed as the king's mentor. Everyone accepted Schillings because he was perceived as partial to the Kuba—his nickname was *Makupkup*, "the pre-eminent Kuba"—although he was also distrusted as an emissary of an intrusive administration. Schillings's use of the income from the special tax to improve the roads (as desired by the government) and to beautify the capital (as desired by the king) was typical for his ambivalent role. Furthermore, the new representativity of indirect rule was cleverly advertised by a picture of the "basket of wisdom," an implement that was linked to the council of the senior titleholders as an emblem of their collective wisdom. Yet the practicalities of implementing the representation of the various "subtribes" in the national council required a thorough study and reorganization of the local political situations in every chiefdom or village cluster all over the kingdom, a task so complex that it was barely completed a few months before independence.

During the fact-finding missions of 1950 and 1951, Mbop Mabinc was very active. He tried but failed to prevent his titleholders from testifying to the administration, especially on the question of tribute. In 1950 two titleholders died in connection with the reorganization of the tribunal at the capital. The following year one very senior titleholder testified about tribute and then suddenly died a few days later after a visit to the king. Poisoning was rumored in all these cases, but the autopsies did not reveal anything of this sort. The following is how a townsman remembered the first episode a few years later.

> In the year 1950 the district commissioner arrived at Nsheng and brought the titleholders together in a council and asked them as follows: "Long ago were you wont to give women, meat, fish, and wrappers to the king?" All the titleholders refused to answer except one of them, Mishambweky, the *nyibiin*, who answered that they did all of this.
>
> But King Mbop Mabinc maKyeen was not at all happy with the words of this person because the commissioner intended to appoint Mishambweky as a judge of the tribunal. Out of anger and spite he [the king] fed Mishambweky some poisoned meat.
>
> And so Mishambweky died.

Indirect Rule in Action in 1953

The following cases dated from August 1 to October 1953 illustrate how decisions were reached by the Kuba government, and how the balance of power between the king and the Bushong councils worked. Normally no colonial agent or administrator attended any of the councils. The administration requested or demanded something from the king, who then put the question to the two councils for ordinary affairs, after which it was up to the colonial administration to accept or reject the results. Because of its stress on representative government after 1951, the decisions arrived at by the councils in the 1950s were only very rarely refused.

First case: "Kwete Mwana." Early in 1940 the king had insisted on Kwete Mwana's relegation because he allegedly had de facto usurped the government of the kingdom between circa 1934 and 1939. Several times during the 1950s some of his friends who were notables and even some officials among the hereditary matrilineal aristocracy proposed that he be allowed to return from exile. Their proposals were rejected several times by the councils. A little later one of the instigators of the proposal died, and public rumor accused the king of having poisoned him. The king won. Although Schillings favored the return of Kwete Mwana, he respected the outcome.

Second case: "The army." The king had visited the school for noncommissioned officers in Luluabourg and was impressed. On his return he summoned all his dignitaries and reported to them that the state wanted more soldiers. He now proposed that the four governors of the Bushong provinces provide two of their children each as recruits and again claimed that the state desired it. The dignitaries retorted: so be it, but the king alone would be responsible for this action because they refused to back him up. The king had no other choice but to call the councils. Meanwhile the women of Nsheng harangued the notables and aristocrats, "Watch out for your children and your nephews." At the first council *ishyaaml* to which the king did not belong, the proposal was rejected. After this the prime minister (*kikaam*) and the two representatives of

> Mishambweky was the last wise man at the capital. He knew so
> many more stories [about the past] than those who tell them today.[15]

During its last colonial years the Kuba kingdom finally saw the real-
ization of two long-needed major investments at Nsheng: an official
school in 1955 and a hospital in 1957. Both came too late to have much of
an effect before independence, for by mid-1959 the turmoil preceding independence reached the territory first with the outbreak of war between

---

Nsheng town met the king several times at night and warned him
that they would not give in, even if he did summon the superior
council *ilaam* over which he presides and where one cannot pub-
licly contradict the king. But Mbop Mabinc did summon the council.
Three days of filibustering followed until the king gave in. Schillings
or his superiors did not intervene and accepted the result.

Third case: "The sticks." The king decided to renovate and extend the outer enclosures of the capital. In order to do this he
wanted its inhabitants to spend two to three hours of corvee
labor a day for about one month. He bypassed the *ishyaaml* council and merely informed the public at an *ilaam* council meeting as
a trial balloon. The main notables then consulted in private with
him and gave in. So when the proposal came up again at *ilaam*, it
was accepted. Once again Schillings did not intervene. But the
townsfolk worked so reluctantly that every day the king himself
had to supervise the job onsite, and soon a string of court cases
had been brought against recalcitrant workers. Yet after about half
the job had been completed, this sabotage was successful, and the
project was stopped. The king then obtained the backing of his
councils to raise laborers from outlying Bushong villages so that
the project was finally carried out after a further six months of
intermittent working.[16]

---

15. Vansina Files, *nyim—after 1920*, told by Makash Victor of Nsheng; translated into
French by Mbope André of Nsheng. My translation follows the French, which includes
additional information, supposedly known by all but not given in the original Bushong.

16. Vansina Notebooks, 17: 62–63, 24: 64–65.

Lulua and Luba and a few months later with the eruption of an outbreak of poison ordeals among the Bushong. Ironically, the same year
also saw the king attain the summit of his reputation among colonials as
he managed to keep the Kuba out of the conflict, play a substantial role
as mediator between the Luba and the Lulua, and stop the outbreak of
the poison ordeals. During these crises he met King Baudouin of the
Belgians at Luluabourg in December. In a surrealistic gesture, the thankful monarch then sent him two peacocks by helicopter as a present to
show his appreciation. And yet Mbop Mabinc was still not quite fully
aware of what was going on or what to expect, for less than three months
before independence he drafted a letter to urge the provincial governor
to appoint a particular Belgian official as the next administrator for
Mweka after independence, but then he never sent it.

Conclusion

The Kuba colonial experience has been exceptional in Congo because
only they were granted indirect rule on a grand scale, even though the
scope of the autonomy left to their own government kept shrinking over
time. Yet this indirect rule still had a great deal in common with colonial rule elsewhere in Congo. After all, its legal basis was the 1910 decree about chiefdoms with its insistence that the chief carry out a string
of duties that turned him into a colonial agent. For all their grand-
standing and ceremony, that is also exactly what happened to the Kuba
king and his councils. Yet everywhere else chiefs lost all credibility as
they became mere passive colonial agents, but the Kuba kings did
not—not among the inhabitants of the capital, nor even among most
rural villagers elsewhere—mainly because their government was representative of most Bushong villages and always preserved some initiative
and autonomy of its own.

Under indirect rule the townspeople at the capital were better protected from various colonial demands than people elsewhere in Congo,
and they enjoyed a more comfortable life than most rural Kuba did. In
general, their colonial experience was not so bitter. But a good part of
the well-being at Nsheng came at the expense of the outlying villagers
who were required to provide tribute and corvee labor for the center.
Hence the villagers paid the price for indirect rule. In addition, they also
bore the full brunt of colonial exploitation, an exploitation similar to
what was practiced elsewhere in the Congolese countryside. The next
two chapters are devoted to their experience.

Further Readings

Beumers E., and H-J Koloss. *Kings of Africa: Art and Authority in Central Africa.* Maastricht, 1992.

Bustin, Edouard. *Lunda under Belgian Rule: The Politics of Ethnicity.* Cambridge, Mass., 1975.

Lemarchand, René. *Political Awakening in the Congo.* Berkeley, Calif., 1964.

Norden, Hermann. *Fresh Tracks in the Belgian Congo.* Boston, 1924.

Young, Crawford. *Politics in the Congo: Decolonization and Independence.* Princeton, N.J., 1965.

Royal Rule According to Its Correspondence

When King Mbop Mabinc maKyeen died ten years after independence, his papers were thrown out to make room for other uses of the footlockers in which they had been kept. Later a presumably small portion of these papers were recovered by Jacques Hymans, an American academic. Today they are kept in the collections of the Memorial Library of the University of Wisconsin–Madison. Most of these turned out to be part of his correspondence between 1920, the year when he became active as the crown prince, and 1969, the year he died. Despite the fact that the surviving letters and messages are only a random part of what was once contained in the royal footlockers, there are enough of them and they seem representative enough to throw a good deal of light on the informal ways in which Mbop Mabinc actually ruled his realm, rather than on how he was supposed to rule it according to official prescriptions and the observations of administrators.

Personal relationships and face-to-face encounters were of great importance in Kuba culture. Hence one expects to encounter a relatively wide range of correspondents in the royal papers, and one can assume Mbop Mabinc had personally met with nearly all of his African correspondents. Moreover, the Kuba letters and messages to and from the king were clearly understood to be official business of one sort or another. Therefore, it is not so surprising to find letters and notes not only from administrators, district commissioners, and territorial agents, but also from agents for the Compagnie du Kasai who paid him an annual retainer, from the local industrial lumber company associated with it, from Bas-Congo-Katanga (BCK) Railway Company personnel, from nearly all the local settlers, and even from small traders or shop managers in faraway places such as Butala. There are also letters and notes from both Presbyterian and Catholic missionaries, although perhaps one would not have expected messages from nuns such as Mother Cecile. By the later 1950s one also finds correspondence with official schools in Luluabourg and even in Léopoldville. Rather more surprising are some the king's contacts with other Westerners. These include two commanders of the Force Publique, an agronomist, and more exotic correspondents such as a freeloader from Katanga, a moviemaker in Belgium, and a family in Los Angeles.

The bulk of the royal correspondents involves only African men—no African women—overwhelmingly Bushong, but no other Kuba apart from a few Kete. Yet such correspondents also include Luba and Lulua, many of whom were already literate by the 1920s. A large number of correspondents are, of course, relatives—mostly sons and nephews (usually begging for money). Another large group is ambitious youths looking for royal patronage in order to obtain jobs ranging from a nomination as judge to a clerical position in the administration or in a shop. After 1949 the king stayed in contact with most of the freshly graduated new elite among the Bushong, both within his realm and far beyond. Another block of correspondents were in official service. These include clerks in the territorial administration or in the kingdom's Native Treasury, judges, clerks supervising the tribunals, schoolmasters, and even lowly agricultural monitors. Beyond these groups one finds Catholic catechists, Presbyterian evangelists, shopkeepers, a soldier or two, and even a bank employee in Elisabethville. It is a sign of the times that some correspondence was exchanged in the 1950s between the king and some major chiefs in central Kasai including Kalamba, the leader of the Lulua (1959). In contrast, not a scrap of correspondence has been found with any of the main modern political leaders in Kasai nor with any of their parties before January 1960. This may be a result of the haphazard rescue of the royal papers, but it is just as likely that there were no such contacts at all.

His papers show the king to be well connected with the milieus of the territorial administration, local commerce, missions, schools, and elsewhere beyond these spheres. This is not what one would have imagined from the part of a supposedly hide-bound "traditional" exemplar of monarchs. That such contacts are missing with the new elites in Kasai beyond the Bushong, including the major provincial politicians of the 1950s, better fits the cliché. But what is perhaps most impressive about these papers are both the very large number of correspondents and their huge social range. Added to the lists of villages, clans, and heads of households, which we know were also kept among the royal papers (although very few of those have survived), this means that Mbop Mabinc came to know practically any person of any direct importance to his realm, whether in it or outside, a necessity for any efficient ruler in a culture based on personal relationships.

The content of these letters also greatly varies. Many items deal with the expected business of indirect rule, such as the census, taxes, tributes, corvee labor, the recruitment of soldiers, the provision of labor for companies or for roadwork, and convocations to the tribunal of the chiefdom, as well as appointments of provincial chiefs, judges, or notables at court. Many items also provide information to the king about what seems to be everybody, information that came from all corners of the country and well beyond it and from all levels of society. That too is obviously a necessary part of government. So are issues concerning schools and pupils, child marriage as crypto-enslavement, the amount of bridewealth, and runaway wives.

Less expected are the number of items about the king's wives, concerning their yearly supplies, payments for their bridewealth, and even their elopements, all handled as official business. Yet they were an essential part of the government, as was shown in a spectacular way by a set of events that unfolded after independence in the dry season of 1960 when many of the royal wives were chased away by a Protestant Kete administrator. As a result, the governance of the whole kingdom crashed, and the administration of Mweka shuddered to a halt.

Then there are a number of documents about the king's and the realm's own treasury. The inventories of twelve footlockers containing the king's treasure in locally produced goods are of obvious significance. Such objects were used as gifts for meritorious chiefs or other subjects and as countergifts for tribute. Most of the other economic items mentioned concern small livestock and also gifts. They are tallies of the increases, decreases, and free gifts to state agents of goats, sheep, chickens, and even eggs.

One also encounters a good number of items about Kuba art objects. Correspondence about the creation of an artist's cooperative, about setting prices by royal decree, about developments at the art school at the capital (where Jules Lyeen, the official royal carver and at the same time a trusted collector of tribute and a friend of the king, taught) are all obvious official business. So are perhaps objects acquired as tribute and thus listed in the inventories already cited. But what about letters from various people such as a BCK woman from Elisabethville and various members of the administration in Kasai who wanted to buy pipes or masks or mats or special textiles? Are such items still part of the official business of indirect rule? No doubt the king considered them as such and viewed these as favors to be paid for in money or in counterfavors from those who counted on their official position to obtain such objects.

Despite initial appearances, the papers of King Mbop Mabinc actually contained rather few private items. Apart from a few notes from what seem to be genuine friends and a record of his own gun permits, these private records consist mainly of various sets of bills, mostly for food or drink or for his car and truck (fuel, maintenance, tires, repairs). In addition, some information about maize prices in the 1950s may also be private since the king seems to have traded himself from time to time in what was after all the hot commodity of the late 1940s and 1950s.

8

Village Life

1911–1950s

This chapter deals with the economic and social experiences of villagers in the Bushong and Kete countryside. It therefore complements the previous chapter, which looked at the history of indirect rule from the top down. Moreover, in sharp contrast to indirect rule that dealt with a situation rather exceptional in colonial Congo, the experiences at the grassroots village level were quite similar to those of rural folk elsewhere in rural Congo, although these diverged more and more over time from the experiences of Congolese who lived as wage laborers or were self-employed in industrial surroundings and in the main cities.

First we look at the economic history of Bushong and Kete villagers as providers of cash crops for export, food for the island of industrial development in Katanga, labor for public works, and labor for taxes to pay as their allotted task within the overall grand scheme of what colonials called "development." Then we turn to an examination of the sociocultural changes that accompanied this colonial development.

Compulsory Cultivation

By 1910 the age of rubber exploitation was ending, and for a while adult male Kuba villagers were left alone, provided they came up with money to pay an annual state tax. Default was punished with a two-month-long jail term. To earn their tax money more and more villagers turned to the production of palm oil and especially palm kernels and continued to sell most of these to the Compagnie du Kasai but at more reasonable prices now that there was competition at Luebo. Taxes were not high, and the district commissioner in Kasai even omitted collecting them in 1915.

But the decree about obligatory labor in February 1917 changed everything. From now on the administration decided what kinds of crops over what acreage each adult male villager was compelled to grow unless he was exempt. Noncompliance of any sort was also punished by a jail term of two months, with the result that by the 1950s about one of every ten men spent some time in jail each year and that most men had done so at one time or another. By then there was even a children's song:

> The man mourns his wife
> They put her in the government jail
> Mishoosh is going to settle our business
> Applaud [him] *owiho*.[1]

Exemptions were eagerly sought but rarely obtained, because only seriously ill people or wage earners for colonial institutions or businesses were exempt. Hence only one or two men enjoyed exempt status in most villages, in sharp contrast to the capital. Here the very first page of a list of gun owners shows that 33 healthy adult men out of 37 who owned a gun in 1939–40 were exempt because they worked for the Josephite mission as cooks, servants for expatriates, laborers, catechists, nurses, or messengers for the state. On that page one other person was listed as exempt because he was ill. Only two men were not exempt, of whom one had left the capital.

In many parts of Kuba country the designated compulsory crops were palm products and continued to be so until independence. But in the 1930s compulsory cultivation of cotton was imposed instead of palm products over a large portion of the kingdom, including parts of the Bushong chiefdom. That effort, however, was abandoned in 1942 after stiff resistance and sabotage by the Bushong, who complained that this crop exhausted the soil. Meanwhile, and starting with the building of the railway, villages along the rail line and some others as well were required to produce foodstuffs such as manioc and maize for the railway navvies first and later for the cities and mines in Katanga. In general,

---

1. Vansina Files, *Literature; songs*: 4.

Arrest Warrant for Tax Delinquency

District of *Kasai* no. 281
  Tax office *of the Bakuba*
    Belgian Congo
  Native tax   Order to arrest
  _____

By virtue of the decree on native taxes, an arrest for a period of
two months
Starting from (2) *18-4-1933* has been
Decreed by the undersigned R. *Van Deuren*
A.T.
against the named *Yamba Pierre*
from the village of Culembonge (no. _____
of the passbook, Folio no. _____ of the register of
taxpayers), because of non payment of the sum
of *45* francs _____ centimes,
representing (3) the *totality*
of his taxes for the year *1932*
Mweka, the *18-4-1933*
The [signed] *A.T. Van Deuren* (4)
—

  1. Date on which the taxpayer has been apprehended
  2. Name, first name, and quality of the official who decreed the
arrest
  3. Totality, first half or second half, as applies
  4. Signature
  _____

  Finances [form] mod. no. 211 _____ 8787

It is likely that Pierre Yamba did not have the funds to pay his
taxes because he had not gathered palm nuts for the Compagnie
du Kasai. If he had, he would have had enough money to pay his
taxes.[2]

2. Hymans Papers of King Bop Mabinc maKyeen, 1933 (available at the Memorial
Library of the University of Wisconsin–Madison). Text in italics is handwritten.

conditions for food sales were better than for palm products because no single large company dominated the market. Starting in 1946 the demand for maize rose to unprecedented heights, and a number of new merchants entered the market, so that the prices offered to the producers by competing European traders rose sharply until the later 1950s so that, perhaps for the first time since 1901, many rural villagers near the rail line began to earn more money than they spent on taxes and basic necessities such as salt or hoes. They might have felt better off, however, were it not that at the same time a widely hated new form of compulsory agriculture known as *mpiki* was foisted upon them.

Each of the crops imposed had its own technical and labor requirements and thereby affected the villagers in different ways. For instance, the production of palm products required men to climb the tall *elais* trees to cut the fruit at its top. They always ran the risk of falling out of the tree, and from time to time some did with severe consequences. After that came the time-consuming and onerous tasks of cooking the nuts, pressing the palm oil out of the fruit by hand, drying the kernel of the fruit, and then cracking it to extract its oil.

The best Kuba technique to press oil was carried out by men. It required more work and a longer time than another method used by women. This was much less time consuming but produced oil of a lesser quality. Still by the 1920s businesses accepted this less pure oil, and hence the second method became the standard one for compulsory cultivation. Similarly an emphasis on speed as well as poor prices for palm kernels pushed the women to cut corners and to leave much waste.

By the late 1920s the companies or settlers began to introduce processing factories equipped with manual oil presses first and with fully mechanized presses a decade or two later. Such factories substantially increased the number of wage earners working for the companies. Yet despite the disadvantages of not doing so, very few Bushong or Kete men took such jobs. Hence most of these jobs went to Luba or Lulua along the rail line. The new system of production replaced most of the tasks women had fulfilled. That meant, though, that boxes of fruit had to be brought to the factory, preferably by truck, which in turn necessitated the availability of roads. So roads first had to be built and then maintained. That was a task that by government decree fell mostly on men's shoulders, although hitherto much of the sort of work this involved—hoeing, weeding, and smoothing the surface of the soil required to keep village public squares, streets, and access roads in good shape—had been women's work.

As it became apparent that artificial plantations of selected palm tree species produced much more fruit per tree and per unit of labor than the existing stands of trees, the government began to mobilize men's labor during the 1930s and even more after 1945 to establish such plantations, albeit to the actual benefit of foreign private companies. Hence the tasks required changed again so that in addition to cutting palm fruit men now also had to work as temporary plantation labor.

With the coming of the railway and oil presses, women spent more and more time growing compulsory food crops such as groundnuts, maize, and manioc as well as foodstuffs for their own family, among which beans were very important. These crops, however, were not at all interchangeable as regards the division of labor between genders and the amount of work to invest. Maize added more work for the men because it required them to hack new fields out of the forests in order to have good soils, whereas this was not necessary with fields for groundnuts and manioc. But manioc required special processing before sale, a very time-consuming process that, like all food processing, was exclusively allotted to women.

Cotton was different again. First, unlike all other imposed crops that were well known to the Kuba, this was a wholly new venture. Second, a

---

Bakwa Kasenga's Palm Fruit Cutters

Luebo (Kasenga) April 8, 1940
The seven *shanshenge* [headmen] Shamba-Mboyo, Pembe-Shamba, Kabana, Shamba-Kamala, Shamba-Kawala, Mutanda-Shamba and Bushaba-Kwete. We have authorized the Shanshenge named Bushaba-Kwete to be our overseer for our labors as [palm] fruit cutters for a trader David Mukeba.
Here follow the thumbprints of all the *Shanshenge*.[3]

---

3. Hymans Papers of King Bop Mabinc maKyeen, 1940. The villagers of this Kete village just north of Luebo were fulfilling their obligations about compulsory labor. Note that they could choose any of the licensed traders as a patron, including Luba ones such as David Mukeba. During the 1950s the same Mukeba was part of the provincial council of Kasai and became a well-known local politician after 1960.

great deal of work had to be invested in it. The fields had to be cleared each year by men but planted and weeded (cotton required much weeding and tending) by women, who also picked the cotton and brought it to the buying stations. The Kuba hated this crop with a passion because cotton both exhausted the soils and took up so much of the time needed for the production of the food crops needed by the villagers. More than any other activity, they sabotaged cotton production whenever they could. Thus, in an endeavor to discourage colonial agronomists, men commonly induced them to select very poor soils for growing the crop, while women found different ways to make the plants wither and die— for instance, by cutting their roots underground.

Then, at the very time that the sale of maize was beginning to ease the life of many villagers, there came the *mpiki*. *Mpiki* was the local expression for the introduction of the peasantry system (*paysannats*), a system by which farmers were to follow a complex form of perennial (rather than shifting) agriculture as had been developed on experimental farms. This was to be carried out on a plot of land that would eventually become the property of the individual farmer who worked it and provide him and his family with a living.

The Bushong villagers first saw a new agronomist arrive in their village. He surveyed a large rectangle of land somewhere in the bush—but usually not far from a road—subdivided it into plots, and assigned one plot each to all adult men in the village as a compulsory field—and never mind that the women were the real farming experts! The system was called *mpiki* from the French term *piquet* after the sticks that were set up as boundary markers for the fields. Every male farmer was said to "own" his field, but he had no control at all over his "property" and knew full well that the land belonged to the domain of his village, not to him.

After this operation a Congolese agricultural monitor was installed in each village, rather like the capita of the rubber age. His job was to teach people modern agriculture—that is, to compel the villagers every single day of the year to do whatever he wanted done on their *mpiki* field, and he could back up his authority by threatening to have recalcitrant villagers fined or arrested.

The Kuba hated the *mpiki* with a vengeance. It was not mainly because the learned agronomists often made gross errors of judgment that led to very poor yields of maize or beans, which then had to be supplemented by hidden farms elsewhere. Instead it was mainly because people bitterly resented the hitherto unprecedented regimentation of their lives and the complete loss of their freedom of action and their free time.

Agricultural monitor intervenes in village court, 1954 (photo by author)

Before World War II they had been compelled to provide this or that crop and had been jailed or fined when they failed to do so or when they failed to pay their taxes. But otherwise they had been left alone. Now there was apparently no escape from the monitor, no letting up of the pressure. The result was that during the later 1950s the *mpiki* system created a more and more intense longing for freedom from control. Later, even twenty years after independence, the Kuba still singled out the *mpiki* as the worst part of the whole colonial regime. For them that was the significance of independence, and it provided the intense emotions that led to wholly unexpected explosions or rural fury in Congo including in Mweka in 1959–60.

Village Labor and Other Impositions

In addition to the payment of a head tax and the compulsory production of crops, villagers also had to provide labor for the government. Legally this was a stipulated amount of time, but in Kasai the law was simply ignored whenever that amount of time was insufficient. At first, porterage was the most common form of commandeered labor. Everyone, but especially the Bushong and Kete, so disliked being porters that they ran away whenever possible without any regard for the status of the person for whose caravan they had been recruited. In 1910 even the vice governor general of Congo could not find carriers in Nsheng, and in 1912 a British consul was stranded on the road while his forcibly recruited porters on that occasion ran away on arrival without even waiting for any payment. As late as 1923, even the Belgian minister for labor was abandoned by his carriers, and when he tried to enroll local Kete they refused to do the job on the grounds that while carrying a litter was a job for men, carrying luggage was women's work.

One can imagine how the news was received during World War I that the government had ordered the recruitment of a substantial number of porters for the armed forces in the Cameroons and in East Africa in addition, of course, to those needed for the local caravans. When press gangs and kidnapping began to occur in Kasai as a result of these orders and chaos threatened, the Presbyterian mission at Luebo and the district commissioner joined forces to call a three-day meeting during which they convinced the chiefs of the region (including Kwet aPe?) to act as recruiters.

The construction of the railway led to the forcible recruitment of lumberjacks and the first mobilization of labor to build roads, both tasks

"Car on the Highway" by Djilatendo, 1930–32 (Thiry, *A la recherche de la peinture nègre*, n.d.)

that were carried out by large gangs supervised by a European. While felling trees and clearing forests were tasks for men, much of the work on the roadbeds and later maintenance was women's work, and whenever there was no supervision much of initial work was actually done by women as well. Building roads remained a major activity during the next twenty years, while later villagers still had to repair the so-called secondary roads every year whenever needed. But at least roads ousted porterage so that by 1940 caravans had practically disappeared.

Much more dreaded than even porterage or compulsory labor was forced recruitment for the colonial army. Periodically the kingdom, like every other territory, was assessed a number of recruits based on the current census. Recruits served seven years and might or might not return to their villages. Before the spread of some literacy, that is, before the 1930s or so, villagers might not hear any news from their soldiers for many years if ever. Hence they viewed army recruitment at best as a new form of slavery and at worst as a death sentence. The king and his officials were very well aware of this, but still they periodically had to require that a designated village furnish one or more recruits while the villagers did all they could to avert such a calamity.

When faced with a peremptory demand, the village council met to designate the families that had to surrender a man each. Even then they tried to beat the system by sending recruits whom they hoped would be rejected as physically unsuitable by the army. In this atmosphere any perceived irregularity in the equal assessment of soldiers between villages and between wards within each village could provoke a rebellious explosion. Exactly this happened when an irate royal official, Miko miBwoon, suddenly demanded a number of recruits from the village of Patambamba in January 1929. Miko miBwoon, a Protestant, wanted to punish the Catholic people of Patambamba who were quarreling with

Building the Road from Luebo to Mweka in 1923

And we stumble on a strange spectacle: hundreds of people swarm over a vast space cleared of forest: a young white man, from Brussels, hastens up and informs us that he is in charge of building a road for wheeled traffic that will go from Mowka [Mweka] to Luebo, capital of the district. Therefore he had to scour the forest which covers many kilometers here and to open a gallery through it more than ten meters wide. Then he has removed the stumps and then leveled the soil; the soil consists of barely loamy sand. To achieve sound leveling one excavates large holes on the side of the roadway and takes soil for the roadbed from them. At the bottom of the hole there are natives with small pots or small baskets; on the lip of the hole there are other natives with the same little baskets which they fill by hand and carry to the road. In line on the road and in close ranks other workers with wooden pestles stamp the soil, while the village headmen encourage them and drummers continually beat their instruments while howling monotonous chants.

It is funny and phenomenal. More than a thousand people working like this with a spoon . . . whereas two hundred workers, even natives, well equipped as they are on the railroad, would do more and better work.[4]

4. Joseph Wauters, *Le Congo au travail* (Brussels, 1926), 140. Note his colonialist and racist tone in spite of this quality as a socialist politician.

their Protestant neighbors near the mission of Bulape. The result was first the murder of the three messengers who came to fetch the recruits and then the inevitable military occupation of the village.

Once the railway was functioning, there came yet another demand for labor by villagers, on top of all of the preceding requirements. Different expatriate businesses of all sorts, including some as far away as south Kasai, began to recruit men on contracts of six months, a year, or even longer. By then the state had officially divided the country into labor recruitment zones, although the territorial administration was not supposed to exert any pressure at all over recruiting. In practice, however, administrators were pressured hard to find "volunteers" for recruitment.

In the Kuba kingdom the first pressure of this kind occurred in 1929, with the result that the king ordered about thirty families to come up with three men each to work at Mweka, soon to be the new capital of the territory. When they arrived there they did not dare tell the territorial administrator that they were not volunteers, so they were enrolled and sent far away by train. However, their families, who interpreted the recruitment order as tantamount to induction into the army, thought they had been wise enough by providing only mature men who were bound to be rejected by the army. The men, however, were found to be fit enough for work as wage labor, whereupon the frustrated families accused the king of having sold their men, even though the same company had previously employed other workers who had all returned safe and sound. Nevertheless, after this incident forcible recruitment of this sort had to be abandoned among the Kuba, mainly because such forceful recruiting was completely illegal. One cannot help but think that it would be hard to find a better illustration of the drawbacks of indirect rule for the Kuba villagers than this story.

Finally, in addition to all the demands by the state, villagers also had to satisfy those of their king. The king assigned an annual tribute that was specified for each village and consisted of durable goods ("dry goods") such as lengths of raffia and dried fish at Shin aNtek, or metal ware, ceramics, salt, and dried mushrooms elsewhere. But the amount demanded was not specified and it varied from year to year. This tribute was collected by the king's representatives, who always took part of the tribute for themselves. The demand for tribute in addition to state taxes and the greedy behavior of the king's men in collecting it were bitterly resented by all the villages who were not free Bushong and hence were not directly represented at the capital. Sometimes, as among the southern

Kete of Kampungu and neighboring villages in the 1920s, discontent broke into open rebellion.

The chorus of complaints from the subordinate polities eventually prompted the reform of 1951 by which tribute was replaced by a small payment in cash. Still, even this so irked the Coofa in the southeast that they hired a lawyer to challenge the practice in court barely a year or two before independence. Along with tribute the king could also order compulsory labor from any village when needed, and the official tribunal enforced such demands. He usually did so for road repair or for construction work at the capital.

And last but not least when the king or any of his representatives were traveling, every village through which they passed along the road was supposed to provide them with the best food and lodgings and to offer them tributary gifts. The following case is perhaps an extreme instance of this. It occurred when Mbop Mabinc, still crown prince, accompanied an American guest from Mweka to Nsheng in 1923.

> Our passage through the villages was a triumphal procession. There is no doubt that Bopé is popular with the people. But the honouring of a royal visitor is as expensive among the Bakuba as elsewhere in the world, for everywhere he received gifts; goats and pigs and chickens and *malufa* [palm wine] and *madiba* [raffia cloth]. I was told that in one village he received two thousand pieces of cloth. Wherever we stopped *bidia* [food] was instantly ready for the

The Case of Pyeem at the Main Native Court

On April 1954 Shanshenge [a Kete village headman] Kwet appeared in order to accuse [the man] Pyeem as follows: "You, judges, why does Pyeem not stitch *kíing* [strings used in building walls] at the capital?" Pyeem said: "It is a lie. I do stitch *kíing*." The witnesses said: "You, judges, it is a lie. He does not stitch *kíing*." The judges said: "Pyeem, you lost: one month in jail; a fine of 150 Francs."[5]

5. Vansina Notebooks, 24: 82–83.

porters, and at one village we were served antelope steaks and
hearts of palm on green leaves, and freshly brewed *pombe* [beer].
Barney and Pierre collected food. Chickens, ducks, and parrots
went into the coop: a couple of sheep were added and plenty of
pineapples. I think they did not pay; was not their master the guest
of the nation?[6]

Even thirty years later one could still see that even lowly ranked canton chiefs on tour were still received with choice foods and the best lodgings. Indeed, even ordinary clerks on official trips expected free food
and lodgings.

All these obligations make one wonder how and when the villagers
found the time to grow or gather their own food, to practice the crafts
needed for their upkeep, and to conduct the local petty trading required
to provide for their clothing, their household utensils and their tools,
and the maintenance of their houses and villages. It was evident that
they only managed to do so by neglecting these time-consuming impositions, especially the compulsory cultivation, whenever they could, even
at the cost of being jailed from time to time for failure to pay taxes or to
come up with the required cash crops.

Before the 1930s the administration lacked the personnel to continually check on the villagers, and the king's officials turned a blind eye. Still,
even by then standards of living had fallen. New houses were considerably smaller than they had been before and they never contained more
than a single room. The diversity of food declined as neither women nor
men had much time left to forage, and women found time only to cultivate the most basic foodstuffs: maize, beans, groundnuts, and some cas-
sava, but not the other vegetables or condiments that were used in earlier
times as a nutritionally rich relish. Hence the quality, if not the quantity,
of their food intake suffered. Yet villagers still managed to produce some
essential utensils including pottery, baskets, mats, or wooden cups and
boxes, and basic tools such as hoes, axes, and knives as well as vegetal
salt, even though by then the marshes where the salty grasses were harvested harbored tsetse flies that infected many a salt maker with sleeping
sickness. As a result, local markets still traded in such goods.

During the Great Depression the situation worsened. To begin
with, many villages lost considerable portions of their domains when
agronomists began to carve out large tracts of land for the 123 new Luba

6. Hermann Norden, *Fresh Tracks in the Belgian Congo* (Boston, [1924]), 224–25.

or Lulua settlements. Then followed a great effort of building roads and the forced relocation of all villages along the new roads. No fewer than 650 miles of road were built by hand between 1923 and 1939, which gives an idea of the colossal commotion caused by this program. It also played havoc with villages' rights of ownership over their own domains and essentially undercut all land tenure law. Later the *mpiki*, with its pretense of individual male land ownership, made matters even worse. By now villagers began to feel that the very foundations of their villages were being eroded and that their lives were becoming ever more insecure.

During the Depression most villages also came under much greater pressure to produce and were now under much closer scrutiny. That meant that the villagers could no longer cheat enough to find the time to satisfy their own needs. This became all the more difficult as the European administration now set out consciously to destroy some of their earlier activities on the grounds that these consumed too much of the labor and time required to meet its own demands. Even initiations into age grades were forbidden on those grounds. Iron smelting, a very labor-intensive activity, was outlawed, and local markets were frowned upon. Yet even so, many villages still managed to produce local commodities that were less time consuming, such as making pottery or plaiting baskets mostly for local consumption.

Around railway stations, mission posts, and at Nsheng, however, villagers and townspeople still managed to produce souvenirs for export (especially cut pile cloth), wooden objects for everyday use, or mats that they sold to local colonials including missionaries or hawked to tourists. The interest among expatriates was great enough to sustain a small but regular trade in such objects. After the missionary sisters had settled at Nsheng in 1938, they set out to acquire pile cloth for export by organizing several ateliers of the local women in a system where the women produced a set number of lengths of cloth per week for a fixed sum. In addition, they also taught needlework in their girls' school so that their pupils also produced pile cloth for them. After World War II, competition among woodcarvers especially became so strong that the Kuba government set up a cooperative arrangement and issued a decree against selling carvings at prices considered to be below cost.

This trade was minor, but it brought in some much needed money. The main beneficiaries were women, because they owned the cloth as well as many of the wooden objects coveted by the curio market, even though they did not produce any of the wooden carvings. Women then spent most of this income on acquiring some by now essential imports for their households as well as some imported clothes. Men used much of this income to pay their head tax and to escape, at least in part, from the treadmill of earning all of one's tax money through compulsory cultivation.

Villagers as Consumers

The availability of imports on which villagers could spend their earnings was very important to the official colonial mind. According to its theories, the desire to own such imports would prompt people to work

---

Selling Souvenirs: A Dream by Albert Mbakam

I dreamt that the capita came to call us: "all of you go to Ibwáncy with your merchandise to sell." Everyone went. When we arrived there we saw a plane flying to and fro without falling. Then we saw a white man who put his hand out and he said: "Come with all your goods for sale and come here. Many white men are going to arrive to buy." We all took our merchandise. After a while we saw five planes filled with whites and those five planes landed and the whites left them. Then we saw a dwarf [this must be the governor general, Léon Pétillon, who was quite small] come out before the others and they all followed, and everyone said that this is the commander in chief. That dwarf asked us the price of something. If you quote him a price he does not answer [haggle], he takes money and gives you what you asked for, even two hundred or four hundred or even one thousand francs. He bought many things. And then these whites board their planes and leave for home. And after that we saw the administrator who told us "Why did you lie about the price, and make our boss pay very much." And he sent policemen to arrest us; and we fled. One of these policemen followed me quite fast to arrest me. When he had come very close to me I changed into a bird and landed somewhere else. When I got up, I had been sleeping.[7]

---

7. Vansina Files, *News and Dreams*, subfile *dreams* 13/XVII (1954).

Tourist art: Royal portrait (*ndop*), 1940s (1953.16.5, collection RMCA Tervuren; photo by
J. Mulders [Inforcongo], © RMCA Tervuren)

for wages and would give them a sense of being rewarded for the cultivation of the compulsory cash crops in particular. During the 1910s the
first commercial centers—that is, clusters of shops for the retail trade—
appeared at major settlements. Later they also sprang up at many points
along the rail line and along all the major roads so that by the 1930s very
few villages were out of reach of a commercial center. Practically every
store in such a center sold "everything," whatever merchandise was in
demand. In return, every store also bought seasonal local produce for
resale. No good description exists of these shadowy, partly open-fronted
emporia smelling of dried fish and palm oil and filled from floor to ceil-
ing with what looked like the most heteroclite collection of items imaginable but was, in fact, packed only with what was in demand.

In these "houses of things," as the Bushong called them, people
bought what had already become absolute necessities in the first decade
after 1900—namely, matches, soap, and salt. But not European food of
any kind, nor any imported textiles yet. They were so opposed to any
form of European food that when Ibanc was destroyed and plundered
in 1900, they threw all foodstuffs, whether canned or not, by the way-
side. Their taste changed slowly, but it did change. From the 1920s onward it became customary for a husband to buy a new wrapper for his
wife yearly, while small quantities of bottled beer and cigarettes also
began to be sold occasionally as expensive, and hence prestigious, sub-
stitutes for palm wine and local tobacco. After the administration forcibly suppressed iron smelting, and less directly iron forging during the
early 1930s, it became unavoidable to buy at least the most essential tools
such as hoes and bush knives annually, even though local smithies still
managed to forge smaller tools from recycled metals and to craft larger
tools such as spears and knives from scrap metal.

By then, shops, especially along the railroad where most of their customers were Tshiluba speakers, had long offered much more than the
basic necessities. There men were tempted by "big ticket" items, especially guns and bicycles, although very few villagers even in the 1950s
could afford them. There also, entrepreneurs might buy some sewing
machines for a tailoring business. The same shops also sold all sorts of
"luxury" items ranging from the useful—blankets, metal footlockers,
enamel basins, hurricane lanterns, and clothes such as wrappers, head-
scarves, and frocks for women, men's short trousers, shirts, and hats
along with shoes and umbrellas for all—to the more fanciful items—
perfumes, beauty creams, beads, sunglasses, earrings and other costume

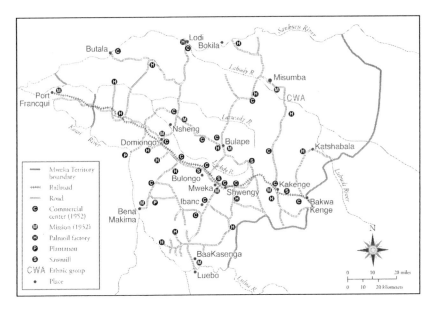

Mweka's modern economy, 1952

jewelry, purses or pocket books, fountain pens, lighters, and even watches or phonographs. There too the extravagant could buy cigarettes and alternative foods such as bottled beer, salted fish, corned beef, margarine, rice, sardines, and locally made hard liquor. But unlike a few people in or near Nsheng, no Bushong or Kete villager ever owned a typewriter or a pickup truck. They had no use for the first, and the second remained simply beyond their means.

The great majority of customers who frequented these shops were Luba or Lulua, who, even before the early 1920s, were already adopting Western clothing everywhere and whenever they could afford it. Kuba villagers were introduced to the new fashions by the Luba/Lulua men whom the missions were then beginning to place there as teachers and proselytizers. The clothes worn by the numerous Protestant evangelists, who tended to be somewhat more formally dressed than their Catholic counterparts, seemed especially sophisticated. By then also a few Bushong or Kete villagers back from military service returned home with new ideas and new goods, and only a few years later the first young men recruited by companies far away as unskilled labor were also returning laden with goods they had bought with their savings after their period of service.

Still, in order to afford such commodities the customers had to have money, and that meant they needed to be wage earners or petty traders. Among the Luba/Lulua the very desire to wear such clothes and thus to imitate westerners was a powerful enough incentive to seek such occupations. Nevertheless most Kuba still prided themselves on their own

Prestige of the Typewriter

It is not known who introduced the first typewriter to Luebo, only that the administration began to use the instrument shortly after 1910. Soon the Congolese in Kasai were considering the typewriter as the chosen instrument of the administration and Djila-tendo's image of "Administrator at Work" in 1930–31 (see chapter 6) epitomizes the whole mysterious business of government as a job in which men were hitting heavy keys on massive Remingtons. Certainly typewriters were a favorite tool of government, not just because they made reports legible but even more because they facilitated the production of copies.

By 1920 the standard requirement of having four copies of nearly every document had become tradition. Even then the machine symbolized the summit of modernity for both expatriates and local people. Indeed, in 1923 a visiting American geographer for whom the Kuba were still the acme of pristine African culture exclaimed that he hoped that the rumor was not true that Mbope Mabinc maKyeen, the crown prince, owned a typewriter!

By the 1950s the king's secretaries at the Kuba court were in possession of several such machines as part of the state's administration. By then the portable typewriter was becoming the hallmark of intellectual distinction. Moreover, these machines were especially highly valued because they could only be bought in the biggest cities or by mail order. Only Congolese intellectuals who had expatriate friends or patrons could obtain such a prized possession. The prestige of typewriters lasted until well after independence when rebels in eastern Congo decorated themselves with black and red typewriter ribbons as a sign of their natural administrative power and their superior intelligence.

finery and still interpreted wage labor as disguised slavery. Only well after the completion of the railway, after the multiplication of commercial centers that followed, and after signs of relative affluence began to appear among the formerly despised Luba/Lulua were Kuba villagers finally attracted to the shops. By then, though, the Depression raged, and the villagers were trapped on an infernal treadmill of compulsory labor and crisis of one sort or another that would not let up before 1947. Under such circumstances most villagers could not afford anything beyond the barest essentials.

When the trade in maize took off beginning in 1947, the situation rapidly improved considerably for the inhabitants of every village near the rail line or near its main feeder roads, and it continued to do so for a good decade before independence loomed and brought the boom to an end in 1959. By 1947 both the Luba and Lulua were enjoying a higher standard of education overall, and many of them found work with employers in the expanding businesses along the rail line. Now at last some young Kuba, especially Kete, began also to be attracted to Western ways of living and were eager to enter the market as "white-collar" labor such as sales clerks or store managers even though they were barely literate considering that that village schools did not amount to much. Meanwhile, selling maize brought more money to all village farmers near the rail line and its feeder roads so that for the first time they too could now afford to buy some coveted extras. Nevertheless, villages such as Shyaam aNyingdy that were too far away from the rail line to benefit from the trade in maize remained as destitute as ever. In the following text, a clerk from the capital Nsheng describes what he estimates to be the poorest village among the ones he knew:

> All around their village the houses are old, except for one new house that belongs to a young boy. Their clothes are made of untreated raffia cloth because they cannot afford to buy imported cloth. Their job is to cut palmfruit. In the village there are plantains, bananas, elais, and raffia palm trees.
>
> The children are dirty. They are not always washed and sometimes they are not washed for a month. The [villagers] lack chairs and/or tables for the messenger of the colonialists. They are the foremost rustics among the rustics. They marry their wives with a bridewealth of 200 to 250 francs which is the cheapest anywhere and they have *nothing* in their village. There are two charms:
> Bomangiem
> Mikomiyool

A Business in Beads

In these regions there are not only the surprising imaginations of the blacks manufacturing innumerable fables, one also meets bold traders.

They all trade in manioc, groundnuts, and palm nuts. But one of them, Mister Lizard, as he is called by the locals[,] made a fortune in a truly original and fantastic fashion. Once he had observed the success with which a few boxes of beads had been sold, he patiently began to write to many European or Asian factories specialized in the manufacture of such articles.

He obtained collections of glass beads from Czechoslovakia, India, and Japan.

His dark shop became a true museum, in which every possible and imaginable bead was arranged in carefully labeled pigeonholes.

In bags the visitor's hand moves beads the size of peas, then there are the beads loved by young Hungarian brides, jewels cherished by Hindu dervishes, glass beads worthy of inspiring an Arabic storyteller, who would see them carried here on a flying carpet, on camelback, or in the stomach of dolphin.

Like any humdrum grocery item, all of this is placed in little bags and weighed on the scales.

Finally he discovered what sort of bead was so eagerly sought by the rich Bakuba; he alone in the region knows who manufactures them. . . . And as the building of the railroad had brought much money in the region he succeeds by this business to siphon off a good portion of it; he sells the bead which cost him 50 cents a piece for as much as 5 francs to the locals.

Moreover there is always an assured future in this business because, traditionally[,] the dead have to be buried with their whole fortune realized in beads. . . .

Very early in the morning I often see a Bakuba notable of high rank, his body anointed in ochre, with a hat shaped out of a pelican's breast [sic], armed with a spear, sitting on the ground to wait for the opening of this fairy tale shop.[8]

---

8. Georges Thiry, *A la recherche de la peinture nègre (Les peintres naïfs congolais Lubaki et Djilatendo)* (Liège, 1982), 42–43. Thiry was in administrative charge of the Mweka post from late 1929 to early 1932.

They expect a great deal from these charms such as immortal life. The main jobs they have at Shamanyigdi are farming maize, manioc, pine apples, beans, groundnuts and some other things (etc.).[9]

Poverty is the correct word to describe such situations even though these villagers did not lack food or a roof over their heads. They were poor as compared to others with regard to the imported goods they owned or consumed and with regard to their overall standard of living. In these villages fewer men than elsewhere were exempt from the ever increasing tentacles of compulsory farming and compulsory labor. Elsewhere wage laborers, modern traders, and the better educated were exempted from those obligations either because they worked for colonial employers or increasingly because they could redeem their obligation by paying the required fee. Hence people in the poorer villages had far less time than elsewhere for keeping their villages in good repair and for maintaining their own comfort. By the 1950s their lifestyle clearly contrasted with that of the more flourishing Bushong or Kete settlements near the rail line. The contrast was even sharper with Luba or Lulua agglomerations or with the inhabitants of the capital of Nsheng.

There is no doubt that between 1920 and 1960 increasing impoverishment was the dominant economic trend in most of the Kuba countryside compared to Nsheng or to those Luba and Lulua settlements that were well integrated in the new market economy or to Congo's main cities. But this impoverishment did not strike all settlements equally hard. It all depended on the precise degree to which any given rural community had been integrated in the wider Congolese and world market. The less integrated a settlement in the modern economy, the worse off it was.

Village Government

The same inequality in development also appeared between the few persons, especially near mission posts, who had been educated well beyond the level of other villagers and the old titled elite of officials and elders of family groups. Catechists, evangelists, returning soldiers, and especially noncommissioned officers had been the first of the new breed to appear in rural villages followed sometimes by a few traders and then

9. Vansina Notebooks, 23 bis: 6 verso–7 recto, text by Kwete Florentin. November 30, 1953.

in the 1930s by the first hated local agricultural monitors. The introduction of such members from a new elite side by side with the old village
leadership was expected to exert a strong impact on village governance.
But surprisingly it did not.

The main reason for this was the crucial role played by the titleholding system on communal ethics. Governance of the village continued as before to be exercised collectively by an assembly that included
both its titleholders and the elders of its constituent wards. This assembly
decided all issues relating to the village, including its response to all outside challenges, and also acted as a tribunal or moot to settle its frequent
internal disputes. It continued to derive its considerable moral authority
from the participation of the whole body of its titleholders. Ambitious
men and women continued to seek one of the half-dozen or so village
titles and still amassed the considerable wealth necessary to obtain them,
out of pride certainly, but also out of a sense of service to their local
community. Thus in the late 1920s we are told of a villager ready to pawn
his niece in order to raise funds to obtain such a title. Even in the 1950s
men still continued to seek titles, even minor ones. For instance, a local
news report from Nsheng mentions that on November 29, 1953, a certain
Mingashang Boniface was installed as the Mbebit, a very minor military
title at the capital. It was only two decades after independence, when
many no longer cared for such titles, that their importance in maintaining the overall moral tone within rural communities really became clear.

Their collective governance gave villages the resilience and the
strength to overcome a succession of setbacks that beset them during the
age of road building. To begin with, not only were villagers conscripted
to build roads but the administration also displaced them, resettled them
along the new roads, and often forced several smaller villages to fuse
together into a single bigger settlement. This disregarded the existing
rights of land tenure and the village ownership of a landed domains.
Often enough a village found itself resettled on someone else's land or
some one else settled on its domain. As a result, a new division of land
often had to be negotiated among several villages. At the same time, the
fused villages all pooled their domains together. The result was that
some villages acquired huge domains but were settled in a small corner
of their land, while others lost most of their lands and eventually were
forced to fuse with a village that was better off.

The fact that almost all of the new arrangements between villages
were sorted out without any recourse to the administration was due
to the quality of the existing institutions. The fusion of villages meant

that their wards settled cheek by jowl on the new site and that their assemblies and titleholders also fused. The main change was the selection of a single village headman by the new assembly. Moreover, in most cases the existing provincial and cantonal structure among the Bushong allowed for successful negotiations about domains between the new settlements.

Nor did the fusion of villages cause much social disruption because they had always been open to the outside world. Even in earlier times men and women of different villages had often intermarried, and villages were therefore linked to most of their neighbors by ties of kinship. Once they were forced to share a single site, these ties facilitated the creation of a single new social network encompassing the newly fused communities. Nor did the growing number of absentee young men who were inducted into the army, left as job recruits, or joined a school pose any problem of reintegration after their return. Indeed, once freed from their obligation nearly all these men tended to return to one of their home villages at least until well into the 1950s when the lure of the big city finally began to draw them to the bright lights and brought the matter of the alienation of youth into the country. Still, it was only long after independence, after the vast majority of young men and women had fled the villages leaving only older people there, that this question became a major issue.

Among the first results of the renewed emphasis on production at all costs during the recession was the abolition of the initiation rituals for boys on the familiar grounds that these took too much time away from farming—even during the dry season and even though women, the main farmers, played no role in the rituals. It was a decision that delighted the missionaries who had lobbied for it and who hoped that this would speed up conversions, which it did not. Instead a whole program of practical and moral education was lost because no new age grades were initiated, as was so much of the old solidarity between age mates that arose out of their common experiences. Thus common working parties among male or female age mates, for instance, to build a house or to bring in a harvest, became steadily rarer. Yet among both men and women, whether initiated or not, the notion of belonging to an age grade survived. Even as late as the 1950s older men of the initiated age class of the deceased still donned masks and danced at funerals when one of their mates died, while women's age classes expressed their solidarity in similar ways, for instance, by contributing lengths of embroidered cloth at the funeral of one of their mates. As to the young noninitiated, they still trouped together to form little clusters of age mates, especially among those who attended the same village or more advanced schools and even bestowed names on such groups.

In 1953, however, the administration relented, and the villages slowly resumed the initiation of their boys and have continued to do so for decades thereafter. But at the capital, where the last initiations dated back to the 1890s, King Mbop Mabinc was unwilling to allow the institution and its ritual to be revived, apparently because he felt that this would somehow increase the prestige of his main councils and his title-holders at the expense of his own.

Village Society: Gender and Slavery

Despite the impact of colonial society on Kuba economy, and despite significant change in other aspects of rural Kuba social relations, their most striking features continued to be their gender relations and a pervasive social stratification even within the village.

Kuba gender relationships were the feature that seemed the most exotic to most colonials and most contrary to their own. The Kuba had been and remained matrilineal despite the laments of some Catholic missionaries who blamed this feature for all social ills and for their lack of success. One misogynist put it as follows:

> This matriarchy is irreconcilable with the principles of a Christian family because the man is put behind the woman and must often reside in her and her family's place, and because the father has no authority over his own children.
> What disorder flows from this situation?[10]

According to him, some of those disorders included the following: "Add to this that matriarchy makes the women conceited and unmanageable. The woman says: 'I marry a man.' Often the man is forced to reside in [the village of] his wife, in a foreign place. The woman says: 'When I marry a man and have a child, then after that I break with him and marry another man.'"[11]

---

10. Prosper Denolf, "Over het ontstaan der Bakubasche beschaving," *Congo* 12, part 1 (1932): 85.

11. Prosper Denolf, "Ontvolking en veelwijverij in Kongo," *Congo* 14, part 1 (1934): 533–34.

Indeed, during the 1910s Althea Brown, a Presbyterian woman missionary, had already observed the high status of Bushong women—mostly with approval. While other women of the royal matrilineage were naturally also held in the highest honor and esteem, the mother of the king was the authority of last resort in the kingdom and enjoyed a status even higher than the king, as her behavior revealed during the epidemics of 1918 and 1919 when she took control of the country. But in this matrilineal system all wholly free women enjoyed a high regard. Within their households Bushong and Kete women pretty much ran their own lives and managed their own finances separately, although they coordinated their household activities with their husbands. All during the period older women continued to act as treasurers for their lineages, which were headed by their brothers or their uncles, and they often were the main agents of their lineages in the financial transactions of matrimonial affairs. Court records also show the women's role in all sorts of lineage matters, a role that sometimes led to violent clashes between brother and sisters, with sisters not hesitating to drag their brothers to court. Moreover, a special woman's court in every village dealt with local cases involving only women.

The unrelenting colonial demands shifted the division of labor by gender only slightly. Thus while Kete women added the job of pressing palm oil or cracking kernels to their roster because it involved cooking, they also sold the end product because marketing had always been their task. However, most contacts with state agents were left to men, mainly it seems because these agents were instructed by their superiors to deal only with men about taxes, labor recruitment, compulsory cultivation, and even schooling. Still, with the passage of time, unequal access of girls to central schools, aggravated by substantial differences in the curriculum for boys and girls, as well as the exclusion of women from almost any skilled or unskilled wage labor, began to affect their status negatively, as was happening elsewhere all over Congo. Nevertheless, even by the end of the colonial period, Kuba women still continued to enjoy a remarkably higher status than those in many other parts of rural Congo.

According to Althea Brown's notes from 1920–22 about the condition of women, marriage was monogamous; women had a voice in the choice of a husband; some young girls between ten and fifteen years old could be married; younger brides stayed in the village of their parents but moved later to that of the husband; an adulterous woman had to pay compensation to her partner's wife (and not just her lover to her husband); wives could initiate a divorce just as husbands did, and divorce was frequent. Indeed, Brown knew some women who had been married six or seven times. Moreover, extramarital affairs were common, and all too many mothers were guilty of pushing their daughters into profitable liaisons or breaking up their marriage in order to obtain more bridewealth from a new suitor. She adds that many women still had servants in the early 1920s or, to put it more bluntly, that they or their husbands still owned some slave women or a woman pawn kept by the husband as a concubine who could not divorce him. All these observations are confirmed by other contemporary authors, sometimes with considerable detail.

When more Bushong and Kete converted ever so slowly, some among them contracted a Christian marriage, but even in the 1950s such unions remained especially uncommon, not because they imposed monogamy, which was not the main problem here, but because they made divorce difficult or impossible since Catholicism outlaws divorce. Not only did Catholic marriages remain rather rare but the bridewealth paid on those occasions seems to have been higher than was otherwise the case.

Despite the very high frequency of divorce, the amount of bridewealth paid at marriage steadily rose over time and rose faster than the rate of inflation overall, at least until the Depression hit. One of the first signs of recovery in 1935 was an increase in the amount of bridewealth paid, and after 1940 the amount rose even more steeply. This development may also indicate that brides were actually becoming scarcer over time. Another indication of such a scarcity was the age of marriage. Already in the early 1920s girls as young as ten years of age were being married, while less than a decade later down payments are mentioned for future marriage with newly born or yet-to-be-born girls. While other evidence from the 1930s also points to such a scarcity, the existing data unfortunately do not allow us to probe this issue any further. After all, the increase in bridewealth may be due not only to a scarcity of brides but to other features as well, such as, for instance, increases in disposable wealth.

Until 1930 or so the colonial authorities left the essential social institutions and practices at the village level alone, mainly because under indirect rule the management of the internal affairs of the kingdom was the responsibility of its ruler. That explains some surprising survivals. Thus as late as the early 1930s one still finds a set of practices dating to the long-gone and much-condemned slave trading days. There were still cases where wives were enticed by their husbands to seduce wealthy

African outsiders so that their husbands could then claim damages for adultery. In the 1920s damages to compensate for adultery were still quite high. An aristocrat could claim the equivalent value of a slave and a commoner one third of that.

Some women were also still pawned for large amounts of valuables because their mother's brothers required the funds to settle debts, to pay fines, or to acquire titles. Women pawns fetched almost ten times the amount given as ordinary bridewealth, both because their marriages could not be dissolved and because a specified number of their children would belong to the husband's lineage rather than to their own. Moreover, their masters could always sell women pawns to other persons. Some Kuba men also became pawns of a creditor, usually a senior chief, because their lineages could not pay a debt or a fine. Many among these pawns were then passed on to the king in lieu of tribute.

In spite of the ban on slave trading and the freeing of slaves at Nsheng in 1910, that trade in humans did not really end. Surreptitiously, poor Luba men from central Kasai still came to sell their daughters outright as slaves to Kuba, although they now pretended to the colonial authorities that this practice was merely another form of marriage. Nevertheless, such women were genuine slaves, all of whose offspring belonged to their master's lineage. Meanwhile more than a few Kuba men still owned one or more male slaves, most of whom had been bought as small children from Luba sellers during the 1910s. The king himself owned several hundred of them, most of them enslaved by chiefs elsewhere as compensation for fines that they were unable to pay and then passed to the king in lieu of tribute just like pawns.

After 1900 the lot of slaves became much better because they no longer had to fear being either sold or sacrificed at a funeral. Although they were servants, they were usually treated like members of the family of their owner. But they suffered even more from the indignity of their status than pawned women because their formal designations as "the person X" rather than just "X" constantly referred to that status. Still, if they felt too badly treated they could always run away, and their owners could not recover them because the colonial government did not recognize any slave status. Actually, the initiative shown by some of these slaves is rather surprising. The slave of a Lele healer who accompanied his master to the capital in order to treat King Kwet Mabinc and then remained behind when the medicine man was dismissed launched a new healing movement of his own among the Bushong, and thus was one of the most enterprising among them.

Such initiatives were more to be expected from favored royal slaves. Some of these achieved considerable power. The most famous slave is perhaps the talented Katshunga (a Lulua child?), who became a royal slave as a young child and soon rose to the position of head manager of the royal treasure house. The king gave him four pawn wives and had a compound built for him at the capital. When tribute and taxes were not forthcoming, he was sent out as royal overseer to Shoowa country, northwest of the capital, to collect them. There he soon acquired a reputation for ruthless brutality. He himself boasted to have killed more than ten people with his own hands. But later, probably in the early 1920s, he was allowed to convert to Protestantism and to leave the king's service altogether. He then returned to Shoowa country as an evangelist and established chapels and schools in most of their villages.

Thanks to the implantation of its new local agents in the 1930s, the colonial administration was finally able to stop female slave trading outright while the number of women offered as pawns gradually diminished and then also disappeared. However, new economic circumstances also played a role in these trends because Luba/Lulua wage earners along the rail line became wealthier than their Kuba neighbors during the 1930s and 1940s and no longer needed to pawn their daughters to raise money or wealth.

During the same decade the administration also finally succeeded in completely suppressing the poison ordeal. Little did it realize that without replacing this practice with one that still permitted the resolution of smoldering social conflicts it inflicted more damage than it prevented. To nearly all the Kuba this action meant that henceforth no deep-rooted social conflicts could be resolved at all. They all continued to fester. In the collective Kuba imagination witches were free to roam at will and to decimate the population with impunity. This was the worst possible nightmare, one that had to be averted at all costs. The next chapter tells us how the Kuba set out to do so.

Conclusion

The colonial government called the results of all the economic pressure it piled on the villages *development* rather than *exploitation*. However, *development* still meant very little even in terms of rising standards of living. By the end of colonial rule practically no Kuba village was better off than when that era began. Quite the contrary! Villagers lived in smaller, more rickety houses and ate less diverse, less nutritious foods. The cloth, the tools, and the utensils they bought were nearly always of poorer quality than previous ones and wore out more quickly. They had lost most of their freedom, as they were always at the beck and call of government agents, as well as that of the king. Surely, had they known the word, the villagers would not have called this *development* but rather the contrary: *underdevelopment*.

What did the colonial regime do for a large village like Kampungu, for instance? By its close there was no piped local water, no electricity, no advanced school, not even a complete elementary school, no health care. There was nothing to show for over half a century of exploitation, except that most of its own industries and its thriving market were gone and that its population was apparently slowly dying out. In many regions elsewhere in the colony rural *development* was broadly similar. When it ended, villagers had become second-class citizens doomed to remain underpaid, overcommandeered, and exploited wherever possible in favor of city dwellers. No wonder then that outbursts of rural radicalism fueled the demand for independence and followed it like fireworks celebrating the end of the colonial age.

FURTHER READINGS

Jewsiewicki, Bogumil. "African Peasants in the Totalitarian Colonial Society of the Belgian Congo." In *Peasants in Africa*, ed. Martin A. Klein, 45–75. Beverly Hills, Calif., 1980.

Jewsiewicki, Bogumil. "Rural Society and the Belgian Colonial Economy." In *History of Central Africa*, vol. 2, ed. David Birmingham and Phyllis Martin, 95–125. London, 1983.

Kellersberger, Julia. *A Life for the Congo: The Story of Althea Brown Edmiston*. New York, 1947.

Likaka, Osumaka. *Rural Society and Cotton in Colonial Zaire*. Madison, Wis., 1997.

Nelson, Samuel Henry. *Colonialism in the Congo Basin, 1880–1940*. Athens, Ohio, 1994.

9

In Pursuit of Harmony

The great swine flu epidemic in 1918–19 was the last of the great plagues that decimated the Kuba. Yet even after it had passed their population did not flourish. The gravest threat facing them from then on until the very eve of independence was a steadily falling birthrate due to venereal disease. The lack of children soon became striking and, as we have seen, led some colonialists to forecast the imminent demise of the Kuba. Obviously the Kuba were well aware that something was terribly wrong: their numbers were dwindling, which told them that their world was out of joint. Their communities were losing their internal *poloo* ("peacefulness," but better translated as "social harmony"). In a nutshell, many children were not conceived or not born alive because an increasing number of witches moved by envy prevented their births. In the view of the Kuba, the only possible remedy to this situation was to restore social harmony, and so, to the horror of the European administration, the Kuba turned to cults that aimed to do so.

The Kuba situation was not unique. Declining birthrates were also prevalent in some other parts of Congo, especially in its Equatorial Province and in Uele to the northeast of the colony. The colonizers gave several reasons to account for these situations, varying from the idyllic to the sternly moralistic. At one end of that spectrum stood the romantic notion that, faced with the colonial situation and rather than accept the loss of their liberty, these peoples preferred to die out rather than procreate.

At the other extreme, the decline was wholly attributed to venereal disease brought on by immoral living—an attitude that reminds us of the one many adopted recently in connection with HIV.

The reasoning of the Belgian senators of 1947 is rather typical: "To examine the demographically deficient tribes one should first submit them to a careful examination to discover the moral spring that no longer functions normally."[1] They then went on to list the general causes of this decline as agreed on by the administration and the Catholic missions: (1) an excess of sexuality; (2) abortions; (3) the effects of the war effort (mobilizations and requisitions that split up households, lack of conception, and the enfeebling of many Africans); (4) the consequences of certain customs (e.g., polygamy, bridewealth, and long-term lactation); (5) compulsory labor and in general all the circumstances that separated man and wife; and (6) the attraction of modern towns and cities. One cannot help but notice that four out of the six reasons blame the situation on the morals of the colonial subjects. Moreover, there was not even a passing comment about actions the public health services might take to remedy or at least mitigate the situation. Yet no European or American doubted that only the provision of better biomedical health care could redress the situation.

While their rulers were lamenting population losses and predicting their extinction, the Bushong and the Kete were also well aware of the looming disaster and had probably been aware long before the colonialists began to worry. The threat of their disappearance in the not too distant future obviously provoked a deep-seated anxiety. Everywhere in the country people experienced the gradual dying out of their villages and the repeated fusions of several smaller settlements into single larger ones that resulted from this. Indeed, by 1950 most existing villages were the product of such fusions. By then, for instance, MBoon a Byeesh, a Bushong village in the north, consisted of four former villages, all of which had coalesced into one well after 1907. Most clans saw whole lineages or clan sections wiped out for lack of offspring. Marriages with pawned girls did not help much because pawned women soon bore no more children than others. Indeed, even healthy foreign Luba slave women were soon infected and had fewer children than their sisters in their own surroundings. Well aware of what was happening, unwilling to meekly accept their own demise, and faced with inaction and what they perceived

1. *Rapport de la mission sénatoriale au Congo* (Brussels, 1947), 62.

as colonial incompetence anyway, Bushong and Kete villages took matters in their own hands by the mid-1920s. Well aware that their own herbal remedies were unable to cope with the situation, they turned for help to cults that promised a restoration of social harmony. But before we follow them let us first sketch the history of medical services.

Medicine and Health

In the latter part of the nineteenth century the role of the state in the provision of public health was considered to be limited to public hygiene and the prevention of major epidemics, both in Belgium and in the Congo Independent State. As in earlier centuries in Europe, the delivery of health in Congo was still left to charitable institutions but now was also joined by corporations employing a large workforce. Hence at first the colonial government did very little in Congo, even though major epidemics were ravaging the country. What it did do was focused almost entirely on fighting sleeping sickness. The first government laboratory to that end opened at Léopoldville as early as 1897, but a rudimentary official medical service was not created until after the takeover by Belgium in 1909. Then World War I intervened, and it was only after its conclusion that mobile medical teams were organized to fight the major epidemics, starting once again with sleeping sickness. Besides these teams the service provided one physician for every district. Hence a very senior government official could still credibly declare in 1919, "Medical assistance to Africans does not exist."[2]

Only in 1922 did the medical service acquire its own internal organization and become autonomous within the overall administration. After that its services improved considerably for a few years until the Depression struck. Then it stagnated until around 1950. Still, the training of European sanitary assistants (as of 1919) and especially of African medical assistants with very advanced training (as of 1936) helped to expand health care by staffing a slowly growing number of rural dispensaries, nearly all of which were built by funds from the local native treasuries or by philanthropic organizations.

Meanwhile also from the 1920s onward, the state partly financed mission congregations, charitable organizations, including two private

2. Jean Stengers, "La Belgique et le Congo," *Histoire de la Belgique contemporaine* (Brussels, 1975), 397.

Belgian universities, and major corporations such as the diamond mining company in Kasai to provide medical assistance in many parts of the colony. Still in Kasai such arrangements left much to be desired, and the provincial council in 1956 bluntly noted that "the massive extension of the medical service" beyond the district capitals dated only from 1950.[3] Indeed, only the last ten years of colonial rule finally saw the

---

Gossip about Medical Care and Adultery

The following item concerns relations between spouses, medical care, and identity papers:

Nsheng, Saturday, October 30, 1953

Quarrel between spouses

The last time Mbop Valentin, secretary general of the local treasury[,] had been caught with the lady teacher of the mission but now he has avenged himself. One day his wife had gone to the mission. On the road she met a Ngende person and she told him all about her misery in the hope of receiving a good medicine for the treatment of gonorrhea (*misho*). The man obeyed poor Angélique's request.

Angélique next saw this person at the market. She asked him why he had refused to give her the medicine a second time. The person advised Angélique to accompany him in the bush to uproot a few bushes appropriate to make indigenous medicine. When they were busy with this the older brother of Valentin, Kwet Michel, found them.

Michel went quickly to accuse them at Valentin's. And without delay this morning Mbop then lodged the whole palaver with the administrator. The man was called to court. He and the woman lost the case. Anyway that man is an idiot, because he did not even carry his identity papers. He was punished with a short prison term.

(by) Shaam aNce Evariste[4]

---

3. *Rapport du conseil provincial du Kasai* (1957), 20.
4. Vansina Files, *Marriage.*

construction of a complete infrastructure for health care, the blueprint of which is still in place with minor modifications today.

But what about the Kuba? No competent medical care at all was available in Kasai until 1906 when a physician settled at the American Presbyterian Christian Mission in Luebo. He completed the first hospital there in 1916. After that the territory of the Bakuba remained utterly neglected until the mid-1920s when a state hospital opened its doors again in Luebo (between 1923 and 1927), a few years before Bena Makima and Nsheng acquired very rudimentary dispensaries without professional medical supervision. Meanwhile the railway company had brought physicians to its camps in Port Francqui (Ilebo) and Mweka in order to treat its personnel from the start of its operations in 1923, and it opened hospitals there in 1930 but they were still reserved for its own personnel only. A year later they abandoned the hospital in Port Francqui to the state, a hospital that declined thereafter to the point that a reporter exclaimed in 1937: "And the hospital? We will honor it greatly by not speaking of it."[5]

Most of the Kuba population beyond the vicinity of Luebo gained more access to biomedical care during the 1930s. A physician settled at the Presbyterian mission in Bulape in 1929 and opened a hospital in 1931–32 with the proceeds from the sale of the mission boat. Then in 1938 the sisters Canonesses of St. Augustine, a missionary order specialized in health care and education, arrived at Nsheng, where they opened a dispensary and started a clinic for nursing mothers and infants. These obviously fulfilled a deeply felt need, for barely three months after their arrival the dispensary already counted 120 daily consultations. They then launched a maternity in 1944. Their medical establishment at Nsheng reached its peak by 1947 with 89,065 consultations at the dispensary, 1,394 patients at an adjacent infirmary ward, 386 deliveries at their maternity, and 335 consultations at the clinic for infant care.

There can be no doubt that as a full-fledged hospital Bulape left a much deeper impact on the territory than the establishment of the sisters at Nsheng, although it was restricted to a limited radius around the mission, a region that normally did not reach quite as far as the capital. Nevertheless the medical work of the sisters also made a significant difference by bringing medical care to the bulk of the Bushong in the middle of the kingdom even if their facilities were no substitute for a proper

5. J. Wannijn, *Une blanche parmi les noirs* (Brussels, 1938), 63.

hospital and a resident physician. Both medical centers soon were a re-sounding success. Large numbers of Kete and Bushong flocked to them, as shown by the statistics for Nsheng just cited for 1947. The antenatal programs, the maternity, and postnatal care soon became very popular among Bushong and Kete women. They were so much appreciated that even as late as 1985 one old lady there still wished to live once again in colonial times because she remembered the excellence of the programs of antenatal care and the maternities.

Despite the distinct improvements during the 1930s, a missionary critic, obsessed by the seeming decline of the Kuba population, bitterly complained about the situation of public health as late as 1949. He noted that the Bas-Congo-Katanga Railway Company hospital in Mweka treated only its railway personnel for free. Villagers did not use the hospital because they could not afford to pay the required fee, even though it amounted to only some five francs a day in 1949, a relatively modest sum. Compared to most other parts of Kasai, the territory now suffered from considerable medical neglect. Everywhere else, the same critic averred, one found hospitals: some run by the government, some by missions, others by the diamond-mining company or the major cotton-buying company, and there were dispensaries in all the towns. In eastern Kasai a well-financed philanthropic agency was in charge, and the situation there was even better. He obviously exaggerated when he went on to claim that meanwhile the Kuba did not even have any ma-ternities and to conclude that the lack of any medical activity to combat the falling birthrates was responsible for the dire demographic situation.

Disenchanted with their relative lack of conversions and with their living conditions at Nsheng, the sisters began to neglect their mission there from 1949 onward and abandoned it completely in 1951 or early 1952. The medical activities reverted to the state's medical service just as a program of renovation of existing medical buildings and equipment started up all over Kasai. At Nsheng this resulted first in the construc-tion of a gleaming new modern dispensary in 1951 staffed by several male nurses and by a Belgian sanitary assistant (1950–53). Then, at last, albeit a mere three years before independence, a full-fledged state hos-pital with a resident physician opened its doors there.

The medical establishment had recognized from the outset that, ma-laria apart, venereal diseases were the most important endemics preva-lent in Congo and that their record in fighting these diseases was poor even after sulfa drugs became available by the mid-1930s. They com-plained that although the treatments were quite efficacious, they could

The Situation at the State Hospital
for Africans of Luebo in 1947

Number of beds: 94
Number of patients hospitalized on October 9, 1947:   289
Lacking:
Electricity;
An adequate operation table;
Running water;
An adequate laboratory;
Baths-showers;
An ambulance with stretchers;
A typewriter.
The sterilization equipment is old fashioned and primitive.

The operation room is far too dark and too small despite the fact that the hospital at Luebo is the one out of all state hospitals in the province of Lusambo where the most surgical operations are undertaken. The dormitories for patients are anti-hygienic and should be painted.

Maternity for Africans at Luebo (where there is a school for midwives).
Number of beds: 24
Average number of deliveries per year: 1,200
Lacking:
A table for confinement;
Closets for instruments;
Baths-showers;
Didactic equipment (illustrations, dummy a.s.o.);
Electricity.

These examples give a general idea of the situation which stands in sharp contrast to the great centers and the exploitation areas of the powerful VICICONGO and OTRACO companies.

Note the very large number of deliveries, indicating a lack of maternities elsewhere. During the same year there were 386 deliveries at Nsheng.[6]

6. *Rapport de la Mission sénatoriale . . .* (Brussels, 1947), 168.

not be given in a satisfactory manner because the patients abandoned further treatment as soon as their outward symptoms had disappeared. Hence in their typically colonialist view the situation required a powerful social service with the authority and the means to track patients and force them to visit the dispensaries that did not exist. Besides, it was useless to treat the population of a town or a camp anyway if one neglected to treat the surrounding villages—and what then about costs?

The treatment for such diseases improved suddenly after World War II with the arrival of the first of the antibiotics, namely the wonder drug penicillin. It was miraculously efficient in general and in particular against venereal disease because no bacteria had yet acquired any resistance to it. Soon everyone in the Kuba area stood in such awe of penicillin injections that they wanted "the needle" for almost any affliction. One typical example of this craze is the case of Madim Corneille, a nurse himself, who managed to overdose on penicillin in 1956 by taking injections to cure an attack of malaria (on which antibiotics have no effect) rather than the quinine he had been prescribed.

The Story of Mbawoot Angelique

This news item shows how poor the provision of health still was in the mid-1950s even at the capital:

> Mbawoot was a good child ever since her youth. She was never married. She was unmarried but bore two children. So she became pregnant again and gave birth to a girl on November 15, 1953, but afterwards she fell ill and eventually entered the dispensary [in Nsheng] on January 5, 1954, where she lost blood for three hours. An ambulance came from Luebo to carry her [there] but she was dead on arrival at Luebo, around five a.m. [the next day]. They telephoned to Mweka and from Mweka they sent a letter, and when the news arrived the whole town lamented "Wóóó."
>
> They hired the pickup of Mishaa miKwet Mikwepy for 1489 frs. and they went to Luebo to fetch her.[7]

---

7. Vansina Notebooks, Kwete Gaston, *The Story of Mbawoot Angélique*, 23: 26–29.

But the resident physician and the fully equipped hospital at Nsheng
arrived too late to turn the demographic situation completely around
before independence. Although nearly all of the persons who came to
the dispensaries or the hospitals newly infected with venereal disease
were now cured very quickly, and even though new additional cases of
sterility were therefore avoided, the cure still did not help people whose
reproductive organs had already been wrecked by these diseases. As a
result, only after independence did the birthrate shoot up, putting an
end to the demographic crisis.

Yet even if this turnaround in the birthrate had happened earlier, it
still remains doubtful whether Bushong and Kete villages would have
abandoned the healing cults from which they sought a remedy for their
plight. No matter how great the popularity of certain medicines and
biomedical programs, the Kuba's understanding of illness was not being
changed by biomedical explanations. Rather, the contrary happened.
They fitted the results of biomedical practices and medications within
their own worldview by equating them with charms and interventions
similar to their own. To them, success or failure, especially in matters of
life and death, were determined without exception by the supernatural
world.

Restoring Harmony

All the Kuba, including the Bushong and the Kete, understood and
assessed the colonial situation, the decline of their own population included, in terms of their own worldview and then acted accordingly to
counter the threats they saw. Hence, before we deal with their concrete
activities we must first examine their worldview—their essential convictions about the ultimate reality in the world. The data show that in spite
of all the missionary activity to alter them, these convictions remained
nearly constant during the whole colonial period. In particular, the Kuba
continued to believe in nature spirits (*ngesh*), witches, and the powers of
charms.

One or more nature spirits resided in the domains of most villages
and were thought to provide for the fertility of plants, animals, and
people alike but also to send illnesses to people who did not observe their
prohibitions. They made their wishes known to their priestesses (rarely
priests) in a dream or possession trance. The spirits were mostly honored through the observation by the villagers of a number of prohibitions, and they were venerated and beseeched in song and dance at the

Ngesh priestess in trance, 1956 (photo by author)

spirit's request or when the villagers and their priestess were in the mood to do so. In the same vein, a village dance was held at the appearance of every new moon to implore fecundity for the women, for they considered the moon to be a nature spirit. Sometimes *ngesh* spirits told their priestesses in dreams how to concoct charms for successful hunts, bountiful crops, or pregnancies.

The Kuba also believed in the existence of pure evil as embodied in witches. Genuine witches were people who secretly attacked and killed other people, usually out of sheer envy. They drew their lethal powers from an organ inside their own body that also provided them with a quintessential selfishness not found in others. Usually they were powerless people, mostly older women, and they tended to attack some of their kin or their neighbors who unknowingly had displeased them in one way or another. Witches were detected by diviners and when identified were subjected to the poison ordeal that killed only those who were guilty; the innocent threw up the poison. Moreover, the corpses of the guilty had to be burned in order to prevent them from being reborn and becoming active witches once again.

Besides innate witchcraft there also existed charms—objects endowed with power for good or for bad. They were made on demand by medicine men, and there was quite a market for them. Many charms were individual. Thus nearly every adult owned protective amulets and other protective power objects. A list of individual charms rumored to be in use in 1953 tells us much about Bushong worries at that time. There were individual charms for healing, for finding a thief, for discovering when food was poisoned, for halting sorcerers with bad charms, for making a given person hate another person, for escaping from jail, for winning court cases, for success in love or business, for bearing a child with ease, for "staving off the bad white man and the black killer," for transgressing food prohibitions without consequences.

Moreover, powerful people, mostly men in leading positions, owned very powerful secret, individual charms that would kill or seriously harm their enemies. Such objects were greatly feared by everyone. As an example of these let us recall the wave of deaths among the royal successors and the lack of fertility among the princesses around 1900 that was attributed to the charm supposedly planted by King Kwet aMbweky just before his demise and also remember the counteraction of King Kwet aPe in 1902 when he obtained another very powerful protective charm from a Zappo Zap medicine man to destroy the effects of the first one.

Besides such individual charms there were also collective charms held for and by a whole community, normally a village or the capital. There were three major collective charms—war charms, charms to promote hunting, and charms against lightning—but all three were also expected to protect the community against witchcraft and outside sorcery as well. On every village square one found a little fenced-in "charm garden," *kiin,* that contained some power objects, such as growing plants, a stone, or a piece of metal, as well as a little shrine house containing one or more horns or pots filled with medicine all in order to attain the triple goal and to provide full protection for the whole village. It was expected that by banning outside evil such *kiin* would provide peaceful social harmony (*poloo*) from which stemmed a good, pleasant, and fertile life for all. Hence a "charm garden" was the first thing to be built on the new site whenever a village moved to another location.

Most Kuba people and certainly most Bushong and Kete also held that their king was a *ngesh,* in this case a priest who could call up the spirits of his predecessors when needed, because after death kings became nature spirits (not ancestors). As a *ngesh* the king controlled the dispensation of fertility and prosperity in all its many forms anywhere in his realm and might use his powers to strike those who displeased him. For instance, the deaths that struck Kampungu and Misumba during their respective rebellions in 1923 and 1925 were attributed to the king's powers. This conviction plus the knowledge that in addition to these powers the king also held powerful charms was continually kept alive during the whole colonial period and well beyond it by all sorts of rumors and gossip about arbitrary royal punishments including murders. That is why his subjects feared him so much. Nevertheless it became self-evident after the war of 1904–5 that the king could no longer fully protect his realm against major disasters such as the colonial occupation, increasing mortality from disease, and a falling birthrate.

Obviously village *kiin* whose specific function was to protect against such disasters were also failing. They needed to be reinforced, if not replaced, by a new sort of cult centered on a new collective charm that would restore social harmony by detecting and neutralizing all evil people, witches and sorcerers alike, since it was believed that they were the cause of all the calamities that threatened the very existence of the community. Specific cults that offered collective charms to procure success in hunting, such as the one named Piip, or to protect in war, such as Tongatonga, on which the Kuba relied during the 1904 revolt, had been known in the country before colonial times. Although as a side effect they also fought evil magic to some extent as well, they were not specifically designed to cope with the demographic catastrophes that seemed to be unfolding in the wake of colonial occupation. Another cult with far more comprehensive aims was needed, and one did appear.

In colonial days at the height of the infamous rubber boom, the earliest known cult aiming at the eradication of all evil, the preservation of life, the restoration of all sorts of harmony, fertility, and the curing of illnesses was reported. That cult was called Nkwiimy. It had been first revealed somewhere in the lands between the Lokenye and Sankuru rivers northeast of the kingdom, and by 1908 it was thriving in Kuba villages east of the Labody River and perhaps elsewhere in the realm. Its propagators proclaimed that their cult destroyed all evil and would as a result usher in a Utopian life for the villages that adopted it, a life full of children, good hunting, bountiful crops, no illness, and nearly no deaths. Inevitably though, a few years after its adoption disenchantment set in, and the specter of the loss of harmony in the village community resulting from a failure to completely eradicate witchcraft and sorcery in the community rose again. At first that was usually countered by further tinkering with the existing cult to restore its efficacy, usually by adding one or several additional specific charms or rituals. When that failed, however, the surge of collective anxiety returned stronger than before. Villagers would begin a desperate search for a new protective cult until one was finally discovered, which would then spread again all over the country.

Kuba villages were not alone in searching for cults with collective charms to destroy evil. With the exception of the Luba/Lulua to the south and southeast, whose settlements were organized in a fundamentally different and much less collective way, all their neighbors lived like the Kuba in well-organized villages with communal rule and shared many of their convictions. Hence, new cults easily diffused among all of them to finally affect quite large areas. In this fashion several cults followed each other during the whole colonial period and beyond until about 1970.

Starting in 1924 a new cult called Lakosh, after the name of the nature spirit or *ngesh* who was said to have revealed it, overran villages in the whole Kuba country. Later and until the late 1940s several waves followed bringing additional charms with minor variants to Lakosh. By 1940 and in spite of all efforts by the territorial administration to stamp out the spread of such feared "secret societies," Lakosh had spread over a huge area stretching nearly from the Equator north of the upper Lokenye River to the source of the Kasai River deep into Eastern

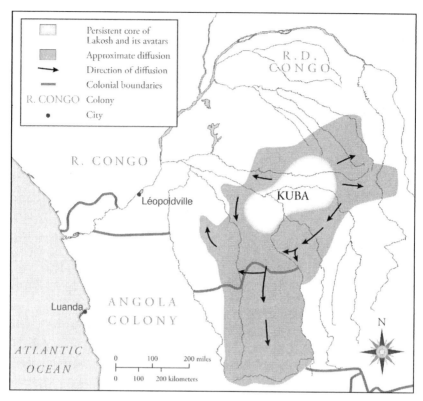

The diffusion of Lakosh, 1924–40

Angola to the south and far into the Kwilu district to the west. And yet, despite its great success, not all villages joined Lakosh even within the Kuba realm. At all times some remained skeptical and preferred another similar cult. Thus, for instance, most Kete villages north of Luebo refused to adopt Lakosh but put their faith in Imeny.

Lakosh remained the dominant cult in the territory until 1950. In that year a visionary known as Bopanga Mukeba revealed that a hitherto unknown spirit or God (no one knows for certain), Miko miYool, had revealed a new cult to him in the Forest of the Spirits to replace Lakosh. This was soon adopted by one village after another. Thus Miko miYool can be seen as one instance of a new wave of cults that swept over rural central Africa after World War II. Some observers have claimed that this wave occurred as a result of the "loss of direction" of rural culture caused by the impact of colonialism in the preceding years. Whatever its merits elsewhere, this argument is not convincing for rural Kasai and certainly not in the Kuba case since their villages, including those where Miko miYool took shape, were still as firmly embedded in the kingdom's structure and values as they had been before—even though it is true that the abolition of the poison ordeal and of age grades in the 1930s were perceived as significant and grievous losses. Moreover, the two most salient characteristics of the new movements appearing after World War II, including Miko miYool, were first its overwhelming continuity with the preceding ones, including Lakosh, and second its approval of modernity such as, for instance, the inclusion of such elements as the pole linked by wire to Miko miYool's shrine that represented the telephone line along which he could send dreams to his adepts. To its practitioners the cult obviously felt more like Lakosh made relevant for modern times than anything else. It certainly did not feel like a novel sort of guidance for those who had lost the bearings of their old world.

Miko miYool did not last nearly as long as its predecessor Lakosh. It disappeared in a dramatic fashion in 1959–60 just before independence. At that point most Bushong villages found themselves under such extreme stress that they suddenly despaired that any cult could ever restore a life of tranquility and harmony. In desperation they therefore turned back to the long outlawed poison ordeals and they conducted no less than five hundred such ordeals, half of which ended in death, before the king and his officials managed to stem this outbreak of desperation.

After independence and starting in 1966, villages replaced Miko miYool either with the old Imeny, now called Kameny, or with Yengayenga, a new cult from across the Sankuru River. The king favored Kameny, which flourished until he died in 1969. Later a few pastors or priests belonging to local mainstream Christian churches took over the management of such cults before they were eventually completely absorbed in the rituals of the new Evangelical movements that arose after 1990.

Cult and Rituals to Restore Harmony

Although local cells of the same cult existed in villages all over the country, each of these was completely autonomous once the officials of a foreign cell had installed the cult in the village and had been paid. Just as the organization of every village was expressed through the specialized duties of its titleholders, so too each cult cell. The cell's leader was called "king of the charms." At the time Miko miYool was introduced there were several titled assistants besides this leader, namely some who made the medicines and the charms to cure and combat diseases, a diviner to

The Healer Bopanga Mukeba

Having summoned him I [agent Stoffelen] succeeded in obtaining the following statements from this astonishing and fanatic young man who started the whole sect.

"I [Bopanga] was still a young child at Kotshe [Koonc] when one night I was taken from my bed and deposed in the forest of the spirits (Lubuya). My charm is mikobe yolo [Miko miYool] and I received it from the spirits to save everyone. This was in 1940.

"I want to give the use of my charm to the whole world, to the Bakuba, to the Batetela, to the Baluba, and to the Basongo Meno.

"Three years ago I began to hand out this medication, but it is only this year that this has taken a great extent. My charm makes any man who is bad good if he only wants to drink it spontaneously.

"All those who want to kill the men of Bula Matadi [the state] should become good again by my charm and those who refuse to drink, I want to give them my charm and it will kill them; or else we should take them and put them in jail, because they do not want to drink.

"That is why I am asking a uniform from Bula Matadi for that purpose and policemen to capture them.

"I made some notebooks in which everyone who buys the charm must write their name and the francs [the amount of money] they pay. I will send most of the money to the office at Mweka. Because I have much work when I am busy healing the ill, to make a weak man strong, to protect the others against eventual difficulties in their affairs, I have taken [hired] a clerk, Kwet Samuel, son of Mingeshi of the Bakuba of Ganda (Imanyi) [village Ngaan, province Imeny]."

. . . The *Bankumbi* [priests] are thought to have the power to immediately heal snake and scorpions bites; Only Bopanga has the power to make many children be born and be born easily; he does not have the power to intervene in court cases.

Bopanga Mukeba is a fanatic, or else very clever, or else very unbalanced. His clerk [titleholder] will accompany him to Mweka.[8]

8. Province du Kasai, *Dossiers sectes secrètes*: Stoffelen to the administrator of the territory of the Bakuba from Bushobe, October 22, 1950.

Medicine man installing a shrine for Miko miYool (photo by author)

uncover both malefactors who use evil charms and witches and who gave an authoritative interpretation for all dreams related to the cult spirit, several male assistants still called *bakwiimy*, as they had been in 1908, and several women titleholders, or *bangaash*, who were the "spouses" of the spirits and who were possessed by Miko miYool just as the village priestesses were by their *ngesh*. Most of these titles and the functions they held in the 1950s already existed in the days of Lakosh and probably earlier.

In each cell, the cult included a myth about its origins, a set of charms kept in an enclosure on the village square with or without a little hut, a whole series of rituals, regular worship in the shape of dances and songs (prayers), and a series of prohibitions in honor of the spirit.

A cult's enclosure was very similar to the village *kiin* while its ordinary worship at the time of the new moon, its prohibitions, and even its revelations in dreams were also quite similar to that of the cult for the village *ngesh*. Thus villagers were quite familiar with the repetitive parts of the cult even though the charms in the enclosure were much more complex than those of *kiin*, the prayers in song were quite different, the prohibitions were more elaborate, and instead of one priestess possessed by the village *ngesh* there were a number of them and a set of medicine men. Still it was the very familiarity with so many of its procedures that gave the villagers the confidence to accept their efficacy.

A cell came to be installed in a village as follows. Some among the village leaders heard favorable reports about a new cult in a neighboring village and went there to ask for the cult. In return for the payment of a significant sum of money, the cell officials of the donor village then came to the recipient settlement with the most sacred charm of their cult (a flat stone in the case of Miko miYool) to *iluk*, the place there where they could camp. There followed much dancing and singing every evening by the visiting and the new titleholders until the following new moon, and the visitors taught local titleholders how to carry out their duties. Once the new moon had arrived, the enclosure for the cult was built on the village square, and the charms and emblems were installed in it. After this a general hunt was organized by the *bakwiimy*, and if no animal was caught the operation was repeated until some game was caught because only such a catch signaled that both the local *ngesh* and the spirit of the cult accepted the new cell. Then there usually followed a ritual to weed out malefactors. As part of this every resident adult in the village, one after the other, would swallow a charm to detect evil charms and witchcraft so as to neutralize or even indirectly kill the malefactors.

Once the cell was installed, the villagers celebrated regular rituals of fertility at every new moon when they danced and honored their spirit. Also once a year they celebrated the planting and harvesting of the first fruits with a ceremony at the spirit's shrine. In addition, titleholders organized particular specialized rituals when needed. Healing rituals were very common. These differed according to the seriousness of the affliction, ranging from a simple prayer to the cult's spirit to a full-fledged dance with songs of prayer by the officials at the patient's house. Ceremonies to purify a villager from a breach of one of the prohibitions imposed by the spirit were nearly as frequent as healing rites. More spectacular, but rarer, were rituals to resolve accusations of witchcraft, to make a divination, to counter a sudden calamity, or a ritual requested by the spirit in a dream or a trance, something that often happened on the eve before a major hunt. Finally, although the cults were collective, devout individuals could also honor its spirit in song or dance in their yard at home when they felt like it. Beyond this, it suffices to point out that the usual techniques used during the rituals of such cults consisted in sacrifices (usually of plants), communion, unction, prayers, and oracles to make it obvious that these cults to restore harmony constitute in fact what we call *religions*.

Apart from their usually scanty myths, cults also proclaimed a doctrine that became more elaborate with the passage of time by means of the accumulation of messages revealed to ordinary cult members in dreams or to *bangaash* in trance. This impact on doctrine was the main reason why anyone who dreamed of Miko miYool was obliged to tell her or his dream to the proper cult officials who then provided an official interpretation. As a result, after a while the detailed belief, doctrine, and ancillary practices of the same cult began to vary somewhat between cells. When a new cult or a new variant of a cult was adopted, it kept most of the rituals, the title, and the organization of the old cult, but its founding myth and doctrine would be somewhat different.

Moreover, as far as we know, these doctrines seemed to become more elaborate over time as the worldview of the Kuba changed under colonial and especially missionary influence. Certainly by the 1950s Christianity had left an obvious impact on the worldview, the claims, the doctrines, and even the epithets of Miko miYool. First the cult proclaimed that the God of Christians, the God of traditionalists, and Miko miYool were the same person. He (it was a he) was the master of the world, and one had to observe his rules to escape misfortune and the attacks by witches or sorcerers. No cult could be rendered to any other spirits but him. No one was allowed to keep any personal charms. That was equated with witchcraft, and Miko miYool kills all witches. Finally, everyone was expected to join the cult, because misfortune upon misfortune would be heaped on unbelievers while believers would lead a happy life. The impact of Catholicism in particular had become strong enough by 1956 that one of the king's two main medicine men, who was also the chief of Miko miYool's cult in Nsheng, attempted to proclaim himself as bishop. No doubt Christianity influenced the cult, but it is just as remarkable that the cult's doctrines had translated some major

A Religious Debate at the Capital in July 1953

The Vision of Mbanc iBushabukwet

This afternoon I learned that a woman named Mbanc iBushabuk-wet, married to the Pokibaan (Mbop aKam), just discovered the charms of an old woman named Pelyeng Bushaming from the Muu ward; and I went there to see and understand what was going to happen.

The story of Mbanc iBushabukwet to the spectators was: "Last night I dreamed of God and all the angels in the sky. God told me to enter and then he opened the heavens. The angels were busy talking with the good God and listen-all-of-you to what He told me: 'Go home and tomorrow you will go to Pelyeng and you must ask her all the charms she owns. They prevent the women and the girls of the village Nsheng from conceiving and know ye that all the Catholic Christians who inhabit Nsheng, even those who stay at the mission, have charms which they have locked into suitcases [suit-case-sized baskets] and hence search carefully for these until you find them.'"

Then this is what the woman added: "You," said the woman Mbanc iBushabukwet, "You are saying that Miko miYool is bad and unimportant; too bad for you. I repeat to you that Miko miYool is still your God who came to save you from your enemies. As for me" added this woman "I confess that I will enter heaven, for I already saw God's divine goodness last night and the place where He dwells."

And I returned home.

Pelyeng Bushaming's Reply

Today I was at Pelyeng Bushaming's to ask her about their faith in Miko miYool. "As for me," answered the woman, "Miko miYool is perhaps one of the ancient magicians who are dead; since he is very wise. I note this because he found a charm I owned. I did not even know that anyone could know where it was hidden.

"As for me, it is not Miko miYool that I have in my life either. I have my nature spirit (*ngesh*) whose name is Mashakl. My nature spirit spoke to me and said: 'Don't take any charm that comes along. Each tree leaf will be of use to you in making charms to treat

tenets of Christian teaching into the Kuba's own previous worldview, and one can observe exactly how it did so.

Restoring Harmony and the Colonial Administration

Until 1921 the colonial administration in Congo-Kasai paid attention only to religious movements that it called "secret sects" when they caused unrest or when the administration believed that they were subversive, for instance, spreading war charms. That had happened in 1915 when Maria Nkoi ("Mary of the leopards"), a prophetess who lived near Lake Mai-Ndombe, claimed to have been given the power to heal. She also announced that the colonial regime would soon be swept aside by the arrival of the Germans. This message created some unrest in the Equatorial province, and as a result she was arrested and deported faraway.

Then in 1921 the prophet Simon Kimbangu appeared in Lower Congo. He was a former evangelist who called for a thorough Africanization and decolonization of the Christian message and who launched the first Independent Congolese Christian church, a church that still flourishes today. Although he did not call for resistance against colonial rule, his message alarmed the colonialists in Lower Congo to the extent that the administration soon arrested him. He was condemned to death, but the sentence was commuted in Brussels to lifelong detention. His

---

men and women.' I have earned much money with these charms. I bought four slaves and around one hundred bars of redwood."

After this speech all of a sudden a wife of the king arrived and told Pelyeng that "I have come so that you make charms for me to conceive a child." Pelyeng ordered her to fetch a stick of sugar cane right away. The woman left and soon returned with a piece of sugar cane; Pelyeng then began to make charms with the sugar cane. "You God" said Pelyeng, "and you Mashakl, my nature spirit, may this woman conceive a child; since both of you gave me this charm."

Thereupon she ordered the woman to place an enema with the liquids that flowed out of the piece of sugar cane.[9]

---

9. Vansina Files, *Religion*: Shaam aNce Evariste, July 10, 1953, *Paganism* (Mbanc iBushabukwet), and July 11, 1953, *Pelyeng Bushaming's Reply*.

most active followers were "relegated"—that is, deported—to other parts of Congo where they spread the new church. Moreover from 1921 onward all territorial administrators in Congo were enjoined to be constantly watching for "secret sects" and to suppress them ruthlessly whenever they appeared, regardless of the theoretical freedom of religion.

A few years later (1924) Lakosh appeared in the territory of the Bakuba and spread from there to adjacent territories, whose administrators immediately sounded the alarm. They all implicitly accused the administrator of the territory of the Kuba of doing nothing at all to stop the movement. But indirect rule prevailed here, the king and his councils were more inclined to encourage than to interfere with the cult, and the territory still enjoyed the special protection of District Commissioner Lode Achten. All that changed when Emile Vallaeys became district commissioner. No sooner did he hear that Lakosh was in the region than he immediately had a local leader arrested near Luebo and wrote to the provincial commissioner to reassure him that "orders have been given to all the territorial administrators to take severe action against the new sect when needed."[10] He actively pursued all signs of such activities in his district.

But René Van Deuren, the administrator in Mweka, still did not react until forced to do so in 1933 by an outsider, a traveling physician. The man denounced a nocturnal manifestation related to the introduction of a "war charm from the adjacent territory of the Lele." Now Van Deuren had no choice but to do something. He went to the villages involved, duly found a charm that reportedly would lessen "the power of the Whites" and might easily be turned into a war charm for a planned insurrection. The same inquest also embarrassingly unveiled not only that some slaves of the successor Mbop Mabinc ma Kyeen were involved but also that Mbop, that staunch ally of the administration, might well be implicated. The result was a sharp warning by District Commissioner Vallaeys to the king that he was expected to combat any "xenophobic movement" by every means at his disposal or else! The result of the whole episode was a belated official admission by the administrator that the Lakosh and Imeny cults were rife in the territory, a warning to all villages that such cults were illegal, a series of fines imposed by the king on various chiefs and on a headman who had been

10. Province du Kasai, *Dossier sectes secrètes. Lukoshi*: August 30, 1931, Vallaeys to governor.

involved in allowing the Lele charm to spread, and unspecified sanctions against the propagators of that war charm.

The cults merely went underground, only to reappear after a few years. By 1936 Vallaeys was once again ordering his administrators to stamp out Lakosh even though Lakosh and related movements were not legally outlawed until a year later. He now underlined that it was a "xenophobic" cult (that is, directed against colonials) and that its aim was to destroy the authority of the colonial establishment as well as the achievements of the missions. And once again Van Deuren had no choice but to destroy the shrines of Lakosh in one village after another, especially when another outsider, a settler this time, again "discovered" some "secret society" among the Kete near Luebo. So Van Deuren continued to "stamp out" the cult and to track the channels by which it had diffused. Finally, just before he went to Europe on leave in 1938, he wrote a general report for the governor and concluded perhaps not so innocently:

> Once again I insist on the fact that no hostile manifestation towards Europeans has been signaled. Nevertheless I have wanted to prove to the natives that these practices [the cults] must cease. In any case the results have been satisfying and Mr. [Gabriel] Hunin, the Assistant Territorial Administrator who will replace me during my leave, has been invited to continue this persecution [underlined twice by the governor and followed by ??], this purification, of the territory, from this nefarious medicine.[11]

Meanwhile, not only was colonial antagonism toward the new religious movements of little or no avail but by its aggressive hostility the administration forced the populations into the very insubordination its officials feared, a situation that Karen Fields has also convincingly documented about the Christian inspired movements in Zambia and Malawi in her *Revival and Rebellion in Colonial Central Africa*. There exists no more blatant demonstration of this truth in Kasai than the questions and answers in this series of police reports from a neighboring territory:

> Q: Who went to Yenga yenga to ask for the charm?
> A: I went myself.
> Q: But did you not know that the State forbade the Bashilele to take the "Lukoshi"?

11. Province du Kasai, *Dossier sectes secrètes*, 1936: 116.

A: Yes, but we have adopted it so that the women bear children and that the men become strong for working.
Q: So, you do not bother with the orders of the State?
A: No, because the women did not have children.[12]

Indeed how could one hope to survive except by ignoring the law? The dilemma is even clearer in the next quote:

Q: Since when do you have the medicine?
A: Since three years.
Q: But the administrator has always forbidden this charm.
A: Yes, I know, and then we did abandon the charm . . .
Q: Since when did you take it up again and why?
A: Since three months and because the women did not have children any longer and to kill much game during the hunt.[13]

Less than a year later the sorry results of this kind of policy became evident. The administrator in charge of that territory now announced "the indifference, the nonchalance, not to say the passive resistance" in carrying out compulsory cultivation. "Despite the presence of police men and agricultural monitors they do not fully finish the jobs," the fields were not well kept, local roads were barely kept passable, with the work hastily done when the colonial agent was near; and the rest houses were in disrepair and, in several instances, almost in ruins. Mysterious charms were planted in and around some rest houses, and no one divulged anything about that. The villagers certainly still kept Lakosh but hid its shrine well. Some villagers escaped into the bush where they stayed for seven months, while many people migrated illegally into another territory in order to escape compulsory cultivation.[14] While the policy of compulsory cultivation was certainly to blame in part for this silent resistance, the unremitting hostility of the administration toward all religious movements was certainly responsible for the attitude of indifference, if not outright hostility, that the population adopted henceforth toward any government order of prescription.

The government's policy concerning religious movements was obviously bankrupt, and many territorial officials in Kasai and especially in

12. Province du Kasai, *Dossier sectes secrètes*, 1937: 105.
13. Province du Kasai, *Dossier sectes secrètes*, 1937: 112. Killing much game was a sign of approval by the nature spirits and a harbinger of fertility.
14. Province du Kasai, *Dossier sectes secrètes*, 1938: 120–21.

Mweka realized this. Yet it remained unchanged, and hence some zeal-
ous officials in search of good points to advance their careers continued
to uncover sinister "secret societies" until the early 1950s. By then, however, Charles Schillings, the official administrative adviser to the king,
was so convinced of the considerable moral value of a movement like
Miko miYool that not only did he not interfere with it but he even went
to ask for the help of cult officials in 1952 when the Native Treasury had
been robbed. And yes, they did recover the money. But he was well
ahead of his time, for the government abandoned the whole policy only
in 1958.

Conclusion

Well aware of the threat of their own extinction for lack of children,
Bushong and Kete villagers did not blame the situation on colonialism
or on any particular colonial foreigner but put it squarely on the loss
of *poloo* (harmony) in their own midst. They perceived witchcraft and
sorcery as flourishing among their own in huge numbers, numbers big
enough to produce such disasters. Foreigners had nothing to do with
this. Hence to restore harmony they turned to collective cults. In their
prayers, songs, and emblems they expressed both their aspirations and
their hatred of witches. They sang "Lakosh who eliminates the witches,
Lakosh who makes the women bear children,"[15] and they wished:
"Miko miYool: if it be a witch, if it be an evil doing sorcerer, cut his
heart out, cut his lungs to pieces."[16] As these villagers experienced it, the
history of colonial times was above all the story of their own struggle for
survival and the return of harmony in a titanic war waged against evil.

From this perspective foreigners were practically irrelevant as far as
these calamities were concerned. But they were a nuisance, an obstacle,
and an aggravation when officials attempted to suppress the cults. The
local people had no choice but to disregard or to circumvent any orders
that interfered with their cult as irrelevancies, whatever the cost might
be in fines, jail, or even the occasional relegation. Colonialists called
such an attitude either passive or underground resistance, as was doing

15. Prosper Denolf, "Ontvolking en veel wijverij in Kongo," *Congo* 14, part 1 (1934):
537.
16. Jan Vansina, "Miko miYool, une association religieuse kuba," *Aequatoria* 22
(1959): 10.

whatever one could to get away with the least amount of forced labor or compulsory farming. Such acts, however, were merely means to survive, not well-thought-out intentions or means to shake off colonial rule, nor were they expressions of a future Congolese national independence, an independence that villagers did not even imagine. That does not mean, however, that the Kuba regarded the colonialists—whether officials, missionaries, or others who mocked people's convictions or interfered with their cults—merely with indifference. Naturally enough, the villagers often hated them just as much as their other tormentors, the agronomists.

On the other hand, though, and despite appearances, these cults were not especially invented to cope with colonial disasters: not only do they seem to have existed before the colonial period but they continued for at least one long decade following independence, after which they became firmly embedded into local mainstream Christian practices. Finally, on the eve of the new millennium, new Pentecostal churches seem to have completely absorbed all aspects of these rituals.

Kete and Bushong used existing religious tools from precolonial times to confront the new colonial disasters. Still, because of the intensity of the calamities they then encountered, they probably used them more intensively than before. Moreover, with the passage of time the cults began to encompass more and more existing religious activities until they became as exclusive as Christianity before eventually becoming part of Christianity. There was nothing exceptional about the attempts of the Kuba to restore harmony by the use of cults so as to cope with colonial disasters and to fight witchcraft. Indeed, not only did the cults that originated in or near the Kuba realm spread to wide swaths of country to the south but broadly similar cults were adopted to fight evil all over Central Africa, including new offshoots of Christianity in places where large numbers of people had converted. All over Central Africa as well, the arrogant adversarial animosity of colonial administrations and missions toward such cults bred deep contempt for their agents. Their scorn helped to fuel a raging rural resentment that eventually exploded by the time of independence in Congo and in its Central African neighbors.

FURTHER READINGS

De Craemer, Willy, Jan Vansina, and Renée Fox. "Religious Movements in Central Africa: A Theoretical Study." *Comparative Studies in Society and History* 18, no. 4 (1976): 458–75.

Fetter, Bruce, ed. *Demography from Scanty Evidence: Central Africa in the Colonial Era.* Boulder, 1990.

Fields, Karen E. *Revival and Rebellion in Colonial Central Africa.* Princeton, N.J., 1985.

Hunt, Nancy. *A Colonial Lexicon of Birth Ritual, Medicalization, and Mobility in the Congo.* Durham, N.C., 1999.

Lyons, Mary-Inez. *The Colonial Disease: A Social History of Sleeping Sickness in Northern Zaire, 1900–1940.* Cambridge, UK, 1992.

Wharton, Conway Taliaferro. *The Leopard Hunts Alone.* New York, 1927.

10

Visions for a Different Future

Reckoned by the calendar, the colonial period constituted only a small fraction of the whole duration of Kuba history. Yet these years were all important, for it was during this period that some Kuba pioneers began to leave their universe and step into a brave new modern world. No, they did not emigrate to a new world across the Atlantic; rather, the modern new world came to Congo and Kasai. In these concluding chapters of our study, we follow the track of how modernity invaded the country. This chapter deals with its foremost foreign agents—the missionaries—and focuses on mission stations and schools, their main tools to graft modernity onto Kuba society. They came to save souls, but in the process they found themselves transmitting Western technology, culture, education, and social institutions and practices in the hope of turning their converts into surrogate Belgians or Americans. The graft began to take, for by 1960 they were beginning to transform their flock, and especially their pupils, culturally from Kuba into Congolese.

Organizing Missions and Their Stations

The colonial administration justified its rule by claiming that its goal was to bring civilization to the benighted Africans. When they spoke of civilization, they referred to their own customs, religion, language,

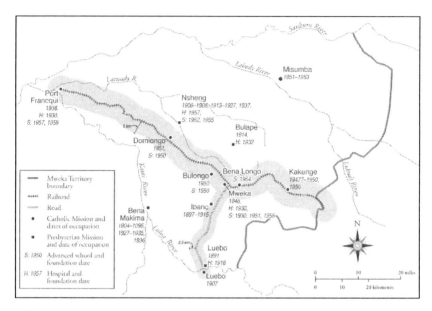

Missions, central schools, and hospitals, 1891–1960

and other habits—that is, the gradual assimilation of Congolese to their own way of life. They strove to make the country's inhabitants adopt literacy, Western dress, food, housing, etiquette, social customs, ethics, and Christianity so as to turn them into surrogate Belgians in all particulars.

While aspiring to confer "civilization" on its subjects, the colonial administration still did not envision spending large amounts of money to achieve it. That task was best left to the private sector, especially the Christian missions, which were expected to transform Africans into "modern" people by a combination of religious conversion, education, and their own example of gracious living. Side by side with the missionaries, private corporations would usher the Congolese into the market economy by providing them with a handsome monetary income stemming from wage labor or from the returns of the compulsory cash crops the companies marketed for profit. From today's vantage point it is evident that the missions succeeded to a large degree in converting the rural Congolese but that the corporations failed.

The first rival missionary parties steamed up the Kasai River by paddleboat in 1891: the American Presbyterian Christian Mission (APCM) would settle at Luebo and the Catholic congregation commonly known as Scheut established themselves at Luluabourg. These men (women followed soon after) had but a single mission: to redeem souls and to set up an organization to do so, their church. Each was convinced that they were God's emissaries and that their task was to bring the "book" (*Biblion*) to the Congolese and be its "good messenger" (*euangelos*), thereby redeeming them both from degrading paganism and from the pernicious falsehoods propagated by their competitors in order to save their souls for all eternity. In their minds they did God's work and acted in God's name. Today they would be called fundamentalists. Even in 1912 a British consul sketched the Catholic fathers of Scheut as follows: "Brusque in the extreme for they are mostly of the peasant class, they are nevertheless indefatigable workers, more especially in regard to their cause, to which they are espoused almost to a degree of fanaticism."[1] The Presbyterians, declared the consul, were sadly wanting in tact. He further added of the Catholics that "power with them is everything" but that was just as true of the Presbyterians.

For all the intensity of their faith, however, these missionaries were not charismatic, with the partial exception of William Sheppard. Apart from the very first year or so of their ministry, they did not wander around the country to proclaim the faith to all and sundry with the help of translators. Rather, they acted like traveling businessmen representing corporations. Both Presbyterians and Catholics began by erecting a set of buildings, called a station, and then by looking for ways to attract people. Both faiths discovered almost immediately that those who flocked to their station were mostly Luba migrant refugees seeking shelter from the ongoing wars in Kasai.

At first Sheppard planned to reach the Kuba court to convert the king because he imagined that all the Kuba would follow. But his congregation missed its early chances. So Ibanc was founded in 1897 as a temporary station until the missionaries could settle at Nsheng. Sheppard's interference in the politics of succession by backing Mishaamilyeng turned out, as we have seen, to be a devastating miscalculation that resulted in long-term enmity between the APCM and the Kuba court. In 1915 Ibanc was abandoned for Bulape, officially because it was closer to the capital but also because the new station lay on the edge of a major concentration of Kete villages. In addition, internal factional politics among the Presbyterians also played a role.

1. H. H. Castens, *Tour in the Bakuba Country*, Command Paper 118427 (London, 1913), 88.

After the epidemics of 1918–19 Kwet Mabinc maKyeen finally implored the mission to settle at his capital in 1920, but by then it was too late. The mission had to request permission from the state to obtain land on which to found its establishment, and District Commissioner Achten refused to grant it. His main reason was the bitter rivalry and sometimes violent clashes that were then ongoing between Protestants and Catholics. Since there was already a Catholic mission at Nsheng, adding a Presbyterian one would merely lead to even greater strife.

Meanwhile, both missions had found that their message did not easily impress the Bushong or the Kete, and that there were few of them compared to the huge numbers of Tshiluba speakers in Kasai, precisely those people who flocked by themselves to the mission stations. Therefore the fathers of Scheut chose to concentrate from the start on the

Church Business

Despite the generosity of the faithful in Belgium and the United States, the construction and the operation of mission stations was never fully financed by them. Nor could the Catholic missions (and the Presbyterian one after 1948) obtain sufficient funds from subsidies paid by the state for the medical facilities and the schools operated by the missions to cover all their costs. Hence both Protestants and Catholics had to raise additional revenues themselves and not just by growing their own vegetables. They needed the more substantial income provided by regular ventures such as plantations of coffee, rubber, or palm trees, carpentry shops, brick making, printing presses, and mills to produce manioc or maize flour, all of which are attested at one station or another in the Kuba area. All missions employed some hired labor, but they all also expected free work from the same adults they instructed in the faith. Thus, along with their other functions, mission stations also became commercial enterprises similar to those of expatriate settlers.

Apart from enterprises such as these, which were as widespread elsewhere in the colony as they were in Kuba country, one business was unique to the Kuba situation: dealing in art. Thus the first Presbyterian missionaries were already buying curios even before they first arrived at Luebo, and a few years later they paid

Luba Kasai, while only a few years later the Presbyterians also decided to follow their lead. So reluctant were the fathers of Scheut to evangelize the Kuba that they only founded a station at Bena Makima when the Compagnie du Kasai offered it to them, free of rent, as part of a commercial alliance. Two years later they left Bena Makima and arrived at Nsheng essentially as subcontractors for the company, but they then abandoned Nsheng another two years later because the company needed them elsewhere.

Later the minister of colonies had to pressure the congregation of Scheut to occupy their station post at Nsheng again. They reluctantly complied theoretically in 1913 but did not re-occupy the station until a year or two later. Indeed, apparently they did not set up a central school there before 1922. But when Kwet Mabinc began to favor the

---

for the printing expenses of their first Kete primer by selling souvenirs at Léopoldville. Catholic and Presbyterian stations alike continued to buy Kuba art for export from the outset throughout the whole colonial period and even decades after that.

Any history of Kuba art during the twentieth century must take such commercial patronage into account, and the Catholic sisters at Nsheng provide the most convincing example of this. During their stay there (1938–51) the sisters ran a business in embroidered lengths of raffia or Kasai velvets for export. They obtained their textiles by putting out work—that is, by buying a set number of pieces a week at a set price from women catechumens in town (some sixty in 1950). In addition, they had the girls in their primary school embroider lengths of cloth or turn them into velvet as part of their instruction in "needle work." Almost from the outset they changed the former aspect of this decoration work by introducing new dyes and by requiring exact reproductions of the geometrical motifs used, which destroyed the dynamic rhythms that turned each piece into its own work of art. Then they began to invent their own Kuba-like motifs and imposed them on their vendors. Something similar happened to the carvings produced at the Josephite art school (1951 onward); carvings were produced that were somewhat inspired by Kuba art but were actually something else altogether.

"Missionary of Scheut" by Djilatendo, 1930–32 (Thiry, *A la recherche de la peinture nègre*, n.d.)

Presbyterians, the local Catholic missionary in charge soon quarreled with him so violently that henceforth the royals ignored the mission. The result was that the Scheutists abandoned Nsheng again in 1927 and retreated to Bena Makima. This seemed to consecrate the failure of Catholic efforts to convert the populations in the very heart of the kingdom, for at that point no more than one percent of Bushong and Kete were Catholic.

Yet the Kuba faithful did not give up. A year or two later the leaders of a cluster of Catholic Kete communities opposed to Protestant Bulape nearby began to badger the superior of the whole Scheutist mission in Kasai with demands to found a station among them, and they continued to pester him for years. Moreover, the king and the court still wanted to have a decent school at Nsheng and lobbied the colonial administration

---

A Remarkable Royal Son

The following text illustrates the competition between the Christian faiths for converts at the court in 1923 and the policy at the court of treating them in an evenhanded way. It also tells us that by 1923 at least one son of a king had been educated at an advanced Catholic school, probably at Luebo.

> And here are the princes, sons of Lukengo. There are some who must be twenty years old and some who are just starting to walk. All have a noble and slightly melancholy air. There is a young prince of a remarkable beauty, a true black Antinoüs [a handsome beauty]. He introduces me to two of his sisters in excellent French and with the gesture of a grand Lord.
>
> Where did he learn the language of Montaigne? "From the mon-père" [Catholic missionaries] answered he. But why, then, does he first go to fetch a necklace with a medal of the Holy Virgin and a fat Bible of the London Bible Society? A prince must be diplomatic. This one wants to be in the good graces of both the "mon-père" and the Protestant missionaries![2]

---

2. Chalux, *Un an Congo belge* (Brussels, 1925), 242.

so relentlessly that by the early 1930s the government also started to urge the Scheutists to reopen their station at the capital.

At that time the Scheutists had just started negotiations with the Josephites, a Belgian teaching order, to take over their more advanced schools in central Kasai, and they soon deflected the pressure to open mission stations in the Kuba area onto these newcomers to the mission field. The Josephites were happy to oblige even though—or perhaps precisely because—Catholics were still rare in this region. Scattered here and there, they were estimated to number no more than a thousand, that is, some 3 percent of the Bushong and Kete population, only a little less than the estimated number of Presbyterians. The Josephites took over Bena Makima in 1936, reopened Nsheng in 1937, and founded a post at Port Francqui the following year. Further expansion was held up by World War II until 1946, when they founded a mission at Mweka.

Six months after their arrival at Nsheng, nuns from the order of the Canonesses of St. Augustine joined them there. In the years that followed, the combined influence of the fathers and the sisters soon exceeded that of the Presbyterians there, in large part because only they taught the much desired official language, French. Nevertheless only a decade later (in 1949) the sisters had become disenchanted with Nsheng. They complained that the Kuba were not always faithful to their conversion, that the population was too sparse, and that were no mass conversions in this region, all of which was true. Hence they saw no future for their apostolate there, and the last nuns left in 1951–52 for Mweka and Port Francqui.

Yet despite the unpromising situation, the Josephites persevered and continued to found new stations. By the time of independence there were six main mission posts in Kuba country and a substantial number of converts, most of whom were alumni from their schools. A few years after independence (1964) this mission field became the Congolese bishopric of Mweka. By then an estimated 10 percent of the Bushong were Catholic as compared to 21 percent for the whole population of the Mweka Territory, Luba/Lulua included, and Catholicism had become the dominant Christian religion among them. But among the Kete, Protestantism held that position. Even then, however, more than three-quarters of all Kuba continued to adhere to their own religion.

Conversion

In view of their limited means, the tactics of conversion were all important for both Presbyterians and Catholics. They were far less influenced by the considerable differences in their specific doctrines and goals than one might think. Moreover, they faced similar challenges. For instance, the ability to read the Bible was crucial to the Presbyterians, but their applicants needed at least two years to master this skill. The Catholics deemed it essential to thoroughly indoctrinate their applicants into the more complex practices of their church and soon discovered that almost three years of instruction were needed to achieve this objective.

Second, a lasting effect of their early maneuvering was the decision by both missionary groups to choose Tshiluba as the language of instruction into the faith, so that by 1909 it was already becoming the unofficial official language for Kasai, a language that was by then being codified in two different "standard" versions: a Presbyterian one and a Catholic one. Consequently by the mid-1920s the Presbyterians abandoned their earlier efforts to use Kete and Bushong, even though by then they had prepared a complete grammar and a dictionary in Bushong. As to Catholic missionaries, they did not even think of using Bushong at all until the very last year before independence.

Both organizations also soon realized that some approaches were particularly effective for attracting people and for promoting orderly conversion. The Presbyterians found that gifts of sea salt brought Kete people to the Luebo mission, and both congregations realized from the outset that young men flocked to their stations for protection from state or company demands. Hence the numerous squabbles between the missionaries and the state administration or the Kuba court. Both confessions obtained an exemption of the hated corvee labor and compulsory agriculture for their salaried workers, and as a result they were never short of candidate catechists/evangelists or of workmen for their stations.

But above all the Catholic and Protestant missions soon began to realize that both schools and a permanent presence in the villages were essential to conversion in the long haul. Schools mattered because children were captive listeners and easy to convince. Moreover, Catholic schools attracted state subsidies that helped to finance the mission post. As to villages, the confessions strove to place more or less well-trained local Christians as resident propagandists in as many villages as possible. The Catholics called these local Christian teachers *catechists* and the Presbyterians *evangelists*. It is they who disseminated the Christian message throughout the country.

They were in charge of the local dissemination of the Christian faiths to the villagers and thus had great influence on the contents of the Christian message as understood by their public. True, they did not

Evangelist convention at Bulape, 1922 (National Presbyterian Heritage Center, Montreat, North Carolina)

translate basic notions such as "sin" into "evil "or "a bad thing," or "Holy Ghost" into "God Breath," because the missionaries carefully selected the translation of such key concepts themselves and allowed no variants. But it was the catechist or evangelist who explained the faith to local audiences, both by expanding on strange official translations and by drawing parallels with local beliefs and practices. Thus "God Breath" was very likely to be understood as a separate nature spirit localized in the breath of an anthropomorphic God, and "sin" became almost or entirely identical with "witchcraft." They also ruthlessly simplified complicated theological points and hence completely distorted them. At one point in a debate between adherents of both religions, the Presbyterian speaker dismissed the Virgin Mary as irrelevant because "one eats the peanut, the shell one throws away," to which the Catholic retort was "No Jesus without a mother," a point reinforced for this audience by analogy to the pivotal position of the Kuba Queen Mother.

Once settled, these folk built a shed in which to preach and teach on the village plaza right next to the *kiin* shrine. The great struggle between the two confessions at the time was their competition for an exclusive official position in every village. Achten vividly reports seeing Kete village plazas near Luebo in 1920 where small and older Catholic sheds stood next to large newer Presbyterian ones, both placed at the usual place for the shrine of a cult to restore harmony—right next to the village *kiin* shrine. No wonder that the Kuba interpreted the two Christian confessions as if they were two new rival cults.

As to the conversion process itself, the Kuba had no problem with the notions of God or revelation. Actually, the Christian message itself was not really new. Biblical stories such as the one about Noah's drunkenness had long ago filtered into the region by hearsay, and earlier in the century Luso-Africans and Ambaquistas had talked a good deal about *Ncyeem* (God). Furthermore, Christian practices were similar enough to those practiced in Kuba cults that it was not particularly hard to understand them. God was thought of as the supreme nature spirit, and biblical stories were his revelations, just as dreams were those of the nature spirits. Likewise, his commandments were prohibitions similar to those always associated with any nature spirit. Protestant hymns were perceived as the danced songs of Kuba cults, Catholic medals recalled protective amulets, baptism resembled initiation, and communion was similar to the collective taking of medicine to abjure witchcraft and sorcery. No doubt

---

Why Does One Become Christian?

A converted Catholic youth answered the question in 1954 in the following succinct way:

> One becomes Catholic or Protestant in order to have a Christian name. Even the pagans assume a name [even] without baptism. [One also converts] [i]n order not to go to hell; [out of] pride to walk in finery, proudly to holy communion; [out of] youthful manliness! or haughtiness. Also for one's comrades. [But] shame about [not having] a name is the main reason.
>
> All the pupils [in the mission school] must be Catholic, [and are] baptized in November during their fourth year. There are some who want to stay as they are. Some don't want to be beaten by their masters [out of] pride.[3]

---

3. Vansina Files, *Religion*, loose sheet, text by Shaam aNce Evariste.

those who were really spreading the message, the indigenous catechists and evangelists, used such analogies in their preaching to telling effect in order to stress the similarities first and the differences later on.

For there were differences. Angels were no problem, but saints posed a conundrum. These obviously were minor nature spirits. But had they once been living people and then became *ngesh* like the Kuba kings, or had they never been living people? Since Kuba do not believe in ancestors but in metempsychosis (rebirth of one's essence), saints were never merely people who lived only once. The two biggest clashes with Kuba religion, however, were Christianity's exclusivity and its stress on personal salvation. The first was only frowned upon because hitherto Kuba cults had never been wholly exclusive. But the notion of individual salvation was anathema because it was completely immoral in Kuba worldview and its ethics. For the Kuba, selfishness was and is the root of all envy, and envy is the one condition that always leads to evil. Even after World War II, Bushong and Kete village leaders still insisted so much on collective restoration that they never adopted the Christian-inspired and fashionable Nzambi wa Malembe cult that was then spreading among the Luba and Lulua along the rail line in Kasai. The cult was unacceptable because it preached *individual* salvation.

Although the Christian message was not exotic from the Kuba point of view and in spite of the intensive propaganda efforts of the churches, it took many years before portions of the Christian worldview became internalized, that is, before they became part of everyone's "natural" convictions. At first the Christian message failed to convince most village communities to join either one of the churches, although a few individuals here and there converted. Gradually, however, Christian notions began to infiltrate the expressions of the local cults to restore harmony. By 1930 at the latest, the absolute supremacy of God (i.e., *Ncyeem*) had become self-evident. A decade later the newest cults to restore harmony claimed both all-encompassing powers and total exclusivity just as the Christian faiths did. Another decade after that, the townspeople at Nsheng had assimilated Catholicism to such a degree that the king's official medicine man, who was then introducing Miko miYool in the town, wanted to be addressed as "bishop."

Despite this gradual infiltration of Christian themes and ideas, however, neither the Bushong nor the Kete rushed to join either of the two churches. Continuing to ponder quite a bit about Christian doctrine, they were often more critical and sometimes more sophisticated than any missionary expected. For instance, when a father asked his children returning from school at the capital what they had learned that day in 1953, they told him the story of creation, whereupon he immediately retorted that this was impossible because a creation from nothing could not occur only once at a single well-defined moment but had to be renewed at every successive moment in order to last.

The Kuba understood that to convert was to join a church and that one joined by undergoing a ritual of initiation, called baptism, after being instructed in the mythical stories and the do's and don'ts associated with them. All of this was familiar to them since this was also the common procedure to enter a new cult, although in the case of a cult whole villages tended to join collectively, whereas in the church case the villagers only admitted a catechist collectively. In both cases the adherence of a village to a given cult was signaled by a new monument, whether it be the Christian school chapel with the house for the catechist nearby or a garden on the plaza for the new cult. In just one documented instance, however, did the demand for Christianity appear to match the clamor for a new cult. That happened to Presbyterianism in and around the capital immediately in the wake of the 1918–19 epidemics. That movement was probably due less to gratitude, however, as the missionaries tended to interpret it, than to the Kuba conviction that it was the Presbyterian cult that had overcome the epidemics.

Although church statistics cannot be trusted for various reasons, it seems that between 1906 and 1920 most Kete and Bushong villages had already chosen one church or the other as their protector, so that rival villages chose rival confessions, while new rivalries also arose between groups of Catholic or Presbyterian villages. By the 1940s nearly every village had its resident catechist or evangelist, and a decade later the number of convinced Christians in some localities had become great enough to somewhat hinder the expansion of Miko miYool and similar cults. When independence came, Christianity was certainly making inroads, especially among the educated youth, but the essential fact remained nevertheless that over three-quarters of the Kuba still believed in their own religion with its familiar and comforting expressions, and they continued to observe its general and moral precepts faithfully and conscientiously. They did so not out of a spirit of resistance, rebellion, spite, or collective frustration, as some have thought, but as a simple practical matter. This approach, they knew, had helped their forebears to cope with the business of living, while so far the Christian denominations had not convinced them that their faith was either more true or more effective in coping with life than the Kuba way was.

Early Schools

Over the time span of the whole colonial period, the provision of education in the Kuba region, as in most of rural Congo, went through three successive phases: first the creation of schools with a rudimentary curriculum, then the adoption of a standardized curriculum for primary schools throughout the country along with the slow multiplication of such schools, and finally a rapid and accelerating development of more advanced secondary education, including full-fledged high schools. Our discussion follows these phases.

Although the missions were there to convert people, the need for literacy especially and hence the provision of schools were so intertwined with this goal that they were part of the missionary enterprise from the outset. With few exceptions education was to remain their monopoly until 1954, when the state began to found its own schools.

Given the importance of reading the Bible, literacy was an essential part of conversion for Protestants. Barely four years after their arrival, the Presbyterians already used a primer in the Kete language that had been printed elsewhere in Congo and paid for by selling Kuba curios in Léopoldville. Soon both confessions realized, however, that school children were far easier to convert than adults, and they gradually focused most of their efforts on schools. The Presbyterians did so enthusiastically, but many missionaries of Scheut were quite reluctant about it. Eventually no one saw anything unusual in the practice of routinely baptizing all the children enrolled at school. Thus in later years pupils in Catholic schools were automatically enrolled as aspirant converts. The following autobiographical snapshot of Mikwepy Anaclet is typical: "In 1942 I entered grade school. A year later I was a catechumen [i.e., a candidate Catholic]. The Father director had given each of us a medal of Saint Benedict."[4]

By an extension of this sort of reasoning, both the Presbyterians and the Catholics turned their mission stations into vast enterprises not unlike the celebrated medieval monasteries. A schoolbook in Belgium painted the following picture of the missionary endeavor: "The Congolese were formerly savage people, but now they are more or less civilized. The missionaries are building chapels, schools, and hospitals in Congo. They instruct the Africans and teach them to read, to write, to

---

4. Vansina Notebooks, Mikwepy Anaclet, *Autobiography*, 5: 7.

draw, to calculate, to speak French, and all manner of crafts. Already many little Africans are baptized and live as good Christian children."[5]

At Luebo the Presbyterians first developed a Sunday school in which willing people of all ages were taught to sing hymns and listen to some Bible stories. Just three years after their arrival there, this was supplemented with an elementary day school for children in 1894. There the pupils were taught to read and write in addition to receiving religious instruction. A home for "abandoned or rescued little girls"—that is, little slave girls bought on the market and emancipated by the missionaries— soon followed in which the boarders learned the practicalities of Western domestic science along with their religious instruction. However, from the outset and as a matter of policy for all their schools, the Protestants carefully refrained from teaching either French or English so as not to expose their pupils to the risks of being flooded with "infidel and agnostic literature."[6]

A year or two after their arrival at Ibanc the missionaries opened another day school there and another boarding home for slave girls they had bought and emancipated. However, the great majority of the Presbyterian pupils everywhere were Luba or Lulua, and even in those early years there were very few Kete or Bushong among them. That situation began to change around Ibanc only after the suppression of the Kuba revolt in 1905.

By then some of the Presbyterian pupils at Ibanc were learned enough to write letters in Tshiluba. At the time all Africans in Kasai considered letter writing to be the very summit of learning, so that the ability to write letters elicited great prestige. Letters were considered to be the most wonderful Western achievement both because they enabled people to communicate complex messages at a distance, which their own signal drums could not equal, and because most messages they knew were orders to be carried out without delay.

His own observation of the potential power of literacy prompted King Kwet aPe to visit Ibanc soon after his return from captivity in Lusambo and to promise that he would send a few Bushong girls to the school, some from his own dynastic lineage. He did so, and the girls

5. Marc Depaepe and Lies Van Rompaey, *In het teken van de bevoogding: De educatieve actie in Belgisch-Kongo (1908–1960)* (Leuven, 1995), 9.

6. Barbara Yates, "Knowledge Brokers: Books and Publishers in Early Colonial Zaire," *History in Africa* 14 (1987): 328.

were followed by a handful of children from patrician families of the capital. Not long after his return from Lusambo, the king also sent his son Joseph Mingashang to the official state school at Lusambo where he became literate and learned some French as well. The youth in Nsheng were so impressed by his ability to write and send letters that they composed the following song, which was still a favorite half a century later.

> The basket of Mwiimy ámbúl [the rain] Mingáshang writes a letter: that they tell my father that I know the Labody and Sankuru River [he saw the rivers when he traveled]

Program of Instruction for the Catholic School of Luebo in 1907

In a letter of April 17, 1907, addressed to the father general superior of the missions of Scheut, the general director of the Compagnie du Kasai confirmed that the company would fund a school at Luebo. The fathers would run the school. Primary education there would be dispensed by "Africans of the mission," but the fathers themselves would be in charge of more advanced teaching. It would be a boys' school, and on graduation the pupils would have to be ready "to render services to the Kasai company later on as clerks, planters, basket weavers and so on. They will be given practical instruction to this effect, each according to his talents." As a sample of what the curriculum should encompass, a copy was added of the official program of studies at the government school of Boma, at that time the most prestigious school in the colony. But that program accounted for only three hours of the school day. Nearly twice that amount of time was spent in a combination of religious instruction and farming in the school gardens. At Luebo the main change to this program was that Tshiluba replaced Lingala. The program of instruction itself was as follows:

Children's Colony at Boma   December 31, 1906
Program of Instruction

I. [First year] Courses.
French, exercising the memory, study of words

The basket of Mwiimy ámbúl likes to travel. I will travel with it,
I will know the literacy of Lusambo.

Mingáshang writes a letter: let them tell my father that I know
the literacy of Lusambo.[7]

Hence in 1933 the first lines in Bushong small children deciphered in
their first reader are perhaps not all that hyperbolic after all: "Today we
are very happy—Today we are beginning to read a new book—The
book that we are beginning to read today is the first book—We already
know all the letters."[8]

Above all, Kwet aPe wanted a school at Nsheng and kept badgering

---

Lingala, simultaneous teaching of reading, writing, spelling arithmetic, exercises concerning the first 20 numbers, then the numbers
from 20 to 100.

II. Courses
French: reading, writing, spelling.
First notions of grammar. Exercises.
Lingala: reading, writing, spelling.
Exercises in recomposition.
Arithmetic: study of the 100 first numbers, many exercises.
The 4 fundamental operations.

III. Courses
French: reading and running translation.
Notions of grammar. Exercises.
Written translation of French and Lingala texts.
Lingala recomposition.
Arithmetic: numerous problems about the 4 operations.
Decimal Numbers.
Rule of three.
Notions of the metrical system.

The Director of the Children's Colony
Signed Corman[9]

---

7. Vansina Files, 27: 9: *Chansons célèbres (ncok* songs), 11, #32, #33, #34.
8. *Nkana Mubala mu Bosha, Bulape* (Luebo, 1933), 4.
9. Compagnie du Kasai Files, *Dima*: annex to letter of April 17, 1907, from Compagnie du Kasai to Scheut.

the missions for a station there since that was the only way to obtain a school. Yet at the same time both he and his successor viewed the Presbyterians as bitter enemies, while the Catholic fathers of Scheut were held to be unreliable. Their first well-organized school in or near the Kuba region was launched only after they settled at Luebo in 1907, in direct competition with the Presbyterians and prompted by the demands of the Compagnie du Kasai, which clamored for trained personnel. When they reluctantly reoccupied their mission post at Nsheng in 1913, the school there remained so rudimentary that the inhabitants of the capital apparently did not even consider they had a genuine school until 1922. And when the mission post was abandoned again, in 1927, that school was again reduced to a rudimentary level. Hence the king and most patricians at Nsheng continued to send some of their children to the Protestant school at Bulape and a few others to the school of Scheut in Luebo.

Standardized Primary Education

Education in Congo acquired its fundamental organization only during the 1920s when a more or less standardized curriculum became official. Early in the decade the so-called foreign missions—that is, the Protestant missions including the APCM—reached an agreement about a common curriculum, while a few years later the lure of state subsidies rallied the so-called national missions—a label covering all the Catholic missions in Congo (and only them)—to accept the official curriculum. In both systems education was now divided between rudimentary village schools and central schools at mission stations. The program of the village school lasted two years. Apart from many hours of religious instruction, it imparted only elementary notions of reading, writing, and arithmetic. The central school lasted a full five years (rarely six), and its program approximated that of grade schools in Belgium or the United States. All these standardized programs still continued to devote only three hours or so a day to the "academic" subjects, religious instruction included, while the rest of the school day was spent on farming the school gardens and on so-called industrial training. This emphasis on vocational training was justified by the need to prepare the children for a future life as farmers. Theoretically it included such useful subjects as farming techniques, bricklaying, or carpentry. But in practice the children were simply set to work for the school to cut costs wherever possible. They did whatever jobs needed to be done, starting with the cultivation of their own food and the building of their own quarters.

And so it came to pass that some Protestant children at Luebo became nurses, typesetters, and even first-rate typists. The Presbyterians recruited their evangelists from their central schools and felt the "Gospel of the hoe" to be all the more appropriate for people whom they

---

The Village School

The following description was written by a missionary who was also an official inspector of schools in Congo, as part of an article in a propaganda volume celebrating the successes of the Catholic Church in Congo. In spite of the idealizing and romanticizing style, the attentive reader perceives the less than glamorous practice as well as the practical goal pursued by the missionaries.

> How is grade school organized? In the villages of the bush one finds the village school. A shed with a roof [of] grass and leaves; a black board and sections of tree trunks serving as benches. Where the population is not so nomadic a brick or stone building covered in tiles or metal sheets has been erected with furniture adapted to it. A school garden and a playground for soccer, a much loved sport, are lacking nowhere. Lessons run from 8 a.m. to noon. The curriculum includes: religion, writing, reading in the local language, the first elements of arithmetic, hygiene, physical education, manual work, and especially farming. It is parceled out according to a fixed schedule established by the missionary doing his rounds in the bush.
>
> Once every three months and more often if possible, the missionary reviews the work achieved, conducts examinations, and gives directives and incentives.
>
> After two or three years of such teaching one has given what is most necessary to the children: mainly order, routine, and perseverance which they have never known in the surroundings of their family. Local life takes them over again and they take part in the communal work of the village until they found their own hearth. Most of the best pupils and of the daring ones try their hand at a central school.[10]

10. P. Hebette, "Het lager onderwijs in Kongo," *De kerk in Kongo en in Ruanda-Urundi* (Brussels, 1950), 43–44.

destined to settle in the villages as a shining example of Christianity there. The missionaries of Scheut behaved in similar ways. These practices would change only very slowly over time, but eventually part of the time spent farming in the gardens would be replaced by organized sport, usually soccer, in the Catholic and later in the official state schools.

To service these establishments, training schools for teachers were needed in both systems. The Presbyterians opened schools of this type at Bulape and Luebo. These seem to have been more or less equivalent to middle schools in the United States. Meanwhile the Scheutist missionaries in central Kasai at first merged this training with the first four years of their own lower seminary—that is, the first of two levels of study for the priesthood—in the same school. The curriculum for teachers there was roughly equivalent to middle school in Belgium.

Then in 1930 Scheut abandoned this approach. They now handed this school over to a specialized Belgian teaching order, the Josephites, who immediately turned this establishment into a proper teacher training school at Luluabourg. In subsequent years the Josephites also assumed responsibility for the mission field and all the schools in Kuba country from 1936 onward. They reopened the school at Nsheng in fall 1937 and were joined there in early spring 1938 by the Canonesses of St. Augustine, an order that was specialized in both health care and teaching.

At Nsheng the fathers set up a central school for boys and the sisters established a school for girls, both with a five-year curriculum that included a smattering of French in the higher classes. In other respects the Josephites raised the quality of education in their central schools for boys almost to the standard set for a complete grade school in Belgium, although their teaching of French was still rudimentary. Nevertheless they still firmly subordinated the dispensation of knowledge to the continued instillation of Christian moral precepts to the point that pupils of other faiths were not welcome nor were those who did not want to convert. Yet at the same time these missionaries also stressed the adequate acquisition of knowledge to a greater extent than what was usual in any mission schools elsewhere.

In other respects, and in contrast to the situation in most schools at this level elsewhere in Congo, the curriculum in both the Presbyterian and Josephite schools was carefully adapted to the local situation, in that it was firmly anchored in the lived experience of their pupils. It avoided implicit references to Belgian or American situations that remained incomprehensible to their pupils. For example, a casual reference to one of the four seasons was usually enough to derail whatever was being taught. Indeed the curriculum here was so careful about this that it excluded any formal exposition of Belgian or American history. It did not include any history at all beyond frequent assertions about how savage the Congolese used to be before Christianity and how colonialism came to save and uplift them. Most pupils thoroughly resented these constant insults but otherwise seem to have had few complaints about the curriculum—except that there was far too little teaching of French.

Unfortunately the standards in the girls' school seem to have been much lower than in the boys' schools. The sisters focused just as strongly on religious subjects as elsewhere, but beyond this they concentrated almost exclusively on training the girls to become the equivalent of Belgian middle-class wives and mothers—rather like the Presbyterians had done with their boarding schools for girls. Such an attitude toward girls' education was never realistic. It only created a genuine handicap that made it much harder for Kuba women to maintain the high economic and social status their mothers had enjoyed in earlier generations. Luckily enough, once the sisters abandoned their mission at Nsheng in 1951–52, the girls came under the supervision of the fathers and joined the boys' classes, where they obtained the same opportunity of learning the boys did.

The greatest weakness at both the rural and central schools of both confessions was poor attendance. In contrast to Luba/Lulua children, Bushong and Kete children often played hooky, and with few exceptions their mothers or mothers' brothers (their fathers did not have that authority) were not keen to force them to attend. At least once, out of desperation, the director of the Bena Makima school wrote directly to the king in 1942 to complain about their lack of attendance, and he even included a list of the main culprits. It did not help much, for when his successor there returned from a long leave he laconically noted in 1954: "A small cloud. Almost no Bakuba at school! However, since my return the pupils are coming back after their . . . vacation." Yet, he also remarks: "The Bakuba were at the head of the welcoming parade. It is pleasure for the missionary to realize how much the black people want their station to be preserved."[11]

Hence, it was not ill will by the adults that kept the children away. Nor was it any lack of appreciation for the education their children

11. François Mbiyangandu, *Histoire du Diocèse de Mweka* (Kimwenza, 2004), 90.

received. They appreciated it so much that by the early 1950s it had become customary at Nsheng for parents whose children graduated from grade school to give a big party where both traditional palm wine and new bottled beer flowed to celebrate the end of the school year. Most likely what tempted these children to play truant so frequently compared to their Luba/Lulua comrades was the fact that Kuba fathers, unlike Luba/Lulua fathers, had little authority and that mothers' brothers, who did have authority, were not part of the same household.

This weakness worried both the missionaries and the kings, especially Mbop Mabinc, to the point that the fathers informed him regularly not only about the size and composition of their classes, but also about the rate of attendance and the diligence of their pupils. Whenever too many of them played truant, the missionaries seem to have called on the king to force them to return to school. That the Kuba were well aware of the inevitable undesirable results of such a situation is revealed in the following dream by Mbop Georges François in 1954: "I dreamed. We had gone somewhere, we found many pupils there, we asked them: 'what are you doing like that?' They answered 'The Reverend Father is going to announce the results.' We have waited for the Father. The Father arrived and announced [the results]. The first one [of the class] was a Muluba and then they all dispersed."[12]

Beyond Basic Education

After World War II the situation of education in Congo rapidly changed. First, state lay schools were founded for European children in the cities, and any discrimination against Protestant schools that wished to receive state subsidies was halted. Since accepting subsidies and school inspections did not require any alteration to their curriculum, the APCM availed itself of these subsidies from 1948 onward. Meanwhile, in 1947, a commission from the Belgian Senate had met demonstrators at Luebo who demanded state lay schools for Africans. Despite bitter opposition from the Catholic Party in Belgium, that demand was gradually fulfilled from 1954 onward. In that year the first official lay grade school opened its doors at Luluabourg, and already the next year a similar school was launched at Nsheng, far ahead of schedule, no doubt as

12. Vansina Files, *News and Dreams* [*carnet* 25: 68]: *Dream of Mbópey Georges François*, September 6, 1954, on loose typed sheet 3 #12.

a result of special pleading on behalf of the king. Thus the king and his grandees finally received what they had wanted for so long: a nonconfessional school. Its curriculum was exactly what was wanted at the time because it stressed the acquisition of knowledge in general and French in particular, exactly as was done in Belgium. But independence intervened before its first batch of students graduated.

Meanwhile, though, the Josephites in Mweka Territory had not been inactive during these years of competition between the Catholic Church and the state over schools. In 1946 they launched a mission station and a primary school at Mweka. Then in 1950 and 1951 they followed this up with four new mission stations in rapid succession, all with schools.

Nearly immediately after the foundation of their new posts, the missionaries followed up by creating various technical training schools

---

A News Item: Scholarly Pretensions

The following bit of gossip from Nsheng in 1956 tells us how much its inhabitants, and especially the young adults, had come to value Western education by then:

> There is a guy here in this town called Bope Jean. He finished the sixth form of grade school and they sent him to the teacher's training school at Domiongo. Going there he stayed two days and then returned. Why did you return? Because the subjects they teach there are more complex and also I returned because of love for my fiancée. But this Bope Jean of which you heard he does not know [understand] a letter in Tshiluba. His friends mock him, saying that this boy does not [even] know how to write. One day he wrote a letter to his friend, a pitiful letter. Instead of writing the name of the guy correctly as Ngenyi Emmanuel he wrote Ngweny Emanul. His friends have given him that nickname to joke. Everyone in town knows this. Ngweny Emanul always provokes smiles.[13]

---

13. Vansina Notebooks, 53: 62–63, 79–80. Text of May 12, 1956, by Kwet Constantin.

there, all state subsidized. Soon Domiongo had an advanced teachers'
training school, Bulongo had a lower seminary (part of the high school)
and technical schools for administrative clerks and joiners, and Mweka
had technical schools for medical auxiliaries, joiners, masons, furniture
makers, and village teachers, as well as a dressmaking school for girls.
Meanwhile a state experimental agricultural station, run by lay people,
had been established at Bena Longo near Mweka with a school for agricultural monitors.

In Kuba eyes, the art school at Nsheng was the most important
among all of these schools. For many years the Josephite missionaries
had dabbled in the development of a Christian liturgical art based on
Kuba motifs and forms. Then in 1949 a new missionary who happened
to also be a trained artist joined them at Mweka. Antonin D'Haenens
was naturally attracted to Kuba decorative art and sculpture, but at the
same time he was convinced that this art needed to be "improved" or
"developed," and he set out to do precisely that. To us today, this argument sounds like the height of paternalist and colonialist arrogance, but
at the time most other colonials found this perfectly reasonable.

The artist soon convinced his colleagues that an art school based on
his principles was absolutely needed in "this country of artists," and he
launched one at the post of Mweka on Christmas 1951, where it seems
he had only Luba/Lulua pupils. Then, only six months later, the school
was suddenly transferred to Nsheng, probably as a result of some pressure related to the wishes of the Kuba court. Although the Kuba government wanted such a school to further foster and legitimize the production of tourist art as a significant source of income, it was not about to
leave this project completely in the hands of the missionaries. So once at
Nsheng the school essentially turned into a joint venture of the artist
missionary and the king. Both parties compromised so that even though
the missionary-artist directed the school, the main teacher for sculpture
was Jules Lyeen, the best known woodcarver in the territory—but also
the son of a former king and an intimate of Mbop Mabinc. On that
basis the school soon flourished and attracted plenty of Bushong youth.

Only two years later, well before anyone had even graduated from
the art school, such a glut of souvenirs were offered for sale, all along the
rail line, that the prices collapsed. The king and his administrative
guide, Schillings, had to stabilize the market by setting up a cooperative
of artists in the kingdom. This succeeded, so that today, more than half
a century later, Kuba art is still an important source of revenue for
Mweka Territory.

By far the most significant among these new schools was Bulongo because the first full-fledged high school was placed there in 1950. This was an outgrowth of the teacher-training school the Josephites had operated at Luluabourg since 1930. First in 1948 they transformed it into a full high school with a curriculum that was essentially identical to the one taught at Josephite high schools in Belgium. In 1950 the whole establishment was transferred to Bulongo between Mweka and Nsheng. Practically the whole new emerging Bushong elite would be trained at this school. Although the first Bushong pupils there had already been enrolled at Luluabourg in 1949, at first rather few eligible youths among them applied because of their reluctance to enter a boarding school and to leave their friends and age mates at home. Moreover, relations between staff and students grew tense at the school during the first years of its relocation at Bulongo, and rumors about this further increased the hesitation of Bushong youth to apply for it. Both the prestige and the fears the school inspired are reflected in the following dreams from 1954.

> Kwet Constantin (September 26, 1954): "I dreamed. We were in class. The teacher called me outside. I went and he told me 'you, you will go to study at Bulong. I was very sad. When I awoke I had been dreaming."
>
> Martin Mingashang (Fall 1954): "He dreamed. They had sent Jerome [Mingashang] away from the school. The Reverend Father had sent him to Bulong. So Martin said 'I too will go with the Father.'"
>
> Mbop Albert (Fall 1954): "He dreamed that he had returned to teacher training school and entered in the year of Mandong Auguste. On arrival he found his friends there. They were just about to complete their studies and he too finished along with them."[14]

The school at Bulongo was reorganized in 1958. By then the value of a high school diploma for a brilliant future had become apparent to all, the king included, and the school immediately offered more places for Bushong youths and attracted more of them. By then the king was also attempting to place youngsters of his lineage at the lay state high school at Luluabourg, and by 1960 even in establishments at Kinshasa. After

14. Vansina Files, *News and Dreams* [carnet 25: 2]: *Dream by Kwet Constantin* on loose typed sheet 1 #5; *Dream by Martin Mingashang*, same file on loose sheet 1 #17; *Dream by Mbop Albert* on loose sheet.

independence Bulongo soon became the most celebrated high school in all of Kasai until all the schools were nationalized in 1973.

Thus the pent-up demand for all sorts of professional training was suddenly met during the last five years of colonial rule, and even though most of the pupils in the new schools along the rail line were Luba or Lulua, the number of Kete and Bushong youths among them rapidly grew as the years went by. Nevertheless these establishments, especially the state grade school at Nsheng and the renovated high school at Bulongo, started so late that they could not be of immediate help to their Kete or Bushong communities during the scramble for influence just before and after independence. Yet, on the other hand, training by Protestants, Catholics, and lay schools alike beyond the grade school level produced just enough alumni by independence day to prevent the kingdom from being torn asunder during the first two years of independence, while still providing a very large measure of autonomy to the mostly Protestant Kete communities.

Obviously the prime movers in the creation of missions and schools were the missionaries, yet Kuba were almost equally important agents. Their catechists, evangelists, and school monitors soon became the prime disseminators of Christianity and the dispensers of Western knowledge to the children in primary schools. Secondly, the kings and their courts actively campaigned for schools and missions to be established and maintained at Nsheng, as did some villages that either wanted to have or already had a mission post or a school. Yet the same villagers did not really enforce school attendance by their children, nor did any Kuba easily convert to Christianity, as the sisters found out among the women at Nsheng. Indeed only a fifth or so of the Kuba population had converted by independence. Regrettably, there remains far too little evidence to document how and why the situation developed as it did. But while one can speculate about the reasons for such results, the one thing that is abundantly clear is that Kuba agency in these processes of conversion and the acquisition of Western knowledge was decisive for their outcome.

FURTHER READINGS

Anstey, Roger. *King Leopold's Legacy*. Oxford, 1966.

Markowitz, Marvin D. *Cross and Sword: The Political Role of Christian Missions in the Belgian Congo, 1908–1960*. Stanford, Calif., 1973.

Roberts, Allen F. "'Fishers of Men': Religion and Political Economy among the Colonized Tabwa." *Africa* 54, no. 2 (1984): 49–70.

Slade, Ruth. *English-Speaking Missions in the Congo Independent State (1878–1908)*. Brussels, 1959.

Yates, Barbara. "The Missions and Educational Development in Belgian Africa, 1876–1908." PhD, Columbia University, 1967.

11

Toward a New World

The first Luso-Africans, and later the first people from overseas, revealed to the Kuba a new world across the oceans in which most things seemed to be vastly different from what they were used to. When these exotic foreigners began to settle in their country, the curious local people keenly scrutinized everything they did and everything they used. All of it was completely novel and hence fascinating, just as any novelty is anywhere else in the world, especially among the young, perhaps because it seems to foretell the future. For some time, then, and just by the mere fact of living there, the incomers demonstrated the possibility of another way of living that they liked to call *modern*, a word that means, strictly speaking, "of the present time." Yet in the new colonial context, the colonialists used the word *modern* to refer not to any novelty in general but only to the particular innovations they were introducing, and especially to their own way of living. In this last chapter we follow the process by which modernization took root and gradually developed in the region alongside the older Kete and Bushong way of life.

Modernization, in its attempt to impart a raft of new attitudes, wants, aspirations, norms, and institutions in tune with the requirements of an industrial world, was a process that went well beyond conversion to Christianity or the adoption of Western knowledge. The acquisition of Western clothes or Western table manners was merely a superficial sign of adherence to a modern way of life, and even a new sense of religion or new abstract knowledge was not enough. To fully succeed in a modern way of life one also had to acquire a new sense of time, as measured by clock and calendar expressed in hours and schedules; a new sense of money, as revenue needed to maintain the modern lifestyle; a new sense of work, as the source for monetary revenue as distinct from leisure; and, most difficult of all, a new sense of the limits of social obligation toward kith and kin. Indeed, even today most Congolese still struggle to balance the obligation to share with those they recognize as kin and the need to hold onto enough income to maintain the standard of living expected of them.

Obviously, then, modernization was too tall an order to be accepted all at once. It was a process. Yet it was not a straightforward accumulation, occurring drop by drop, as it were, through the adoption of one modern thing after another until by the end of the process that way of living had become modern. In particular, one should not confuse the acquisition of new foreign goods with the development of a modern way of living, as so many of the early colonialists did. Thus the early adoption of sea salt and matches did not affect the daily way of life of Bushong or Kete in any significant way, nor did it ineluctably lead to a subsequent craving for Western costumes, cigarettes, bicycles, or the standard of living of a storekeeper.

The process started with observing the behavior of the foreigners from overseas at Luebo along the Sankuru River and at various trading posts. Soon thereafter the Presbyterians pioneered active instruction into how to live the modern life. The Catholics followed them only some years later. But neither demonstration nor instruction met with immediate acceptance among the Kuba, for the obstacles were just too formidable. Moreover, the adoption of even the outward appearance in dress, food, or housing erased important expressions of Kuba identity and consequently provoked resistance. So, despite the fascination with things modern, acceptance of a modern way of living remained quite slow for a long time. But by the late 1940s, as the economic and social context had become more favorable, the new way of living began to spread faster. Suddenly, between 1950 and 1952, a breakthrough occurred at Nsheng when trendsetting young men among the elite at the capital embraced the modern way of life they had learned at boarding school, thereby legitimizing it. In the following sections we deal successively with the introduction of a modern lifestyle, resistance to it, and the final breakthrough of modernization.

Introduction of a Modern Lifestyle

The missions were not only the demonstrators but also the first main teachers and disseminators of a modern lifestyle. They were eager to spread the whole of their way of living to their disciples because they seem to have found it impossible to wholly dissociate the essentials of a Christian way of life from the way they themselves lived in the Western industrial world. Thus Christianity seemed to require not just faith but dresses, table manners, and, implicitly, money. Hence, missionary preaching turned into an apostolate of modernity as well as one of conversion and of education.

From the very moment in 1895 when the Presbyterians opened a home for little girls in Luebo, they planned to train the girls for years in the niceties of American domestic science. The first priority was to teach the girls how to dress, then how to take care of their clothes, how to be polite, and incidentally how to become consumers of modern things. In Kuba country at Ibanc the African American Edmiston Brown family was a living advertisement for the new way of life. Ibanc became the first magnet of modernization and remained so as late as Djilatendo's days in the early 1930s when Mweka, the capital of the modern rail line settlements, began to take over.

At Ibanc, Alonzo Edmiston, eager to promote development, used his earlier experience as a schoolboy on a farm in Tuscaloosa, Alabama, and as a farmhand on the plantation of the Alabama State Hospital to organize an industrial school focused on agriculture. He set out to teach the selection of seed, the rotation of crops, the preservation of the soil, and up-to-date methods of cultivation. As with so many development projects, however, the local Bushong and the Kete knew better than he did how to farm in this region. Yet he also introduced new varieties of corn, garden vegetables, mangos, citrus fruit trees, and domestic pigeons, and some of that caught on. Some of the corn varieties, cabbages, tomatoes, and mango and lemon trees are still planted today, while one giant dove cote survived in Ibanc until at least 1932. Edmiston's goat and chicken clubs, run by young people at the station who competed for prizes handed out at an annual mission fair, were equally stunning innovations, but they were too much part of a foreign mentality at the mission station itself to survive its closure in 1915.

When Ibanc was abandoned, the Protestants continued their apostolate of modernity at Bulape, where it reached the Kete and some Bushong. But Bulape never succeeded as well in this as its predecessor had, because these populations did not share the thirst for innovation at any cost shown by the Luba/Lulua people who had surrounded Ibanc. Indeed, not only did a Luba/Lulua community survive at Ibanc after the missionaries left in 1915 but the place continued to be a magnet for modern and fashionable lifestyles. By 1923 African porters all around central Kasai vaunted it as the Paris of Kuba land, and it was here that the Lulua tailor Djilatendo settled a year or two before he became one of the first two Congolese painters in 1930. There his paintings of planes,

The Presbyterian Mission at Ibanc Demonstrates Gracious Living

When the ethnologist Leo Frobenius visited the Presbyterian mission at Ibanc in August 1905, he was astonished by what he saw in the main residence of the missionaries. And what he saw had all been rebuilt, refurnished, and reequipped in barely eight months after the mission station had been totally destroyed during the Kuba revolt. As he wrote:

> How surprised I was when I entered this Mission station. Neither before nor afterwards have I seen such lovely luxury allied to comfort as in the station of the Baptist [Presbyterian] mission in these countries. There are drapes, real drapes, in the windows. On the walls framed images. In the master bedroom beautiful beds and chests of drawers, in the dining room a genuine sideboard. In addition rugs and easy chairs. . . . We had lunch in an unadorned natural fashion without affectation. Cleanly dressed little girls served us. On good quality tableware we had first class delicatessen: oyster soup, lamb's roast, a delicate chicken fricassee, little plum tarts, as I said, a genuine feast.
>
> The Baptists [Presbyterians] unquestionably wanted to underline the human aspects as such. They attempt to erase race distinctions. When they travel these missionaries do not sleep in beds, and twice a week they eat local dishes with their fingers, albeit on fine porcelain plates.[1]

---

1. Leo Frobenius, *Im Schatten des Kongostaates* (Berlin, 1907), 229–30.

steamboats, cars, bicycles, couples in European dress, and even an administrator at a typewriter betrayed his fascination with spectacular innovations.

Meanwhile the earliest African practitioners of a modern life throughout the land were the hated capitas of the Compagnie du Kasai who set an example of all its social drawbacks. They were soon followed by the evangelists and the catechists who settled Bushong and Kete villages to disseminate not just Christianity and literacy but modernity as well, and they did attract attention. Already by the 1920s there were evangelists well dressed in Western costumes in all parts of the country. Their behavior demonstrated a style of life that was a simplified but thorough copy of Western habits that they had observed or had learned about from the servants in colonial households. The range of their innovations included houses, furniture, clothes, food, tools and utensils, and many household routines. Yet despite all its simplicity, their style of living still implied more or less regular access to money, be it through wage labor or trade. Somewhat later, especially after the construction of the railway, a number of African personnel in government service, local store managers, military veterans, nurses, and clerks followed their example by adopting a similar but secularized lifestyle. But at that time most of these folk were still Luba or Lulua, even in Kuba milieus. Only from the late 1930s onward were they joined by some Kete and Bushong.

So sharp was the contrast between the Luba modernizers and the Kuba that foreign observers were all struck by it, often attributing it to a supposedly innate Kuba conservatism. But that made no sense. The Kuba were exceptionally interested in technology, as shown by their arts and their material culture, and they appreciated technological innovations. As early as the late 1890s they were copying foreign drinking cups or plates, had already adopted the pencil as a way of making preliminary tracings on masks before decorating them, and used artificial blue and other foreign colors in their art as soon as they could lay hands on them. Like other Congolese the Kuba were also eager to ride bicycles, use mirrors, operate sewing machines, or play gramophones. They even imagined that their spirits also made use of technological innovations. By 1950, for instance, every shrine for Miko miYool had a long pole with a rope attached to it, signifying the magic telephone line used by the spirit to send dreams to his devotees. And yet they were slow to adopt the new way of life. Therefore it was not any innate conservatism with regard to innovation that was responsible for this huge difference of

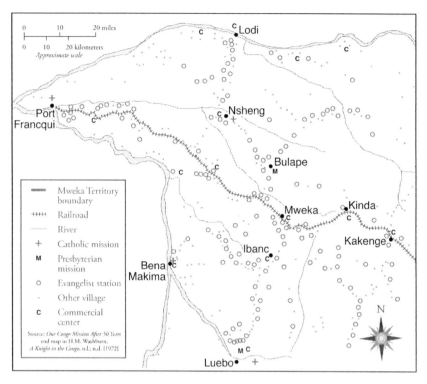

Apostles of modernity: Evangelist stations, 1941

receptivity between Kuba and Luba/Lulua toward modern ways of life. Rather, the big difference flowed from equally large social and cultural differences.

Outward Appearance and Modernity

We started this chapter with a brief glimpse of the formidable social and cultural obstacles that hindered the adoption of a modern way of life among the Kete and Bushong. Yet most of these obstacles were eventually overcome, and by the end of the period the modern way of life was well entrenched and expanding. It is neither practical, nor are the sources sufficiently detailed, to construct the annals of the acceptance of a modern way of life year by year, especially before the breakthrough around 1950. But we can use changes in outward appearance and especially in dress as an indicator to trace the underlying changes in attitudes and practices.

Outward appearance and dress especially were an important marker of common identity among all the Kuba, whatever the sub-groups, as well as an indication of status or wealth. In late precolonial times any Kuba man, wherever in the realm, wore a small conical woven hat fixed in the hair with a long standardized needle, an outfit of sewn skirts worn in a certain way, a special belt of raffia, and a standard-ized parade knife at the side. Kuba women wore a similar outfit, yet their skirts were sewn in a different way, their belts differed, they wore neither hat nor knife, and they sported different ornaments. For men, status was indicated by the exact sort of hat and knife one wore, by one's personal jewelry, and by the technical quality of one's dress. Hence, to adopt Western clothes was to erase all outward manifestation of Kuba identity as distinct from that of other Africans—except for body scarifi-cation. To do so amounted almost to a repudiation of that Kuba iden-tity. To adopt Western dress was a momentous choice, and one should therefore not be surprised that in his autobiography Georges Kwete Mwana discusses his decision to do so definitively in 1938 in a special section following hard on the heels of the one devoted to his conversion to the Catholic religion.

Hence, few or no Kete or Bushong persons were willing at first to adopt any of these novelties, and every one of their leaders seems to have frowned on doing so. Conversely, to adopt Western dress, and es-pecially tailored clothing, was a sign of adherence to the ranks of those allied to the foreigners from overseas. Those Lulua men who sided with the "modern" party of Kalamba Mukenge and later Luba refugees were quite eager for Western ways from the very start of the colonial pres-ence, at a time when Kete and Bushong were only interested in blankets.

Around 1900 printed cotton cloth began to attract some attention, but it was still considered to be too extravagant an expense. At the capi-tal, however, King Kwet aPe attempted to appropriate this cloth as a status symbol. Around 1908 he ruled that cotton cloth could only be used to sew some of the panels that made up the formal costumes that royals and aristocrats were entitled to wear. Although Western dress for adults was by then quite common at Ibanc, and later among evangelists, it still made no headway at all among either Kuba or Kete, even those living close to Luebo. Indeed, Torday recounts how in 1908 a Bushong veteran of the colonial army found nothing more urgent to do on his re-turn home than to shed his uniform, and in the 1920s village elders were still scolding young men as spendthrifts when they returned with West-ern cloth from wage labor stints outside of the realm.

Old-fashioned finery, 1956 (photo by author)

And yet from the late 1920s onward, Kuba women seem to have become so attached to wraps, especially the expensive Dutch wraps with their steadfast colors, that they now expected to receive one new wrap a year from their husbands as part of their upkeep. Although Kuba women with their knee-length skirts were not concerned, the wrap fashion may well be indirectly connected with a Catholic missionary propaganda offensive during that decade to make Lulua women cover their bodies more than they were wont to do. The Scheutists even designed a skirt for minimum decency and required all women in their flock to wear it, a practice that kept tailors like Djilatendo's in business for many years.

Still, throughout the 1930s very few if any villagers or common townsfolk at Nsheng wore anything but their raffia outfits, and it was generally believed that the king had forbidden Western dress altogether. In 1937 only the sons of kings, and probably the members of his own matrilineage, were allowed to wear tailored clothing. Kwete Mwana is described as wearing "linen trousers, silk shirt and felt hat."[2] But change came soon thereafter. A year later, when the sisters opened their school, they required their girls to wear dresses or blouses, and a few years later most of the boys at the central mission schools also began to wear shirts and short trousers.

Wearing European Costume.

In his memoirs Georges Kwete Mwana recalls when he began to wear Western dress. It was the same year that he converted to Catholicism:

> I started to wear European clothes constantly only from 1938 onward. [Before that] since 1936 I only wore them when I went to Mweka to present the monthly accounts of the tax collection [he was then a tax collector].
>
> [The following] gives an idea about the expense involved. As a person in charge of the census [and the collection of taxes], they gave me 50 francs per month and later on 75 francs. A shirt cost 6 or 7 francs. A suit could cost up to 150 francs, and I remember having bought one for 200 francs.[3]

---

2. Jeanne Wannijn, *Une blanche parmi les noirs* (Léau, 1938), 51. Also see 52, 56–57, and photo.

3. Georges Kwete Mwana, *Autobiographie* (manuscript, ca. 1971), 31–32.

During the 1940s men's tailored clothing began spreading outside of schools into many villages, and more women were now wont to wear their wraps when they were not at work. These changes indicated a greater availability of wage labor, more extensive schooling, and a general willingness by the villagers to enter little by little into a modern economy.

This was the background for the sudden breakthrough of the new way of living at Nsheng by 1952. By then anyone with a job or a position in the modern sector started to wear tailored clothes as his or her daily costume, and so did most of the royal male and female successors. In that year Hollywood came to film "traditional Africa" at the capital, and the fact that the king found it necessary to order everyone to wear Kuba costume is an indication that some, at least, were no longer doing so. In another sign of the times, two years later a Bushong veteran of World War II was buried there in full uniform.

Western costume is a good indicator of how much the modern way of life had by now spread, because it required the overcoming of so many social and economic obstacles. The following texts from the mid-1950s speak eloquently about the transition to the modern world as expressed in Western clothing. The first is a dream by Mikwepy Anaclet, one of the trendsetting young elite men at the time:

> I dreamed that I had washed my clothes and had put them out in the sun to dry. I had taken a packet of blue washing powder and put it near my clothes but the king came to my mother's brother Mbop Albert. He asked for my packet of blue washing powder; my uncle gave it to him. Later I checked the clothes: the packet was not there. I reprimanded my uncle: "Why did you give my blue to the king? He, he has much money to buy things."[4]

Even this innocuous story brings out a few important points about the new way of life. The washing powder "belongs" to him in the Western world, but in the Kuba world it belongs even more to his mother's brother, the male head of his lineage. The complaint is not that the uncle gave away what was not his to give, but that he gave it to a person who could buy his own. The reason that he did so was, of course, his awe for the king's power, a greater awe than the modern Anaclet felt. In those years the issues of both owning and sharing kept cropping up all

---

4. Vansina Files, *News and Dreams: Dream by Mikwepy Anaclet* 1953/1954, on loose sheet.

the time, because Bushong norms relating to both commodities and money itself were still in force.

But the wage earners, especially those who enjoyed greater social consideration, were beginning to dispute these norms. Thus, around the time of the dream just quoted, a schoolboy of Anaclet's lineage on his way to school tried to borrow Anaclet's briefcase, a then rare and prestigious status symbol of a senior clerk. When the latter refused, the boy instead borrowed a footlocker for which his classmates proceeded to ridicule him. This incident, trivial on the surface, illustrates a fundamental clash of values that remains, to the present day, unresolved; on the one hand, the Kuba premise of group solidarity and sharing; on the other, the modern capitalist premise of exclusive ownership. Even innocuous innovations, the dream suggests, may be the start of a slippery slope; that is, they are the first steps in a process. Once something new is adopted, one also has to adopt related items too: clothes require washing, and washing requires special powder, in the same way that bicycles require the tools and the knowledge to repair them.

The second text, a news item, dates from three years later. It tells how the king suddenly tried, once again as he had done several times before, to restrict the wearing of Western costume. Kwet aMbo, a son of Mbop Mabinc, had stolen 2,000 francs from the royal treasury. At the same time, he married, paid a bridewealth of 600 francs, and bought a photograph for 200 francs. When the king checked his finances he discovered the shortfall and was then told what his son had been up to. The son's behavior was all the more suspicious because he was not "working for money." The king then pressured Kwet aMbo and the latter's mother as treasurer for her lineage to reimburse him. To prevent such behavior in the future, he also decreed the following: "You, my children, you will no longer wear any European clothes at all, because the day one wants to dress in such clothes is the day one wants to steal."[5] His point was well taken: theft or fraud by young men wishing to adopt a modern style of living had been notorious during the preceding two decades, and by this time it had become abundantly clear that to pursue

---

5. Vansina Files, *News and Dreams: News item 1956* on loose sheet 107 # ix. The resulting situation became exactly the opposite of what it had been in 1937: now everyone was free to dress in Western costume except for the king's sons, whereas then only his sons could do so. But it was a sign of the new times that the children did not obey him on the spot. Western costumes were there to stay.

the modern way of life required a regular income either from wage labor in the industrial market economy or from trade linked to it.

This need explains a steady stream of news items in the 1950s about thefts in money or in goods. Shortfalls, usually by the clerks in charge of the shops, had become so common that theft began to seem the natural and inevitable outcome of a position as store manager. Thus one Kwet André dreamed that a white man came to hire him as a store clerk to sell

---

The Woman and the Monkey Dance

Although jotted down as recently as the 1950s, this extract of a folktale about a woman and the monkey dance is quite critical of modernization, in this case signaled by both dress and food. By this time the public mentality toward both had changed considerably. In 1904 when Ibanc was burned and looted, foreign food was left untouched. By the 1940s, sardines had become a valued prestige dish for young Bushong. Still, a decade later, older heads had this to say:

> The monkeys danced and asked her: "Do you have children in the village"—"yes"—"What gender?"—"A girl"—"Dress her in clothes similar to ours and she will dance as we do. She only has to show this to the village nearby and sing our [the monkeys'] song: 'Good day to you all, stay at home, I am going to our village Biyombo. In our village we eat canned meat. Those [cans of] fish hurt our belly, but the Whites prefer them. At home we drink water from iron pipes yet if you drink this it does not fill you. The drummer [for this dance] becomes angry [because he remains thirsty].'"

The reference to Biyombo is quite scornful. Biyombo was a small region south of the Lulua River downstream from Luebo particularly despised for its rustic ways. But in this story the name really refers to the city of Luebo, inhabited by people, as thoughtless as monkeys, because they forsake tried and trusted ways for newfangled Western silliness.[6]

---

6. Vansina Files, *Literature*, loose sheet.

goods: "And yet I cannot even read nor speak the language [French]. But the white man retorted: 'No matter. I will show you how to do the job.' I went with him and he showed me how to do the work; after a few days we made our accounts and I had fallen short."[7]

One other major obstacle to the adoption of a Western style of life, even in clothing, had to do with social aspirations. From the outset the ideal of young Luba/Lulua, and later especially those who lived along the rail line, was to become "like whites." That was not so for most Bushong or the Kete of all ages or either gender, even as late as the 1950s. Like their elders, many young Bushong or Kete still dreamed of a title and of the leadership as well as the social consideration within their own communities attached to it. Indeed, before independence most Kuba still aspired to service as a titleholder, at least according to reminiscences dating from the 1980s. Even in the 1950s few were ready to embrace a modern lifestyle at the expense of that cherished social solidarity. And the few who tried seemed unaware that they could not have it both ways.

The Breakthrough of Modernity

The sudden breakthrough of a new style of living at the Bushong capital resulted from the coalescence of two different developments: the gradual accumulation of wage labor positions that just then reached a critical mass when a group of young men with middle school education returned to town in 1952.

Training for crafts useful to the modern sector was almost as old as that sector itself. The missions first trained some people in low-level crafts such as carpentry, bricklaying, service in a Western household, or casual labor. A little later, they produced men with enough literacy to become stock keepers, low-level clerks, and even store managers. Yet they did not provide skilled blue-collar training. Only the railway company at Mweka could provide such training in the territory of the Bakuba. Besides workers for their repair shop and telephonists, they had, for instance, already trained at least one fully competent electrician there in 1930–31.

But all these jobs went to Luba speakers from central Kasai. Most Bushong and Kete missed out on such training essentially because they

---

7. Vansina Files, *News and Dreams: Dream by Kwet André* on loose typed sheet 11.

continued for many years to equate wage labor with slave labor. Only army recruits and a few other men who had been forcibly recruited to work outside their territory landed jobs in the modern economy. Nevertheless, little by little a few of them did acquire some skills for the modern sector. Indeed, several lists of central Kuba (excluding Kete) gathered in 1953 reveal that by then far more of them had acquired skills and positions in the modern sector of the economy than their colonial reputation as dyed-in-the-wool traditionalists foresaw. By then, in fact, a full 10 percent of those adult men at Nsheng who were not directly tied to the court held prestigious occupations as traders, nurses, teachers, or clerks, while another 12 percent held low-level jobs as tailors, mechanics, truck drivers, carpenters, and masons, and that does not include any of the local policemen.

Nor were the Kuba as isolated as their reputation would have it. Although their numbers were still small, a few Bushong were even then working in the modern colonial sector of the economy elsewhere in Kasai, in the main cities of Katanga and in smaller towns all across the southern half of Congo. But this was still a recent enough development by the mid-1950s that some ordinary experiences in industrial settings were nonetheless big news to the people of Nsheng. In one tale of woe a young man who returned from Katanga explained that he had been sacked merely because of a disagreement over the notion of time: he was frequently late for work and, yes, he had perhaps skipped a few days as well.

All in all, by then, from one fifth to one quarter of the ordinary men at Nsheng were employed in the modern sector, dressed in Western clothes, and followed a more or less inconspicuous modern way of living that others still considered to be inferior and barely acceptable by 1952 when the first small group of well-born young men returned after graduation from the teacher's training boarding school. They had conspicuously adopted the modern style of living and instantly became trendsetters at the capital. Yet they were not the first Bushong to do so.

Since Joseph Mingashang had gone to boarding school in Lusambo around 1905, two other sons of kings had acquired some Western education and made use of it for the benefit of the court. Jules Lyeen, son of King Mbop Mabinc maMbeky and a famous woodcarver, was the older of the two. Despite his education he never accepted Western ways and used his education only to assist the kings as a census taker and tribute collector when he was not practicing his art. The second son, Georges Kwete Mwana, son of King Kwet Mabinc maKyeen, however, was radically different. Essentially an autodidact, he not only became literate and numerate but then proceeded to acquire a good mastery of French. As he grew up he became his father's favorite son, and by the mid-1930s he was old enough to work for both the Kuba government and for the Belgian administration in various positions for which literacy, a good knowledge of French, and an equally good knowledge of Bushong custom was required. He converted in 1938, consciously adopted a wholly Western way of life, and never abandoned this thereafter. Whatever his motivation for this rather sudden shift in belief and lifestyle a year before his father's death, he soon became the model of a Westernized Bushong. He remained very influential even after he was forced to leave the capital and then the territory in 1940 shortly after the accession of King Mbop Mabinc maKyeen, at least until he was formally exiled in 1948 to the Kwilu district. Then his political setbacks prevented him from becoming a trendsetter for the lower-status workers in the modern sector among the Bushong or Kete and their leader.

Kwete Mwana was exiled one year before the "class of 1949" left for Luluabourg. These young men admired his achievement and strove to emulate it. When four years later they returned from their school, times had changed, and they found themselves to be instant trendsetters at the capital. Their status and their attitude made a modern lifestyle not only acceptable but also desirable, a way of life equal to and as fashionable as that of the older patricians in town. The low-status wage earners who had hitherto been rather diffident about their situation now enthusiastically followed the new lead, so that the new ways became very quickly dominant among the whole younger generation.

The Western intellectual baggage of that handful of young men was still modest—only a little more than what would be a middle school education today. But they knew French, they were up-to-date in the affairs of Congo as a whole, they were used to Western dress, they led a half-Western lifestyle, they were at home in the cosmopolitan city, and they were broadly nationalist. The process of modernization had turned them not into Westerners but into Congolese at ease anywhere in the country. They returned home with dreams for great achievements as wise administrators, wily traders, or great teachers. These men looked forward, their arena was the whole Congo, and among themselves they were already discussing ways to prepare for a future independence in terms fairly similar to Lievin Kalubi's letter nearly a decade earlier (see chapter 6).

Mikwepy Anaclet, a leader of the "class of 1949" (photo by author)

When they came home, they were immediately recognized as the vanguard of a new elite, and they were well aware of it. Yet they did not dismiss out of hand the old elite who had sired them. They might be Congolese nationalists, but at the same time they were Bushong from Nsheng who appreciated the reputation for supernatural power and splendor associated with their kingdom throughout Kasai, a prestige that redounded on them, too, as if they were prominent titleholders and they were well aware that the king closely followed their educational progress.

On the other hand, though, they still set themselves apart. Defining themselves as the first true Bushong intellectuals, they formed a closely knit group like one of the old-fashioned age sets. They even referred to themselves as the "class of 1949," the date when they first went to Luluabourg. In their view that was the moment when, as Bushong pioneers, they were the first to step into the modern world and to show others how to follow in their footsteps for years thereafter.

Modern Life at Nsheng in the Mid-1950s

What exactly was this modern new way of life the "class of 1949" was so proud of, and how did it differ from the older practices? First, the handful of new elite men divided their time into work and leisure. They were employees in white-collar jobs such as school teachers, administrative clerks for the government or for the Kuba court, clerks for tribunals, and skilled nurses. Not many years later, some were already unemployed and behaved as such, looking for other jobs such as store managers or trying to launch a small business of their own rather than to become farmers or hunters or even blue-collar truck drivers. White-collar employment, in return for an income, was the foundation for their lifestyle, and that by itself already set them apart from the rest of the population.

The new youth liked to stand out by their appearance and their novel leisure activities. While the women usually sported blouses with wraps, the men wore Western apparel with shoes, trousers, shirts, and hats. Indeed these men were nearly obsessed by their wish to have the best wardrobe. For example, a man once dreamed that his friend boasted nine shirts while the dreamer himself only had five. In another dream, a friend arrived with a lot of money from Bena Makima wearing a jacket made out of a woolen piece of cloth for the back and cotton cloth in front. Again the dreamer was outclassed, but at least he had good taste, in contrast to his friend, the nouveau riche. In yet another dream a young dandy was satisfied that he had been able at least to buy the same shirt as the one his friend owned. Matters of dress, such as a dispute over a loaned shirt and hat, for example, were sometimes serious enough to end up as court cases.

Apart from the age-old pastime of strolling around town with their friends, the leisure activities of the new young men included playing soccer, a sport to which they had been introduced at school. But they also loved to organize parties to mark such modern occasions as the end of the school year or Catholic first communion. Most memorable among such occasions, though, were the rare performances by bands from

Kinshasa. These allowed the modern youth to indulge in urban dances such as the rumba and take in the latest hit songs with the messages of modernity they carried.

All of this stood in sharp contrast to the splendors of Kuba formal costume dress, the occasional official ballet performances that mobilized the whole town, or other large-scale ceremonial occasions. While the new youth did come to such occasions as spectators, they eschewed attendance at the frequent spontaneous informal dances accompanied by impromptu singing when the moon stood high in the sky, or informal occasions such as the bawdy celebration of abundant fertility held in honor of newborn twins.

Just as important for the future as their acculturation to Congolese urban ways were the aspirations of the new elite. They were no longer interested in the values and careers that had fascinated their elders. The new men wanted to achieve the status of those colonials around them who seemed to be the most respected, but they focused only on positions that they could hope realistically to achieve. They dreamed of becoming priests, mechanics, administrators, and ship captains, and at the time clear paths to achieve such goals had just opened up. They did not yet aspire to become physicians or lawyers, for instance, because by the mid-1950s those professions did not seem accessible yet. They also wanted to become wealthy enough to own a pickup truck, just as Kwakong, a Bushong trader at Nsheng, had managed to do, so that then they could look down on lesser people. This attitude stands out in several dreams about this widely coveted truck among which the dream of Mingashang Martin was only the most arrogant:

> He dreamed that they were traveling in the pickup of Kwakong Symphorien and when they stopped at the [imaginary] brick house, one or other out of town rustic put his bicycle in the car. Symphorien ordered "Martin hit him." Martin hit him. They drove on and then another one was going to put his [large] basket with chickens in the car. They hit him too. And then they finally could go their way with the pickup.[8]

To fully appreciate this text one must realize first that this dream, in fact, faithfully describes the behavior of certain truck drivers for colonial

---

8. Vansina Files, *News and Dreams: Dream by Mingashang Martin*, February 15, 1953, on loose sheet.

Leisure Activities in the News

Parties on November 15 and November 29, 1953

We have been very happy for the children of Nsheng who have finished school. We went to Makash. He gave us wine and food. His child Georges was drunk and behaved like an animal. After that he vomited everything he had eaten and drunk.

This Sunday we have been quite happy because of the children who took their first Holy Communion. We had a lot to drink, alcohol, bottled beer, palm wine [from the oil palm] and from the raphia palm, and food. We also danced the Mading (Maringa, a.k.a. Rumba) until the evening.[9]

Note the mix of Western and local drinks. At the same events fashionable young men would smoke only cigarettes. They were not to be caught enjoying a local pipe!

A Band at Nsheng in 1953

This afternoon we heard a truck coming from the direction of Domiongo. Then it arrived at the quarter with the new houses and it stopped. After a good ten minutes we heard the band [perform] with an excellent big sound: they were singing songs. Oh! Those people of Léopoldville!

All of the capital hurried to go there, as if they were off to the wars. All the people at the food market scattered and filled the road to the truck like a column of driver ants. But we, the young men, we ran very fast after the truck because of the music . . . and the brass went *yiwa yiwa*. When it was time to sleep all became quiet. And so, now, we are trying to find out what the words were they sang [because the song was in Lingala, the language of Kinshasa].

9. Vansina Files, *News and Dreams*, subfile #3 *News:* loose sheets for November 15 and November 29, 1953.

A band performed today at noon with four songs. After that the king sent them all to the house of the titleholder Mbyeeng because of the multitude and because there is a nice view there and also [there is room] to dance. First we paid fifteen francs and then we were allowed to enter the compound. And the king did send goats as food for the party. There were many people there and the band was really good.[10]

Soccer News

Foundation of the first soccer club at Nsheng Spring 1953:

> All the young men of Nsheng paid five francs each. With this money we have bought a football for Sport, but those who have not paid are not allowed to play football. Bityet Benoit is the treasurer.

The soccer match of September 20, 1953:

> Yesterday evening there was a football match between the young men of Nsheng and the pupils at the Native Art school of Reverend Father Antoine from 4.30 p.m. to 5 p.m. [*sic*] It was a hard fought match for both sides.
>
> But thanks to the power of the prayers of the Reverend Father Superior, the pupils of the art school scored one to nil against the men from Nsheng.
>
> Still this is not right because the Reverend Brother whistled for each foul of the Nsheng side but there was no whistling for the fouls of the artists.
>
> Therefore we remain angry. But next week we will play again against them and we will equal their courage.

The reader will note the explanation of the outcome on two levels of reality: first a supernatural one, then a pragmatic one. This was then (and remains today) typical for the interpretation of soccer matches, the difference between Christians and others being merely the difference between the power of prayer and the power of charms.[11]

The soccer match of May 10, 1956:

10. Vansina Files, *News and Dreams*, subfile #35 *News:* loose sheets. News items by Florentin Kwete, September 1953.

11. Vansina Files, *News and Dreams*, subfile #35 *News:* loose sheets. First text reported by Mikwepy Anaclet, second one by Florentin Kwete on September 20, 1953.

businesses, and second that this Martin was Mbop Mabinc maKyeen's son and hence as a *mwaanyim* could be expected to be more arrogant than others—at least in the old-fashioned system to which he obviously still subscribed in part.

This last observation tells us that despite their modern aspirations and wider worldview, the new elite was still steeped in some of the core values of the old-fashioned system including its sense of hierarchy. Despite their thirst for innovation, none of these young men broke completely with their kin or the larger social groups at home. They all admired Kuba art and boasted about it, and a few revered the older Kuba social and political organization as an expression of age-old wisdom that needed to be remembered. And so, even though their new lifestyle and aspirations led to some friction with those who had authority over them, such as their mothers' brothers or even the king, they did not break with them.

Rather, their relationships with these authority figures became quite ambiguous. Their dreams and their gossip showed them to still stand in awe of the king and his mysterious powers, and they all saw him as the bulwark of Kuba values and institutions against the Belgian administration. They fully realized that he closely followed their careers, and they appreciated that, but at the same time they deplored his general interventions against the modern style of living as expressed in his ban on adobe houses or his fulminations against modern dress. Then again, they did appreciate his occasional and unexpected gifts of food for modern parties, and they all vaguely realized that in some sense their way of living depended on the Kuba order that he personified.

The Pupils of the sixth form [of the state school] played a match against those from the art school. Those from the sixth form won with a score of four goals to none. The arbiter was a European, the master mason who is building the houses of the hospital at Tung aKosh (Shin bukung). The father Director of the Art school was very angry. He told the pupils that today you will not eat something tasty. Why then did the little children win?[12]

---

12. Vansina Notebooks, 53: 73, 56: 10, Report of May 16, 1956, by Kwet Constantin.

In fact, to a large extent their adherence to the most essential Kuba values and their lingering respect for the old-fashioned norms and social institutions explain why a way of life that clashed to such an extent with the previous way of life did not lead to permanent friction or social breakdown. In part this was due to their acceptance of the decisions of local courts, which resolved not only quarrels between modern young men and others, but also those among competing young men, such as a case concerning the distribution of an inheritance. The titleholding judges decided on the merits of the case and according to precedent, regardless of the degree to which the parties had accepted or rejected the modern lifestyle, and as a result everyone abided by their decision. That kept the inevitable frictions between modern and older within bounds.

Second, members of the new elite were truly adept at turning old precedents to a new advantage, that is, getting what they wanted while avoiding a clash. The following example is typical. One day the news—or was it a scandal?—broke that one Mingambengl Benoît had just married not a Bushong but a Luba woman from a village on the rail line and brought her to Nsheng, and yet there were no protests. There were none because what he had done was in line with past practice. Wealthy men had long taken Luba concubines whose offspring then belonged to the lineage of the father and hence strengthened it. Mingambengl's action was the same, except that it raised the status of the Luba woman from a pawn or slave status to that of legitimate spouse. It looked like something old, but in fact it was something new because the Luba wife's family kept quite a few rights as well as significantly more influence over the children. Maneuvers similar to this helped just as much as the courts did to allow the new way of life to coexist with the old-fashioned one—and thereby to begin to subvert it.

The modernity adopted by the Kuba in the 1950s was one that was then spreading out from the main cities of the country, not least Kinshasa. It was not the modern living proposed by the Ambaquistas, nor the lifestyle taught and propagated by the missions at the beginning of the twentieth century, a variety hopelessly unrealizable in the concrete living conditions and living standards of the time and place. Even the more simplified version that was gradually worked out by such Africans as the evangelists in the 1910s, or the railway personnel in the 1920s, then altered by those Africans who worked within the modern economy of Kasai, did not fully fit the Kuba situation. The notion of modernity continued to be a moving target, and the movement toward it a process that developed and even today keeps developing over time and according to place. By the 1950s Bushong and Kete had created their own modernity, a way of life that was remarkable in being quite congenial to the almost standardized urban Congolese way of life, and at the same time one that was growing deep local roots by means of creative compromises such as Benoît Mingambengl's marriage. Such compromises enlarged social horizons yet stressed continuity and hence could appease the old-fashioned as well. After independence such dynamics allied to the further spread of

Gender Emancipation

Those considered to belong to the modern elite at Nsheng were men. Unlike them, even young women with a complete grade school education still did not aspire to any goal beyond Bushong society and culture. The following dream of the most ambitious girl among them is revealing:

> Elizabeth dreamed that "I received a gun from Maxi Schillings [the son of the administrator]. I went with it to track a leopard that I had wounded earlier on. My reason for killing this animal was to be invested with the title of Cikl. But when I came very close to the beast I became afraid and in its evil way the leopard killed my dog."[13]

Elizabeth's ambition was one of gender emancipation. One realizes this as soon as one is aware that Cikl is the second most senior title in Kuba hierarchy and one that had always been reserved for men; moreover, the Cikl in 1954 was reputed to be a very wealthy man. In her dream she wanted to gain the title for herself by her own heroism with the aid of a gun. But despite the goal and the modern means, the most striking part of her dream is that what she wanted was success in the old-fashioned way, not in the new world. After all, her goal was the familiar one to achieve high status in its titleholding system (Cikl) by an act of extraordinary old-fashioned bravery (the leopard). In her dream only the gun was really new.

---

13. Vansina Files, *News and Dreams: Elizabeth's Dream,* June 5, 1954, on small loose sheet 49.

Western education would gradually rally all the Bushong and the Kete to the new modern way of life and its new aspirations of progress.

Rushing into an Uncertain Future Called Independence

The 1950s were heady days. What had been drowsy became dynamic, and change became hectic during the last colonial years. Business boomed, schools blossomed, living standards grew by leaps and bounds especially in the towns, colonial society seemed to open up to Western-educated Congolese, more and more students graduated from technical schools and even from high schools, while more and more infrastructures were built faster and faster, especially in Luluabourg and Mweka. Everything seemed possible. King Baudouin's visit to Luluabourg in 1955 was a genuine triumph. The Bushong especially relished the private interview he gave to their king, whose hand he shook in public. The year 1955 was also the time when half a dozen Bushong women went to Belgium to exhibit their embroidery skills in Brussels.

The cities were the great success story. Like magnets, they drew skilled blue-collar and white-collar labor from the countryside around them. Luluabourg mushroomed faster than anyone had dreamed of. Between 1940 and 1958 its population increased more than twenty-two-fold, and despite its best efforts the administration failed miserably to slow the flow of immigration. Officials could only frantically attempt to keep up with the infrastructures needed. On a much smaller scale, Mweka also became the focus of a flight to the city. By the early 1950s the dream of many a Bushong youth, even at Nsheng, was to find work as a mechanic in Mweka. At the same time, and even though they constituted only a mere 1.5 percent of its population in 1958, more than two thousand Kuba had settled by then in Luluabourg, and a number of others lived in the cities of Katanga and Kinshasa. The good times seemed to roll on forever. Less than six months before independence a bridge over the Lulua River was inaugurated at Luebo, while funds became available to asphalt the main street of Mweka and to provide the town with both running water and electricity. Obviously, even then the colonial administration was not yet conscious of what independence would mean for its routine operations.

And yet there had been clouds on the horizon as early as 1953 when people in Mweka learned with misgivings that the émigré Lulua in Katanga had created their tribal association Lulua Frères to fight the better-educated Luba Kasai for jobs and influence. In 1957 the economic boom suddenly ground to a halt, and for the first time ever provisions had to be made for the unemployed in Luluabourg and in Mweka. A year later all eyes focused on the urban elections in Luluabourg, which triggered such tensions between Lulua and Luba Kasai in and around the city that they exploded by mid-1959 into a full-scale civil war. From then on and until independence, the administration in Kasai ran essentially from emergency to emergency to cope with the war, with the demands of Congolese leaders and their parties, with the organization of a cascade of elections, and finally with the installation of their own successors.

The usual colonial life also abruptly ended for the Kuba by the fall of 1959, when the Luba/Lulua civil war nearby, and rumors about the unexpected coming of independence, led to such panic in the Bushong countryside that a large number of villages suddenly sought a solution in a large-scale administration of the poison ordeal. Only the discovery and the destruction of all witches in their midst, they thought, could remove the threats that now beset them. Once they had started, they continued to administer the ordeal during the following six months and gave it to some five hundred people, half of whom died. It soon became evident that the colonial administration was powerless to cope with this situation, both because their soldiers had their hands full with the civil war between Lulua and Luba and because they lacked the moral authority required to end the slaughter.

Rather, it was the king who managed to stop the practice. During the same months he prevented the civil war in central Kasai from spilling over into the Kuba villages of the southeastern part of the kingdom, he also served as one of the mediators between Lulua and Luba Kasai for the colonial establishment. Ironically, by early 1960 the prestige and power of Kuba kingship in colonial times had never been so high. Less than three months before independence, the king, and perhaps the provincial administration as well, seems to have expected that some form of Belgian control would somehow continue beyond independence, as is attested, for instance, by a letter he wrote on April 6, 1960, but did not send to the provincial governor:

> Sir,
>
> Respectfully I take the liberty to solicit your benevolent intervention in favor of Mister Joseph Croonen, assistant territorial administrator, former head of the region of Mushenge and presently stationed at TSHIKAJI.
>
> Considering that Mister Croonen enjoyed the whole trust and the consideration of all the BAKUBA and that his departure is

much regretted by the population of the Bushongo, I allow myself
to solicit your benevolent intervention with regard to his return to
Mweka Territory.

In the hope that you will be inclined to grant a favorable outcome to this request, and with my thanks in anticipation, please, Sir,
accept the expression of my respectful and wholly devoted feelings.

The Nyimi [king] Bushongo'
Not signed
MBOPE Mabintshi Makena.[14]

Independence came on June 30. The same day a new executive administrator backed by an elected council took over in Mweka Territory.
He was a Presbyterian Kete from Bulape, a man dead set against the
continuing existence of the kingdom. Not much more than two months
after his accession to office he sent the soldiers of his garrison to occupy
Nsheng and chase the royal wives out of their quarters in the name of
the very Presbyterian desire to stamp out the scandal of royal polygamy.
Thereupon the king's government, in which these women played an irreplaceable role, immediately ceased to function. Chaos resulted. Mbop
Mabinc hastened to inform one of the ministers in the provincial government of Kasai at Luluabourg, who was a Bushong from Nsheng, to
ask for the support of the provincial government. He also called upon
army officers of his acquaintance to intervene. The Luba/Lulua civil
war still absorbed everyone's energy, however, and nothing happened
very quickly.

Then in December, while the territory was still in complete chaos,
the fugitive prime minister of Congo, Patrice Lumumba, appeared unexpectedly in Mweka. He gave his last political speech there and then
sped northward to Lodi, where he was captured as he was about to cross
the Sankuru River. A few months later the Congolese crisis abated somewhat, and the king managed to have the Kete administrator dismissed
and replaced with a young Bushong intellectual, one of that "class of
1949" who had nourished such high hopes for the future only eight years
earlier.

In sharp contrast to its arrival in the late nineteenth century, colonialism left suddenly and with a bang. That arrival had been so slow and
affected the daily life of most Kuba so gradually before 1902 that it does

14. A letter drafted but not mailed. Hymans Papers of King Bop Mabinc maKyeen,
1960 (available at the Memorial Library of the University of Wisconsin–Madison).

not make sense to insist on a precise date for its beginning. In contrast, events in 1960 went very quickly. The civil war in Kasai and the poison ordeal in Bushong villages show that colonial control had already begun to recede about a year before the official date of the handover on June 30, 1960. From that very first day of independence, compulsory farming and forced labor collapsed, including the maintenance of roads. Two years later that lack of maintenance had rendered most roads impassable, and the rural economy was slowly being throttled. By then daily life had completely changed, to the chagrin of the many who had appreciated colonial stability, not just among the privileged at Nsheng but now even among the villagers. Yet despite all the disturbances, the dynamics of turning Kuba into Congolese continued unabated until our own days.

Further Readings

Anstey, Roger. *King Leopold's Legacy*. Oxford, 1966.

Markowitz, Marvin D. *Cross and Sword: The Political Role of Christian Missions in the Belgian Congo, 1908–1960*. Stanford, Calif., 1973.

Roberts, Allen F. "'Fishers of Men': Religion and Political Economy among the Colonized Tabwa." *Africa* 54, no. 2 (1984): 49–70.

Slade, Ruth. *English-Speaking Missions in the Congo Independent State (1878–1908)*. Brussels, 1959.

Yates, Barbara. "The Missions and Educational Development in Belgian Africa, 1876–1908." PhD, Columbia University, 1967.

Conclusion

The Experience of Being Colonized

T his narrative about the history of colonial experiences among the Bushong and Kete is now over. And so it is time to look back at the whole sweep of this book and to ask ourselves a few questions that flow from the choice to write about "being colonized" and about the value of "the experience of the Bushong and Kete" as an introduction to the history of the period in the whole of Congo.

The very first question a reader raised was whether being colonized accounts for all the changes the Bushong and Kete faced between 1880 and 1960. Would some of those changes have happened anyway, even if they had not been colonized? This sort of question is called counterfactual because it deals with a situation that did not happen. The short reply is that precisely because it did not happen, any answer except for "we don't know" has to be mere fiction limited only by the imagination of the speaker. Yet when their underlying reasoning is comparative, counterfactual questions can sometimes be useful to disentangle various factors that led to a given outcome. Thus one might posit: *if* Kasai had become part of Angola, *then* the Kuba would have learned Portuguese, Luanda would have been their capital and *then* . . . because that is what happened to people in Angola. "*If* the Kuba had never been integrated into any colony," however, is an extremely unlikely presupposition given the known history of Africa. But it is one that might be invoked to justify a comparison with, say, Bhutan or Thailand to conclude that the Kuba still would have been affected by the global market economy.

Well and good, but the real evidence is that all change for whatever reason among the Kuba between 1899 and 1960 was so affected by the colonial situation that it is spurious to try to figure out how it could have been different otherwise. Colonialism was an essential attribute for every other process occurring at the time, something that colored everything else. And yes, being colonized was the essence of Kuba history during that period.

Does that mean, the same reader asked, that by 1960 Kuba people no longer defined themselves as "people of the king," as they did in 1880, but as "colonized Congolese"? Yes and no. By 1960 they defined themselves toward other Congolese as "Bakuba," a label imposed by others that became part of the colonial gallery of ethnic identities, almost from its inception. When asked by anyone outside of Congo they would call themselves Congolese and feel themselves to be that. Only in local situations did they still distinguish between Kete or Bushong. So, yes, colonialism influenced their identities.

The next question raised by the title of this book is one of agency. "Being colonized" sounds passive, and "experience" is ambiguous. To what extent did ordinary Bushong or Kete affect their own destinies? The answer is quite complex. The reader will first notice that the leading actors are not always the same. They vary from chapter to chapter and even within chapters: sometimes they are the colonizers, sometimes not. Because this is a history from below, we are emphasizing agency from below, that is, from somewhere among the colonized, not from the colonialist top down. Agents vary from individuals and villagers to kings and the Kuba establishment, and so do the points of view we follow. Most of the time, though, the dominant agents are the kings and the Kuba councils of titleholders at the capital, so that their views dominate in the narrative as well as in the sources. Before dismissing this as yet another elite point of view, although admittedly one below the top level, the reader should keep in mind that the opinions of the councils usually reflected those of their constituents, that is, most Bushong villages, and thus they are closer to the grass roots than is apparent at first. As to the king, the main reason why he still enjoyed genuine authority at the end of the period flows from the conviction that he used his agency above all to further the interests of his villagers.

So the question of agency is quite complex, and one can sympathize with another reader who concluded that this book views the history of colonial rural Congo neither from the top down nor from the bottom up but largely from the periphery—even though, of course, several chapters do tell it from the perspective of ordinary villagers. But even this statement remains rather vague. If one understands this book as a general colonial history from below because it focuses on "the experience of the Kete and the Bushong," one is actually creating two monolithic blocks in one's mind: "the elites" and "the masses," blocks that did not exist as such. By the end of the book perceptive readers will be well aware that, in fact, the experiences of all the Kete and of all the Bushong were not the same. Obviously the aristocrats and courtiers in Nsheng led a different and easier life than almost any Bushong villager, while the Kete inhabitants of villages on the doorstep of the Presbyterian missions of Luebo and Bulape were better protected from colonial demands than others and also were much better placed to benefit from Western schooling and health care. Carried to the extreme, such observations conclude that every person's experiences have differed somewhat from those of every other person. In real life there are no "grass roots" or "popular masses" to contrast as a single block against an equally unreal single experience of top-down colonizers.

On further thought one becomes keenly aware, however, that throughout the colonial period none of the colonized subjects have ever shared the same fate in equal measure. They never have been equal losers in the colonial situation. One soon discovers that there have been winners and losers among them just as there have been winners and losers among their colonial masters. Moreover, once one starts to label who was what, one soon finds out that the identification of "winners" and "losers" can shift with the passage of time. "Losers" from a perspective contemporary with the time of the events may become "winners" over a longer-term perspective and vice versa. For example, in the era of the slave trade and of bonded labor the Luba of Kasai were the great losers, yet by the end of the colonial period many of them were among the greatest winners in Congo, while in the Congo of today they do not look much better off than the Kuba who once were "losers."

As one reads this study anew in this light, it also becomes quite obvious that the differences between winners and losers at the time were particularly pronounced among the Kuba because their society was so hierarchical at the onset of the colonial period. Wherever possible their leaders at all levels passed as many burdens as they could onto the lowest ranking and the least powerful of their subjects, and to a certain extent indirect rule made this easier. Thus the recruits for the colonial army who were peremptorily demanded from a village were often chosen by the titleholders in the village council from among the weaker of the clan sections that resided there. Still, as the period rolled on, the range of winning or losing lessened somewhat, and all sorts of unexpected effects began to appear. Some of the losers, such as noncommissioned officers who returned to their villages after seven years of military service, became winners there while some early winners became sudden losers.

When one rereads this study with the rising or falling fortunes of individuals or groups in mind, it becomes possible to reintroduce the shifting inequalities over time between people, and one obtains an even more complex and realistic perspective of Bushong and Kete communities than I have presented here. As a result, one also comes that much closer to understanding lives as they were lived and the differences between individual people. Thus it is clear by now that even after World War II when conditions improved overall, the main experiences of persons at the bottom of the heap were still leagues apart from those at the top. For example, at that time the experience of a pawned woman belonging to a middle-level household in Nsheng was still one of almost unrelieved misery and drudgery compared to that of a young princess in the ward of the successors, which consisted mostly in rounds of socializing and shopping. Or compared to most wives, whose status was falling compared to that of their husbands mostly because the colonial administration bypassed them but also because they had less access to schooling and jobs; yet their status remained considerable because they continued to hold the purse strings for their lineages.

Given the wide divergence of different experiences, what then does it mean to say that this book focuses on "the colonial experience of the Bushong and Kete"—that is, on a generalization? It means that we are relying on that part of all the experiences that they shared with each other. Their shared experiences consisted of what happened either to all of them or to large sets of them. This book has been built on such shared experiences, and those shared experiences bring us closer than any other approach to a concrete understanding of what life was actually like in that colonial period. In other words, the book rests on inductive generalizations, and without a generalizing process it could not have been written. Furthermore, in so far as most Bushong and Kete have shared many of their common experiences of colonial rule with other rural Congolese, the experiences described here are also representative, and therefore valid, generalizations for rural Congo in general.

During the colonial period the Bushong and Kete were well aware of being colonized, but one may well ask if they saw any inner coherence to the flow of the colonial experiences that they underwent? Were they, for instance, aware of colonialism as a process, as single-minded straightforward progress toward a well-defined goal? Did the colonial establishment not continually claim that it was gradually implanting what it called "civilization"? All the evidence indicates that during most of the era successive or simultaneous colonial actions appeared to the Bushong and Kete as totally arbitrary and that they experienced the process as a confusing sequence of oscillations between the threat of social chaos caused by colonial exploitation and their own attempts to restore harmony. After the initial conquest, the sequence of these oscillations seems to have signified nothing more to them than a perennial struggle to retain, to restore, or to expand the established colonial order for the benefit of the foreign colonialists first and the royal establishment at Nsheng after that. Beyond this no one seemed quite aware that colonialism was advancing toward any kind of ultimate goal.

Only after World War II did some among the educated young Bushong and Kete men and women realize that colonialism was a process by which more and more Congolese who had been properly schooled were gradually gaining access to positions of increasing importance in the colony and partaking more and more of its material benefits. They realized that they could be the new winners. It was not a novel vision. Rather, it had already been familiar to most Luba Kasai some two generations earlier and had ever since guided their efforts to reach always higher positions in the colonial world and to profit from them. Yet it was only in the early 1950s that some Kuba youths along with the Luba intelligentsia began to realize that colonialism might well come to an early end and that Congolese like themselves would then take over the existing system and benefit from it.

It was only after the colonial period was long gone that Bushong and Kete began to acquire an overall opinion of what it had meant to them. One would expect that, barring a few royals and aristocrats, all the others, especially rural villagers, would condemn the period and stress its hardships. One would expect it, but one would be wrong, at least according to some fifty older Bushong villagers from the heart of the country who were questioned in 1985 by the Bushong sociologist Lobo Bundwoong Bope, precisely twenty-five years after the colonial period ended and exactly a century after Ludwig Wolf's first visit. When asked to assess the colonial era, nearly all these villagers stressed the crucial importance of indirect rule. They emphasized the respected status of their kingdom under colonial rule and stressed the physical and moral order that reigned at the time, particularly the integrity of the local tribunals. Once in this nostalgic vein, they also waxed eloquent about the absence of hunger, formal prostitution, and discrimination among Africans, the rarity of theft (forgetting about all those shortfalls in the shops!) and corruption, the availability of medical care, the punctuality in the payment of wages, and the availability of decent wages for teachers—all, of course, in contrast to the situation in 1985.

Indeed, praise for the late colonial experience in 1985 was so strong that, despite his professional academic detachment, Lobo felt obliged to insert the following ambiguous statement in his text:

> It is evident that colonization was not a good thing. On the one hand there were many disadvantages to it, but on the other hand there were also some advantages. Here is the opinion of an old man: "I know that the situation at the onset of colonization was difficult, but it became normal later on."[1]

And it was not only the Kuba who uttered such favorable opinions about "the good old times." Similar opinions are still voiced by most other Congolese today. Obviously such opinions merely reflect people's experience of a very painful and considerable decline in living standards that began right after independence and still continue today. Yet many older rural Congolese, Kuba included, have never realized that the very decline in living standards that caused them to proclaim how much better life had been in colonial times was, in fact, the fatal flaw in the colonial system, a flaw so severe that neither the colonial economy nor colonial government could have survived the end of that period.

That flaw had been the colony's reliance on coercion or the threat of coercion—a feature that was also vividly remembered and roundly condemned by the very same people Lobo interviewed once he began to ask opinions about jail, the use of the whip, or the *mpiki* agricultural program. The evidence shows that living standards in most of rural Congo and among the Kuba began to fall from the very first day of independence onward and in some places even earlier, soon after colonial

---

1. Lobo Bundwoong Bope, "Afrikanische Gesellschaft im Wandel: Soziale Mobilität und Landflucht am Beispiel der Region Mweka in Zaire" (doctoral dissertation, University of Linz, Frankfurt, 1991), 179 and, more generally, 177–79.

coercion came to an end. No more *mpiki*, no more jail, no more commandeered labor on the roads—but as a result barely two or three years later most roads had become impassable for lack of maintenance, motor transport could no longer get through, and, except along the railway, the flood of commerce that sustained the general standard of living dwindled to a trickle. Hence, paradoxically, the very praise heaped on the quality of life in the late colonial period actually amounted to its utter condemnation.

This book has attempted to provide an introduction to colonial history in a more concrete and realistic way than has been usual hitherto. It does so in the hope that this would allow readers to develop a genuine feeling for life as it was lived in those days by the majority of Congolese. At the very least, all readers of this book will immediately spot the false so-called lessons of history. They will easily refute the fallacies of current clichés about Congo's history so favored today by journalists, among others. The worst cliché centers on violence. This cliché justifies today's outbreaks in eastern Congo as "natural" by suggesting that violence in Congo is atavistic, as shown by the appalling violence that occurred during the colonial conquest and the exploitation of the country, as well as by similar bursts of violence after independence—as if most parts of Congo had not been peaceful for well over a century. Readers will now also need no help spotting the crass ignorance of the cliché that reduces the colonial period to a time of unspeakable atrocities under Leopold II followed by a breakdown into utter chaos at independence, which then somehow leads to and explains the failed state of the country today.

Rather than such "lessons of history," this book, its author hopes, will prompt most readers to come to their own assessments and to draw their own conclusions about colonial Congo. That is as it should be, even though such assessments and conclusions will only be provisional. At this point, readers should be reminded that this book is only an introduction: no single book can either capture all the facets of the phenomenon known as colonialism or give a fully balanced account of the colonial history of Congo. To obtain more profound insights in these subjects the curious student of history—and let there be many of them—will have to pursue the subject further. That is why lists of further readings have been provided. But even if this book just manages to capture the imagination and the interest of most of its readers and thereby raises greater understanding, awareness, and perhaps sympathy for the lives of Congolese then and now, it will not have been written nor read in vain.

INDEX

255 56, 261; Western medicine as analogous to traditional, 252

currency, 89 90, 91, 92, 117

Cwa (nomads), 6, 46, 193, 195

De Cock, Jacques-Paul-Félix (Ibulbul), 93, 96 98, 100, 102, 136

decolonization, 176 77. *See also* independence

Democratic Republic of Congo (Congo-Kinshasa), 4, 10

d'Haenens, Antonin, 294

disease, 144 45, 153; colonial activity linked to, 138, 140 41, 145; dysentery, 138, 142 44, 145, 147; European contact and contagion of, 142, 145, 147; infertility and, 242, 245; influenza, 142; population decline linked to, 137 45, 242 45; venereal disease, 140 42, 147, 244, 245, 249 52; World War I and, 142 43, 145

divorce, 50, 142, 239 40

Djilatendo, 161, 162 63, 301 2; works by, *160, 222, 232, 290*

dress or appearance: assimilation and, 271 72, 300, 306, 309, 312; and Kuba identity, 299, 304; linked to Christian conversion and values, 305 6; modernity and adoption of Western modes, 120, 299, 303 10; prohibitions on, 15, 115, 308, 318; social status and, 304, 314; traditional production of raffia cloth, 51 52, 123; traditional style, 304, *305*

dysentery, 138, 142 44, 145, 147

economics: colonial development and lower standard of living, 242 43; of colonization, 59 60; commercial monopoly, 59 60, 63, 84 85, 117 (*see also* Compagnie du Kasai); currency and exchange, 89 90, 91, 92, 117; Great Depression, 161 68; King Mbop Mabinc maKyeen's speech on "The Chase for Money," 187; "poverty" and lifestyle, 234 35; retail trade and villagers as consumers, 228, 230 31, 234; social impacts of wage economy, 239, 242, 299, 302, 307 12; taxation (*see* taxation); traditional Kuba villages as collective-oriented, 47, 51 53, 161, 299; wage labor and cash economy, 215, 217,

224, 229 33, 272, 302, 307 (*see also* social impacts of wage economy *under this heading*); World War I and, 125; World War II and, 123 24

Edmiston, Alonzo, 300

education: access to, 156, 175, 321; and adoption of Western lifestyle, 272, 284 85, 300, 310 14, 321; attendance at school, 291 92; compulsory labor as, 125; as conversion, 284 85; and employment opportunities, 233, 294 95, 310 12; gender and, 239, 285 86, 290 91, 320; high schools, 284, 294 96; initiation rituals as moral and social, 237; Kuba kings as advocates of, 189 90, 200, 285 86, 292; Kwet Mabinc as advocate of, 200; language of instruction, 156, 279, 284, 285; map of school locations, *272*; missions and responsibility for, 156, 168, 284 92; political unrest and, 171, 329; standardization of, 288 91; state responsibility for, 174, 196, 292 93; truancy and, 291 92, 296; vocational and professional, 290, 293, 296

elephants, 11 12, 30, 59

The Elephant Who Walked on Eggs (Badibanga), 163

Elisabeth, queen of Belgium, 155, 195

Elisabethville uprising, 170 71

Elisofon, Eliot, 183

epidemics. *See* disease

fertility: cults and restoration of harmony, 252 53, 256, 261 62, 315; infertility as result of witchcraft or curses, 80 83, 140 41, 254 55; king's role in, 185, 255; lineal descent and cultural emphasis on, 30 31, 49 50, 146; venereal disease and infertility, 141 42

first contact: and crystallization of colonial relationship, 35 43

food shortages, 226; as cause of population decline, 136 37; diversion of labor to rubber production linked to, 102, 104, 107 8

Franck, Louis, 181 82, 185

French, knowledge of, 168

friendships, colonial context and, 55 56